# Introduction to

# MACROECONOMICS

## FOURTH EDITION

## EDWIN G. DOLAN
Ph.D. Yale University

# BVT

The publisher of affordable textbooks

# BVT

The publisher of affordable textbooks

## INTRODUCTION TO MACROECONOMICS, FOURTH EDITION

ISBN: 978-1-60229-962-7

**PROJECT DEVELOPMENT MANAGER:** Brae Buhnerkemper

**PROJECT DEVELOPMENT ASSISTANT:** Brandi Cornwell

**MANAGING EDITOR:** Joyce Bianchini

**SENIOR DEVELOPMENT EDITOR:** Rhonda Minnema

**PHOTO RESEARCHER:** Della Brackett

**COVER DESIGN TEAM:** Jason James
Brae Buhnerkemper
Dan Harvey
Della Bracket

**ILLUSTRATIONS:** Dan Harvey

**TYPESETTER:** Dan Harvey

**TEXT AND COVER PRINTING:** Quad/Graphics

**SALES MANAGER:** Robert Rappeport

**MARKETING MANGER:** Richard Schofield

**PERMISSIONS COORDINATOR:** Suzanne Schmidt

**ART DIRECTOR:** Linda Price

# Table of Contents

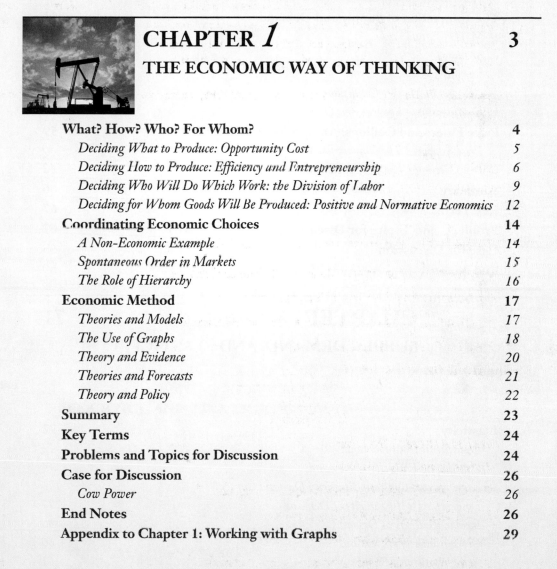

# PART 2  An Overview of Macroeconomics

## CHAPTER 4    97
### IN SEARCH OF PROSPERITY AND STABILITY

## CHAPTER 5    123
### THE CIRCULAR FLOW OF INCOME AND EXPENDITURE

# CHAPTER *6*     149
## MEASURING ECONOMIC ACTIVITY

# PART 3  Banking, Money, and the Financial System

## CHAPTER 7                                             177
### THE BANKING SYSTEM AND REGULATION

## CHAPTER 8                                             205
### MONEY AND CENTRAL BANKING

# PART 4  Macroeconomic Policy

## CHAPTER 9    229
### PRICES AND REAL OUTPUT IN THE SHORT RUN

# CHAPTER *10*   **253**

## STRATEGIES AND RULES FOR MONETARY POLICY

# CHAPTER *11*   **283**

## FISCAL POLICY

# CHAPTER *12*                                                     315

## FIGHTING INFLATION AND DEFLATION

# Preface

THE TWO YEARS leading up to this fourth edition of *Introduction to Macroeconomics* from BVT Publishing have seen the most dramatic events in the global economy in more than half a century. In response to these events, the book has been thoroughly revised. Nearly a third of the entire book, including most of the key chapters on macroeconomic policy, is new. The new material is not simply added on to what was already there. An unintended, but beneficial consequence of the revision is that the chapter outline ends up shorter by two chapters. That should make it easier than before to get through the entire book in a single semester.

As in the past, the macroeconomics volume begins with three introductory chapters that cover basic economic ideas, supply and demand, and elasticity. These chapters make it possible to use the book in either "macro-first" or "micro-first" course sequencing. Students who have already had microeconomics can skip the first three chapters or treat them as review.

Chapters 4, 5, and 6 cover basic ideas of macroeconomics. The structure of these chapters is unchanged from previous editions, although new charts and cases have been added to reflect current events. Economic data are brought up through mid-2009. During the life of the edition, instructors will be able to find tables and charts updated to 2010 and beyond, in PowerPoint slide form, on the BVT Publishing web site (www.bvtpublishing.com).

Chapter 7 is a completely new discussion of the financial system and bank regulation. It explains the evolution of the banking system from the traditional "originate-to-hold" model to the modern "originate-to-distribute" model. In doing so, it explains key concepts of modern finance, including securitization and subprime mortgage lending. The final sections of the chapter cover bank regulation and the problems that led up to the recent financial crisis. Chapter 8 introduces basic concepts of banking and Chapter 9 covers the aggregate supply and demand model. These chapters are subject to only minor revisions.

The final three chapters of the book are completely rewritten to provide students with a better perspective on current developments in macroeconomics.

Chapter 10 looks at strategies for the conduct of monetary policy. It begins by explaining why lags, forecasting errors, and time-inconsistency render policymaking in the real world much more difficult than the aggregate supply and demand model by itself implies. That is followed by a discussion of alternative policy rules, including monetary targeting, inflation targeting, and exchange rate targeting.

Chapter 11, on fiscal policy, is completely rewritten. It pays much more attention than before to lags, forecasting errors, multiplier uncertainty, and other practical problems of policy. Most of the chapter is devoted to short-run fiscal stabilization, but the final section also looks at longer run issues of macroeconomic imbalances and sustainability of the federal debt and deficit.

Finally, Chapter 12 looks at tools for fighting inflation and deflation. Some of the material on inflation, inflationary recession, and hyperinflation was covered in previous editions. The second half of the chapter is devoted to a greatly expanded discussion of deflation. New topics include the liquidity trap, quantitative easing, productivity-driven supply-side deflation, and asset price bubbles.

Users of earlier editions may wonder what has happened to the material previously covered in the two chapters that have been omitted from the new chapter outline. Little substantive material has been lost. Instead, it is reorganized. Productivity, previously covered in Chapter 14, is now discussed in Chapters 4 and 12. The money supply/money demand approach to interest rate determination now appears in an appendix to Chapter 10. That appendix is recommended for courses that have a high percentage of students who plan to major in economics. Otherwise, it can be omitted without loss of continuity.

As always, I thank the entire publishing and editorial staff of BVT Publishing for their highly professional support. They are a pleasure to work with, and I hope that all students and instructors who use this book benefit as much as I have from their unique and innovative approach to textbook publishing.

## Features of This Edition

- *State of the art pedagogy*: An abundance of case studies introduce and illustrate the subject matter of every chapter.
- *Integrated international economics:* As the world economy itself comes closer together, international economics must be more closely integrated into the principles course. Accordingly, topics relating to international economics are not exclusively confined to Chapter 7, which outlines the theory of international trade. In addition, numerous examples and cases drawn from international economic experience are included throughout the book.

## Supplements for Instructors

1. **Study Guide.** The Study Guide has hands-on applications and self-testing programs. Students can gain an advantage by reinforcing their reading and lecture notes with the following study guide features:

- *Where You're Going:* The objectives and terms for each chapter are recapped to tie concepts together.

- *Walking Tour:* The "Walking Tour" section provides a narrative summary of the chapter and incorporates questions on key points. Answers are given in the margin.

- *Hands On:* Geographical and numerical exercises clarify concepts and better prepare students for tests and quizzes.

- *Economics in the News:* A news item illustrates how concepts covered in the chapter could appear in the real world. Questions and answers reinforce the concepts.

- *Questions for Review:* These questions and answers follow the key chapter concepts, preparing students for the self-test.

- *Self-Test:* Extra test preparation increases a student's understanding and ability to succeed.

- *Careers in Economics:* Formerly an appendix in the text, this material provides students with an understanding of where the study of economics could lead them.

2. **Instructor's Manual.** The expanded Instructor's Manual contains material that can be easily included in lectures. The manual also includes all of its traditional elements, including instructional objectives, lecture notes, and suggestions.

3. **Test Bank.** The accompanying Test Bank has been expanded to include 150 questions per chapter in a variety of formats, including multiple choice, true/false, and essay questions.

4. **PowerPoints.** This edition is accompanied by a greatly expanded set of PowerPoint transparencies. Beginning with this edition, the transparencies for each chapter include coverage of all graphical material in the text, sometimes supplemented by additional material, as well.

5. **Customize This Book.** If you have additional material you'd like to add (handouts, lecture notes, syllabus, etc.) or simply rearrange and delete content, BVT Publishing's custom publishing division can help you modify this book's content, to produce a book that satisfies your specific instructional needs. BVT Publishing has the only custom publishing division that puts your material exactly where you want it to go, easily and seamlessly. Please visit www.bvtpublishing.com or call us at 1-800-646-7782 for more information on BVT Publishing's Custom Publishing Program.

## Supplements for Students

BVT Publishing is pleased to provide students with a free, comprehensive online tutorial which can be found at www.bvtstudents.com. This web site offers the following:

1. **eBook Editions.** Save time, money and paper by purchasing an eBook version of this text directly from our convenient online store, located on our student web site.

2. **Shopping Cart.** For the student's convenience and pocketbook, the student web site also contains a shopping cart where they have the added option of purchasing the traditional paper textbook directly from the publisher if they prefer.

3. **Self Testing.** Students can test their knowledge of this book's content on our student web site. The Self Test questions are designed to help improve students' mastery of the information in the book.

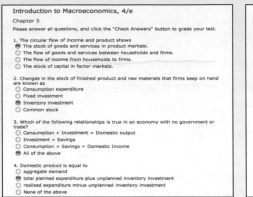
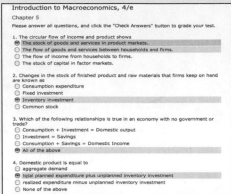

4. **Flash Cards.** The Flash Cards are an easy way for students to spot-check their understanding of common and important terms, as well as effectively retain the information.

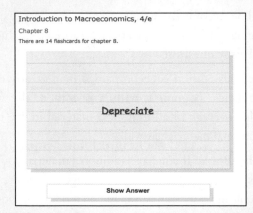
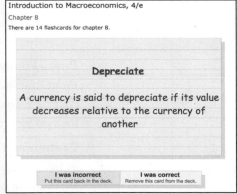

5. **Chapter Summaries.** The Chapter Summaries are another tool designed to give the students an overview of each chapter's content, further aiding the students in content comprehension and retention.

# About the Author

EDWIN G. DOLAN was born in Oklahoma and grew up in a small town in Oregon. He attended Earlham College and Indiana University, where he majored in Russian Studies as an undergraduate and later earned a Masters degree from Indiana University's Russian and East-European Institute. After earning a doctorate in economics from Yale University, he taught at Dartmouth College, the University of Chicago, George Mason University and Gettysburg College.

In 1971, he published his first book, TANSTAAFL: The Economic Strategy for Environmental Crisis, which, although long out of print, continues to be cited as a classic in its field. That slim volume was followed by a number of other textbooks covering principles of economics, money and banking, and problems of microeconomic policy. Combined world-wide sales of these books total more than a million copies.

As economic and political changes accelerated in the Soviet Union during the Gorbachev era, Professor Dolan returned to his early interest in Russia and Eastern Europe. He began teaching in Moscow in 1990. In 1993, he and his wife founded the American Institute of Business and Economics, an independent, not-for-profit MBA program that continues operation to this day. Since leaving Moscow in 2001, he has taught global macroeconomics, managerial economics, money and banking, and other courses in Latvia, Hungary, Croatia, Bulgaria, the Czech Republic, and Estonia. When not lecturing abroad, he makes his home in Washington's San Juan Islands, where he is active in the Community Education program of Skagit Valley College. Hobbies include tennis, horseback riding, woodworking, and bridge.

# PART 1

# *Introduction to Economics*

# CHAPTER *1*

# The Economic Way of Thinking

**After reading this chapter, you will understand the following:**

1. What is the subject matter of economics?
2. Four fundamental economic choices:
   – What will an economy produce?
   – How will goods and services be produced?
   – Who will produce which goods and services?
   – For whom will goods be produced?
3. How are economic choices coordinated?
4. How do economists use theory, graphs, and data in their work?

I T WAS A turbulent year for the world economy. In the first half of the year, oil prices rose to a record high, as did prices for a range of other commodities from wheat and corn to gold. Later in the year, prices of these same commodities fell sharply. At the same time other prices—those for housing in many countries, the prices of stocks traded on the New York Stock Exchange, and the exchange rate of the dollar against the euro—also displayed unprecedented volatility. Many factors lay behind these swings in prices—the weather in Australia, political events in Venezuela, a presidential election in the United States, and the onset of a global financial crisis. How can we understand all of these complex, yet interrelated, events?

This chapter will take the first steps toward a systematic way of thinking about the economy by introducing a few big ideas that apply to events in all markets, in all countries, at all times. The biggest of all the ideas that underlie this economic way of thinking is **scarcity**. Scarcity means any situation in which there is not enough of something to fill everyone's wants. For example, corn grown in the U.S. Midwest is scarce because there is not enough of it to fully meet the competing needs of Chinese consumers, who want to eat more corn-fed pork

**Scarcity**

A situation in which there is not enough of a resource to meet all of everyone's wants

as they become wealthier, and U.S. drivers, who are burning more corn-based ethanol in their cars. The scarcity of corn affects people's choices about how to use not only corn but also other scarce goods. The effects on markets for wheat and oil are relatively direct. The effects on exchange rates and stock markets are not quite so easy to trace, but they are no less important. Scarcity and the way people deal with it are the central topics of **economics**, which is commonly defined as the social science that seeks to understand the choices people make in using scarce resources to meet their wants.

Economics, as its definition makes clear, is a study not of things or money or wealth but of *people*. Economics is about people because scarcity itself is a human phenomenon. Deposits of crude oil lay undisturbed in the ground for millions of years before they became the object of human wants. Only at that point did they become scarce in the sense that economists understand the term.

The focus on the human dimension of scarcity and choice is part of what makes economics a social science. In addition, economics is a social science because people do not attempt to solve the problem of scarcity in isolation. Instead, they can meet their wants much more effectively by trading with one another. As they trade, each person gives up something of value to others in such a way that each person gains from the exchange. Some economists think exchange is even more important than scarcity as a defining characteristic of economics.[1]

The wide range of topics covered by economics can be divided into two main branches. The example of corn prices is an application from **microeconomics**. The prefix *micro*, meaning "small," indicates that this branch of economics deals with the choices of small economic units such as households, firms, and government agencies. Although microeconomics studies individual behavior, its scope can be worldwide, as when it focuses on global trade in goods such as cars and crude oil.

Economics also has another branch, known as **macroeconomics**. The prefix *macro*, meaning "large," indicates that this branch deals with larger-scale economic phenomena. Typical problems in macroeconomics include how to maintain conditions in which people who want jobs can find them, how to protect the economy against the distortions caused by widespread price increases (inflation), and how to provide for a continued increase in living standards over time. Choices studied by macroeconomics include those made by governments—for example, choices among alternative policies concerning taxes, expenditures, budget deficits, and the financial system. However, because macroeconomic phenomena like inflation represent the end result of millions of individual choices regarding the prices of particular goods and services, macroeconomics ultimately rests on a microeconomic foundation.

Whether one is dealing with microeconomics or macroeconomics, whether with domestic or international economic relationships—all economic analysis comes down to a special way of thinking about how people interact with one another as they choose how to use scarce resources.

## What? How? Who? For Whom?

Among the most important economic choices people make are those concerning what goods will be produced, how they will be produced, who will do which jobs, and for

**Economics**

The social science that seeks to understand the choices people make in using scarce resources to meet their wants

**Microeconomics**

The branch of economics that studies the choices of individual units—including households, business firms, and government agencies

**Macroeconomics**

The branch of economics that studies large-scale economic phenomena, particularly inflation, unemployment, and economic growth

whom the results of production will be available. Each of these choices is made necessary because of scarcity, and each can be used to introduce a key element of the economic way of thinking.

## Deciding What to Produce: Opportunity Cost

The first choice is that of what goods to produce. Although the number of goods and services that could be produced in any real economy is immense, the basic concept of choice can be illustrated with an economy in which there are just two alternative goods. Suppose these goods are cars and education. For many students, going without a car (or driving a used car instead of a new one) is a sacrifice that must be made in order to get a college education. The same trade-off faced by an individual student is also faced by the economy as a whole: Not enough cars and education can be produced to satisfy everyone's wants. Somehow it must be decided how much of each good to produce.

The impossibility of producing as much of everything as people want reflects a scarcity of the productive resources that are used to make all goods. Many scarce productive resources must be combined to make even the simplest of goods. For example, making a car requires steel, glass, paint, welding machines, land for factories, and the labor of autoworkers. For convenience, all the various productive resources can be grouped into three basic categories called **factors of production**: labor, capital, and natural resources. **Labor** includes all of the productive contributions made by people working with their minds and muscles. **Capital** includes all the productive inputs created by people—including tools, machinery, buildings, and intangible items, such as computer software. **Natural resources** include anything that can be used as a productive input in its natural state—for example, farmland, building sites, forests, and mineral deposits.

Productive resources that are used to satisfy one want cannot be used to satisfy another at the same time. Steel, concrete, and building sites used for automobile factories cannot also be used for classrooms. People who are employed as teachers cannot spend the same time working on an automobile assembly line. Even the time students spend in class and studying for tests represents use of a factor of production that could otherwise be used as labor in an auto plant. Whenever the inputs to production have more than one possible use, producing one good means forgoing the opportunity to produce something else instead. Economists express this basic truth by saying that everything has an **opportunity cost**. The opportunity cost of a good or service is its cost in terms of the forgone opportunity to pursue the best possible alternative activity with the same time or resources.

In our two-good economy, the opportunity cost of producing a college graduate can be stated in terms of the number of cars that could have been produced by using the same labor, capital, and natural resources. Suppose that the opportunity cost of educating a college graduate is four Toyota Camrys. Such a ratio (graduates per car or cars per graduate) is a useful way to express opportunity cost when only two goods are involved. More typically, though, we deal with situations in which there are many goods. Having more of one means giving up a little bit of many others.

In an economy with many goods, opportunity costs can be expressed in terms of a common unit of measurement, money. For example, rather than saying that a college

---

**Factors of production**

The basic inputs of labor, capital, and natural resources used in producing all goods and services

**Labor**

The contributions to production made by people working with their minds and muscles

**Capital**

All means of production that are created by people—including tools, industrial equipment, and structures

**Natural resources**

Anything that can be used as a productive input in its natural state, such as farmland, building sites, forests, and mineral deposits

**Opportunity cost**

The cost of a good or service measured in terms of the forgone opportunity to pursue the best possible alternative activity with the same time or resources

education is worth four Camrys or that a Camry is worth one-fourth of a college education, we could say that the opportunity cost of a car is $25,000 and that of a college education is $100,000.

Useful as it is to have a common unit of measurement, great care must be taken when opportunity costs are expressed in terms of money because not all out-of-pocket money expenditures represent the sacrifice of opportunities to do something else. At the same time, not all sacrificed opportunities take the form of money spent. *Applying Economic Ideas 1.1*, which analyzes both the out-of-pocket expenditures and the opportunity costs of a college education, shows why.

The importance of opportunity cost will be stressed again and again in this book. The habit of looking for opportunity costs is one of the distinguishing features of the economic way of thinking.

## Deciding How to Produce: Efficiency and Entrepreneurship

A second basic economic choice is that of how to produce. There is more than one way to produce almost any good or service. Cars, for example, can be made in highly automated factories, using a lot of capital equipment and relatively little labor; or they can be built one by one in smaller shops, using a lot of labor and only a few general-purpose machines. Toyota Camrys are built the first way, Tesla Roadsters the second way. The same kind of thing could be said about education. Economics can be taught in a small classroom with one teacher and a blackboard serving twenty students; or it can be taught in a large lecture hall in which the teacher uses video technology to address hundreds of students.

**Economic efficiency**

A state of affairs in which it is impossible to make any change that satisfies one person's wants more fully without causing some other person's wants to be satisfied less fully

**EFFICIENCY**   Efficiency is a key consideration in deciding how to produce. In everyday usage, efficiency means producing with a minimum of expense, effort, and waste. Economists use a more precise definition. **Economic efficiency**, they say, refers to a state of affairs in which it is impossible to make any change that satisfies one person's wants more fully without causing some other person's wants to be satisfied less fully.[2]

Although this formal definition of economic efficiency may be unfamiliar, it is actually closely related to the everyday notion of efficiency. If there is some way to make you better off without making me worse off, it is wasteful (inefficient) to pass up the opportunity. If I have a red pen that I am not using, and you need one just for a minute, it would be wasteful for you to buy a red pen of your own. It is more efficient for me to lend you my pen;

Automation in the car industry can produce many cars with little labor

**Applying Economic Ideas 1.1**
# THE OPPORTUNITY COST OF A COLLEGE EDUCATION

How much does it cost you to go to college? If you are a resident student at a typical four-year private college in the United States, you can answer this question by making up a budget like the one shown in Figure A. This can be called a budget of out-of-pocket costs because it includes all the items—and only those items—that you or your parents must actually pay for in a year.

Your own out-of-pocket costs may be much higher or lower than those listed. Chances are, though, that these are the main categories that first come to mind when you think about the costs of college. As you begin to think more like an economist, you may find it useful to restate your college budget in terms of opportunity costs. Which of the items in Figure A represent opportunities that you have forgone in order to go to college? Are any forgone opportunities missing? To answer these questions, compare Figure A with Figure B, which shows a budget of opportunity costs.

Some items are both opportunity costs and out-of-pocket costs. The first three items in Figure A show up again in Figure B. To spend $14,000 on tuition and fees and $1,200 on books and supplies, you must give up the opportunity to buy other goods and services—to buy a car or rent a ski condo, for instance. To spend $1,100 getting to and from school, you must pass up the opportunity to travel somewhere else or to spend the money on something other than travel. Not all out-of-pocket costs are also opportunity costs, however. Consider the last two items in the out-of-pocket budget. By spending $7,000 on room, board, and personal expenses during the year, you are not really giving up the opportunity to do something else. Whether or not you were going to college, you would have to eat, live somewhere, and buy clothes. Because these are expenses that you would have in any case, they do not count as opportunity costs of going to college.

Finally, some items are opportunity costs without being out-of-pocket costs. Think about what you would be doing if you were not going to college. If you were not going to college, you probably would have taken a job and started earning money soon after leaving high school. As a high-school graduate, your earnings would be about $16,000 during the nine months of the school year. (You can work during the summer even if you are attending college.) Because this potential income is something that you must forgo for the sake of college, it is an opportunity cost even though it does not involve an outlay of money.

Which budget you use depends on the kind of decision you are making. If you have already decided to go to college and are doing your financial planning, the out-of-pocket budget will tell you how much you will have to raise from savings, money earned, parents' contributions, loans, and scholarships to make ends meet. But if you are making the more basic choice between going to college and pursuing a career that does not require a college degree, the opportunity cost of college is what counts.

What are opportunity costs of your education?

| Figure A | Budget of Out-of-Pocket Costs | Figure B | Budget of Opportunity Costs |
|---|---|---|---|
| Tuition and fees | $14,000 | Tuition and fees | $14,000 |
| Books and supplies | 1,200 | Books and supplies | 1,200 |
| Transportation to and from home | 1,100 | Transportation to and from home | 1,100 |
| Room and board | 7,000 | Forgone income | 16,000 |
| Personal expenses | 1,400 | | |
| **Total out-of-pocket costs** | **$24,700** | **Total opportunity costs** | **$32,300** |

it makes you better off and me no worse off. If there is a way to make us both better off, it would be all the more wasteful not to take advantage of the opportunity. You lend me your bicycle for the afternoon, and I will lend you my volleyball. If I do not ride a bicycle very often and you do not play volleyball very often, it would be inefficient for us both to own one of each item.

The concept of economic efficiency has a variety of applications. One such application centers on the question of *how* to produce. **Efficiency in production** refers to a situation in which it is not possible, given available productive resources and existing knowledge, to produce more of one good without forgoing the opportunity to produce some of another good. The concept of efficiency in production, like the broader concept of economic efficiency, includes the everyday notion of avoiding waste. For example, a grower of apples finds that beyond some certain quantity, using more water per tree does not increase the yield of apples; so using more than that amount would be wasteful. Better to transfer the extra water to the production of, say, peaches. That way, more peaches can be grown without any reduction in the apple crop.

The economist's definition also includes more subtle possibilities for improving the efficiency of production in cases where the waste of resources is less obvious. For example, it is possible to grow apples in Georgia. It is also possible, by selecting the right tree varieties and using winter protection, to grow peaches in Vermont. Some hobbyists do grow both fruits in both states. However, doing so on a commercial scale would be inefficient even if growers in both states followed the most careful cultivation practices and avoided any obvious waste, like using too much water. To see why, suppose that initially apple and peach trees were planted in equal numbers in the two states. Then compare this with a situation in which 500 fewer struggling peach trees had been planted in Vermont, and 500 thriving apple trees had been planted instead. At the same time, suppose 500 fewer heat-stressed apple trees had been planted in Georgia, and peaches had taken their place. The second alternative would increase the output of both fruits without increasing the total land, labor, and capital used in fruit production. This shows that the original distribution of trees was inefficient.

**HOW TO INCREASE PRODUCTION POTENTIAL**    Once efficiency has been achieved, more of one good can be produced only by forgoing the opportunity to produce something else, assuming that productive resources and knowledge are held constant. Over time, accumulating more resources and finding new ways of putting them to work can expand production potential.

In the past, discovery of new supplies of natural resources has been an important way of increasing production potential. Population growth has always been, and still is, another way. However, as the most easily tapped supplies of natural resources are depleted and as population growth slows in most parts of the world, capital will increasingly be the factor of production that contributes most to the expansion of production potential.

The act of increasing the economy's stock of capital—that is, its supply of productive inputs made by people—is known as **investment**. Investment involves a trade-off of present consumption for future consumption. To build more factories, roads, and computers, we have to divert resources from the production of bread, movies, hair-

## Efficiency in production

A situation in which it is not possible, given available knowledge and productive resources, to produce more of one good without forgoing the opportunity to produce some of another good

## Investment

The act of increasing the economy's stock of capital—that is, its supply of means of production made by people

cuts, and other things that satisfy immediate wants. In return, we put ourselves in a better position to satisfy our future wants.

Increased availability of productive resources is not the only source of economic growth, however. Even more important are improvements in human knowledge—the invention of new technology, new forms of organization, and new ways of satisfying wants. The process of looking for new possibilities—making use of new ways of doing things, being alert to new opportunities, and overcoming old limits—is called **entrepreneurship**. It is a dynamic process that breaks down the constraints imposed by existing knowledge and limited supplies of factors of production.

**Entrepreneurship**

The process of looking for new possibilities—making use of new ways of doing things, being alert to new opportunities, and overcoming old limits

Entrepreneurship does not have to mean inventing something or starting a new business, although it sometimes does. It may mean finding a new market for an existing product—for example, convincing people in Germany that Japanese sushi makes a quick and tasty lunch. It may mean taking advantage of price differences between one market and another—for example, buying hay at a low price in Pennsylvania, where growing conditions have been good in the past year, and reselling it in Virginia, where the weather has been too dry.

Households can be entrepreneurs, too. They do not simply repeat the same patterns of work and leisure every day. They seek variety—new jobs, new foods, and new places to visit. Each time you try something new, you are taking a step into the unknown. In this sense, you are an entrepreneur.

Entrepreneurship is sometimes called the fourth factor of production. However, entrepreneurship differs from the three classical factors of production in important ways. Unlike labor, capital, and natural resources, entrepreneurship is intangible and difficult to measure. Although entrepreneurs earn incomes reflecting the value that the market places on their accomplishments, we cannot speak of a price per unit of entrepreneurship; there are no such units. Also, unlike human resources (which grow old), machines (which wear out), and natural resources (which can be used up), the inventions and discoveries of entrepreneurs are not depleted as they are used. Once a new product or concept has been invented—such as gasoline-electric hybrid power for cars, text messaging on cell phones, or life insurance as a form of financial investment, the required knowledge does not have to be created again (although, of course, it may be supplanted by even better ideas). All in all, it is more helpful to think of entrepreneurship as a process of learning better ways of using the three basic factors of production than as a separate factor of production.

## Deciding Who Will Do Which Work: the Division of Labor

The questions of what will be produced and how to produce it would exist even for a person living in isolation. Even the fictional castaway Robinson Crusoe had to decide whether to fish or hunt birds; and if he decided to fish, he had to decide whether to do so with a net or with a hook and line. In contrast, the economic questions of who will do which work and for whom output will be produced exist only for people living in society—another reason economics is considered one of the social sciences.

The question of who will do which work is a matter of organizing the social division of labor. Will everyone do everything independently—be a farmer in the morning, a tailor in the afternoon, and a poet in the evening? Or will people cooperate—work together, trade goods and services, and specialize in one particular job? Economists answer these questions by pointing out that it is more efficient to cooperate. Doing so allows a given number of people to produce more than they could if each of them worked alone. Three things make cooperation worthwhile: teamwork, learning by doing, and comparative advantage.

First, consider *teamwork*. In a classic paper on this subject, Armen Alchian and Harold Demsetz used the example of workers unloading bulky crates from a truck.[3] The crates are so large that one worker alone cannot move them at all without unpacking them. Two people, each working independently, would take hours to unload the truck. If they work as a team, however, they can easily pick up the crates and stack them on the loading dock. This example shows that even when everyone is doing the same work, and even when little skill is involved, teamwork pays.

A second reason for cooperation applies when there are different jobs to be done and different skills to be learned. In a furniture plant, for example, some workers operate production equipment, others use office equipment, and still others buy materials. Even if all the workers start out with equal abilities, each gets better at a particular job by doing it repeatedly. *Learning by doing* thus turns workers of average productivity into specialists, thereby creating a more productive team.

A third reason for cooperation comes into play after the process of learning by doing has developed different skills, and it also applies when workers start out with different talents and abilities—the principle of division of labor according to *comparative advantage*. **Comparative advantage** is the ability to do a job or produce a good at a relatively lower opportunity cost than someone else.

**Comparative advantage**

The ability to produce a good or service at a relatively lower opportunity cost than someone else

The following example will illustrate the principle of comparative advantage. Suppose two clerical workers, Bill and Jim, are assigned the job of getting out a batch of personalized letters to clients. Jim is a whiz. He can prepare a letter in five minutes and stuff it into an envelope in one minute. Working alone, he can finish ten letters in an hour. Bill is slow and clumsy. It takes him ten minutes to prepare a letter and five minutes to stuff it into the envelope. Alone, he can do only four letters an hour. In summary form:

Jim: Prepare one letter in five min.     Stuff one envelope one in min.
Bill: Prepare one letter in ten min.     Stuff one envelope five in min.

Without cooperation, the two workers' limit is fourteen letters per hour between them. Could they do better by cooperating? It depends on who does which job. One idea might be for Jim to prepare all the letters while Bill does all the stuffing because that way they can just keep up with each other; but at five minutes per letter, that kind of cooperation cuts their combined output to twelve letters per hour. It is worse than not cooperating at all.

Instead, they should divide the work according to the principle of comparative advantage. Even though Bill is slower at preparing the letters, he has a *comparative advantage* in preparation because the opportunity cost of that part of the work is lower for him: The ten minutes he takes to prepare a letter is equal to the time he needs to stuff two envelopes. For Jim, the five minutes he takes to prepare a letter could be used to stuff five envelopes. For Bill, then, the opportunity cost of preparing one letter is to forgo stuffing *two* envelopes, whereas for Jim the opportunity cost of preparing one letter is to forgo stuffing *five* envelopes.

Because Bill gives up fewer stuffed envelopes per letter than Jim, the principle of comparative advantage says that Bill should spend all his time preparing letters. If he does, he can produce six letters per hour. Meanwhile Jim can spend forty-five minutes of each hour preparing nine letters, and the last fifteen minutes of each hour stuffing all fifteen envelopes. By specializing according to comparative advantage, the two workers can increase their total output to fifteen letters per hour, the best they can possible do.

In this example, the principle of comparative advantage points the way toward an efficient division of labor between two people working side by side. However, the principle also has broader implications. It can apply to a division of labor between individuals or business firms working far apart—even in different countries. In fact, the earliest application of the principle was to international trade (see *Who Said It? Who Did It? 1.1*). Today comparative advantage remains one of the primary motiva-

## Who Said It? Who Did It? 1.1
## DAVID RICARDO AND THE THEORY OF COMPARATIVE ADVANTAGE

David Ricardo was born in London in 1772, the son of an immigrant who was a member of the London stock exchange. Ricardo's education was rather haphazard, and he entered his father's business at the age of fourteen. In 1793, he married and went into business on his own. These were years of war and financial turmoil. The young Ricardo developed a reputation for remarkable astuteness and quickly made a large fortune.

In 1799, Ricardo read Adam Smith's *The Wealth of Nations* and developed an interest in political economy (as economics was then called). In 1809, his first writings on economics appeared. These were a series of newspaper articles on "The High Price of Bullion," which appeared during the following year as a pamphlet. Several other short works added to his reputation in this area. In 1814, he retired from business to devote all his time to political economy.

Ricardo's major work was *Principles of Political Economy and Taxation*, first published in 1817. This work contains, among other things, a pioneering statement of the principle of comparative advantage as applied to international trade. Using a lucid numerical example, Ricardo showed why, as long as wool can be produced comparatively less expensively in England, it was to the advantage

Ricardo's comparative advantage describes exporting wool and importing wine between England and Portugal

of both countries for England to export wool to Portugal and to import wine in return, even though both products could be produced with fewer labor hours in Portugal.

International trade is only one topic in Ricardo's *Principles*. The book covers the whole field of economics, as it then existed, beginning with value theory and progressing to a theory of economic growth and evolution. Ricardo held that the economy was growing toward a future "steady state." At that point, economic growth would come to a halt, and the wage rate would be reduced to the subsistence level. This gloomy view and the equally pessimistic views of Ricardo's contemporary, Thomas Malthus, gave political economy a reputation as "the dismal science."

Ricardo's book was extremely influential. For more than half a century thereafter, much of the writing on economic theory published in England consisted of expansions and commentaries on Ricardo's work. Economists as different as Karl Marx, the revolutionary socialist, and John Stuart Mill, a defender of liberal capitalism, took Ricardo's theories as their starting point. Even today, there are "neo-Ricardian" and "new classical" economists who look to Ricardo's works for inspiration.

tions for mutually beneficial cooperation, whether on the scale of the workplace or on that of the world as a whole.

Whatever the context, the principle of comparative advantage is easy to apply provided one remembers that it is rooted in the concept of opportunity cost. Suppose there are two tasks, A and B, and two parties, X and Y (individuals, firms, or countries), each capable of doing both tasks, but not equally well. First ask what is the opportunity cost for X of doing a unit of task A, measured in terms of how many units of task B could be done with the same time or resources. Then ask the same question for Y. The party with the lower opportunity cost for doing a unit of task A has the comparative advantage in doing that task. To check, ask what is the opportunity cost for each party of doing a unit of task B, measured in terms how many units of task A could be done with the same time or resources. The party with the lower opportunity cost for doing a unit of task B has the comparative advantage in doing that task. Both A and B will be better off if each specializes according to comparative advantage.

## Deciding for Whom Goods Will Be Produced: Positive and Normative Economics

Together, the advantages of team production, learning by doing, and comparative advantage mean that people can produce more efficiently by cooperating than they could if each worked in isolation. Cooperation raises yet another issue, however: For whom will goods be produced? The question of the distribution of output among members of society has implications in terms of both efficiency and fairness.

**EFFICIENCY IN DISTRIBUTION**   Consider first a situation in which production has already taken place and the supply of goods is fixed. Suppose, for example, that 30 students get on a bus to go to a football game. Bag lunches are handed out. Half the bags contain a ham sandwich and a root beer; the other half contain a tuna sandwich and a cola. What happens when the students open their bags? They do not just eat whatever they find—they start trading. Some swap sandwiches; others swap drinks. Maybe there is not enough of everything to give each person his or her first choice. Nevertheless, the trading makes at least some people better off than they were when they started. Moreover, no one ends up worse off. If some of the students do not want to trade, they can always eat what was given to them in the first place.

This example shows one sense in which the "for whom" question is partly about efficiency: Starting from any given quantity of goods, their distribution can be improved through trades that result in better satisfaction of some people's preferences. As long as it is possible to trade existing supplies of goods in a way that permits some people to satisfy their wants more fully without making others worse off, **efficiency in distribution** can be improved even while the total quantity of goods remains fixed.

Efficiency in distribution and efficiency in production are two aspects of the general concept of economic efficiency. When both aspects are taken into account, the relationship between distribution and efficiency is not restricted to situations in which the total amount of goods is fixed in advance. That is so because the rules for distribu-

**Efficiency in distribution**

A situation in which it is not possible, by redistributing existing supplies of goods, to satisfy one person's wants more fully without causing some other person's wants to be satisfied less fully

tion affect the patterns of production. For example, suppose rewards for providing nursing care are increased relative to the rewards for producing clothing. As a result, some people will switch jobs, so that more nursing care and less clothing is produced. Another reason is that rules for distribution affect incentives for entrepreneurship. If there are great rewards for discovering new ways of doing things, people will make greater efforts to improve products, methods of production, and means of distribution.

**FAIRNESS IN DISTRIBUTION**     Efficiency is not the whole story when it comes to the question of for whom goods will be produced. One can also ask whether a given distribution is fair. Questions of fairness often dominate discussions of distribution.

One widely held view judges fairness in distribution in terms of equality. This concept of fairness is based on the idea that all people, by virtue of their shared humanity, deserve a portion of the goods and services turned out by the economy. There are many versions of this concept. Some people think that all income and wealth should be distributed equally. Others think that people have an equal right to a "safety net" level of income but that inequality in distributing any surplus beyond that level is not necessarily unfair. Still others think that certain goods, such as health care and education, should be distributed equally but that it is fair for other goods to be distributed less equally.

An alternative view, which also has many adherents, judges fairness not in terms of how much each person receives but instead, in terms of the process through which goods are distributed. In this view, fairness requires that certain rules and procedures be observed, such as respect for property or nondiscrimination on grounds of race and gender. As long as those rules are followed, any resulting distribution of income is viewed as acceptable. In this view, equality of opportunity is emphasized more than equality of outcome.

**POSITIVE AND NORMATIVE ECONOMICS**     Some economists make a sharp distinction between questions of efficiency and fairness. Discussions of efficiency are seen as part of **positive economics**, the area of economics that is concerned with facts and the relationships among them. Discussions of fairness, in contrast, are seen as part of **normative economics**, the area of economics that is devoted to judgments about whether particular economic policies and conditions are good or bad.

Normative economics extends beyond the question of fairness in the distribution of output. Value judgments also arise about the fairness of the other three basic choices faced by every economy. In choosing what will be produced, is it fair to permit production of alcohol and tobacco but to outlaw production of marijuana? In choosing how to produce, is it fair to allow people to work under dangerous or unhealthy conditions, or should work under such conditions be prohibited? In choosing who does which work, is it fair to limit access to specific jobs according to age, gender, race, or union membership? As you can see, normative issues extend to every corner of economics.

Positive economics, rather than offering value judgments about outcomes, focuses on understanding the processes by which the four basic economic questions are or could be answered. It analyzes the way economies operate, or would operate, if certain institutions or policies were changed. It traces relationships between facts, often looking for regularities and patterns that can be measured statistically.

**Positive economics**

The area of economics that is concerned with facts and the relationships among them

**Normative economics**

The area of economics that is devoted to judgments about whether economic policies or conditions are good or bad

Most economists consider positive economics their primary area of expertise, but normative considerations influence the conduct of positive economics in several ways. The most significant of those influences is the selection of topics to investigate. An economist who sees excessive unemployment as a glaring injustice may study that problem; one who sympathizes with victims of job discrimination may take up a different line of research. Also, normative views are likely to affect the ways in which data are collected, ideas about which facts can be considered true, and so on.

At one time it was thought that a purely positive economics could be developed, untouched by normative considerations of values and fairness. Within its framework, all disputes could be resolved by reference to objective facts. Today that notion is less widely held. Nevertheless, it remains important to be aware that most major economic controversies, especially those that have to do with government policy, have normative as well as positive components and to be aware of the way each component shapes the way we think about those controversies.

## Coordinating Economic Choices

To function effectively, an economy must have some way of coordinating the choices of millions of individuals regarding what to produce, how to produce it, who will do each job, and for whom the output will be produced. This section discusses how households, businesses, and the government interact in the coordination of economic choices.

### A Non-Economic Example

You, like almost everyone, have probably had the experience of shopping at a supermarket where there are several long checkout lines. In such a situation, you and other shoppers want to get through the checkout process as fast as possible. The store, too, would like to avoid a situation in which customers in some lines have a long wait for service while the cashiers in other lines stand idle for lack of customers. How can this be done?

One way would be for the store to follow the example of the U.S. Customs service at New York's busy Kennedy International Airport where an employee is on duty to direct arriving passengers to the agent with the shortest wait. Supermarkets, however, do not usually work that way. Instead, supermarkets leave shoppers to decide for themselves which line to join based on information from their own observations. As you approach the checkout area, you first look to see which lines are the shortest. You then make allowance for the possibility that some shoppers have carts that are heaped full, while others have only a few items. Using your own judgment based on your own observations, you head for the line you think will be fastest.

The coordination system used by the Customs Service at JFK airport is an example of coordination by **hierarchy**. Hierarchy is a way of achieving coordination in which individual actions are guided by instructions from a central authority. The approach used in supermarkets is an example of coordination by **spontaneous order**. Under this system, coordination is achieved when individuals adjust their own actions as they see best in response to cues received from their immediate environment. This

**Hierarchy**

A way of achieving coordination in which individual actions are guided by instructions from a central authority

**Spontaneous order**

A way of achieving coordination in which individuals adjust their actions in response to cues from their immediate environment

method is *orderly* because it achieves an approximately equal waiting time in each checkout line. It is *spontaneous* in that coordination is achieved without central direction. Even though no shopper has the specific goal of equalizing the lines, approximate equalization is the end result.

## Spontaneous Order in Markets

**Market**

Any arrangement people have for trading with one another

In economics, markets are the most important example of the coordination of decisions through spontaneous order. A **market** is any arrangement people have for trading with one another. Some markets have formal rules and carry out exchanges at a single location, such as the New York Stock Exchange. Other markets are more informal, such as the word-of-mouth networks through which domestic workers get in touch with people who need their services. Despite the wide variety of forms that markets take, they all have one thing in common: They provide the information and incentives people need to coordinate their decisions.

Just as shoppers need information about the length of checkout lines, participants in markets need information about the scarcity and opportunity costs of various goods and factors of production. Markets rely primarily on prices to transmit this information. If a good or factor of production becomes scarcer, its price is bid up. The increase in the price tells people it is worth more and signals producers to make greater efforts to increase supplies. For example, when platinum first began to be used in catalytic converters to reduce pollution from automobile exhaust, new buyers entered the market. As automakers began to compete with makers of jewelry and other traditional users, platinum became more difficult to acquire. Competition for available supplies bids up the price of platinum. This provided buyers with a cue that the value of platinum had increased and provided an incentive to be careful with its use. At the same time, producers learned that, where possible, they should increase the quantity of platinum mined.

Instead, suppose a new technology were to reduce the cost of producing platinum, for example, by allowing extraction of platinum from mine wastes that were discarded in earlier periods when platinum was less valuable. Markets would transmit information about the reduced cost in the form of a lower price. People could then consider increasing the quantity of platinum they use.

In addition to knowing the best use for resources, people must also have incentives to act on that information. Markets provide incentives to sell goods and productive resources where they will bring the highest prices and to buy them where they can be obtained at the lowest prices. Profits motivate business managers to improve production methods and to design goods that match consumer needs. Workers who stay alert to opportunities and work where they are most productive receive the highest wages. Consumers are motivated to use less expensive substitutes where feasible.

Adam Smith, often considered the father of economics, saw coordination through markets as the foundation of prosperity and progress. In a famous passage in *The Wealth of Nations*, he called markets an "invisible hand" that nudges people into the economic roles they can play best (see *Who Said It? Who Did It? 1.2*). To this day, an appreciation of markets as a means of coordinating choices remains a central feature of the economic way of thinking.

**Who Said It? Who Did It? 1.2**
## ADAM SMITH ON THE INVISIBLE HAND

Adam Smith is considered the founder of economics as a distinct field of study, even though he wrote only one book on the subject: *The Wealth of Nations,* published in 1776. Smith was fifty-three years old at the time. His friend David Hume found the book such hard going that he doubted that many people would read it. Hume was wrong—people have been reading it for more than two hundred years.

The wealth of a nation, in Smith's view, is not a result of the accumulation of gold or silver in its treasury, as many of his contemporaries believed. Rather, it is the outcome of the activities of ordinary people working and trading in free markets. To Smith, the remarkable thing about the wealth produced by a market economy is that it is not a result of any organized plan but that it is rather the unintended outcome of the actions of many people, each of whom is pursuing the incentives the market offers with his or her own interests in mind. As he put it:

*It is not from the benevolence of the butcher, the brewer, or the baker that we expect our dinner, but from their regard to their own interest ... Every individual is continually exerting himself to find out the most advantageous employment for whatever capital he can command ... By directing that industry in such a manner as its produce may be of the greatest value, he intends only his own gain; and he is in this, as in many other cases, led by an invisible hand to promote an end which was no part of his intention. \**

Much of the discipline of economics as it has developed over the past two centuries consists of elaborations on ideas found in Smith's work. The idea of the "invisible hand" of market incentives that channels people's efforts in directions that are beneficial to their neighbors remains the most durable of Smith's contributions to economics.

_____

\* Adam Smith, *The Wealth of Nations* (1776), Book 1, Chapter 2.

## The Role of Hierarchy

Important as markets are, they are not the only means of achieving economic coordination. Some decisions are guided by direct authority within organizations, that is, by the mechanism of hierarchy. Decisions made by government agencies are one important example. Government decisions are often implemented, not through the spontaneous choices of individuals, but via directives issued by a central authority: pay your taxes, do not dump toxic wastes in the river, and so on. Business firms, especially large corporations, are another important example of the hierarchical form of organization. The Toyota Motor Corporation uses directives from a central authority to make many important decisions—for example, the decision to build a new hybrid version of its popular Camry in Kentucky rather than in Japan.

Although governments and corporations use hierarchical methods to make choices within their organizations, they deal with one another and with individual consumers through markets. Markets and hierarchies thus play complementary roles in achieving economic coordination. Some economies rely more on markets, others on government or corporate planning. At one extreme, the centrally planned economy of North Korea places heavy emphasis on government authority. Economies like that of the United States make greater use of markets, but no economy uses one means of coordination to the exclusion of the other. Government regulatory agencies in the United States establish laws to control pollution or protect worker safety; on the other hand, North Korea uses small-scale markets to distribute some goods. Large corporations use commands from higher authority to make many decisions, but they also often subcontract with outsiders through the market; and they sometimes encourage their own divisions to deal with one another on a market basis.

In short, wherever one turns in economics, the question of coordination arises. Understanding economic coordination means understanding the complementary roles of markets, on the one hand, and of government and corporate hierarchies, on the other.

## Economic Method

We have seen that economists have a distinctive way of thinking about the world based on the concepts of scarcity, choice, and exchange. They also have some distinctive methods of approaching problems and expressing the conclusions that they reach. We will conclude the chapter with a few comments about method.

### Theories and Models

Economists try to understand the choices people make in terms of the context in which the choices are made. The relationships they propose between choices and context are called **theories** or **models**. The terms mean almost the same, although economists tend to use the term theory to refer to more general statements about economic relationships and the term model to refer to more particular statements, especially those that take the form of graphs or mathematical equations.

**Theory**

A representation of the way in which facts are related to one another

**Model**

A synonym for theory; in economics, often applied to theories that are stated in graphical or mathematical form

Economics needs theories and models because facts do not speak for themselves. Take, for example, the fact that in the spring of 2008 U.S. farmers planted more acres in corn than ever before. Economists have a theory as to why this happened. They relate the change in crop patterns to a record-high price for corn at the time of planting. The relationship between the price of corn and the choice of what crop to grow is seen as a particular instance of a broader theory according to which an increase in the price of any good, other things being equal, leads producers to increase their output of the good.

The theory, as stated, is a simple one. It relates crop choices to just one other fact, the price of corn. A more complete theory would bring in other factors that influence choice, such as the prices of gasoline, for which corn-based ethanol is a substitute; the price of soybeans, which can be grown on the same land

Choosing to plant corn is generally based on the price of corn compared to other crops.

as corn; tax advantages provided by Congress to producers of biofuels; and so on. Where does one draw the line? How much detail does it take to make a good theory?

There is no simple answer to this question because adding detail to a theory involves a trade-off. On the one hand, if essential details are left out, the theory may fail altogether to fit the facts. On the other hand, adding too much detail defeats the purpose of understanding because key relationships may become lost in a cloud of complexity. The only real guideline is that a theory should be just detailed enough to suit the purpose for which it is intended, and no more.

By analogy, consider the models that aircraft designers use. A scaled-down wind-tunnel model made to test the aerodynamics of a new design would need to represent the shapes of the wings, fuselage, and control surfaces accurately, but it would not need to include tiny seats with tiny tables and magazine pockets. On the other hand, a full-scale model built for the purpose of training flight crews to work on the new plane would need seats and magazine pockets, but it would not need wings.

In much the same way, the theories and models presented in this book are designed to highlight a few key economic relationships. They are helpful in understanding economics in the same way that playing a flight simulation game on a laptop computer is helpful in understanding the basics of flying. Professional economists use more detailed models, just as professional pilots train with complex flight simulators rather than with simple computer games. Nevertheless, the basic principles learned from the simple models should not contradict those that apply to the more complex ones. In the simple games, just as in the complex simulators, adjusting the rudder makes the plane turn and adjusting the elevators makes it climb or dive.

## The Use of Graphs

The theories introduced so far have been stated in words. Words are a powerful tool for developing understanding, but they are even more powerful when pictures supplement them. Economists support their words with pictures called graphs. An example will illustrate how economists use graphs to represent theories.[4]

**THE PRODUCTION POSSIBILITY FRONTIER**    Recall our earlier discussion of the trade-off between education and cars. Figure 1.1 shows the trade-off in graphical form for an economy in which only those two goods are produced. The horizontal axis measures the quantity of education in terms of the number of college graduates produced per year; the vertical axis measures the production of cars. Any combination of education and cars can be shown as a point in the space between the two axes. For example, production of 10 million graduates and 5 million cars in a given year would be represented by point E.

In drawing this graph, supplies of productive resources and the state of knowledge are assumed to remain constant. Even if all available resources are devoted to education, there is a limit to the number of graduates that can be produced in a year: twenty million. The extreme possibility of producing twenty million graduates and no cars is shown by point A. Likewise, the maximum number of cars that would be produced if no resources were put into education is eighteen million cars, shown by point B. Between those two extremes is a whole range of possible combinations of education

**FIGURE 1.1     PRODUCTION POSSIBILITY FRONTIER**

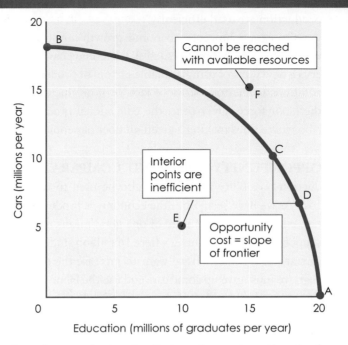

This figure shows combinations of cars and education that can be produced in a simple economy in which they are the only two products. Quantities of available factors of production and the state of existing knowledge are assumed to be fixed. If all factors are devoted to education, 20 million college graduates can be produced each year (point A). If all factors are devoted to making cars, 18 million cars can be produced each year (point B). Other combinations of the two goods that can be produced using available factors efficiently, such as those represented by points C and D, lie along a curve called a production possibility frontier. The slope of the frontier indicates the opportunity cost of education in terms of cars. Interior points, such as E, represent inefficient use of resources. Beginning from such a point, more of one good can be produced without producing less of the other. Points outside the frontier, such as F, cannot be reached using available factors of production and knowledge.

**Production possibility frontier**

A graph that shows possible combinations of goods that can be produced by an economy given available knowledge and factors of production

and cars. Those intermediate possibilities are shown by points such as C and D, which fall along a smooth curve. The curve is known as a **production possibility frontier**.

**EFFICIENCY AND ECONOMIC GROWTH**     The production possibility frontier is a boundary between the combinations of education and cars that can be produced and those that cannot, using given knowledge and productive resources. As such, it serves nicely to illustrate the concept of efficiency in production. Points inside the frontier, such as point E, represent inefficient production. Beginning from such a point, more cars can be made without cutting the output of education (shown by a vertical move toward the frontier); more education can be produced without cutting the output of cars (a horizontal move toward the frontier); or the output of both goods can be increased (a move up and to the right toward the frontier).

Points such as A, B, C, and D that are on the frontier represent efficient production. Starting from any of those points, it is not possible to produce more of one good without producing less of the other. For example, in moving from C to D, output of education is increased but output of cars falls. Points such as F that lie outside the frontier cannot be reached even when the currently available knowledge and factors of production are used efficiently.

Over time, however, economic growth can stretch the production possibility frontier outward so that points such as F become possible. As mentioned earlier, the discovery of new ways of using available factors of production is one source of growth. So are additions to the total stock of factors of production—for example, through growth of the labor force. Over time, the educational process itself improves the quality of the labor force, thus making a given number of people capable of producing more.

**OPPORTUNITY COST AND COMPARATIVE ADVANTAGE**    The production possibility frontier can also be used to represent the concept of opportunity cost. As we have seen, once the economy is producing efficiently at a point on the frontier, choosing to make more of one good means making less of the other. For example, suppose we start at point C, where 16 million students graduate each year and 10 million cars are being made. If we want to increase the output of graduates to 18 million per year, we must give up some cars and use the labor, capital, and natural resources freed in this way to build and staff classrooms. In moving from point C to point D, we trade off production of 4 million cars for the extra 2 million graduates. Over that range of the frontier, the opportunity cost of each extra graduate is about two cars. The slope of the frontier shows the opportunity cost of graduates, measured in terms of cars.

As more graduates are produced and the economy moves down and to the right along the frontier, the frontier becomes steeper and the opportunity cost of producing graduates increases. A major reason is that not all factors of production—especially not all workers—are alike. Suppose we start all the way up at point B, where no education is produced, and transfer enough resources to education to open one small college. The first people we would pull off the assembly line to staff the classrooms would be those who have a comparative advantage in teaching. By the time enough resources have been transferred to education from the auto industry to reach point D, the most suitable recruits for academic life have already been used. Increasingly, to produce still more education we have to take some of the best production workers with no assurance that they will be good teachers. The opportunity cost of increasing the output of education (shown by the slope of the frontier) is correspondingly greater.

## Theory and Evidence

Theories are of no use in explaining relationships among facts unless they fit those facts. Theory building is a matter of constantly comparing proposed explanations with evidence gleaned from observations of the actual choices people make—that is, with empirical evidence. When **empirical** evidence is consistent with the relationships proposed in a theory, confidence in the validity of the theory is increased. When evidence is not consistent with the theory, the theory needs to be reexamined. The relationships proposed in it may be invalid, or they may be valid only under circumstances different from those that prevailed when the observations were made. The theory then needs to be modified by changing the proposed relationships or adding detail.

**Empirical**

Based on experience or observation

Government agencies and private firms generate mountains of empirical data on economic activity. Economists constantly examine those data in an effort to confirm theories or find inconsistencies that point the way to better theories. Statistical analysis of empirical economic data is known as **econometrics**—the science of economic measurement.

**Econometrics**

The statistical analysis of empirical economic data

## Theories and Forecasts

Economic theories can help us understand things that happened in the past—trends in crop patterns over the past decade, the effects of new, twenty-first century communication technologies, and so on; but understanding the past is not always enough. People also want forecasts of future economic events.

Within limits, economic theory can be useful here, too. Any theory that purports to explain a relationship between past events provides a basis for predicting what will happen under similar circumstances in the future. To put it more precisely, economic theory can be used to make **conditional forecasts** of the form "If A, then B, other things being equal." Thus, an economist might say, "If gasoline prices rise, and if at the same time consumer incomes and the prices of other goods do not change, purchases of low-mileage vehicles will fall."

**Conditional forecast**

A prediction of future economic events in the form "If A, then B, other things being equal"

Thousands of economists make a living from forecasting. Decision-makers in business and government use economic forecasts extensively. Forecasts are not perfect, however; and forecasters sometimes make conspicuous mistakes. There are at least three reasons for the mistakes.

First, insufficient attention is sometimes paid to the conditional nature of forecasts. The news might report, for example, that "economists predict a drop in SUV sales," yet people keep right on buying big vehicles. In such a case, the news report may have failed to note the forecasters' precautionary comments. The forecasters may have said that SUV sales would drop in response to a gas price increase if consumer incomes and technology remained the same; but consumers got richer and new technology made SUVs less gas-hungry, so SUV sales did not fall after all.

Second, a forecast may be invalid because the theory on which it is based is incorrect or incomplete. Economists do not always agree on what theory best fits the facts. Some theories give more weight to one fact, others to different facts. The competing theories may imply conflicting forecasts under some conditions. At least one of the forecasts will then turn out to be wrong. Finding out which theories yield better forecasts than others is an important part of the process through which valid theories are distinguished from inadequate ones.

Third, economic forecasts can go wrong because some of the things that business managers and government officials most want to know are among the hardest to predict. For example, a competent economist could produce a fairly accurate forecast of vehicle sales based on certain assumptions about incomes and the prices of gasoline and other goods. However, what the marketing people at General Motors would like to know is what will happen to the social image of SUVs: Will they continue to be a symbol of high status, or will they become an embarrassment in a more environmentally conscious society? Social attitudes are not among the variables that economists can forecast accurately.

Despite these limitations, most economists take the view that well-founded conditional forecasts, for all their limitations, are a better basis for business and public policy decisions than whims and guesswork. Still, they caution against relying too heavily on forecasts.

## Theory and Policy

Economists are often asked to use their theories to analyze the effects of public policies and forecast the effects of policy changes. The government may, for example, be considering new measures to aid unemployed workers, new responses to global warming, or new measures to regulate international trade. How will the effects of such policies be spread through the economy? How will they affect people's lives?

Economists have their own characteristic way of thinking about public policy, just as they have their own way of thinking about other topics. In particular, economists are concerned with identifying both the direct and indirect effects of policy, as well as any indirect or unintended consequences. They are also constantly alert to both the long-term and short-term effects of policy. For example:

- Unemployment compensation has the intended effect of aiding unemployed workers; but it also has the unintended effect of increasing the number of workers who are unemployed because workers receiving compensation can afford to take their time finding just the right new job. Many observers see generous unemployment compensation in some parts of Europe as one reason unemployment rates there are higher than in the United States.

- Regulations intended to improve the fuel efficiency of automobiles encourage production of cars that weigh less, but the lighter cars are somewhat less safe. Increased highway deaths among drivers of the lighter cars may thus be an unintended consequence of efforts to save fuel.

- After widespread banking failures in the 1980s, U.S. regulators made rule changes intended to stabilize the banking system by strengthening the balance sheets of commercial banks. Those regulations also raised the cost of bank loans relative to loans from other sources outside the banking system. As an unintended consequence, much lending activity, including home mortgage lending, moved to an emerging "shadow banking system" consisting of mortgage brokers, securitized loans, and special purpose financial vehicles. When a crisis came, the new financial system turned out, in some ways, to be not more but less stable than the old one.

While policies may have unintended consequences, it would be wrong to conclude that the government should never act simply because its actions may do some harm as well as some good. Sometimes the harm may outweigh the good, and sometimes not. What is important, economists say, is that policy-makers look at the whole picture, not just part of it, before they make a decision. As Henry Hazlitt once put it, the whole of economics can be reduced to a single lesson:

*The art of economics consists in looking not merely at the immediate but at the longer effects of any act or policy; it consists in tracing the consequences of that policy not merely for one group but for all groups.*[5]

As you progress through your study of economics—both the macro and micro branches—you will repeatedly encounter examples of the way economic theory can help understand the choices people make and the complex effects of policies intended to regulate those choices.

## Summary

1. **What is the subject matter of economics?** Economics is a social science that seeks to understand the choices people make in using scarce resources to meet their wants. Scarcity is a situation in which there is not enough of something to meet everyone's wants. *Microeconomics* is the branch of economics that studies choices that involve individual households, firms, and markets. *Macroeconomics* is the branch of economics that deals with large-scale economic phenomena, such as inflation, unemployment, and economic growth.

2. **What considerations underlie the choice of what an economy will produce?** Producing more of one good requires producing less of something else because productive resources that are used to produce one good cannot be used to produce another at the same time. Productive resources are traditionally classified into three groups, called *factors of production*. *Labor* consists of the productive contributions made by people working with their hands and minds. *Capital* consists of all the productive inputs created by people. *Natural resources* include anything that can be used as a productive input in its natural state. The *opportunity cost* of a good or service is its cost in terms of the forgone opportunity to pursue the best possible alternative activity with the same time or resources.

3. **What considerations underlie the choice of how to produce?** Goods and services can be produced in many different ways, some of which are more efficient than others. *Economic efficiency* refers to a state of affairs in which it is impossible to make any change that satisfies one person's wants more fully without causing some other person's wants to be satisfied less fully. *Efficiency in production* refers to a situation in which it is not possible, given the available productive resources and existing knowledge, to produce more of one good or service without forgoing the opportunity to produce some of another good or service. Once efficiency has been achieved, production potential can be expanded by increasing the availability of resources or by improving knowledge. The process of increasing the economy's stock of capital is known as *investment*. The process of looking for new possibilities—making use of new ways of doing things, being alert to new opportunities, and overcoming old limits—is known as *entrepreneurship*.

4. **What considerations underlie the choice of who will do which work?** Economic efficiency is greatly enhanced by cooperation with others. Three things make cooperation worthwhile: teamwork, learning by doing, and comparative advantage. Teamwork can enhance productivity even when there is no specialization. Learning by doing improves productivity even when all workers start with equal talents and abilities. Comparative

advantage comes into play when people have different innate abilities or, after learning by doing, have developed specialized skills. Having a *comparative advantage* in producing a particular good or service means being able to produce it at a relatively lower opportunity cost than someone else.

5. **What considerations underlie the choice of for whom goods will be produced?** In part, deciding for whom goods will be produced revolves around issues of efficiency. *Efficiency in distribution* refers to a state of affairs in which, with a given quantity of goods and services, it is impossible to satisfy one person's wants more fully without satisfying someone else's less fully. Efficiency is part of *positive economics*, the area of economics that is concerned with facts and the relationships among them. *Normative economics* is the area of economics that is devoted to judgments about which economic conditions and policies are good or bad.

6. **What mechanisms are used to coordinate economic choices?** The two principle methods of coordinating choices are *hierarchy* and *spontaneous order*. Markets are the most important example of spontaneous order. The internal decisions made by large corporations and units of government are the most important examples of hierarchy.

7. **How do economists use theory, graphs, and evidence in their work?** A *theory* or *model* is a representation of the ways in which facts are related to one another. Economists use graphs to display data and make visual representations of theories and models. For example, a *production possibility frontier* is a graph that shows the boundary between combinations of goods that can be produced and those that cannot, using available factors of production and knowledge. Economists refine theories in the light of *empirical* evidence, that is, evidence gleaned from observation of actual economic decisions. The economic analysis of empirical evidence is known as *econometrics*. Economic models are often used to make *conditional forecasts* of the form "If A, then B, other things being equal."

## Key Terms

## Problems and Topics for Discussion

1. **Opportunity cost** Gasoline, insurance, depreciation, and repairs are all costs of owning a car. Which of these can be considered opportunity costs in the context of each of the following decisions?

a. You own a car and are deciding whether to drive 100 miles for a weekend visit to a friend at another university.

b. You do not own a car but are considering buying one so that you can get a part-time job located 5 miles from where you live.

In general, why does the context in which you decide to do something affect the opportunity cost of doing it?

2. **Comparative advantage in international trade** Suppose that in the United States a car can be produced with 200 labor hours while a ton of rice requires 20 labor hours. In China, it takes 250 labor hours to make a car and 50 labor hours to grow a ton of rice. What is the opportunity cost of producing rice in each country, stated in terms of cars? What is the opportunity cost of cars, stated in terms of rice? Which country has a comparative advantage in cars? Which in rice?

3. **Efficiency in distribution and the food stamp program** The federal food stamp program could have been designed so that every low-income family would receive a book of coupons containing so many bread coupons, so many milk coupons, and so on. Instead, it gives the family an allowance that can be spent on any kind of food the family prefers. For a given cost to the federal government, which plan do you think would better serve the goal of efficiency in distribution? Why?

Now consider a program that would allow families to trade their food stamps for cash (some such trading does occur, but it is restricted by law) or one in which poor families are given cash, with which they can buy whatever they want. Compare these alternatives with the existing food stamp program in terms of both positive and normative economics.

4. **Spontaneous order in the cafeteria** Suppose that your college cafeteria does not have enough room for all the students to sit down to eat at once, so it stays open for lunch from 11:30 a.m. to 1:30 p.m. Consider the following three methods of distributing diners over the two-hour lunch period in such a way that everyone can have a seat.

a. The administration sets a rule: First-year students must eat between 11:30 and 12:00, sophomores between 12:00 and 12:30, and so on for juniors and seniors.

b. The lunch period is broken up into half-hour segments with green tickets for the first shift, blue tickets for the second, and so on. An equal number of tickets of each color is printed. At the beginning of each semester an auction is held in which students bid for the ticket color of their choice.

c. Students can come to the cafeteria whenever they want. If there are no empty seats, they have to stand in line.

Compare the three schemes in terms of the concepts of (1) spontaneous order and hierarchy, (2) information and incentives, and (3) efficiency.

5. **A production possibility frontier** Bill Schwartz has four fields spread out over a hillside. He can grow either wheat or potatoes in any of the fields, but the low fields are better for potatoes and the high ones are better for wheat. Here are some combinations of wheat and potatoes that he could produce:

| Number of Fields Used for Potatoes | Total Tons of Potatoes | Total Tons of Wheat |
|---|---|---|
| All 4 | 1,000 | 0 |
| Lowest 3 | 900 | 400 |
| Lowest 2 | 600 | 700 |
| Lowest 1 | 300 | 900 |
| None | 0 | 1,000 |

Use these data to draw a production possibility frontier for wheat and potatoes. What is the opportunity cost of wheat, stated in terms of potatoes, when the farmer converts the highest field to wheat production? What happens to the opportunity cost of wheat as more and more fields are switched to wheat?

# Case for Discussion

## Cow Power

As natural resources go, it doesn't have much glamour; but unlike oil, the United States has plenty of it. We're talking about cow manure. The average cow puts out about 30 gallons a day. Multiply that by something like 8 million cows on the nation's 65,000 dairy farms, and you have—well, what do you have— a big problem or a big opportunity?

In the past, manure would, on balance, have been considered a problem. True, it makes good fertilizer, but with big drawbacks. Most dairy farms stored it in open lagoons before spreading it on fields. The smelly lagoons created a nuisance to neighbors. What is more, they were a big source of methane, a greenhouse gas that, pound for pound, contributes 10 times more to global warming than carbon dioxide.

Methane burns, however; and that's where cow manure becomes an opportunity. If farmers pump it into an anaerobic digester instead of into an open lagoon, it produces a purified gas that can either be burned on the farm to produce electricity or transported by pipeline to be burned elsewhere.

Marie and Earl Audet's dairy farm in Bridport, Vermont, expects to sell $200,000 worth of cow power a year to Central Vermont Public Service, the local electric utility. There are other benefits as well. The process also produces a clear liquid that can be used as fertilizer; and the farm will save another $50,000 by using the dry, odorless, fluff that is left over from the digester as bedding for the cows, in place of expensive sawdust.[6]

Cow power is not a free lunch, however. To make the economics favorable to farmers, Central Vermont Public Service pays them 12 cents per kilowatt-hour, a 4-cent premium over the normal rate. The utility makes up the difference by selling premium-priced "green electricity" to customers who want to feel they are doing something for the planet. Other state and federal agencies subsidize an estimated 100 cow power digesters elsewhere in the country.

Boosters of cow power hope the need for subsidies will disappear as costs of manufacturing the digesters fall and as gas and electric prices continue to rise. "The business model of producing energy along with food will transform the economics of rural America," said Michael T. Eckhart, president of the American Council on Renewable Energy, based in Washington.[7]

## QUESTIONS

1. Based on the information given in the case, do you think the out-of-pocket costs of producing electricity from cow manure are greater, less, or about the same as the cost of conventional power sources? On what information in the case do you base your answer?

2. Anaerobic digestion of cow manure reduces harm to neighbors (less smell) and harm to the environment (less greenhouse gas). How do these benefits enter into the calculation of the opportunity cost of producing cow power? Do these benefits tend to make the opportunity cost greater than, or less than, the out-of-pocket costs?

3. Based on information in the case, do you think the growth of the cow power industry is based on the principle of spontaneous order or that of hierarchy? Or, is it a little bit of both? Explain your reasoning.

## End Notes

1. The Austrian economist Ludwig von Mises suggested that *catallactics*, meaning the science of exchange, would be a better term than *economics*, which has the original meaning of household management. For better or worse, the term catallactics has never come into wide use.

2. Efficiency, defined this way, is sometimes called Pareto efficiency after the Italian economist Vilfredo Pareto.

3. Armen A. Alchian and Harold Demsetz, "Production, Information Cost, and Economic Organization," *American Economic Review* (December 1972): 777–795.

4. A review of basic graphical concepts, including axes, points and number pairs, slopes, and tangencies, is provided in the appendix to this chapter.

5. Henry Hazlitt, *Economics in One Lesson* (New York: Arlington House, 1979), 17.

6. Martha T. Moore, "Cows Power Plan for Alternative Fuel," *USA Today,* Dec. 6, 2006, http://www.usatoday.com/news/nation/2006-12-03-cow-power_x.htm.

7. Claudia H. Deutsch, "Tapping Latent Power in What's Left Around the Barnyard," *New York Times,* July 4, 2006. http://select.nytimes.com/search/restricted/article?res=F20B13FD39540C778CDDAE0894DE404482

# Appendix to Chapter 1:
# WORKING WITH GRAPHS

Which is smarter—a computer or the human brain? The computer certainly does some things faster and more accurately, say, dividing one twenty-digit number by another. The human brain, however, is programmed to solve other kinds of problems with speed and accuracy beyond the ability of most computers. Working with pictures is one of the areas in which the human brain excels. Three key abilities give the brain a comparative advantage where pictures are involved.

1.  An ability to store and retrieve a vast number of images quickly and accurately (Think of how many people's faces you can recognize.)

2.  An ability to discard irrelevant detail while highlighting essentials (Think of how easily you can recognize a politician's face in a political cartoon drawn with just a few lines.)

3.  An ability to see key similarities between patterns that are not exactly the same (That is why you can usually match two pictures of a person taken 20 years apart.)

Graphs are an invaluable aid in learning economics precisely because they make use of these three special abilities of the human brain. Graphs are not used to make economics harder but to make it easier. All it takes to use graphs effectively as a learning tool is the inborn human skill in working with pictures plus knowledge of a few simple rules for extracting the information that graphs contain. This appendix outlines those rules in brief. Additional details and exercises can be found in the *Study Guide* that accompanies this textbook.

## Pairs of Numbers and Points

The first thing to master is how to use points on a graph to represent pairs of numbers. The table in Figure 1A.1 presents five pairs of numbers. The two columns are labeled "*x*" and "*y*." The first number in each pair is called the *x value* and the second the *y value*. Each pair of numbers is labeled with a capital letter. Pair A has an *x* value of 2 and a *y* value of 3, pair B has an *x* value of 4 and a *y* value of 4, and so on.

The diagram in Figure 1A.1 contains two lines that meet at the lower left-hand corner; they are called *coordinate axes*. The horizontal axis is marked off into units representing the *x* value and the vertical axis into unit representing the *y* value. In the space between the axes, each pair of numbers from the table can be shown as a point. For example, point A is found by going two units to the right along the horizontal axis and then three units straight up, parallel to the vertical axis. That point represents the *x* value of 2 and the *y* value of 3. The other points are located in the same way.

The visual effect of a graph usually can be improved by connecting the points with a line or a curve. By doing so, the relationship between *x* values and *y* values can be seen at a glance: As the *x* value increases, the *y* value also increases.

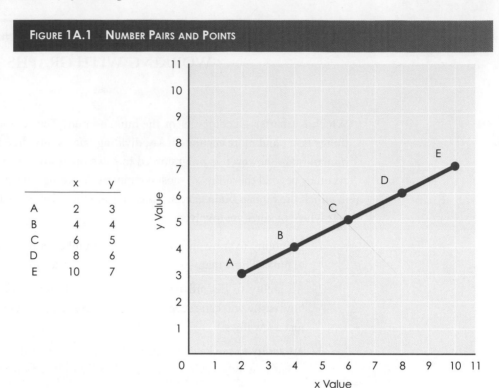

**FIGURE 1A.1   NUMBER PAIRS AND POINTS**

|   | x | y |
|---|---|---|
| A | 2 | 3 |
| B | 4 | 4 |
| C | 6 | 5 |
| D | 8 | 6 |
| E | 10 | 7 |

Each lettered pair of numbers in the table corresponds to a lettered point on the graph. The x value of each point corresponds to the horizontal distance of the point from the vertical axis; the y value corresponds to its vertical distance from the horizontal axis.

**Slope**

For a straight line, the ratio of the change in the y value to the change in the x value between any two points on the line

**Positive slope**

A slope having a value greater than zero

**Direct relationship**

A relationship between two variables in which an increase in the value of one variable is associated with an increase in the value of the other

## Slopes and Tangencies

The lines or curves used in graphs are described in terms of their slopes. The **slope** of a straight line between two points is defined as the ratio of the change in the y value to the change in the x value between the two points. In Figure 1A.2, for example, the slope of the line between points A and B is 2. The y value changes by six units between these two points, whereas the x value changes by only three units. The slope is the ratio 6/3 = 2.

The slope of a line between the points (x1, y1) and (x2, y2) can be expressed in terms of a simple formula that is derived from the definition just given:

$$\text{Slope} = (y_2 - y_1)/(x_2 - x_1)$$

Applied to the line between points A and B in Figure 1A.2, the formula gives the following result:

$$\text{Slope} = (7 - 1)/(4 - 1) = 6/3 = 2$$

A line such as that between A and B in Figure 1A.2, which slopes upward from left to right, is said to have a **positive slope** because the value of its slope is a positive number. A positively sloped line represents a **direct relationship** between the variable represented on the x axis and that represented on the y axis—that is, a relationship in which an increase in one variable is associated with an increase in the other. The relationship

**FIGURE 1A.2   SLOPES OF LINES**

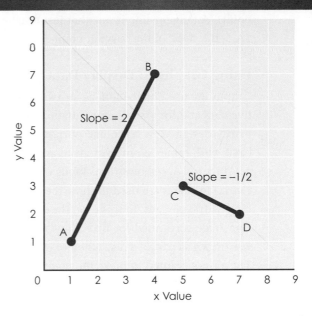

The slope of a straight line drawn between two points is defined as the ratio of the change in the *y* value to the change in the *x* value as one moves from one point to the other. For example, the line between points A and B in this figure has a slope of +2, whereas the line between points C and D has a slope of –1/2.

**Negative slope**

A slope having a value less than zero

**Inverse relationship**

A relationship between two variables in which an increase in the value of one variable is associated with a decrease in the value of the other

of the age of a tree to its height is an example of a direct relationship. An example from economics is the relationship between family income and expenditures on housing.

When a line slants downward from left to right, like the one between points C and D in Figure 1A.2, the *x* and *y* values change in opposite directions. Going from point C to point D, the *y* value changes by –1 (that is, decreases by one unit) and the *x* value changes by +2 (that is, increases by two units). The slope of this line is the ratio –1/2.

When a negative number gives the slope of a line, the line is said to have a **negative slope**. Such a line represents an **inverse relationship** between the *x* variable and the *y* variable—that is, a relationship in which an increase in the value of one variable is associated with a decrease in the value of the other variable. The relationship between the temperature in the room and the time it takes the ice in your lemonade to melt is an example of an inverse relationship. To give an economic example, the relationship between the price of gasoline and the quantity that consumers purchase, other things being equal, is an inverse relationship.

The concepts of positive and negative slopes, and of direct and inverse relationships, apply to curves as well as to straight lines. However, the slope of a curve, unlike that of a straight line, varies from one point to the next.[1] We cannot speak of the slope

---

[1] Economists try to be consistent, but in talking about lines and curves, they fail. They have no qualms about calling something a "curve" that is a straight line. For example, later we will encounter "demand curves" that are as straight as a stretched string. Less frequently, they may call something a line that is curved.

**Tangent**

A straight line that touches a curve at a given point without intersecting it

of a curve in general, but only of its slope at a given point. The slope of a curve at any given point is defined as the slope of a straight line drawn tangent to the curve at that point. (A **tangent** line is one that just touches the curve without crossing it.) In Figure 1A.3, the slope of the curve at point A is 1 and the slope at point B is –2.

## Using Graphs to Display Data

Graphs are used in economics for two primary purposes: for visual display of quantitative data and for visual representation of economic relationships. Some graphs are primarily designed to serve one purpose, some the other, and some a little of both. We begin with some common kinds of graphs whose primary purpose is to display data.

Figure 1A.4 shows three kinds of graphs often used to display data. Part (a) is *pie chart*. Pie charts are used to show the relative size of various quantities that add up to a total of 100 percent. In this case, the quantities displayed are the percentages of U.S. foreign trade accounted for by various trading partners. In the original source, the graph was drawn as part of a discussion of U.S. trade with Canada, Japan, and Western Europe. The author wanted to make the point that trade with these countries is very important. Note how the graph highlights Canadian, Japanese, and Western European trade with the U.S. and, at the same time, omits details not relevant to the discussion by lumping together the rest of Europe, Africa, the rest of Asia, and many other countries under the heading "rest of the world." In reading graphs, do not just look at the numbers; ask yourself, "What point is the graph trying to make?"

Part (b) of Figure 1A.4 is a *bar chart*. Bar charts, like pie charts, are used to display numerical data (in this case, unemployment rates) in relationship to some non-numerical

**FIGURE 1A.3    SLOPES OF CURVES**

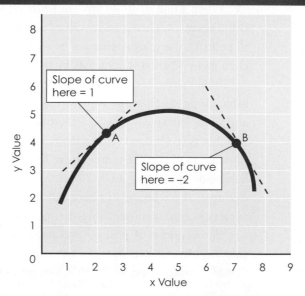

The slope of a curve at any point is defined as the slope of a straight line drawn tangent to the curve at that point. A tangent line is one that just touches the curve without crossing it. In this figure, the slope of the curve at point A is 1, and the slope at point B is –2.

**FIGURE 1A.4    USING GRAPHS TO DISPLAY DATA**

(a)

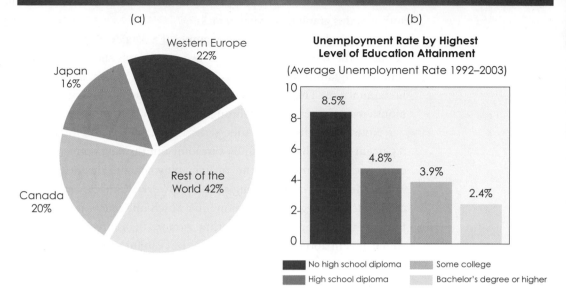

(b)

**Unemployment Rate by Highest
Level of Education Attainment**

(Average Unemployment Rate 1992–2003)

(c)

**Civilian Unemployment Rate**
(1980–2003)

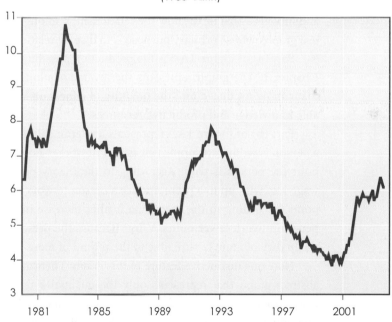

This figure shows three common kinds of data display graphs. The *pie chart* in part (a) is used when the data items sum to 100 percent. The *bar chart* in part (b), like the pie chart, is used when reporting numerical data that are associated with nonnumerical categories (in this case educational attainment). The bar chart does not require data items to sum to 100%. The *time-series graph* in part (c) shows the values of one or more economic quantities on the vertical axis and time on the horizontal axis.

SOURCE: Part (a), U.S. Council of Economic Advisers, *Economic Report of the President* (Washington, D.C.: Government Printing Office, 2002), Table B-105, 397; part (b), Bureau of Labor Statistics, *Current Population Survey*; and part (c), Bureau of Labor Statistics, *The Employment Situation*.

classification of cases (in this case, educational attainment). Bar charts are not subject to the restriction that data displayed must total 100 percent. What point do you think the author of this graph was trying to make?

Part (c) of Figure 1A.4 is an example of a data display graph very common in economics—the *time-series graph*. A time-series graph shows the values of one or more economic quantities on the vertical axis and time (years, months, or whatever) on the horizontal axis. This graph shows the ups and downs of the U.S. unemployment rate by month over the period 1980 through 2003.

Note one feature of this time-series graph: the scale on the vertical axis begins from 3 percent rather than from 0. By spreading out the data points in the range 3 to 11 percent, one can show the trend of unemployment in greater detail. The advantage of greater detail has an offsetting danger, however. Careless reading of the graph could cause one to exaggerate the amount by which unemployment rises during a recession. For example, the unemployment line is more than three times higher above the horizontal axis in 2003 than in 2000. However, careful reading of the graph shows that the unemployment rate was actually only about half again as high (6 percent versus 4 percent) in 2003 as in 2000. The moral of the story: Always examine the vertical and horizontal axes of a graph carefully.

## Using Graphs to Display Relationships

Some graphs, rather than simply recording observed facts, attempt to represent theories and models—that is, to show the relationships among facts. Figure 1A.5 shows two typical graphs whose primary purpose is to display relationships.

Part (a) of Figure 1A.5 is the production possibility frontier that we encountered in Chapter 1. The graph represents the inverse relationship between the quantity of cars that can be produced and the quantity of education that can be produced, given available knowledge and productive resources.

Part (b) of Figure 1A.5 represents a relationship between the quantity of labor that a person is willing to supply (measured in worker-hours per year) and the wage rate per hour the person is paid. According to the theory portrayed by the graph, raising the wage rate will, up to a point, induce a person to work more hours; but beyond a certain point (according to the theory), a further increase in the wage will actually cause the person to work fewer hours. Why? Because the person is so well off, he or she prefers the luxury of more leisure time to the reward of more material goods.

Note one distinctive feature of this graph: There are no numbers on the axes. It is an abstract graph that represents only the qualitative relationships between the hours of labor supplied per year and the wage rate. It makes no quantitative statements regarding how much the number of hours worked will change as a result of any given change in wage rate. Abstract graphs are often used when the point to be made is a general one that applies to many cases, regardless of quantitative differences from one case to another.

## Packing Three Variables into Two Dimensions

Anything drawn on a flat piece of paper is limited to two dimensions. The relationships discussed so far fit a two-dimensional framework easily because they involve just two variables. In the case of the production possibility frontier, the two are the quantity of

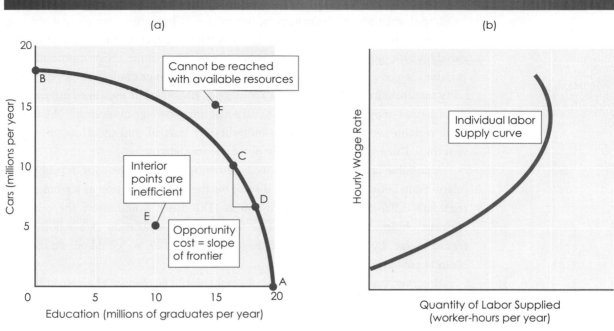

Relational graphs are visual representations of theories, that is, of relationships among facts. Two typical relational graphs are shown here. Part (a) is the production possibility frontier discussed in Chapter 1. It relates quantities of cars to quantities of education that can be produced with given factors of production and knowledge. Part (b) represents a theory of individual labor supply, according to which an increase in the hourly wage rate, after a point, will cause a person to reduce the quantity of labor supplied. Part (b) is an abstract graph in that it shows only the general nature of the relationship, with no numbers on either axis.

education (horizontal axis) and the quantity of cars (vertical axis). In the case of the labor supply, they are hours worked per year (horizontal axis) and wage rate per hour (vertical axis), but reality does not always cooperate with geometry. Often one must take three or more variables into account in order to understand relationships among facts.

A number of methods have been devised to represent relationships involving three or more variables. For example, a map of the United States might use coordinates of latitude and longitude to indicate position, contour lines to indicate altitude and shadings of various colors to indicate vegetation. An architect might use a perspective drawing to give the illusion of three dimensions—height, width, and depth—on a flat piece of paper. This section deals with one simple method of packing three variables into two dimensions. Although the method is a favorite of economists—it will be used in dozens of graphs in this book—we will show its generality by beginning with a non-economic example.

**A Non-Economic Example**    The example concerns heart disease, the leading cause of death in the United States. The risk of heart disease is closely linked to the quantity of cholesterol in a person's blood. Studies have indicated, for example, that a 25 percent reduction in cholesterol can cut the risk of death from heart attack by nearly 50 percent. Knowing this, millions of people have had their cholesterol levels tested and, if results were found to be high, have undertaken programs of diet, exercise, or drug therapy to reduce their risk of heart disease.

Important though cholesterol is, however, just knowing your cholesterol level is not enough to tell you your risk of dying of a heart attack in the coming year. Other variables also enter into the risk of heart disease. One of the most important of these variables is age. For example, for men aged 20 with average cholesterol levels, the mortality rate from heart disease is only about 3 per 100,000. For men aged 60, the mortality rate rises to over 500 per 100,000, still assuming average cholesterol. We thus have three variables with which to deal—mortality, cholesterol, and age. How can we represent these three variables using only two-dimensional graphs?

A possible approach would be to draw two separate graphs. One would show the relationship between age and heart disease for the male population as a whole, without regard to differences in cholesterol counts. The other would show the relationship between cholesterol and heart disease for the male population as a whole, without regard to age. By looking from one diagram to the other, we could get an idea of the entire three-variable relationship.

However, such a side-by-side pair of graphs would be clumsy. There must be a better way to represent the three variables in two dimensions. The better way, shown in Figure 1A.6, is to use cholesterol and mortality as the $x$ and $y$ axes, and to take age into account by plotting separate lines for men of various ages. That chart is far easier to interpret than the side-by-side pair would be. If you are a man and know your age and cholesterol count, you just pick out the appropriate line and read off your risk of mortality. If you do not like what you see, you go on a diet.[2]

The multi-curve graph is a lovely invention. One of the great things about it is that it works for more than three variables. For example, we could add a fourth variable, gender, to the graph by drawing a new set of lines in a different color to show mortality rates for women of various ages. Each line for women would have a positive slope similar to the men's lines; however, it would lie somewhat below the corresponding line for men of the same age because women, other things being equal, experience lower mortality from heart disease.

Shifts in Curves and Movements Along Curves    Economists use three-variable, multi-curve graphs often enough that it is worth giving some attention to the terminology used in discussing them. How can we best describe what happens to a man as he ages, given the relationship shown in Figure 1A.6?

One way to describe the effects of aging would be to say, "As a man ages, he moves from one curve to the next higher one on the chart." There is nothing at all wrong with saying that; but an economist would tend to phrase it a bit differently saying, "As a man ages, his cholesterol-mortality curve shifts upward." The two ways of expressing the effects of aging have exactly the same meaning. Preferring one or the other is just a matter of habit.

---

[2] We could instead have started with the age-mortality chart and drawn separate lines for men with different cholesterol levels. Such a chart would show exactly the same information. We could even draw a chart with cholesterol and age on the axes, and separate contour lines to represent various levels of mortality. The choice often depends on what one wants to emphasize. Here, we emphasize the cholesterol-mortality relationship because cholesterol is something you can do something about. You cannot do anything about your age, so we give age slightly less emphasis by not placing it on one of the two axes.

**FIGURE 1A.6   THREE VARIABLES IN TWO DIMENSIONS**

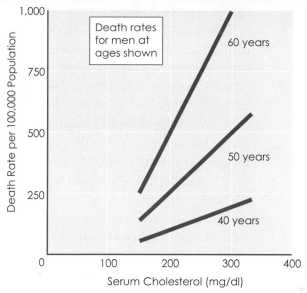

This graph shows a common way of representing a three-variable relationship on a two-dimensional graph. The three variables in this case are serum cholesterol (a measure of the amount of cholesterol in the blood), age, and death rate from heart disease for the U.S. male population. The relationship among the three variables is most easily interpreted, if all three variables are included in one graph, by drawing separate cholesterol-death rate lines for each age group. As a man ages, his cholesterol-death rate line shifts upward.

If we express the effects of aging in terms of a shift of the cholesterol-mortality curve, how should we express the effects of a reduction in cholesterol for a man of a given age? An economist would say it this way: "Cutting a man's cholesterol count through diet or exercise will move him down along his cholesterol-mortality curve."

Before you finish this book, you will see the phrases "shift in a curve" and "movement along a curve" a great many times. How can you keep them straight? Nothing could be easier.

- If you are talking about the effect of a change in a variable that is shown on one of the coordinate axes of the diagram, the effect will be shown as a movement along one of the curves. For example, the effect of a change in cholesterol (horizontal axis) on mortality (vertical axis) is shown by a movement along the line for a given age.

- If you are talking about the effect of a change in a variable that is not shown on one of the coordinate axes of the diagram, the effect will be shown by a shift in one of the curves. For example, the effect of a change in age (not the unit for either axis) on mortality (vertical axis) is shown by a shift in the curve relating cholesterol to mortality.

## Study Hints

So much for the basic rules of graphics. Once you master them, how should you study a chapter that is full of graphs?

The first—and most important—rule is to *avoid trying to memorize graphs as patterns of lines*. In every economics course, at least one student comes to the instructor after failing an exam and exclaims, "But I learned every one of those graphs! What happened?" The reply is that the student should have learned economics instead of memorizing graphs. Following are some hints for working with graphs.

After reading through a chapter that contains several graphs, go back through the graphs one at a time. Cover the caption accompanying each graph, and try to express the graph's "picture" in words. If you cannot say as much about the graph as the caption does, reread the text. Once you can translate the graph into words, you have won half the battle.

Next, cover each graph and use the caption as a guide. Try to sketch the graph on a piece of scratch paper. How are the graph's axes labeled? How are the curves labeled? What are the slopes of various curves? Are there important points of intersection or tangencies? If you can go back and forth between the caption and the graph, you will find that the two together are much easier to remember than either one separately.

Finally, try going beyond the graph that is shown in the book. If the graph illustrates the effect of an increase in the price of butter, try sketching a similar diagram that shows the effect of a decrease in the price of butter. If the graph shows what happens to the economy during a period of rising unemployment, try drawing a similar graph that shows what happens during a period of falling unemployment. This is a good practice that may give you an edge on your next exam.

**Making Your Own Graphs**   For some students, the hardest test questions to answer are ones that require original graphs as part of an essay. Suppose the question is, "How does a change in the number of students attending a university affect the cost per student of providing an education?" Here are some hints for making your own graph.

1. Write down the answer to the question in words. If you cannot, you might as well skip to the next question. Underline the most important quantities in your answer, such as "The larger the *number of students* who attend a college, the lower the *cost per student* of providing them with an education because fixed facilities, such as libraries, do not have to be duplicated."

2. Decide how you want to label the axes. In our example, the vertical axis could be labeled "cost per student" and the horizontal axis "number of students."

3. Do you have specific numbers to work with? If so, the next step is to construct a table showing what you know and use it to sketch your graph. If you have no numbers, you must draw an abstract graph. In this case, all you know is that the cost per student goes down when the number of students goes up. Your graph would thus be a negatively sloped line.

4. If your graph involves more than one relationship between quantities, repeat steps 1 through 3 for each relationship you wish to show. When constructing a graph with more than one curve, pay special attention to points at which you think the curves should intersect. (Intersections occur whenever both the x and y values of the two relationships are equal.) Also, note the points at which you think two curves ought to be tangent (which requires that their slopes be equal), the points of maximum or minimum value, if any, and so on.

5. When your graph is finished, try to translate it back into words. Does it really say what you want it to?

**A Reminder**    As you read this book and encounter various kinds of graphs, turn back to this appendix now and then. Do not memorize graphs as patterns of lines; if you do, you will get lost. If you can alternate between graphs and words, the underlying point will be clearer than if you rely on either one alone. Keep in mind that the primary focus of economics is not graphs; it is people and the ways in which they deal with the challenge of scarcity.

# CHAPTER 2

# Supply and Demand: the Basics

WE BEGAN THE preceding chapter with a discussion of recent record-breaking ups and downs in the prices of commodities, ranging from corn and wheat to crude oil and gold. These are just a few among millions of goods and services for which prices, quantities sold, and other market conditions vary from day to day and from year to year. Whether they are goods that we ourselves buy and sell, or goods that our employers, neighbors, or family members buy and sell, the changing market conditions affect our lives in many ways. The factors determining market prices and quantities are thus central to any discussion of economics.

**Supply**

The willingness and ability of sellers to provide goods for sale in a market

**Demand**

The willingness and ability of buyers to purchase goods

**Law of demand**

The principle that an inverse relationship exists between the price of a good and the quantity of that good that buyers demand, other things being equal

Economists use the term **supply** to refer to sellers' willingness and ability to provide goods for sale in a market. **Demand** refers to buyers' willingness and ability to purchase goods. This chapter will show how supply and demand work together to determine the prices of goods and services.

# Demand

According to the **law of demand**, the quantity of a demanded good tends to rise as the price falls and to fall as the price rises. We expect this to happen for two reasons. First, if the price of one good falls while the prices of other goods stay the same, people are likely to substitute the cheaper good. Second, when the price of one good falls while incomes and other prices stay the same, people feel a little richer. They use their added buying power to buy a bit more of many things, including, in most cases, a little more of the good whose price went down.

The terms *demand* and *quantity demanded*, as used in economics, are not the same as *want* or *need*. For example, I think a Porsche is a beautiful car. Sometimes when I see one on the street, I think, "Hey, I want one of those!" Alas, my income is limited. Although in the abstract I might want a Porsche, there are other things I want more. Thus, the quantity of Porsches I demand at the going price is zero.

On the other hand, I might *need* dental surgery to avoid losing my teeth. However, suppose I am poor. If I cannot pay for the surgery or find someone to pay for it on my behalf, I am out of luck. The quantity of dental surgery I demand, therefore, would be zero, however great my need for that service. Demand, then, combines both willingness and ability to buy. It is not desire in the abstract, but desire backed by the means and the intent to buy.

## The Demand Curve

The law of demand states a relationship between the quantity of a good that people are willing and able to buy, other things being equal, and the price of that good. Figure 2.1 represents this relationship for a familiar consumer good, chicken. It would be possible to discuss the demand for chicken of a single consumer; but more frequently, as in the following discussion, we focus on the total demand for the good by all buyers in the market.

The figure shows the demand relationship in two different ways. First look at part (a). The first row of the

The demand curve is based upon quantity and price.

## FIGURE 2.1 A DEMAND CURVE FOR CHICKEN

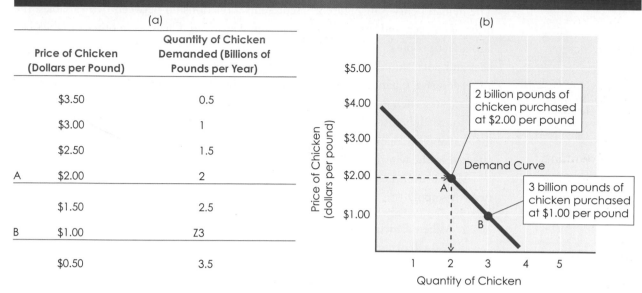

|  | Price of Chicken (Dollars per Pound) | Quantity of Chicken Demanded (Billions of Pounds per Year) |
|---|---|---|
|  | $3.50 | 0.5 |
|  | $3.00 | 1 |
|  | $2.50 | 1.5 |
| A | $2.00 | 2 |
|  | $1.50 | 2.5 |
| B | $1.00 | Z3 |
|  | $0.50 | 3.5 |

Both the table and the chart show the quantity of chicken demanded at various prices. For example, at a price of $2.00 per pound, buyers are willing and able to purchase 2 billion pounds of chicken per year. This price-quantity combination is shown by row A in part (a) and point A in part (b).

**Demand curve**

A graphical representation of the relationship between the price of a good and the quantity of that good that buyers demand

**Change in quantity demanded**

A change in the quantity of a good that buyers are willing and able to purchase that results from a change in the good's price, other things being equal, shown by a movement from one point to another along a demand curve

table shows that when the price of chicken is $3.00 a pound, the quantity demanded per year is 1 billion pounds. Reading down the table, we see that as the price falls, the quantity demanded rises. At $2.50 per pound, buyers are willing and able to purchase 1.5 billion pounds per year; at $1.50, 2.5 billion pounds; and so on.

Part (b) of Figure 2.1 presents the same information in graphical form. The graph is called a **demand curve** for chicken. Suppose we want to use the demand curve to find out what quantity of chicken will be demanded at a price of $2.00 per pound. Starting at $2.00 on the vertical axis, we move across, as shown by the arrow, until we reach the demand curve at point A. Continuing to follow the arrow, we drop down to the horizontal axis. Reading from the scale on that axis, we see that the quantity demanded at a price of $2.00 per pound is 2 billion pounds per year. That is the quantity demanded in row A of the table in part (a).

The effect of a change in the price of chicken, other things being equal, can be shown as a movement from one point to another along the demand curve for chicken. Suppose that the price drops from $2.00 to $1.00 per pound. In the process, the quantity that buyers plan to buy rises. The point corresponding to the quantity demanded at the new, lower price is point B (which corresponds to row B of the table). Because of the inverse relationship between price and quantity demanded, the demand curve has a negative slope.

Economists speak of a movement along a demand curve as a **change in quantity demanded**. Such a movement represents buyers' reactions to a change in the price of the good in question, other things being equal.

## Shifts in the Demand Curve

The demand curve[1] in Figure 2.1 represents a relationship between two variables: the price of chicken and the quantity of chicken demanded. Changes in other variables can also affect people's purchases of chicken, however. In the case of chicken, the prices of beef and pork would affect demand. Consumer incomes are a second variable that can affect demand. Changes in expectations about the future are a third; and changes in consumer tastes, such as an increasing preference for foods with low carbohydrate content, are a fourth. The list could go on and on—the demand for ice is affected by the weather; the demand for diapers is affected by the birthrate; the demand for baseball tickets is affected by the won-lost record of the home team; and so on.

How are all these other variables handled when drawing a demand curve? In brief, two rules apply.

1.  When drawing a single demand curve for a good, such as the one in Figure 2.1, all other conditions that affect demand are considered to be fixed or constant under the "other things being equal" clause of the law of demand. As long as that clause is in force, the only two variables at work are quantity demanded (on the horizontal axis) and price (on the vertical axis). Thus, a movement along the demand curve shows the effect of a change in price on quantity demanded.

2.  When we look beyond the "other things being equal" clause and find that there is a change in a variable that is not represented on one of the axes, such as the price of another good or the level of consumer income, the effect is shown as a shift in the demand curve. In its new position, the demand curve still represents a two-variable price-quantity relationship, but it is a slightly different relationship than before because one of the "other things" has changed.

These two rules for graphical representation of demand relationships are crucial to understanding the theory of supply and demand as a whole. It will be worthwhile to expand on them through a series of examples.

**CHANGES IN THE PRICE OF ANOTHER GOOD**    We have already noted that the demand for chicken depends on what happens to the price of beef, as well as what happens to the price of chicken. Figure 2.2, which shows demand curves for both goods, provides a closer look at this relationship.

Suppose that the price of beef is initially $3.00 per pound and then increases to $4.50 per pound. The effect of this change on the quantity of beef demanded is shown in part (a) of Figure 2.2 as a movement along the beef demand curve from point A to point B. Part (b) of the figure shows the effect on the demand for chicken. With the price of beef higher than before, consumers will tend to buy more chicken *even if the price of chicken does not change.* Suppose the price of chicken is $2.00 per pound. When beef was selling at $3.00 a pound, consumers bought 2 billion pounds of chicken a year (point A′ on demand curve $D_1$). After the price of beef goes up to $4.50 a pound, they will buy 3.5 billion pounds of chicken a year, assuming that the price of chicken does not change (point B′ on demand curve $D_2$).

**FIGURE 2.2 EFFECTS OF AN INCREASE IN THE PRICE OF BEEF ON THE DEMAND FOR CHICKEN**

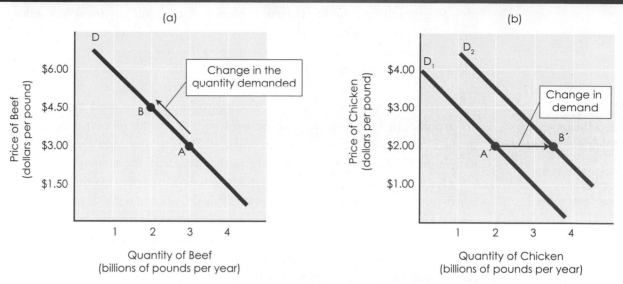

An increase in the price of beef from $3.00 to $4.50 per pound, other things being equal, causes a movement from point A to point B on the beef demand curve—a decrease in the quantity of beef demanded. With the price of chicken unchanged at $2.00 per pound, consumers will substitute chicken for beef. That will cause an increase in the demand for chicken, which is shown as a shift in the chicken demand curve from $D_1$ to $D_2$.

### Change in demand

A change in the quantity of a good that buyers are willing and able to purchase that results from a change in some condition other than the price of that good, shown by a shift in the demand curve

### Substitute goods

A pair of goods for which an increase in the price of one causes an increase in demand for the other

A rise in the price of beef would cause consumers to buy more chicken regardless of the initial price of chicken. If the price of chicken had started out at $3.00 a pound and remained there while the price of beef went up, consumers would have increased their chicken consumption from 1 billion pounds a year to 2.5 billion pounds a year. At a price of $1.00 a pound for chicken, the quantity would have risen from 3 billion pounds to 4.5 billion pounds, and so on. We see, then, that a change in the price of beef causes the entire demand curve for chicken to shift. The "other things being equal" clause of the new demand curve, $D_2$, incorporates a price of $4.50 a pound for beef, rather than the price of $3.00 a pound assumed in demand curve $D_1$.

Earlier we explained that economists refer to a movement along a demand curve as a "change in quantity demanded." The corresponding term for a shift in a demand curve is a **change in demand**. A change in quantity demanded (a movement along the curve) is caused by a change in the price of the good in question (the variable on the vertical axis). In contrast, a change in demand (a shift in the demand curve) is caused by a change in some variable other than the price of the good in question (one that does not appear on either axis).

In the example in Figure 2.2, people bought more chicken when the price of beef went up, replacing one meat with the other in their dinners. Economists call such pairs of goods **substitutes** because an increase in the price of one causes an increase in the demand for the other—a rightward shift in the demand curve.

Consumers react differently to price changes when two goods tend to be used together. One example is cars and gasoline. When the price of gasoline goes up, people's selection of cars will be affected. In particular, they will buy fewer low-mileage, large SUVs even if there is no change in the price of those vehicles. An increase in the price of gasoline thus causes a movement upward along the gasoline demand curve and a *leftward* shift in the demand curve for SUVs. Pairs of goods that are related in this way are known as **complements**.

**Complementary goods**

A pair of goods for which an increase in the price of one results in a decrease in demand for the other

Whether a given pair of goods is a substitute or complement good depends on buyers' attitudes toward those goods; these terms do not refer to properties of the goods themselves. Some people might regard cheese and beef as substitute sources of protein in their diets; others, who like cheeseburgers, might regard them as complements.

One more point regarding the effects of changes in the prices of other goods is also worth noting: In stating the law of demand, it is the price of a good *relative to those of other goods* that counts. During periods of inflation, when the average level of all prices rises, distinguishing between changes in *relative prices* and changes in *nominal prices*— the number of dollars actually paid per unit of a good—is especially important. When the economy experiences inflation, a good can become relatively less expensive even though its nominal price rises, provided that the prices of other goods rise even faster.

Consider chicken, for example. Between 1950 and 2005 the average retail price of a broiler rose by almost 40 percent, from $.59 per pound to $1.05 per pound. Over the same period, however, the average price of all goods and services purchased by consumers rose by about 600 percent. The relative price of chicken thus fell during the period even though its nominal price rose. The drop in the relative price of chicken had a lot to do with its growing popularity on the dinner table.

**CHANGES IN CONSUMER INCOMES**    The demand for a good can also be affected by changes in consumer incomes. When their incomes rise, people tend to buy larger quantities of many goods, assuming that the prices of those goods do not change.

Figure 2.3 shows the effect of an increase in consumer income on the demand for chicken. Demand curve $D_1$ is the same as the curve shown in Figure 2.1. Suppose now that consumer income rises. With higher incomes, people become choosier about what they eat. They do not just want calories; they want high-quality calories from foods that are tasty, fashionable, and healthful. These considerations have made chicken increasingly popular as consumer incomes have risen.

More specifically, suppose that after their incomes rise, consumers are willing to buy 2.5 billion pounds of chicken instead of 1 billion pounds at a price of $3.00 per pound. The change is shown as an arrow drawn from point A to point B in Figure 2.3. If the initial price of chicken had been $2.00 per pound, even more chicken would be bought at the new, higher level of income. At the original income level and a price of $2.00, the amount purchased would be 2 billion pounds, as shown by point C. After the increase in incomes, buyers would plan to purchase 3.5 billion pounds, shown by the arrow from point C to point D.

Whatever the initial price of chicken, the effect of an increase in consumer income is shown by a shift to a point on the new demand curve, $D_2$. The increase in demand for chicken that results from the rise in consumer income thus is shown as a shift in the

**FIGURE 2.3   EFFECTS OF AN INCREASE IN CONSUMER INCOME ON THE DEMAND FOR CHICKEN**

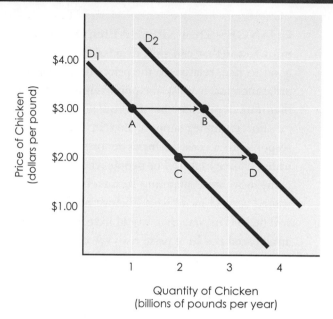

Demand curve $D_1$ assumes a given level of consumer income. If their incomes increase, consumers will want to buy more chicken at any given price, other things being equal. That will shift the demand curve rightward to, say, $D_2$. If the prevailing market price at the time of the demand shift is $3.00 per pound, the quantity demanded increases to 2.5 billion pounds (B) from 1 billion (A); if the prevailing price is $2.00 per pound, the quantity demanded will increase to 3.5 billion pounds (D) from 2 billion (C); and so on.

entire demand curve. If consumer income remains at the new, higher level, the effects of any changes in the price of chicken will be shown as movements along the new demand curve. There is, in other words, a chicken demand curve for every possible income level. Each represents a one-to-one relationship between price and quantity demanded, given the assumed income level.

In the example just given, we assumed that an increase in income would cause an increase in the demand for chicken. Experience shows that this is what normally happens. Economists, therefore, call chicken a **normal good**, meaning that when consumer income rises, other things being equal, people will buy more of it.

There are some goods, however, that people will buy less of when their income rises, other things being equal. For example, as the economy slipped into a deep recession in 2008, sales of new shoes fell, but demand for shoe repair services increased sharply. Hormel Foods Corp. reported a surge in sales of staple products like Spam and Dinty Moore beef stew, even while demand for its upscale single-serving microwaveable foods fell. Goods like shoe repair services and Spam, for which demand increases as consumer income falls, are called **inferior goods**. When consumer income rises, the demand curve for an inferior good shifts to the left instead of to the right. As in the case of substitutes and complements, the notions of

**Normal good**

A good for which an increase in consumer income results in an increase in demand

**Inferior good**

A good for which an increase in consumer incomes results in a decrease in demand

inferiority and normality arise from consumer choices; they are not inherent properties of the goods themselves.

**CHANGES IN EXPECTATIONS**      Changes in buyers' expectations are a third factor that can shift demand curves. If people expect the price of a particular good to rise, relative to the prices of other goods, or expect something other than a price increase to raise the opportunity cost of acquiring the good, they will step up their rate of purchase before the change takes place.

For example, suppose that in May, consumers rush to buy airline tickets in response to a series of news reports indicating that prices will be raised for tickets ordered after June 1. The people who buy their tickets in May would probably include many who were planning to travel late in the summer and ordinarily would have waited several more weeks before making their purchase. Thus, many more tickets will be sold in May than would have been sold at the same price if consumers had not anticipated the June price rise. We can interpret the surge in ticket sales in May as a temporary rightward shift in the demand curve.

**CHANGES IN TASTES**      Changes in tastes are a fourth source of changes in demand. Sometimes these changes occur rapidly, as can be seen, for example, in such areas as popular music, clothing styles, and fast foods. The demand curves for these goods and services shift often. In other cases, changes in tastes take longer to occur but are more permanent. For example, in recent years consumers have been more health conscious than they were in the past. The result has been reduced demand for cigarettes and foods with high content of trans fats, along with increased demand for fish, organic vegetables, and exercise equipment.

# Supply

## The Supply Curve

We now turn from the demand side of the market to the supply side. As in the case of demand, we begin by constructing a one-to-one relationship between the price of a good and the quantity that sellers intend to offer for sale. Figure 2.4 shows such a relationship for chicken.

**Supply curve**

A graphical representation of the relationship between the price of a good and the quantity of that good that sellers are willing to supply

The positively sloped curve in Figure 2.4 is called a **supply curve** for chicken. Like demand curves, supply curves are based on an "other things being equal" condition. The supply curve for chicken shows how sellers change their plans in response to a change in the price of chicken, assuming that there are no changes in other conditions—the prices of other goods, production techniques, input prices, expectations, or any other relevant condition.

Why does the supply curve have a positive slope? Why do sellers, other things being equal, plan to supply more chicken when the prevailing market price is higher than they plan to supply when the price is lower? Without going too deeply into a discussion of microeconomic theory, we can consider some common-sense explanations here.

## FIGURE 2.4   A SUPPLY CURVE FOR CHICKEN

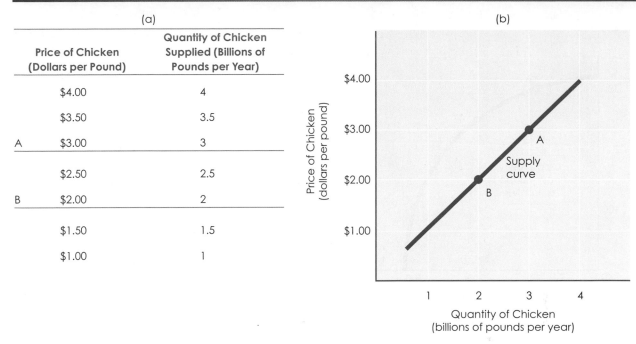

| (a) | |
|---|---|
| **Price of Chicken (Dollars per Pound)** | **Quantity of Chicken Supplied (Billions of Pounds per Year)** |
| $4.00 | 4 |
| $3.50 | 3.5 |
| A    $3.00 | 3 |
| $2.50 | 2.5 |
| B    $2.00 | 2 |
| $1.50 | 1.5 |
| $1.00 | 1 |

Parts (a) and (b) of this figure show the quantity of chicken supplied at various prices. As the price rises, the quantity supplied increases, other things being equal. The higher price gives farmers an incentive to raise more chickens, but the rising opportunity cost of doing so limits the supply produced in response to any given price increase.

One explanation is that the positive slope of the supply curve represents *producers' response to market incentives*. When the price of chicken goes up, farmers have an incentive to devote more time and resources to raising chickens. Farmers who raise chickens as a sideline may decide to make chickens their main business. Some people may enter the market for the first time. The same reasoning applies in every market. If parents are finding it hard to get babysitters, what do they do? They offer to pay more. If a sawmill cannot buy enough timber, it raises the price it offers to loggers, and so on. Exceptions to this general rule are rare.

Another explanation is that the positive slope of the supply curve reflects *the rising cost of producing additional output in facilities of a fixed size*. A furniture factory with a fixed amount of machinery might be able to produce more chairs only by paying workers at overtime rates to run the machinery for more hours. A farmer who is trying to grow more wheat on a fixed amount of land could do so by increasing the input of fertilizer and pesticides per acre, but beyond a certain point each unit of added chemicals yields less additional output.

Finally, the positive slope of the supply curve can be explained in terms of *comparative advantage and opportunity cost*. Figure 2.5a shows a production possibility frontier for an economy in which there are only two goods, tomatoes and chicken. Farmers can choose which product they will specialize in, but some farmers have a comparative

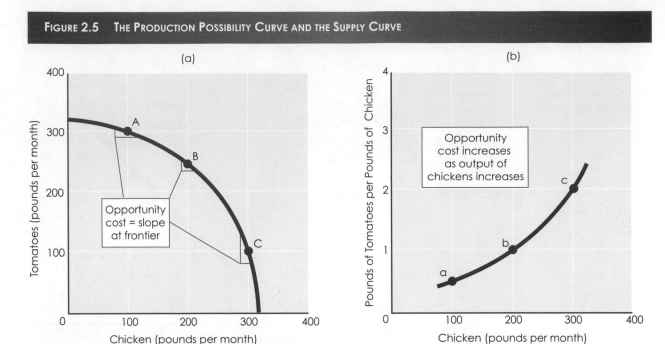

**FIGURE 2.5   THE PRODUCTION POSSIBILITY CURVE AND THE SUPPLY CURVE**

This figure offers an interpretation of the supply curve in terms of the production possibility frontier for an economy in which two goods are produced, tomatoes and chicken. Part (a) shows a production possibility frontier. The slope of the frontier, at any point, shows the opportunity cost of producing an additional pound of chicken measured in terms of the quantity of tomatoes that could have been produced using the same factors of production. The frontier curves because some farmers have a comparative advantage in producing tomatoes and others have a comparative advantage in producing chicken. As more chicken is produced, those with the greatest comparative advantage in producing chicken are the first to stop producing tomatoes. Because the frontier gets steeper as more chicken is produced, the opportunity cost rises, as shown in part (b). The curve in part (b) can be interpreted as a supply curve, in the sense that an incentive, in the form of a higher price, will cause factors of production to be shifted from tomatoes to chicken despite the rising opportunity cost of producing chicken.

advantage in growing tomatoes, others in raising chickens. Beginning from a situation in which only tomatoes are produced, farmers with the strongest comparative advantage in raising chickens—that is, those who are able to produce chicken at relatively the lowest opportunity cost—will switch from tomatoes to chicken even if the price of chicken is low. As the point of production moves along the frontier, the price of chicken must rise to induce farmers with relatively higher opportunity costs to make the switch. The slope of the frontier, at any point, represents the opportunity cost of producing more chicken for a farmer who finds it worthwhile to switch from tomatoes to chicken just at that point.

In Figure 2.5, the slopes at points A, B, and C in part (a) are graphed on a new set of axes in part (b). The graph can be interpreted as a supply curve if it is noted that the price of chicken must rise relative to the price of tomatoes to induce more farmers to switch to chicken as the opportunity cost rises.

Each of these common-sense explanations fits certain circumstances. Together, they provide an intuitive basis for the positive slope of the supply curve.

### Change in supply

A change in the quantity of a good that suppliers are willing and able to sell that results from a change in some condition other than the good's price; shown by a shift in the supply curve

### Change in quantity supplied

A change in the quantity of a good that suppliers are willing and able to sell that results from a change in the good's price, other things being equal; shown by a movement along a supply curve

## *Shifts in the Supply Curve*

As in the case of demand, the effects of a change in the price of chicken, other things being equal, can be shown as a movement along the supply curve for chicken. Such a movement is called a **change in quantity supplied**. A change in a condition other than the price of chicken can be shown as a shift in the supply curve. Such a shift is referred to as a **change in supply**. Four sources of change in supply are worth noting. Each is related to the notion that the supply curve reflects the opportunity cost of producing the good or service in question.

**CHANGES IN TECHNOLOGY**   A supply curve is drawn on the basis of a particular production technique. When entrepreneurs reduce the opportunity costs of production by introducing more efficient techniques, it becomes worthwhile to sell more of the good than before at any given price. Figure 2.6 shows how an improvement in production technology affects the supply curve for chicken.

**FIGURE 2.6   SHIFTS IN THE SUPPLY CURVE FOR CHICKEN**

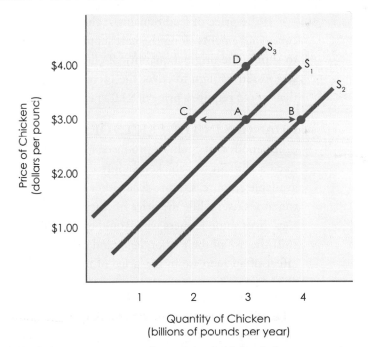

Several kinds of changes can cause the supply of chicken to increase or decrease. For example, a new production method that lowers costs will shift the curve to the right, from $S_1$ to $S_2$. The shift is to the right because, taking into account the new, lower cost of production per unit, producers will be willing to supply more chicken at any given price. An increase in the price of inputs, other things being equal, will shift the curve to the left, from $S_1$ to $S_3$. The shift is to the left because, taking into account the new, higher price of inputs, producers will be willing to supply less chicken at any given price. Changes in sellers' expectations or in the prices of competing goods can also cause the supply curve to shift.

Supply curve $S_1$ is the same as the one shown in Figure 2.4. It indicates that farmers will plan to supply 3 billion pounds of chicken per year at a price of $3.00 per pound (point A). Now suppose that the development of a faster-growing bird reduces the amount of feed used in raising chickens. With lower costs per unit, farmers will be willing to supply more chicken than before at any given price. They may, for example, be willing to supply 4 billion pounds of chicken at $3.00 per pound (point B). The move from A to B is part of a shift in the entire supply curve from $S_1$ to $S_2$. Once the new techniques are established, an increase or decrease in the price of chicken, other things being equal, will result in a movement along the new supply curve.

**CHANGES IN INPUT PRICES**    Changes in input prices are a second item that can cause supply curves to shift. An increase in input prices, other things being equal, increases the opportunity cost of producing the good in question; hence, it tends to reduce the quantity of a good that producers plan to supply at a given price. Refer again to Figure 2.6. Suppose that starting from point A on supply curve $S_1$, the price of chicken feed increases and no offsetting changes occur. Now, instead of supplying 3 billion pounds of chicken at $3.00 per pound, farmers will supply, say, just 2 billion pounds at that price (point C). The move from A to C is part of a leftward shift in the supply curve, from $S_1$ to $S_3$.

If the price of feed remains at the new level, changes in the price of chicken will cause movements along the new supply curve. For example, farmers could be induced to supply the original quantity of chicken—3 billion pounds—if the price of chicken was raised enough to cover the increased cost of feed. As you can see in Figure 2.6, that would require a price of $4.00 per pound for chicken (point D).

**CHANGES IN THE PRICES OF OTHER GOODS**    Changes in the prices of other goods that could be produced using the same factors of production can also produce a shift in the chicken supply curve. In our earlier example, farmers could use available resources to produce either chickens or tomatoes. Suppose that the price of tomatoes rises while the price of chicken stays at $3.00. The rise in the price of tomatoes gives some farmers who would otherwise have produced chickens an incentive to shift the use of their labor, land, and capital to the production of tomatoes. Thus, the effect of an increase in the price of tomatoes can be shown as a leftward shift in the chicken supply curve.

**CHANGES IN EXPECTATIONS**    Changes in expectations can cause supply curves to shift in much the same way that they cause demand curves to shift. Again, we can use farming as an example. At planting time, a farmer's selection of crops is influenced not so much by current prices as by the prices expected at harvest time. Expectations over a time horizon longer than one growing season also affect supply. Each crop requires special equipment and know-how. We have just seen that an increase in the price of tomatoes gives farmers an incentive to shift from chicken to tomatoes. The incentive will be stronger if the price of tomatoes is expected to remain at the higher level. If it is, farmers are more likely to buy the special equipment needed for that crop and to learn the necessary production techniques.

# The Interaction of Supply and Demand

Markets transmit information, in the form of prices, to people who buy and sell goods and services. Taking these prices into account, along with other knowledge they may have, buyers and sellers make their plans.[2] As shown by the demand and supply curves, buyers and sellers plan to buy or sell certain quantities of a good at any given price.

Each market has many buyers and sellers, each making plans independently. When they meet to trade, some of them may be unable to carry out their plans on the terms they expected. Perhaps the total quantity of a good that buyers plan to purchase is greater than the total quantity that suppliers are willing to sell at the given price. In that case, some of the would-be buyers must change their plans. Perhaps planned sales exceed planned purchases at the given price. In that case, some would-be sellers will be unable to carry out their plans.

## Market Equilibrium

**Equilibrium**

A condition in which buyers' and sellers' plans exactly mesh in the marketplace, so that the quantity supplied exactly equals the quantity demanded at a given price

Sometimes no one is surprised. The total quantity of a good that buyers plan to purchase exactly matches the total quantity that producers plan to sell. When buyers' and sellers' plans mesh when they meet in the marketplace, no buyers or sellers need to change their plans. Under these conditions, the market is said to be in **equilibrium**.

Supply and demand curves, which reflect the plans of sellers and buyers, can be used to give a graphical demonstration of market equilibrium. Figure 2.7 uses the same supply and demand curves as before, but this time both curves are drawn on the same diagram. If the quantity of planned sales at each price is compared with the quantity of planned purchases at that price (either the table or the graph can be used to make this comparison), it can be seen that there is only one price at which the two sets of plans mesh. That price—$2.00 per pound—is the equilibrium price. If all buyers and sellers make their plans with the expectation of a price of $2.00, no one will be surprised and no plans will have to be changed.

## Shortages

**Excess quantity demanded (shortage)**

A condition in which the quantity of a good demanded at a given price exceeds the quantity supplied

**Inventory**

A stock of a finished good awaiting sale or use

What will happen if for some reason people base their plans for buying or selling chicken on a price other than $2.00 a pound?[3] Suppose, for example, that they base their plans on a price of $1.00. As Figure 2.7 shows, at that price buyers will plan to purchase chicken at a rate of 3 billion pounds per year, but farmers will plan to supply only 1 billion pounds. When the quantity demanded exceeds the quantity supplied, as in this example, the difference is an **excess quantity demanded** or, more simply, a **shortage**. In Figure 2.7 the shortage is 2 billion pounds of chicken per year when the price is $1.00 per pound.

In most markets the first sign of a shortage is a drop in the **inventory**, that is, in the stock of the good in question that has been produced and is waiting to be sold or used. Sellers plan to hold a certain quantity of goods in inventory to allow for minor changes in demand. When they see inventories dropping below the planned level, they change

**FIGURE 2.7    EQUILIBRIUM IN THE CHICKEN MARKET**

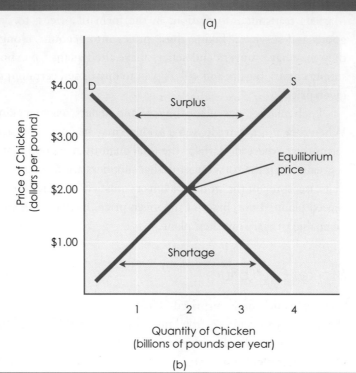

(a)

(b)

| Price (per Pound) | Quantity Demanded (Billions of Pounds) | Quantity Supplied (Billions of Pounds) | Shortage (Billions of Pounds) | Surplus (Billions of Pounds) | Direction of Pressure on Price |
|---|---|---|---|---|---|
| $3.50 | 0.5 | 3.5 | — | 3 | Downward |
| $3.00 | 1 | 3 | — | 2 | Downward |
| $2.50 | 1.5 | 2.5 | — | 1 | Downward |
| $2.00 | 2 | 2 | — | — | Equilibrium |
| $1.50 | 2.5 | 1.5 | 1 | — | Upward |
| $1.00 | 3 | 1 | 2 | — | Upward |
| $0.50 | 3.5 | 0.5 | 3 | — | Upward |

This figure shows the supply and demand curves for chicken presented earlier in graphical and numerical form. The demand curve shows how much buyers plan to purchase at a given price. The supply curve shows how much producers plan to sell at a given price. At only one price—$2.00 per pound—do buyers' and sellers' plans exactly match. That is the equilibrium price. A higher price causes a surplus of chicken and puts downward pressure on price. A lower price causes a shortage and puts upward pressure on price.

their plans. Some may try to rebuild their inventories by increasing their output if they produce the good themselves; or, if they do not make it themselves, they may order more from the producer. Some sellers may take advantage of the strong demand for their product to raise the price, knowing that buyers will be willing to pay more. Many sellers will do a little of both. If sellers do not take the initiative, buyers will—they will offer to pay more if sellers will supply more. Whatever the details, the result will be an upward movement along the supply curve as both price and quantity increase.

As the shortage puts upward pressure on price, buyers will change their plans, too. Moving up and to the left along their demand curve, they will cut back on their planned purchases. As both buyers and sellers change their plans, the market will move toward equilibrium. When the price reaches $2.00 per pound, both the shortage and the pressure to change buying and selling plans will disappear.

In the markets for most goods, sellers have inventories of goods ready to be sold. There are exceptions, however. Inventories are not possible in markets for services—haircuts, tax preparation, lawn care, and the like. Also, some goods, such as custom-built houses and machine tools that are designed for a specialized need, are not held in inventories. Sellers in these markets do not begin production until they have a contract with a buyer.

In markets in which there are no inventories, the sign of a shortage is a queue of buyers. The queue may take the form of a line of people waiting to be served or a list of names in an order book. The queue is a sign that, given the prevailing price, buyers would like to purchase the good at a faster rate than that at which producers have planned to supply it. However, some plans cannot be carried out—at least not right away. Buyers are served on a first-come, first-served basis.

The formation of a queue of buyers has much the same effect on the market as a decrease in inventories. Sellers react by increasing their rate of output, raising their prices, or both. Buyers react by reducing the quantity they plan to purchase or by offering a higher price. The result is a movement up and to the right along the supply curve and, at the same time, up and to the left along the demand curve until equilibrium is reached.

## Surpluses

Having considered what happens when buyers and sellers initially expect a price below the equilibrium price, we now turn to the opposite case. Suppose that for some reason buyers and sellers of chicken expect a price that is higher than the equilibrium price—say, $2.50 per pound—and make their plans accordingly. Figure 2.7 shows that farmers will plan to supply 2.5 billion pounds of chicken per year at $2.50, but their customers will plan to buy only 1.5 billion pounds. When the quantity supplied exceeds the quantity demanded, there is an **excess quantity supplied** or a **surplus**. As Figure 2.7 shows, the surplus of chicken at a price of $2.50 per pound is 1 billion pounds per year.

**Excess quantity supplied (surplus)**

A condition in which the quantity of a good supplied at a given price exceeds the quantity demanded

When there is a surplus of a product, sellers will be unable to sell all that they had hoped to sell at the planned price. As a result, their inventories will begin to grow beyond the level they had planned to hold in preparation for normal changes in demand.

Sellers will react to the inventory buildup by changing their plans. Some will cut back their output. Others will lower their prices to induce consumers to buy more and thus reduce their extra stock. Still others will do a little of both. The result of these changes in plans will be a movement down and to the left along the supply curve.

As unplanned inventory buildup puts downward pressure on the price of chicken, buyers change their plans too. Finding that chicken costs less than they had expected, they buy more of it. In graphical terms, they move down and to the right along the demand curve. As that happens, the market is restored to equilibrium.

In markets in which there are no inventories, surpluses lead to the formation of queues of sellers looking for customers. Taxi queues at airports are a case in point. At some times of the day, the fare for taxi service from the airport to downtown is more than high enough to attract a number of taxis that is equal to the demand. A queue of cabs waiting for passengers then forms. In some cities drivers who are far back in the queue try to attract riders by offering cut-rate fares. Often, though, there are rules against fare cutting. The queue then grows until the next peak period when a surge in demand shortens it.

## Changes in Market Conditions

On a graph, finding the equilibrium point looks easy. In real life, though, it is a moving target. Market conditions, by which we mean all the items that lie behind the "other things being equal" clause, change frequently. When they do, both buyers and sellers revise their plans; and market prices and quantities adjust.

**RESPONSE TO A SHIFT IN DEMAND**    We will first consider a market's response to a shift in demand. Suppose, for example, that television news broadcasts a warning that eating chicken meat might transmit a new virus. The result would be an immediate decrease in demand for chicken. Part (a) of Figure 2.8 interprets this case in terms of the supply-and-demand model.

As the figure is drawn, the chicken market is initially in equilibrium at $E_1$. There, the price is $3.00 per pound, and the quantity produced is 2 billion pounds per year. Now the temporary change in tastes caused by the health warning shifts the demand curve to the left, from $D_1$ to $D_2$. (There is a shift in the demand curve rather than a movement along it because a change in tastes is not one of the items represented by the axes of the diagram.) What will happen next?

At the original price of $3.00 per pound, there will be a surplus of chicken. The supply curve shows that at that price chicken farmers will plan to produce 2 billion pounds per year. However, according to the new demand curve, $D_2$, consumers will no longer buy that much chicken at $3.00 per pound. Instead, given their new tastes, they will buy only 1 billion pounds at that price.

The price does not stay at $3.00 for long, however. As soon as the demand curve begins to shift and the surplus begins to develop, chicken inventories rise above their planned levels, putting downward pressure on the price. As the price falls, producers revise their plans. They move down and to the left along their supply curve, reducing the quantity supplied. (There is a movement along the supply curve, not a shift in the curve, because the producers are responding to a change in the price of chicken, the variable shown on the vertical axis. Nothing has happened to change the "other things being equal" conditions, such as technology, input prices, and so on, which could cause the supply curve to shift.)

As farmers move downward along their supply curve in the direction shown by the arrow in part (a) of Figure 2.8, they eventually reach point $E_2$, where their plans again mesh with those of consumers. At that point the price has fallen to $2.25 per pound and production to 1.5 billion pounds. Although health-conscious consumers would not have bought that much chicken at the old price, they will do so at the

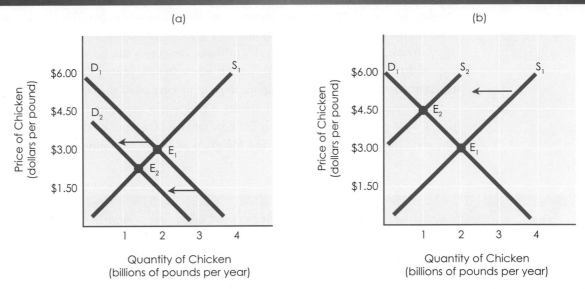

FIGURE 2.8   EFFECTS OF CHANGING CONDITIONS IN THE CHICKEN MARKET

Part (a) of this figure shows the effects of a decrease in demand for chicken caused by a health warning about the safety of eating chicken. Initially the market is in equilibrium at $E_1$. The change in tastes causes a shift in the demand curve. At the original equilibrium price of $3.00 per pound, there is a temporary surplus of chicken. This causes inventories to start to rise and puts downward pressure on the price. As the price falls, producers move down along their supply curve to a new equilibrium at $E_2$. There both the price and quantity of chicken are lower than before the shift in demand. Part (b) shows the effects of a decrease in supply caused by an increase in the price of chicken feed. The shift in the supply curve causes a shortage at the initial price of $3.00 per pound. The shortage puts upward pressure on price. As the price rises, buyers move up and to the left along the demand curve until a new equilibrium is reached at $E_2$. In each case, note that only one curve needs to shift to bring about the new equilibrium.

new, lower price. $E_2$ thus is the new equilibrium point. Later, if the health scare proves to be baseless, the demand curve will shift back $D_1$, and the market price and quantity will return to their original values.

**RESPONSE TO A SHIFT IN SUPPLY**   The original equilibrium might be disrupted by a change in supply rather than by a change in demand. For example, beginning from a condition of equilibrium, increased demand for corn used to make ethanol fuel could cause the price of chicken feed, also made with corn, to increase. That would shift the supply curve to the left while the demand curve remained unchanged, as shown in part (b) of Figure 2.8.

Given the new supply curve, there will be a shortage of chicken at the original price. Inventories will decline, and the prices will rise in response. As the price increases, producers will move upward and to the right along their new supply curve, $S_2$; and consumers will move upward and to the left along their demand curve, $D_1$, which remains in its original position. A new equilibrium is established when the price reaches $4.50 per pound.

One of the most frequent mistakes people make in learning the supply-and-demand model is to think that *both* curves always must shift in order to restore equilibrium. The examples given in Figure 2.8 show clearly that this is not the case. In part (a), after the demand curve shifts, a movement along the supply curve is enough to establish the new equilibrium. No shift in the supply curve is needed. Similarly, in part (b), after the supply curve shifts, the demand curve does not need to shift to reach the new equilibrium.

However, in the turmoil of real-world markets, cases can be found in which both curves do shift at once. This will happen when two separate changes in conditions occur at the same time, one acting on the supply curve and the other on the demand curve. *Economics in the News 2.1* provides a real-world example. It shows how wheat prices were pushed upward in early 2008 by two simultaneous changes in market conditions. One was increasing demand for grain as food and animal feed in India and

### Economics in the News 2.1
## WHEAT PRICES SOAR ON RISING DEMAND, DROUGHT

The United Nations World Food Program is a lifeline for 73 million people in more than 80 countries around the world. WFP assistance does a lot of good; but, not surprisingly, its help does not come cheap. The agency began 2008 with a budget of $2.9 billion, enough to do the job, it was thought. The year was less than a quarter gone, however, before a new disaster struck that led to an appeal for $500 million in extra funds.

This time it was neither natural disaster nor war that led to the emergency appeal. Instead, it was high prices for grain, especially wheat, which hit an all-time high of over $12 a bushel in March, and also for corn, rice, and other staple foods. What was behind the run-up in prices?

A dwindling supply of wheat eventually led to higher prices.

Supply was one problem. In 2007, a serious drought affected Western Australia, one of the world's great wheat producing regions. This caused inventories around the world to fall to dangerously low levels. Then, in the spring of 2008, the bad weather news continued, this time with more dry weather in the wheat producing states of Kansas, Oklahoma, and Texas in the United States. A threat of strikes in wheat-producing regions of Argentina made matters even worse.

Weather was not the only factor affecting supply. Worried about energy dependence and global warming, the U.S. Congress, late in 2007, passed an energy bill that contained generous subsidies for corn-based ethanol. Corn competes with wheat for cropland, so a record acreage planted in corn meant reduction in the planting of wheat.

Demand-side events were also at work to push up wheat prices in 2008. India, the world's biggest wheat importer, and China, also a major importer, were among the fastest growing economies. Increased urbanization and millions of consumers emerging from poverty were not only eating more wheat in the form of bread but also eating more grain-fed meat, as well.

Some countries in East Africa, Southeast Asia, and South America began to see food riots. Josette Sheeran, head of the WFP, warned that the rise in world food prices was creating a "new face of hunger."[a] She said, "There is food on shelves, but people are priced out of the market. There is vulnerability in urban areas we have not seen before. There are food riots in countries where we have not seen them before."

Toward the end of 2008, the food crisis began to ease. This time, the dominant factor was a slowdown in demand as a result of the spreading global economic crisis. Long-term planners in agencies like the UN World Food Program worried that the relief from high prices was only temporary, however. Sooner or later, growth would resume in the giant economies of South and East Asia. When it did, the world's poorest consumers, like those in Sub-Saharan Africa, would once again feel the pinch of supply and demand.

_____
[a] Cited by Amando Doronilla, "Analysis: New Face of Hunger," *The Phillippine Enquirer*, March 26, 2008,

China. That shifted the demand curve to the right. At the same time, bad weather in major wheat-producing regions of the United States and Australia shifted the supply curve to the left. Either change acting alone would have been enough to raise the price. Both changes acting together had an especially sharp impact. Later in the year, the price fell again. This time the dominant factor was a drop in demand as a result of the growing global economic crisis.

### Equilibrium as Spontaneous Order

The way that markets move toward a new equilibrium following a disturbance is an example of economic coordination through spontaneous order. In the case we have been following, the disturbance began either with a change in health consciousness among consumers or with a change in the weather. To make the adjustment to new conditions, the decisions of thousands of farmers, wholesalers, retailers, as well as that of millions of consumers, must somehow be coordinated. How can that be done?

In a market economy, no central planning agency or regulatory bureaucracy is needed. The required shift in the use of scarce resources is brought about through information and incentives transmitted in the form of changing market prices. The trend toward low-carbohydrate, high-protein diets in the early 2000s is a typical example. As demand for beef, chicken, and other high-protein foods rose, farmers responded to higher prices by raising more chickens and cattle. Labor, capital, natural resources, and entrepreneurial energy flowed into chicken and beef production without any central authority giving an order. At the same time, investments in donuts, a high-carb food that had boomed in the 1990s, slowed substantially.

The process was remarkably smooth for so vast a shift in resource use. Behind the scenes, surpluses and shortages nudged choices in the needed directions, but at no time did shortages occur in the acute form of empty meat coolers at the super market or lines of chicken-hungry consumers stretching down city streets. Similarly, slack demand for donuts signaled entrepreneurs to turn away from building new outlets, but it did not give rise to mountains of rotting donuts that had to be dumped into landfills.

No one *intended* this process of adjustment. Equilibrium is not a compromise that must be negotiated by a committee of consumers and producers. Just as shoppers manage to equalize the length of supermarket checkout lines without the guidance of a central authority, markets move toward equilibrium spontaneously, through the small, local adjustments that people make in their efforts to serve their own interests. As Adam Smith might have put it, we have not the benevolence of Tyson Foods or the Beef Industry Council to thank for our dinner; instead it is their self-interest that puts the right food on our table.

## Price Floors and Ceilings: An Application

Economics—both macro and micro—encompasses a great many applications of the concepts of supply and demand. Although each situation is unique, each to some extent draws on ideas developed in this chapter. This section, which uses the model to analyze the effects of government-imposed price floors and ceilings, provides some examples. Many more will be added in later chapters.

## Price Supports: the Market for Milk

In our earlier example of the market for beef, a decrease in demand caused a surplus, which in turn caused the price to decrease until the surplus was eliminated. Markets are not always free to respond by adjusting prices, however. The market for milk is a case in point.

The market for milk is supported by a floor price subsidy.

Figure 2.9 shows the market for milk in terms of supply and demand curves. The quantity of milk is measured in hundredweight, the unit used for bulk milk sales, equal to roughly 12 gallons. Suppose that initially the market is in equilibrium at point $E_1$. The wholesale price of milk is $13 per hundredweight, and 110 million hundredweight is produced per year. Then suppose that a trend in taste away from high-cholesterol foods shifts the demand curve for milk to the left. The result would be a surplus of milk at the $13 price, as shown by the arrow in Figure 2.9.

At this point a new factor comes into operation that was not present in our earlier discussion of the chicken market. In that case, chicken prices were free to fall in response to a surplus, but in the milk market they are not. Instead, an elaborate set of government-imposed controls and subsidies puts a floor under the price of milk. As part of the controls, the government agrees to pay a minimum price for all milk that cannot be sold at that price on the open market. In our example, the support price is assumed to be $13.

With the demand curve in its original position $D_1$, there was no surplus and the government did not need to buy any milk. However, with the demand curve in position $D_2$, there is a surplus of 40 million hundredweight per year. Under the price support law the government must buy this surplus and store it in the form of powdered milk, cheese, butter, and other products with long shelf lives. Without price supports, the shift in demand would cause the price of milk to fall to the new equilibrium price of $10 per hundredweight. When price supports are applied to a product at a level higher than the equilibrium price, however, the result is a persistent surplus. The effects of the price support can be understood in terms of conflicting signals sent to producers and consumers. To consumers, the price of $13 says, "Milk is scarce. Its opportunity cost is high. Hold your consumption down." To producers, it says, "All is well. Incentives are unchanged. Feel free to continue

**FIGURE 2.9   PRICE SUPPORTS FOR MILK**

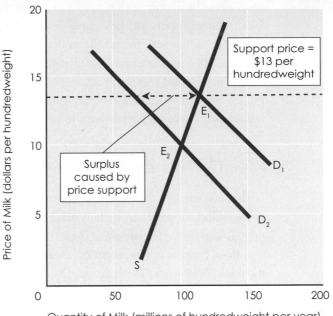

Suppose that initially the market for milk is in equilibrium at $E_1$. A shift in tastes away from high-cholesterol foods then shifts the demand curve to $D_2$. If the price were free to fall, there would be a temporary surplus that would push the price down to a new equilibrium at $10 per hundredweight. Instead, suppose that the government maintains a support price for milk at a level higher than the equilibrium price, as it did for many years ($13 per hundredweight in this example). The government would then need to buy the surplus milk and stores it in the form of powdered milk, butter and cheese to keep the price from falling.

using scarce resources to produce milk." Without price supports, a drop in the price to $10 would send a different set of messages. Consumers would hear, "Milk is cheaper and more abundant. Although it is not cholesterol free, give in to temptation! Drink more of it!" Producers would hear, "The milk market is not what it once was. Look at your opportunity costs. Is there perhaps some better use for your labor, capital, and natural resources?"

During the 1980s and 1990s, the government's price support was consistently higher than the equilibrium price. The program became very expensive, more than $1,000 per U.S. family by some estimates, enough to buy each family its own cow. From time to time the government has tried to eliminate the milk surplus by shifting the supply curve to the left so that it would intersect the demand curve near the support price. Under one program, for example, farmers were encouraged to sell their cows to be slaughtered for their meat, thereby reducing the size of dairy herds; but such programs have failed to eliminate the milk surplus. The chief reason is the dairy farmers' entrepreneurial response to the high price of milk. The government's efforts to cut the size of herds were largely offset by increased output per cow as a result of genetic improvements and better farm management practices. The government accumulated mountains of surplus dairy products.

Then, during the early years of the twenty-first century, conditions in the milk market changed. Increasing demand from emerging-market countries and rising feed costs caused shifts in both supply and demand curves. By 2005, the support price had fallen below the market price and the surplus had disappeared. This, too, had unintended consequences for public policy. Under the U.S. Department of Agriculture's Commodity Supplemental Food Program, as many as 100,000 mothers, children, and elderly people had received packages of free milk powder drawn from government surpluses. Suddenly these vast stocks were threatened with exhaustion, and officials were left scrambling to find other ways to aid needy citizens.

## Price Ceilings: the Case of Rent Control

In the milk market, the government maintains a support price that has often been above the equilibrium price. In certain other markets, a price ceiling below the equilibrium price is imposed. An example of the latter situation is rent control in housing markets.

Rent control in one form or another has been used in several major U.S. cities, including New York, Washington, D.C., San Francisco, and Los Angeles. The controls vary from one city to another; however, in all cases law, at least for some categories of apartments, establishes maximum rents. The purpose of rent control is to aid tenants by preventing landlords from charging "unreasonably high" rents. What is unreasonably high is determined by the relative political strength of landlords and tenants rather than by the forces of supply and demand.

**INTENDED EFFECTS**    Figure 2.10 interprets the effects of rent control in terms of supply and demand. For the sake of simplicity, it is assumed that the supply of rental housing consists of units of equal size and rental value. Part (a) of the figure shows the effects of rent control in the short run. Here the short run means a period that is too short to permit significant increases or decreases in the supply of rental housing. (The short-run supply curve, which is drawn as a vertical line, indicates that a change in price will not result in any change in the quantity of apartments.[4])

Under the conditions shown, the equilibrium rent per standard housing unit is $1,250 per month for each of the 200,000 units in the city. Now suppose that a rent ceiling of $500 is imposed. The result is a gain to tenants of $750 per unit per month. The total sum transferred to tenants (that is, the benefit to them from below-market rents) is $750 per unit multiplied by 200,000 units, or $150 million, in all. In graphical terms, that sum is equal to the area of the shaded rectangle in Figure 2.10. The benefit to tenants at the expense of landlords is the principal intended effect of rent control.

**UNINTENDED EFFECTS**   The policy of rent control, which aims to benefit tenants at the expense of landlords, provides a classic illustration of the law of unintended consequences. In the short run, when the stock of apartments is fixed, the unintended consequences stem from the apartment shortage created by the controls. The shortage occurs because the quantity demanded is greater at the lower ceiling price than at the higher equilibrium price.

## FIGURE 2.10  EFFECTS OF RENT CONTROL

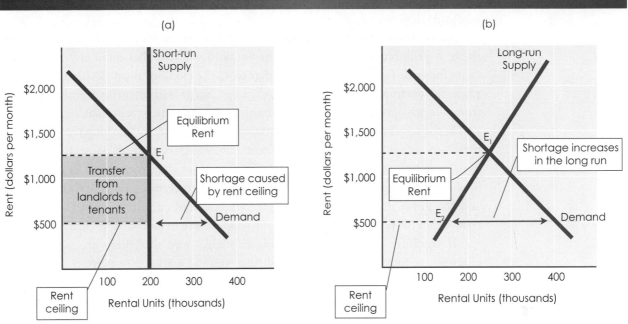

Part (a) shows the short-run effects of rent control. In the short run, the supply of rental apartments is considered to be fixed. The equilibrium rent is $1,250 per month. A rent ceiling of $500 per month is then put into effect. One possible outcome is that landlords will charge disguised rent increases, which will bring the true price back to $1,250 per month. If such disguised increases are prohibited, there will be a shortage of 350,000 units at the ceiling price. Part (b) shows the long run effects when there is time to adjust the number of units in response to the price. If the ceiling price is enforced, landlords move down their supply curve to $E_2$. The shortage then becomes even more severe than in the short run.

The greater quantity demanded has several sources. First, people who would otherwise own a house or condominium may now want to rent. Second, people who would otherwise live in non–rent-controlled suburbs may now seek rent-controlled units in the city. Third, each tenant may want more space, which results in a demand for more of the standardized units shown in Figure 2.10.

The shortage creates a problem for both landlords and tenants: How will the limited supply of apartments be rationed among those who want them? Both landlords and tenants devise a number of creative responses—*entrepreneurial* responses, as an economist would say.

One response on the part of landlords is to seek disguised rent increases. These may take the form of large, nonrefundable "key deposits" or security deposits. As an alternative, they may sell old, used furniture or drapes at inflated prices as a condition for renting the apartment. Finally, the costs of certain maintenance or security services for which the landlord might otherwise have paid may be transferred to tenants.

Tenants, too, may get into the act. When they decide to move, they may sublet their apartments to other tenants rather than give up their leases. Now it is the tenant who collects the key money or sells the old drapes to the subtenant. The original tenant may have moved to a distant city but maintains a bank account and a post office box for use in paying the rent. The subtenant is instructed to play the role of a "guest" if the landlord telephones.

Advocates of rent control view these responses as cheating and often try to outlaw them. If prohibitions are enforced, the landlord will find that there are many applicants for each vacant apartment. In that case, the landlord must decide to whom to rent the apartment. The result will often be discrimination against renters who are from minority groups, who have children, or who have unconventional lifestyles.

In the long run, rent control has other unintended effects. The long run in this case means enough time for the number of rental units to grow through construction of new units or shrink through abandonment of old ones (or their conversion to condominiums). Other things being equal, the higher the rent, the greater the rate of construction; and the lower the rent, the greater the rate of abandonment or conversion. This is reflected in the positively sloped long-run supply curve in part (b) of Figure 2.10.

If landlords enforce rent controls in such a way that there are no disguised charges, the number of rental units shrinks and the market moves from $E_1$ to $E_2$. At $E_2$, the unintended effects that appeared in the short run become more pronounced. The intensity of housing discrimination increases relative to the short-run case because the difference between the number of units available and the number sought by renters increases. Graphically, that difference is shown by the horizontal gap between the supply and demand curves at the ceiling price. In the short run, there is a shortage of 50,000 units; in the long run, the shortage increases to 75,000 units.

Rent controls are often defended as being beneficial to the poor; but when all of the unintended effects of rent control are taken into account, one may question whether poor families really benefit. In cases in which disguised rent increases are possible, the true cost of rental housing is not really decreased. Further, it is hard to believe that the tendency of landlords to discriminate against minority group members, single-parent families, and tenants with irregular work histories will benefit the poor. The most likely beneficiaries of rent control are stable, middle-class families who work at the same jobs and live in the same apartments for long periods.

Why does rent control persist as a policy, given its many seemingly perverse unintended consequences? Some economists explain the popularity of rent control in terms of the political power of the middle-class tenants who are most likely to benefit from rent controls and who see "helping the poor" as nothing more than a convenient cover for their own self-interest. Some explain their popularity in terms of the short time horizon of government officials: The adverse effect on tenants of ending rent control would appear very quickly, whereas such benefits as increased construction of new apartments would materialize only long after the next election. Others attribute the popularity of rent control to the simple fact that many voters do not give much thought to the policy's unintended consequences. Whatever the reason, it appears that very gradually rent control is weakening its hold, even in New York, long home of the strongest controls. In the past decade, some 10 percent of the 1 million or so apartments once covered by New York's rent controls have left the system; and the trend is expected to continue.

THIS CHAPTER HAS covered the basics of the supply-and-demand model and described a few applications of that model. There are many more applications in both macro- and microeconomics. In macroeconomics, the supply-and-demand model can be applied to financial markets, labor markets, and the problem of determining the rate of inflation and real output for the economy as a whole. In microeconomics, the model can be applied to product markets, markets for productive resources, and policy issues ranging from pollution to farm policy to international trade, to name just a few. As the great economist Alfred Marshall once put it, nearly all of the major problems of economics have a "kernel" that reflects the workings of supply and demand (see *Who Said It? Who Did It? 2.1*).

When one takes a detailed look at the underpinnings of the model, it appears to fit some kinds of markets more closely than others. The fit is best for markets in which there are many producers and many customers, the goods sold by one producer are much like those sold by others, and all sellers and buyers have good information on market conditions. Markets for farm commodities, such as wheat and corn, and financial markets, such as the New York Stock Exchange, meet these standards reasonably well.

### Who Said It? Who Did It? 2.1
### ALFRED MARSHALL ON SUPPLY AND DEMAND

Alfred Marshall, often considered to have been the greatest economist of his day, was born in London in 1842. His father was a Bank of England cashier who hoped the boy would enter the ministry. Young Marshall had other ideas, however. He turned down a theological scholarship at Oxford to study mathematics, receiving his M.A. from Cambridge in 1865.

While at Cambridge, Marshall joined a philosophical discussion group. There he became interested in promoting the broad development of the human mind. He was soon told, however, that the harsh realities of economics would prevent his ideas from being carried out. Britain's economic potential as a country, it was said, could never allow the masses sufficient leisure for education. This disillusioning episode appears to have triggered Marshall's fascination with economics.

At the time, the classical school founded by Adam Smith and David Ricardo dominated British economics. Marshall had great respect for the classical writers. Initially, he saw his own work as simply applying his mathematical training to strengthen and systematize the classical system. Before long, however, he was breaking new ground and developing a system of his own. By 1890, when he brought out his famous *Principles of Economics*, he had laid the foundation of what we now call the neoclassical school.

In an attempt to explain the essence of his approach, Marshall included the following passage in the second edition of his *Principles*:

> In spite of a great variety in detail, nearly all the chief problems of economics agree in that they have a kernel of the same kind. This kernel is an inquiry as to the balancing of two opposed classes of motives, the one consisting of desires to acquire certain new goods, and thus satisfy wants; while the other consists of desires to avoid certain efforts or retain certain immediate enjoyment ... in other words, it is an inquiry into the balancing of the forces of demand and supply.

Marshall's influence on economics—at least in the English-speaking world—was enormous. His *Principles* was the leading economics text for several decades, and modern students can still learn much from it. As a professor at Cambridge, Marshall taught a great many of the next generation's leading economists. Today his neoclassical school continues to dominate the profession. It has received many challenges, but so far it has weathered them all.

However, even in markets that do not display all of these features, the fit is often close enough so that the supply-and-demand model provides useful insights into what is going on. The rental housing market is an example. Not all rental units are, in fact, alike, even when measurement is standardized for objective characteristics such as floor space. Nevertheless, most economists would agree that applying the supply-and-demand model to that market could lead to valid conclusions about the effects of rent control. Thus, the supply-and-demand model serves a precise analytical function in some markets and a broader, more metaphorical function in others. That flexibility makes the model one of the most useful items in the economist's tool kit.

# Summary

1.  **How does the price of a good or service affect the quantity of it that buyers demand?** Economists use the term *demand* to refer to the willingness and ability of buyers to purchase goods and services. According to the *law of demand*, there is an inverse relationship between the price of a good and the quantity of it that buyers demand. The *quantity demanded* is the quantity that buyers are willing and able to pay for. The law of demand can be represented graphically by a negatively sloped *demand curve*. A movement along the demand curve shows a change in the quantity demanded.

2.  **How do other market conditions affect demand?** A change in any of the variables covered by the "other things being equal" clause of the law of demand causes a shift in the demand curve; this is known as a *change in demand*. Examples include changes in the prices of goods that are *substitutes* or *complements* of the good in question as well as changes in consumer incomes, expectations, and tastes.

3.  **How does the price of a good affect the quantity supplied by sellers?** *Supply* refers to sellers' willingness and ability to offer products for sale in a market. In most markets an increase in the price of a good will increase the quantity of the good that sellers are willing to supply.

This relationship can be shown as a positively sloped *supply curve*. The higher price gives producers an incentive to supply more, but rising opportunity costs set a limit on the amount they will supply at any given price.

4.  **How do changes in other market conditions affect supply?** A change in any of the items covered by the "other things being equal" clause of the supply curve will shift the curve. Examples include changes in technology, changes in the prices of inputs, changes in the prices of other goods that could be produced with the same resources, and changes in expectations.

5.  **How do supply and demand interact to determine the market price of a good or service?** In a market with a positively-sloped supply curve and a negatively-sloped demand curve, there is only one price at which the quantity of a good that sellers plan to supply will exactly match the quantity that buyers plan to purchase. That is known as the *equilibrium* price. At any higher price there will be a *surplus*, and at any lower price there will be a *shortage*.

6.  **Why do market prices and quantities change in response to changes in market conditions?** A change in any market condition that shifts the supply or demand curve will change the equilibrium price and quantity in a market. For example, the demand curve may shift to the right as a

result of a change in consumer incomes. This causes a shortage at the old price, and the price begins to rise. As the price rises, suppliers move up along the supply curve to a new equilibrium. No shift in the supply curve is required. On the other hand, better technology may shift the supply curve to the right. In that case, there is a surplus at the old price, and the price will fall. As the price decreases, buyers will move down along their demand curve to a new equilibrium. No shift in the demand curve is required.

7. **How do price supports and price ceilings affect the operation of markets?** A price support prevents the market price from falling when the demand curve shifts to the left or the supply curve shifts to the right. The result may be a lasting surplus. A price ceiling prevents the price from rising to its equilibrium level. The result may be a permanent shortage. The total quantity supplied may then be less than the quantity that buyers would like to purchase at the ceiling price or even at the equilibrium price.

## Key Terms

## Problems and Topics for Discussion

1. **A shifting demand curve**   A vending machine company has studied the demand for soft drinks sold in cans from machines. On a 70-degree day consumers in the firm's territory will buy about 2,000 cans at a price of $0.75. For each $.05 rise in price, the quantity sold falls by 200 cans per day; for each 5-degree rise in the temperature, the quantity sold rises by 150 cans per day. The same relationships hold for decreases in price or temperature. Using this information, draw a set of curves showing the demand for soft drinks on days when the temperature is 60, 70, and 85 degrees. Then draw a separate diagram with temperature on the vertical axis and quantity on the horizontal axis. Draw a line representing the relationship between temperature and quantity when the price is $0.75. Next, draw additional temperature-quantity lines for prices of $0.50 and $1.00. Do the two diagrams give the same information? Discuss. (Note: If you have any trouble with this exercise, review the appendix to Chapter 1, "Working with Graphs," especially the section entitled "Packing Three Variables into Two Dimensions.")

2. **Demand and the relative price of motor fuel in the 1980s**   In 1979 and 1980, the nominal price of motor fuel rose much more rapidly than the general price level, pushing up the relative price of motor fuel. As we would expect, the quantity sold decreased. In 1981 and 1982, the relative price leveled off and then began to fall; but the quantity sold continued to fall. Which one or more of the following hypotheses do you think best explains the behavior of motor fuel sales in 1981 and 1982? Illustrate each hypothesis with supply and demand curves.

   a. In the 1970s the demand curve had the usual negative slope. However, in 1981 and 1982, the demand curve shifted to an unusual positively sloped position.

b. The demand curve had a negative slope throughout the period. However, the recession of 1981 and 1982 reduced consumers' real incomes and thus shifted the demand curve.

c. The demand curve has a negative slope at all times, but the shape depends partly on how much time consumers have to adjust to a change in prices. Over a short period, the demand curve is fairly steep because few adjustments can be made. Over the long term, it has a somewhat flatter slope because further adjustments, such as buying more fuel-efficient cars or moving closer to the job, can be made. Thus, the decreases in fuel sales in 1981 and 1982 were delayed reactions to the price increases that occurred in 1979 and 1980.

3. **Shortages, price controls, and queues**   During the late 1980s and early 1990s, economic reforms initiated by Soviet President Mikhail Gorbachev began to raise consumer incomes; but the Soviet government continued to impose price ceilings on basic goods like food, clothing, and household goods. As a result, there were severe shortages of many goods and long lines at all kinds of stores became common. Then, in January 1992, the new Russian government, under President Boris Yeltsin, removed retail price controls on most goods. Within a month, prices more than doubled on average and lines disappeared. Analyze these events using the supply and demand model. First draw a supply and demand diagram for some common good, i.e., butter, showing the market in equilibrium before the beginning of the Gorbachev reforms. Next, use shifts of the appropriate curves to show why the combination of rising incomes plus price ceilings produced shortages and lines. Finally, show what happened when price controls were removed in 1992.

4. **Eliminating queues through flexible pricing**   You are a member of the Metropolitan Taxi Commission, which sets taxi fares for your city. You have been told that long lines of taxis form at the airport during off-peak hours. At peak hours, on the other hand, few taxis are available and there are long lines of passengers waiting for cabs. It is proposed that taxi fares from the airport to downtown be cut by 10 percent during off-peak hours and increased by 10 percent during peak hours. How do you think these changes would affect the queuing patterns of taxis and passengers? Do you think the proposal is a good one from the passengers' point of view? From the cabbies' point of view? From the standpoint of economic efficiency? What do you think would happen if the Taxi Commission stopped setting fares altogether and allowed passengers and drivers to negotiate any price they wanted? Discuss.

5. **Rent control**   Turn to part (b) of Figure 2.10, which shows the long-run effects of rent control. If the controls are enforced and there are no disguised rent charges, landlords move down the supply curve to $E_2$. Buildings are abandoned or converted because of the low rent they bring in. Now consider some alternative possibilities.

a. Suppose that the controls are poorly enforced so that landlords—through key deposits, furniture sales, or some other means—are able to charge as much as the market will bear. What will the resulting equilibrium price and quantity be, taking both open and disguised rental charges into account?

b. Now suppose that the controls are enforced so that landlords really cannot collect more than $500 per month. However, the controls are not enforced against tenants who sublet. What will the equilibrium quantity and price be, including both the rent paid to landlords and the disguised rental payments made by subtenants to their sublessors?

## Case for Discussion

The hottest topic at a recent exposition for suppliers and users of off-road heavy equipment was tire shortages. Booming Chinese demand for raw materials meant that mining companies in China, Russia, and Indonesia were stocking up on new earth moving equipment and wearing tires out faster on equipment they already owned.

While demand soared, supply had a hard time keeping up. Building a new production line for large tires can take more than two years. The *Financial Times* reported that some tire makers were reactivating mothballed production lines for old-fashioned bias-ply tires. While not as good as modern radial tires, they were good enough to satisfy demand from customers who just wanted something "black and round," according to Prashant Prabhu, president of the earth-mover and industrial tire business of Michelin, the French tire maker. Prabhu also said his company was revising its pricing for large tires to take the shortage into account. Other suppliers have been buying tires of unknown, possibly inferior, quality from Russia and China.

According to *Light and Medium Truck Magazine*, the shortages of huge off-road tires were spilling over into the market for heavy-duty truck tires. In addition to sharply increased demand, it blamed rising prices for materials, including both natural and synthetic rubber. The magazine predicted that the shortage would last two years or more.

Expectations, based on past experience, were a significant factor slowing the adjustment of supply to the shortage. In 2000–2003, demand for heavy-duty tires from equipment makers had dropped by more than 50 percent, leaving some tire makers with serious overcapacity. The fear that recent high demand might not last led some manufacturers to take a "wait-and-see" attitude, but world demand for tires did hold up. In 2008, Canadian miners, trying to meet orders for strip-mined coal and oil shale, were still struggling to keep their giant vehicles rolling—using every little trick from keeping their roads free of sharp rocks to even digging up tires discarded years ago, but now, perhaps, capable of being reconditioned and used again.

SOURCES: *Financial Times*, Materials squeeze leads to tyre shortage, By James Mackintosh Published: April 28 2005 03:00; *Light and Medium Truck Magazine*, May 2005,

http://www.ttnews.com/lmt /May05/tire.asp (May 22, 2005); *Rental Management Online*, http://www.rentalmanagement-mag.com/newsart.asp?ARTID=1776, May 22, 2005; *Business Edge*, "Tire Shortage Poses Challenges to Miners," March 7, 2008, http://www.businessedge.ca/article.cfm/newsID/17370.cfm.

## QUESTIONS

1. Beginning from a position of equilibrium, use supply and demand curves to show how the tire market is affected by an increase in demand for earth-moving equipment. Does the supply curve shift? The demand curve? Both? Explain.

2. Now draw a diagram that has two supply curves, one that applies to the short run and the other to the long run. How does the long-run impact of an increase in demand differ from the short-run impact?

3. As the world fell into recession in 2008 and 2009, demand for earthmoving equipment decreased sharply. How would this affect the market for tires?

## End Notes

1. Before continuing, the reader may want to review the Chapter 1 appendix, "Working with Graphs," especially the section entitled "Packing Three Variables into Two Dimensions."

2. The "plans" referred to need not be formal or thought out in detail, and are subject to change. A consumer might, for example, make out a shopping list for the supermarket based on the usual prices for various foods, but then revise it to take into account unexpected price increases or sales on certain items. On specific occasions, consumer decisions may even be completely impulsive, with little basis in rational calculation. The model of supply and demand does not require that every decision be based on precise analysis, but only that consumer intentions, on the average, are influenced by prices and other economic considerations.

3. Why might buyers and sellers enter the market expecting a price other than the one that permits equilibrium? It may be, for example, that market conditions have caused the supply or demand curve to shift unexpectedly, so that

a price that formerly permitted equilibrium no longer does so. It may be that buyers or sellers expect conditions to change, but they do not change after all; or, it may be that government policy has established a legal maximum or minimum price that differs from the equilibrium price. Later sections of the chapter will explore some of these possibilities.

4.  This is a fairly restrictive assumption. In practice, a small number of housing units can move into or out of the rental market quickly in response to changing conditions. "Mother-in-law apartments" in private homes are an example. If conditions in the rental market are unfavorable, the owners of such units may simply leave them vacant. Allowing for such fast-reaction units means that the short-run supply curve, while still quite steep, would not be vertical. However, a vertical short-run curve simplifies the geometry while capturing the essential features of the situation.

# CHAPTER *3*

# Supply, Demand, and Elasticity

**After reading this chapter, you will understand the following:**

1. How the responsiveness of quantity demanded to a price change can be expressed in terms of elasticity
2. How elasticity of demand is related to revenue
3. How elasticity applies to changes in market conditions other than price
4. How elasticity is useful in interpreting issues of taxation and other public policies

**Before reading this chapter, make sure you know the meaning of the concepts:**

1. Supply and demand
2. Demand, quantity demanded
3. Supply, quantity supplied
4. Substitutes and complements
5. Normal and inferior goods

HOW MUCH DID you pay for this textbook? Was it more expensive or less expensive than the books you buy for other courses? As a student, you probably have a strong desire to pay less for your books if you can. Have you ever wondered why your professors sometimes choose books that are so expensive?

This chapter will help you understand the effect of price on choices that people make among alternative goods—like different textbooks, different foods, or different modes of transportation. It will focus on the concept of *elasticity*, a word economists use to say how sensitive such choices are to price. As a student, your choice of textbook is probably very sensitive to price—your demand is *elastic*, to use the economist's term. However, your professor, who does not pay for the books, cares less about how much they cost. Your professor's demand may be *inelastic*. In the following pages you will learn how to define, measure, and apply the important concept of elasticity.

# Elasticity

The responsiveness of quantity demanded to a change in price can be expressed in many ways, depending on the units of measurement that are chosen. Consider the demand for chicken, an example used in the preceding chapter. A study of the budget of a single American household might find that an increase of ten cents per pound would decrease consumption by 1 pound per week. A study done in France might find that a price increase of 1 euro per kilogram would decrease consumption of all consumers in the city of Lille by 25,000 kilos per month. Are the findings of these studies similar? It is hard to tell because the units used are different. It would require more information, and some calculations, to know whether the sensitivity of demand to price as measured in different countries using different currencies are the same. A further problem with the examples given is that they do not tell us where prices or quantities started. Ten cents a pound is not a very large increase—if it refers to premium free-range, boneless, chicken breasts that began at $3.49 a pound. One euro per kilogram might represent a doubling of the price, however, for a low-quality, commercial grade of chicken.

To avoid confusion arising from the choice of different units of measurement and differing starting points for price changes, it is useful to standardize. One common way of doing so is to express all changes as percentages. Suppose, for example, that the studies of both American and French consumers found that a 20 percent increase in price was associated with a 10 percent decrease in quantity demanded. Stating changes in percentages would take into account the size of a price change relative to the starting or ending price and quantity. The percentages would also stay the same regardless of whether the original data were stated in dollars per pound, euros per kilo, or any other measurement.

The use of percentages to express the response of one variable to a change in another is widespread in economics. The term **elasticity** is used to refer to relationships expressed in percentages. Like equilibrium, elasticity is a metaphor borrowed from physics. Much as equilibrium calls to mind a pendulum that has come to rest hanging straight down, elasticity conjures up the image of a rubber band that stretches by a certain percentage of its length when the force applied to it is increased by a given percentage. This chapter introduces several applications of elasticity in economics.

## Price Elasticity of Demand

The **price elasticity of demand** is the ratio of the percentage change in the quantity of a good demanded to a given percentage change in its price. Figure 3.1 presents five demand curves showing different degrees of price elasticity of demand. In part (a), the quantity demanded is strongly responsive to a change in price. In this case, a decrease in price from $5 to $3 causes the quantity demanded to increase from three units to six.

Changes in price and quantity are reflected in the **revenue** earned from sale of the product. Revenue means the price times the quantity sold. In part (a) of Figure 3.1, the percentage change in quantity demanded is greater than the percentage change in price, so the drop in price causes total revenue from sales of the good to increase. On a supply-and-demand diagram, revenue can be shown as the area of a rectangle drawn under the demand curve, with a height equal to price and a width equal to quantity

**Elasticity**

A measure of the response of one variable to a change in another, stated as a ratio of the percentage change in one variable to the associated percentage change in another variable

**Price elasticity of demand**

The ratio of the percentage change in the quantity of a good demanded to a given percentage change in its price, other things being equal

**Revenue**

Price multiplied by quantity sold

## FIGURE 3.1    PRICE ELASTICITY OF DEMAND

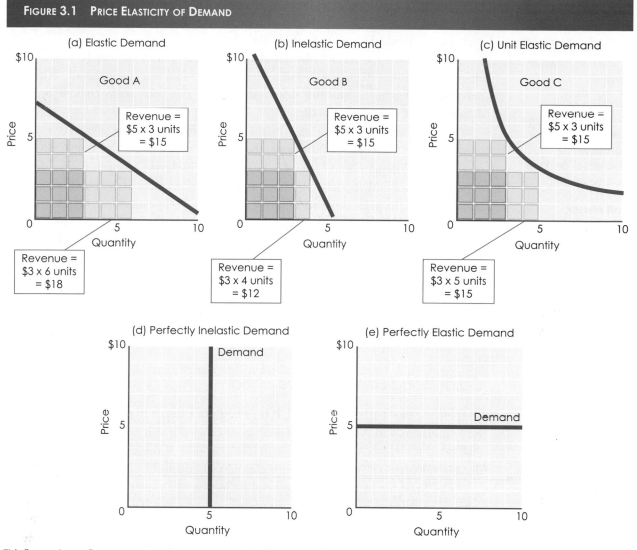

This figure shows five examples of demand curves with various degrees of elasticity over the indicated range of variation of price and quantity. The examples illustrate elastic, inelastic, unit elastic, perfectly inelastic, and perfectly elastic demand. For the first three cases, the revenue change associated with a change in price is shown. When demand is elastic, a price decrease causes revenue to increase. When demand is inelastic, a price decrease causes revenue to decrease. When demand is unit elastic, revenue does not change when price changes.

**Elastic demand**

A situation in which quantity demanded changes by a larger percentage than price, so that total revenue increases as price decreases

demanded. In this case, comparison of the shaded rectangles representing revenue before the price reduction ($5 per unit × 3 units = $15) and afterward ($3 per unit × 6 units = $18) shows that revenue is greater after the price has been reduced. When the quantity demanded changes by a greater percentage than price, so that a price decrease causes total revenue to increase, demand is said to be **elastic**.

Part (b) of Figure 3.1 shows a case in which the quantity demanded is only weakly responsive to a change in price. Here, a $2 decrease in price, from $5 to $3 per unit, causes the quantity demanded to increase by just one unit—from three to four. This

**Inelastic demand**

A situation in which quantity demanded changes by a smaller percentage than price, so that total revenue decreases as price decreases

**Unit elastic demand**

A situation in which price and quantity demanded change by the same percentage, so that total revenue remains unchanged as price changes

**Perfectly inelastic demand**

A situation in which the demand curve is a vertical line

**Perfectly elastic demand**

A situation in which the demand curve is a horizontal line

time the percentage change in quantity demanded is less than that in price. As a result, the decrease in price causes total revenue to fall (again note the shaded rectangles). In such a case, demand is said to be **inelastic**.

Part (c) shows a case in which a change in price causes an exactly proportional change in quantity demanded, so that total revenue does not change at all. When the percentage change in quantity demanded equals the percentage change in price, demand is said to be **unit elastic**.

The final two parts of Figure 3.1 show two extreme cases. Part (d) shows a vertical demand curve. Regardless of the price, the quantity demanded is five units—no more, no less. Such a demand curve is said to be **perfectly inelastic**. Part (e) shows a demand curve that is perfectly horizontal. Above a price of $5, no units of the good can be sold; but as soon as the price drops to $5, there is no limit on how much can be sold. A horizontal demand curve like this one is described as **perfectly elastic**. The law of demand, which describes an inverse relationship between price and quantity, does not encompass the cases of perfectly elastic and inelastic demand; and we do not expect market demand curves for ordinary goods and services to fit these extremes. Nevertheless, we will see that perfectly elastic and inelastic curves sometimes provide useful reference points for theory building, even though they do not resemble real-world market demand curves.

## Calculating Elasticity of Demand

In speaking of elasticity of demand, it is sometimes enough to say that demand is elastic or inelastic, without being more precise. At other times, it is useful to give a numerical value for elasticity. This section introduces one of the most common methods used to calculate a numerical value for elasticity of demand.

The first step in turning the general definition of elasticity into a numerical formula is to develop a way to measure percentage changes. The everyday method for calculating a percentage change is to use the initial value of the variable as the denominator and the change in the value as the numerator. For example, suppose the quantity of California lettuce demanded in the national market is initially 12,000 tons per week and then demand decreases by 4,000 tons per week; we say that there has been a 33 percent decrease (4,000/12,000 = .33). The trouble with this convention is that the same change in the opposite direction gives a different percentage. By everyday reasoning, an increase in the quantity of lettuce demanded from 8,000 tons per week to 12,000 tons per week is a 50 percent increase (4,000/8,000 = .5).

Decades ago the mathematical economist R. G. D. Allen proposed an unambiguous measure of percentage changes that uses the midpoint of the range over which change takes place as the denominator. To find the midpoint of the range over which a change takes place, we take the sum of the initial value and the final value and divide by 2. In our example, the midpoint of the quantity range is (8,000 + 12,000)/2 = 10,000). When this value is used as the denominator, a change of 4,000 units becomes a 40 percent change (4,000/10,000 = .4). Using $Q_1$ to represent the quantity before the change and $Q_2$ to represent the quantity after the change, the midpoint formula for the percentage change in quantity is

$$\text{Percentage change in quantity} = \frac{Q_2 - Q_1}{(Q_1 + Q_2)/2}$$

The same approach can be used to define the percentage change in price. Suppose that in our case, the price of lettuce increased from about $700 per ton to about $900 per ton. Using the midpoint of the range, or $800, as the denominator [(700 + 900)/2 = 800], we conclude that the $200 increase in price is a 25 percent increase (200/800 = .25). The midpoint formula for the percentage change in price is

$$\text{Percentage change in price} = \frac{P_2 - P_1}{(P_1 + P_2)/2}$$

**THE MIDPOINT FORMULA FOR ELASTICITY**    Defining percentage changes in this way allows us to write a useful formula for calculating elasticities. We can simplify the formula by omitting the terms "/2", which cancel out. With $P_1$ and $Q_1$ representing price and quantity before a change, and $P_2$ and $Q_2$ representing price and quantity after the change, the midpoint formula for elasticity is

$$\text{Price elasticity of demand} = \frac{(Q_2 - Q_1)/(Q_1 + Q_2)}{(P_2 - P_1)/(P_1 + P_2)} = \frac{\text{Percentage change in quantity}}{\text{Percentage change in price}}$$

Following is the complete calculation for the elasticity of demand for lettuce when an increase in price from $700 per ton to $900 per ton causes the quantity demanded to fall from 12,000 tons per day to 8,000 tons per day:

$P_1$ = price before change = $700

$P_2$ = price after change = $900

$Q_1$ = quantity before change = 12,000

$Q_2$ = quantity after change = 8,000

$$\text{Elasticity} = \frac{(8{,}000 - 12{,}000)/(8{,}000 + 12{,}000)}{(\$900 - \$700)/(\$700 + \$900)}$$

$$= \frac{-4{,}000/20{,}000}{200/1{,}600}$$

$$= \frac{-.2}{.125}$$

$$= -1.6$$

Because demand curves have negative slopes, price and quantity change in opposite directions. As a result, this formula yields a negative value for elasticity. When the price decreases, the term $(P_2 - P_1)$, which appears in the denominator of the formula, is negative, whereas the term $(Q_2 - Q_1)$, which appears in the numerator, is positive. When the price increases, the numerator is negative and the denominator is positive. However, in this book we follow the widely used (but not universal) practice of dropping the minus sign when discussing price elasticity of demand. For example, we will refer to the elasticity of demand for lettuce in our example as approximately 1.6 over the range studied.

A numerical elasticity value such as 1.6 can be related to the basic definition of elasticity in a simple way. That definition stated that price elasticity of demand is the ratio of the percentage change in quantity demanded to a given percentage change in price. Thus, an elasticity of 1.6 means that the quantity demanded will increase by 1.6 percent for each 1 percent change in price. An elasticity of 3 would mean that quantity demanded would change by 3 percent for each 1 percent change in price, and so on.[1]

**ELASTICITY VALUES AND TERMINOLOGY**    Earlier in the chapter we defined *elastic, inelastic, unit elastic, perfectly elastic,* and *perfectly inelastic* demand. Each of these terms corresponds to a numerical value or range of values of elasticity. A perfectly inelastic demand curve has a numerical value of 0 since any change in price produces no change in quantity demanded. The term *inelastic* (but not perfectly inelastic) *demand* applies to numerical values from 0 up to, but not including, 1. *Unit elasticity,* as the name implies, means a numerical value of exactly 1. *Elastic demand* means any value for elasticity that is greater than 1. *Perfectly elastic* demand, represented by a horizontal demand curve, is not defined numerically; as the demand curve becomes horizontal, the denominator of the elasticity formula approaches 0 and the numerical value of elasticity increases without limit.

## Varying- and Constant-Elasticity Demand Curves

The midpoint formula shows elasticity of demand over a certain range of prices and quantities. Measured over some other range, the elasticity of demand for the same good may be the same or different, depending on the shape of the demand curve, as shown in Figure 3.2.

Part (a) of Figure 3.2 shows a demand curve that, like most of those in this book, is a straight line. The elasticity of demand is not constant for all ranges of price and quantity along this curve. For example, when measured over the price range $8 to $9, the elasticity of demand is 5.66; when measured over the range $2 to $3, it is .33. (The calculations are shown in the figure.)

The calculations illustrate the general rule that elasticity declines as one moves down and to the right along a straight-line demand curve. It is easy to see why. With such a demand curve, a $1 reduction in price always causes the same absolute increase in quantity demanded. At the upper end of the demand curve, a $1 change is a small percentage of the relatively high price, while the change in quantity is a large percentage of the relatively low quantity demanded. At the lower end of the curve, however,

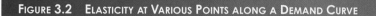

**FIGURE 3.2    ELASTICITY AT VARIOUS POINTS ALONG A DEMAND CURVE**

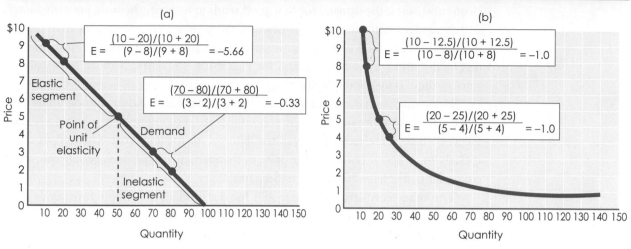

Elasticity varies along a straight-line demand curve, as part (a) of this figure illustrates. At the upper end of the curve, where the price is relatively high, a $1 change in price is a relatively small percentage change; and because the quantity demanded is low, the corresponding change in quantity is relatively large in percentage terms. Demand is thus elastic near the top of the demand curve. At the lower end of the curve, the situation is reversed: a $1 change in price is now a relatively large change in percentage terms, whereas the corresponding change in quantity is smaller in percentage terms. Thus demand is inelastic. As part (b) shows, a curved demand curve can be drawn such that elasticity is constant for all ranges of price and quantity change.

the situation is reversed: A $1 change is now a large percentage of the relatively low price, while the increase in quantity is smaller in relation to the relatively larger quantity demanded. Because it is percentages, not absolute amounts that matter in elasticity calculations, a linear demand curve is less elastic near the bottom than near the top.

If the demand curve is not a straight line, other results are possible. There is an important special case in which the demand curve has just the curvature needed to keep elasticity constant over its entire length. Such a curve is shown in part (b) of Figure 3.2. As can be seen from the calculations in the figure, elasticity is 1.0 at every point on that curve. It is possible to construct demand curves with constant elasticities of any value. Econometric studies of demand elasticity often look for the constant-elasticity demand curve that most closely approximates buyers' average sensitivity to price changes as revealed by market data over time.

## Determinants of Elasticity of Demand

The fact that elasticity often varies along the demand curve means that care must be taken in making statements about the elasticity of demand for a good. In practice, what such statements usually refer to is the elasticity, measured by the midpoint formula or some alternative method, over the range of price variation that is commonly observed in the market for that good. With this understanding, we can make some generalizations about what makes the demand for some goods elastic and the demand for others inelastic.

**SUBSTITUTES, COMPLEMENTS, AND ELASTICITY**    One important determinant of elasticity of demand is the availability of substitutes. When a good has close substitutes, the demand for that good tends to be elastic because people willingly switch to the substitutes when the price of the good goes up. Thus, for example, the demand for corn oil is elastic because other cooking oils can usually be substituted for it. On the other hand, the demand for cigarettes is inelastic because for a habitual smoker there is no good substitute.

This principle has two corollaries. One is that the demand for a good tends to be more elastic the more narrowly the good is defined. For example, the demand for coffee as a whole is inelastic. However, the demand for medium-roast Colombian coffee is likely to be elastic because if the price of that particular type rises, people can switch to similar coffee from Nicaragua or Sumatra.

The other corollary is that demand for the product of a single firm tends to be more elastic than the demand for the output of all producers operating in the market. As one example, the demand for cigarettes as a whole will be less elastic than the demand for any particular brand. The reason is that one brand can be substituted for another when the price of a brand changes.

The complements of a good can also play a role in determining its elasticity. If something is a minor complement to an important good (that is, one that accounts for a large share of consumers' budgets), demand for it tends to be inelastic. For example, the demand for motor oil tends to be inelastic because it is a complement to a more important good, gasoline. The price of gasoline has a greater effect on the amount of driving a person does than the price of motor oil.

**PRICE VERSUS OPPORTUNITY COST**    Elasticity measures the responsiveness of quantity demanded to the monetary price of a good. In most cases, the price, in money, is an accurate approximation of the opportunity cost of choosing a good; but that is not always the case. We mentioned one example at the beginning of the chapter: The price of a textbook is an opportunity cost to the student who buys it; but it is not an opportunity cost to the professor who assigns it because the students pay for the book, not the professor. As a result, publishers have traditionally assumed that professors will pay little attention to the price of the text, and demand will be

Textbook prices are opportunity costs for students.

highly inelastic. However, in recent years students have increasingly been making their influence felt, so that price-elasticity of demand for textbooks may be increasing.

The textbook market is a relatively small one, but there are other much more important markets where the responsibility for choice does not lie with the party who bears the opportunity cost. Medical care provides many examples. Doctors choose what drug to offer to patients, but either the patient or the patient's insurance company pays for the drug. As a result, demand for drugs is very inelastic; and doctors sometimes prescribe expensive brand-name drugs when cheaper generic drugs are available to do the same job.

Business travel is still another example of the separation of price and opportunity cost. Business travelers do not pay for their own airline tickets, hotels, and meals, so their demand for these services tends to be inelastic. When vacationers purchase the same services, they bear the full opportunity cost. Not surprisingly, business travelers often choose more expensive options. In many cases airlines and hotels take advantage of the separation of price and opportunity cost by charging different rates to business and vacation travelers.

**TIME HORIZON AND ELASTICITY**     One of the most important considerations determining the price elasticity of demand is the time horizon within which the decision to buy is made. For several reasons, demand is often less elastic in the short run than in the long run.

One reason is that full adjustment to a change in the price of a good may require changes in the kind or quantity of many other goods that a consumer buys. Gasoline provides a classic example. When the price of gasoline rises, people can cut out some nonessential driving; but the total quantity of gasoline demanded is not much affected. Short-run demand elasticity for gasoline has been estimated as about .25, that is, just one quarter of one percent reduction in quantity demanded for each 1 percent increase in price. As time goes by, though, consumers can make many kinds of adjustment to the higher price. They can buy fewer fuel-hungry SUVs and more higher-mileage hybrid cars. They can change their jobs or move in order to shorten their daily commute. They can switch to public transportation, if it is available; or if it is not, they can demand that local governments expand public transportation options. The long-run demand for gasoline is estimated to be about .6 to .8, considerably higher than the short-run elasticity.

Another reason elasticity tends to be greater in the long run than in the short run is that an increase in the price of one good encourages entrepreneurs to develop substitutes, which, as we have seen, can be an important determinant of elasticity. To take an example from history, consider the response to what has been called America's first energy crisis: a sharp increase in the price of whale oil, which was widely used as lamp fuel in the early nineteenth century. At first candles were the only substitute for whale-oil lamps, and not a very satisfactory one. People, therefore, cut their use of whale oil only a little when the price began to rise. The high price of whale oil, however, spurred entrepreneurs to develop a better substitute, kerosene. Once kerosene came onto the market, the quantity of whale oil demanded for use as lamp fuel dropped to zero. Today market forces are spurring the development of many alternative forms of energy, ranging from ethanol as a motor fuel to wind, wave, and solar energy for generating electricity.

A final reason for greater elasticity of demand in the long run than in the short run is the slow adjustment of consumer tastes. The case of beef and chicken, featured in the preceding chapter, provides an example. Chicken, originally the more expensive meat, achieved a price advantage over beef many years ago; but eating lots of beef was a habit. Gradually, though, chicken developed an image as a healthy, stylish, versatile food; and finally it overtook beef as the number-one meat in the United States.

## Income Elasticity of Demand

Determining the response of quantity demanded to a change in price is the most common application of the concept of elasticity, but it is by no means the only one. Elasticity can also be used to express the response of demand to any of the conditions covered by the "other things being equal" assumption on which a given demand curve is based. As we saw in the preceding chapter, consumer income is one of those conditions.

**Income elasticity of demand**

The ratio of the percentage change in the quantity of a good demanded to a given percentage change in consumer incomes, other things being equal

The **income elasticity of demand** for a good is defined as the ratio of the percentage change in the quantity of that good demanded to a percentage change in income. In measuring income elasticity, it is assumed that the good's price does not change. Using $Q_1$ and $Q_2$ to represent quantities before and after the change in income, and $y_1$ and $y_2$ to represent income before and after the change, the midpoint formula for income elasticity of demand can be written as follows:

$$\text{Income elasticity of demand} = \frac{(Q_2 - Q_1)/(Q_1 + Q_2)}{(y_2 - y_1)/(y_1 + y_2)} = \frac{\text{Percentage change in quantity}}{\text{Percentage change in income}}$$

For a normal good, an increase in income causes demand to rise. Because income and demand change in the same direction, the income elasticity of demand for a normal good is positive. For an inferior good, an increase in income causes demand to decrease. Because income and demand change in opposite directions, the income elasticity of demand for an inferior good is negative.

Some of the considerations that determine price elasticity also affect income elasticity. In particular, whether a good is considered to be normal or inferior depends on how narrowly it is defined and on the availability of substitutes. For example, a study by Jonq-Ying Lee, Mark G. Brown, and Brooke Schwartz of the University of Florida looked at the demand for frozen orange juice.[2] Orange juice considered as a broad category is a normal good; people tend to consume more of it as their income rises. However, when the definition is narrowed so that house brand and national brand frozen orange juice are treated as separate products, the house brand product turns out to be an inferior good. As their incomes rise, consumers substitute the higher-quality national brands, which have a positive income elasticity of demand.

## Cross-Elasticity of Demand

Another condition that can cause a change in the demand for a good is a change in the price of some other good. The demand for chicken is affected by changes in the price of beef, the demand for SUVs by changes in the price of gasoline, and so on. The

**Cross-elasticity of demand**

The ratio of the percentage change in the quantity of a good demanded to a given percentage change in the price of some other good, other things being equal

**cross-elasticity of demand** for a good is defined as the ratio of the percentage change in the quantity of that good demanded to a given percentage change in the price of another good. The midpoint formula for cross-elasticity of demand looks just like the one for price elasticity of demand, except that the numerator shows the percentage change in the quantity of one good while the denominator shows the percentage change in the price of some other good.

Cross-elasticity of demand is related to the concepts of substitutes and complements. Because lettuce and cabbage are substitutes, an increase in the price of cabbage causes an increase in the quantity of lettuce demanded; the cross-elasticity of demand is positive. Because SUVs and gasoline are complements, an increase in the price of gasoline causes a decrease in the quantity of SUVs demanded; the cross-elasticity of demand is negative. The previously mentioned study of frozen orange juice found a positive cross-elasticity of demand between house brand and national brand juices, indicating that the two are substitutes.

## Price Elasticity of Supply

**Price elasticity of supply**

The ratio of the percentage change in the quantity of a good supplied to a given percentage change in its price, other things being equal

Elasticity is not confined to demand; it can also be used to indicate the response of quantity supplied to a change in price. Formally, the **price elasticity of supply** of a good is defined as the percentage change in the quantity of the good supplied divided by the percentage change in its price. The midpoint formula for calculating price elasticity of supply looks like the one for determining price elasticity of demand, but the Qs in the numerator of the formula now refer to quantity *supplied* rather than quantity *demanded*. Because price and quantity change in the same direction along a positively sloped supply curve, the formula gives a positive value for the elasticity of supply. Figure 3.3 applies the elasticity formula to two supply curves, one with constant elasticity and the other with variable elasticity.

In later chapters we will look in detail at the considerations that determine the elasticity of supply for various products. Two of those considered are especially important, however, and deserve some discussion here.

One determinant of the elasticity of supply of a good is the mobility of the factors of production used to produce it. As used here, *mobility* means the ease with which factors can be attracted away from some other use, as well as the ease with which they can be reconverted to their original use. The trucking industry provides a classic example of mobile resources. As a crop such as lettuce or watermelons comes to harvest in a particular region of a country, hundreds of trucks are needed to haul it to market. Shippers compete for available trucks, driving up the price paid to truckers in the local market. Independent truckers throughout the country learn—from their own experience, from trucking brokers, and from Internet sites— where they can earn the best rates for hauling produce. It takes only a modest rise in the price for hauling a load of Georgia watermelons to attract enough truckers to Georgia to haul the crop to market. When the harvest is over, the truckers will move elsewhere to haul peaches, tomatoes, or whatever.

In contrast, other products are produced with resources that are not so mobile. Petroleum provides a good example. When oil prices rise, producers have an incentive

## FIGURE 3.3 CALCULATING PRICE ELASTICITY OF SUPPLY

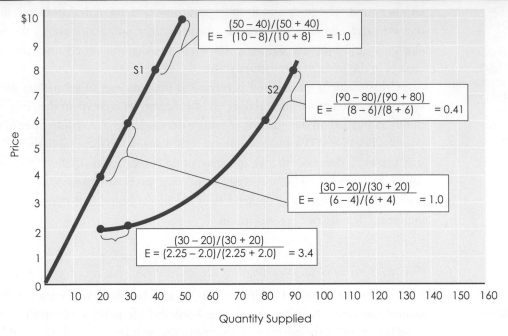

$$E = \frac{(50-40)/(50+40)}{(10-8)/(10+8)} = 1.0$$

$$E = \frac{(90-80)/(90+80)}{(8-6)/(8+6)} = 0.41$$

$$E = \frac{(30-20)/(30+20)}{(6-4)/(6+4)} = 1.0$$

$$E = \frac{(30-20)/(30+20)}{(2.25-2.0)/(2.25+2.0)} = 3.4$$

This figure gives four examples of the way price elasticity of supply is calculated. Price elasticity of supply is shown for two ranges on each of the two supply curves. Supply curve $S_1$, which is a straight line passing through the origin, has a constant elasticity of 1.0. Supply curve $S_2$, which is curved, is elastic for small quantities and inelastic for larger ones.

to drill more wells. However, given limited numbers of drilling rigs and other highly specialized equipment, not to mention limited numbers of sites worth exploring, even a doubling of oil prices has only a small effect on oil output. Factor mobility in this industry is limited in the other direction, too. Once a well has been drilled, the investment cannot be converted to a different use. Thus, when world demand falls, as it did in the late 1990s, and again beginning in late 2008, prices fall sharply but the quantity of oil produced falls by much less than price.

A second determinant of elasticity of supply is time. As in the case of demand, price elasticity of supply tends to be greater in the long run than in the short run. In part, the reason for this is connected with mobility of resources. In the short run, the output of many products can be increased by using more of the most flexible inputs—for example, by adding workers at a plant or extending the hours of work. Such short-run measures often mean higher costs per unit for the added output, however, because workers added without comparable additions in other inputs (such as equipment) tend to be less productive. If a firm expects market conditions to warrant an increase of supply in the long run, it will be worthwhile to invest in additional quantities of less mobile inputs such as specialized plants and equipment. Once those investments have been made, the firm will find it worthwhile to supply the greater quantity of output at a lower price than in the short-run case because its costs per unit supplied will be lower. The Case for Discussion at the end of Chapter 2, which discussed the market for heavy-duty tires, provides an example of the difference between short-run and long-run elasticity of supply.

## Applications of Elasticity

Elasticity has many applications in both macro- and microeconomics. In macroeconomics, it can be applied to financial markets, to the aggregate supply and demand for all goods and services, and to foreign exchange markets, to name just a few. In microeconomics, elasticity plays a role in discussions of consumer behavior, the profit-maximizing behavior of business firms, governments' regulatory and labor policies, and many other areas. To further illustrate elasticity, we conclude this chapter with applications featuring the problems of tax incidence and drug policy.

### Elasticity and Tax Incidence

Who pays taxes? One way to answer this question is in terms of *assessments*—the issue of who bears the legal responsibility to make tax payments to the government. A study of assessments would show that property owners pay property taxes, gasoline retailers pay gasoline taxes, and so on. However, looking at assessments does not always settle the issue of who bears the economic burden of a tax—or, to use the economist's term, the issue of **tax incidence**.

The incidence of a tax does not always coincide with the way the tax is assessed because the economic burden of the tax, in whole or in part, often can be passed along to someone else. The degree to which the burden of a tax may be passed along depends on the elasticities of supply and demand. Let's consider some examples.

**Tax incidence**

The distribution of the economic burden of a tax

**INCIDENCE OF A GASOLINE TAX**　First consider the familiar example of a gasoline tax. Specifically, suppose that the state of Virginia decides to impose a tax of $1 per gallon on gasoline beginning from a situation in which there is no tax. The tax is assessed against sellers of gasoline, who add the tax into the price paid by consumers at the pump.

Figure 3.4 uses the supply-and-demand model to show the effects of the tax. Initially, the demand curve

How do supply and demand affect gasoline prices?

intersects supply curve $S_1$ at $E_1$, resulting in a price of $2 per gallon. The supply curve is elastic in the region of the initial equilibrium. The elasticity of supply reflects the fact that we are dealing with the gasoline market in just one state; only a slight rise in the price in Virginia is needed to divert additional quantities of gasoline from elsewhere in the nation because of the wide geographic reach of the wholesale gasoline market. The

**FIGURE 3.4  INCIDENCE OF A TAX ON GASOLINE**

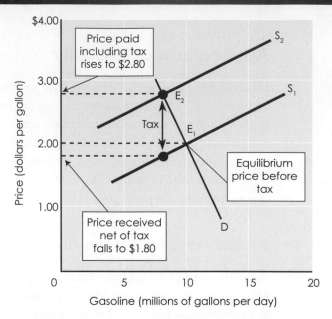

S₁ and D are the supply and demand curves before imposition of the tax. The initial equilibrium price is $2 per gallon. A tax of $1 per gallon shifts the supply curve to S₂. To induce sellers
to supply the same quantity as before, the price would have to rise to $3. However, as the
price rises, buyers reduce the quantity demanded, moving up and to the left along the
demand curve. In the new equilibrium at E₂, the price rises only to $2.80. After the tax is paid,
sellers receive only $1,80 per gallon. Thus, buyers bear $.80 of the tax on each gallon and sellers the remaining $.20. Buyers bear the larger share of the tax because demand, in this case,
is less elastic than supply.

retail gasoline market is more local. If the price in Virginia rises, some consumers living
near the border may cross a state line to fill up in Maryland or North Carolina; but most
people will continue to fill up in Virginia. In the short run, they have only limited ways
to save gas, such as cutting back on non-essential trips. As a result, demand for gasoline
is less elastic than the supply in the region of the initial equilibrium.

The effect of the tax is to shift the supply curve to the left until each point on the new
supply curve is exactly $1 higher than the point for the corresponding quantity on the old
supply curve. (We could instead say that the supply curve shifts *upward* by $1.) Because
sellers must now turn over $1 to the state government for each gallon of gas sold, they
would have to get $3 per gallon to be willing to sell the same quantity (10 million gallons
per day) as initially. However, when sellers attempt to pass the tax on to motorists,
motorists respond by reducing the amount of gas they buy. As the quantity sold falls, sellers move down and to the left along supply curve S₂ to a new equilibrium at E₂.

In the new equilibrium, the price is $2.80 per gallon—just $.80 higher than the
original price. The new price includes the $1 tax, which sellers add to their net price
of $1.80 per gallon—a net price that is $.20 less than before. The amount of the
tax—$1 per gallon—is shown by the vertical gap between the supply and demand

curves. The economic burden of the tax is divided between buyers and sellers, but in this case it falls more heavily on the buyers.

**INCIDENCE OF A TAX ON APARTMENT RENTS**    In the preceding example, the incidence of the gasoline tax falls more heavily on buyers than on sellers because demand is less elastic than supply. If the elasticities are reversed, the results will also be reversed, as can be seen in the case of a tax on apartment rents.

In Figure 3.5, the market for rental apartments in Ogden, Utah (a small city) is initially in equilibrium at $500 per month. The supply of rental apartments is inelastic. An increase in rents will cause a few new apartments to be built, whereas a reduction will cause a few to be torn down; but in either case, the response will be moderate. On the other hand, demand is fairly elastic because potential renters consider houses or condominiums a fairly close substitute for rental apartments.

Given this situation, suppose that the local government decides to impose a tax of $250 per month on all apartments rented in Ogden. This tax, like the gasoline tax, is assessed against landlords, who include the tax payment in the monthly rental they charge to tenants. As in the previous example, the tax shifts the supply curve to the left until each point on the new supply curve lies above the corresponding point on the old supply curve by the amount of the tax. (Again, we could instead say the supply curve

**FIGURE 3.5    INCIDENCE OF A TAX ON APARTMENT RENTS**

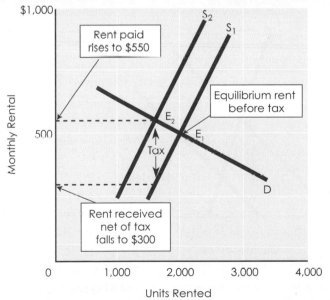

This figure shows the incidence of a tax imposed in a market in which supply is less elastic than demand. Initially, the equilibrium rent is $500 per month. A $250-per-month tax on apartment rents shifts the supply curve to $S_2$. The new equilibrium is at $E_2$. Landlords end up absorbing all but $50 of the tax. If they tried to pass more of the tax on to renters, more renters would switch to owner-occupied housing, and the vacancy rate on rental apartments would rise.

shifts upward by the amount of the tax.) After the shift, the market reaches a new equilibrium at $E_2$. There the rental price paid by tenants rises to only $550 per month, as indicated by the intersection of the new supply and demand curves. Landlords succeed in passing only $50 of the $250 monthly tax along to tenants. Their net rental income, after turning over the tax receipts to the town government, is now just $300, down from $500 before imposition of the tax. In this case, because supply is inelastic and demand is elastic, suppliers bear most of the incidence of the tax and buyers only a little.

**INCIDENCE AND TAX REVENUE**    When the government considers imposing a tax on gasoline, cigarettes, apartments, or any other item, the price elasticity of demand and supply is important, not only for how the burden is shared between buyers and sellers, but also for how much tax revenue the government collects. When buyers or sellers are more responsive to changes in price (when demand or supply is more elastic), a tax will generate less revenue for the government.

Figure 3.6 compares the markets for two items: milk and pork. The elasticities of supply are similar, but the price elasticities of demand differ. Pork has many obvious substitutes—beef, chicken, turkey, and other meats. Milk has few substitutes, so its demand is more inelastic. The markets for milk and pork are shown in Figure 3.6. The equilibrium price of milk is $0.50 per gallon and 12 million gallons are sold each year at this price. The milk market equilibrium is point $E_1$ on the left panel of Figure 3.6.

**FIGURE 3.6    COMPARISON OF THE MARKETS FOR MILK AND PORK**

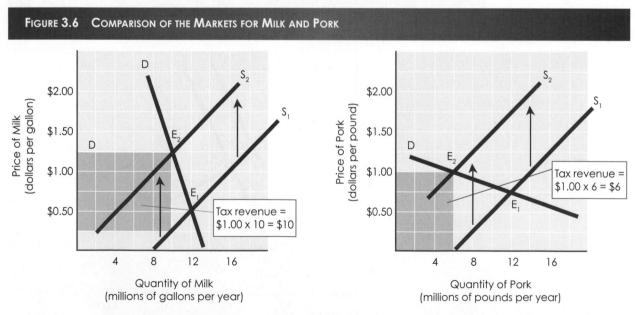

A tax imposed on a good that has an inelastic demand will generate more tax revenue than a tax on a good with elastic demand, assuming similar supply conditions. The diagrams above compare the effects of a $1.00 tax on the markets for milk (inelastic demand) and pork (elastic demand). In the market for milk, the tax reduces the equilibrium quantity by 2 million gallons, from point $E_1$ (12 million gallons) to $E_2$ (10 million gallons). Therefore, the government collects a total of $10 million from the milk tax. The same $1.00 tax on pork causes a large reduction in the quantity sold, from 12 million pounds (point $E_1$) to 6 million pounds (point $E_2$). This means the government will only collect $6 million, as only 6 million pounds of pork are sold at the new equilibrium.

The equilibrium (shown by the point $E_1$ on the right panel of Figure 3.6) is $0.75 per pound, and 12 million pounds are sold each year.

Suppose now that the government imposes a $1.00 tax on each product. In the milk market, where demand is inelastic, the tax leads to a small decrease in the quantity, from 12 to 10 million gallons. The government collects $1.00 on each gallon of milk sold, for tax revenue of $10 million on the 10 million gallons sold after the tax. In the market for pork, the tax leads to a larger reduction in the quantity people buy, from 12 to 6 million pounds. The government will collect a total of $6 million from the tax on pork, collecting $1.00 on each of the 6 million pounds sold. When comparing the two taxes, the government collects more revenue from the tax on milk. Today, governments rely for most of their revenue on broad-based taxes like income taxes, sales taxes, and value-added taxes. In past centuries, however, taxes on individual goods were more important than they are now. In those days, taxes on goods with highly inelastic demand, like salt, tobacco, and matches, were especially popular.

## Elasticity and Prohibition

In the case of gasoline and apartment rents, a tax led to a reduction in the quantity consumed, which we characterized as an unintended consequence of the tax. In a few cases, the reduction in quantity consumed may be an *intended* consequence of the tax. Modern taxes on tobacco products are one example: because tobacco is regarded as harmful, a reduction in quantity consumed is seen as desirable. Taxes on environmentally harmful products, such as the chemicals responsible for ozone depletion, are another example.

Prohibition is a more extreme policy aimed at reducing the quantity of a product consumed. Alcoholic beverages were subject to prohibition in the United States during the 1920s; and drugs like marijuana, heroin, and cocaine are subject to prohibition today. Prohibition is a common method of environmental regulation as well. For example, use of the pesticide DDT and lead additives for gasoline are not just taxed but also completely prohibited in the United States.

On the surface, a policy of prohibition may seem very different from a tax; since unlike a tax, prohibition raises no tax revenue for the government. However, if we use economic analysis to look below the surface, we see some similarities as well as differences between taxation and prohibition.

First, passage of a law prohibiting production and sale of a good does not make it impossible to supply the good; it simply makes it more expensive to do so. After the prohibition is in effect, the supplier must consider not only the direct costs of production but also the extra costs of covert

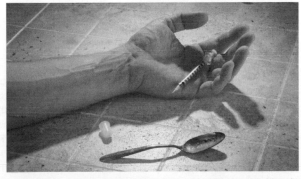

Drugs like heroin and cocaine are subject to prohibition in the United States.

transportation and distribution systems, the risk of fines or jail terms, the costs of hiring armed gangsters to protect illegal laboratories, and so on. From the law-breaking supplier's point of view, these costs can be seen as an implicit tax. If the price rises by enough to cover them, the good is still supplied. Thus, the effect of prohibition of a good is to shift its supply curve to the left until each point on the new supply curve lies above the corresponding point on the old curve by a distance equal to the extra costs associated with evading the prohibition.

Second, the effects of the prohibition, like those of a tax, depend on the elasticities of demand and supply. This is illustrated in Figure 3.7, which compares the effects of prohibition on the U.S. markets for DDT and cocaine. The demand for DDT is shown as elastic because effective substitutes are available at a price only a little higher than the banned pesticide. The demand for cocaine is shown as inelastic, in part because once people become addicted, they will find it hard to cut back on their use of the drug even if its price rises sharply.

In the case of elastic demand for DDT (Figure 3.7a), even a weakly enforced prohibition, which raises costs of illegal supply only a little, will sharply reduce the

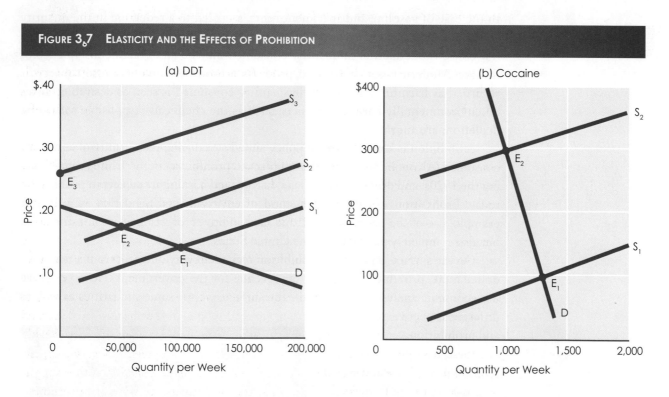

**FIGURE 3.7   ELASTICITY AND THE EFFECTS OF PROHIBITION**

(a) DDT

(b) Cocaine

A law prohibiting production and sale of a good, like a tax on the good, shifts its supply curve to the left. The new supply curve will lie above the old supply curve at any given quantity by a distance equal to the cost of evading the prohibition. The effects on price, quantity, and revenue depend on the elasticity of demand. Part (a) uses DDT to illustrate prohibition of a good with elastic demand. A weakly enforced prohibition ($S_2$) raises the price, reduces the quantity, and reduces total revenue earned by producers from sale of the product. A strongly enforced prohibition reduces quantity and revenue to zero ($S_3$). Part (b) uses cocaine to illustrate prohibition of a good with inelastic demand. In this case, even strong efforts to enforce prohibition do not reduce quantity sold to zero. Because quantity sold increases by a smaller percentage than price increases, there is an increased total revenue and expenditure on the good.

quantity sold. Such a weak prohibition, represented by a shift in the supply curve from $S_1$ to $S_2$, is already enough to reduce the total revenue earned by producers (price times quantity sold) from $14,000 per week to $8,500 per week. A more vigorously enforced prohibition, as represented by supply curve $S_3$, raises the cost of supply by enough to eliminate use of the product altogether.

In the case of cocaine, with its inelastic demand, even a strongly enforced prohibition has a small effect on quantity sold. This case is represented in Figure 3.7b by a shift in the supply curve to $S_2$. Because quantity demanded is not much affected by the price increase, total revenue from the sale of cocaine rises sharply, from $130,000 per week at equilibrium $E_1$ to $300,000 per week at equilibrium $E_2$. As long as demand is inelastic, increasing strictness of enforcement, which drives the supply curve still higher, will make the sales revenue of drug suppliers increase still further.

Elasticity of demand is important in understanding the intended and unintended consequences of prohibition. The intended consequence, of course, is to reduce or eliminate use of the product. As we see, the more elastic the demand for the product, the more successful is the policy of prohibition in achieving its intended effects. The unintended effects of prohibition are those associated with the change in revenue that the policy produces. These are very different in the case of elastic and inelastic demand.

Where demand is elastic, there is a moderate loss of revenue to DDT producers and a small rise in the cost of growing crops as farmers switch to more expensive pesticides. Neither has major social consequences. Chemical companies will offset the loss of revenue from producing DDT by increased revenue from production of substitutes. The increased cost of growing crops is offset by the benefits of a cleaner environment.

On the other hand, where demand is inelastic, the intended consequences are smaller and the unintended consequences greater. With inelastic demand, prohibition increases total expenditure on the banned product. The social consequences may be severe. First, users of cocaine must spend more to sustain their habit. At best this means impoverishing themselves and their families; at worst it means an increase in muggings and armed robberies by users desperate for cash. Second, the impact of the prohibition on suppliers must be considered as well. For suppliers, the increase in revenue does not just mean an increase in profit (although profits may increase) but also an increase in expenditures devoted to evading prohibition. In part, the result is simply wasteful, as when drug suppliers build special submersible boats that are discarded after a single one-way smuggling voyage rather than shipping their product cheaply by normal transportation methods. Worse, another part of suppliers' increased expenditures takes the form of hiring armies of thugs to battle the police and other suppliers, further raising the level of violence on city streets, or bribing government officials, thereby corrupting the quality of government.

The issue of drug prohibition, of course, involves many normative issues that reach far beyond the concept of elasticity. One such issue is whether people have a right to harm themselves through consumption of substances like tobacco, alcohol, or cocaine; or whether, instead, the government has a duty to act paternalistically to prevent such harm. Another concerns the relative emphasis that should be placed on prohibition versus treatment in allocating resources to reduce drug use. The analysis given here cannot answer such questions. However, it does suggest that the law of unintended consequences applies in the area of drug policy as elsewhere, and that elasticity of demand is important in determining the nature and severity of those consequences.

# Summary

1. **How can the responsiveness of quantity demanded to a price change be expressed in terms of elasticity?** *Elasticity* is the responsiveness of quantity demanded or supplied to changes in the price of a good (or changes in other factors), measured as a ratio of the percentage change in quantity to the percentage change in price (or other factor causing the change in quantity). The *price elasticity of demand* between two points on a demand curve is the percentage change in quantity demanded divided by the percentage change in the good's price.

2. **How is the elasticity of demand for a good related to the revenue earned by its seller?** If the demand for a good is elastic, a decrease in its price will increase total revenue. If it is inelastic, an increase in its price will increase total revenue. When the demand for a good is unit elastic, revenue will remain constant as the price varies.

3. **How can elasticity be applied to changes in market conditions other than price?** The concept of elasticity can be applied to many situations besides movements along demand curves. The *income elasticity of demand* for a good is the ratio of the percentage change in quantity demanded to a given percentage change in income. The *cross-elasticity of demand* between goods A and B is the ratio of the percentage change in the quantity of good A demanded to a given percentage change in the price of good B. The *price elasticity of supply* is the ratio of the percentage change in the quantity of a good supplied to a given change in its price.

4. **What determines the distribution of the economic burden of a tax?** The way in which the economic burden of a tax is distributed is known as the *incidence* of the tax. The incidence depends on the relative elasticities of supply and demand. If supply is relatively more elastic than demand, buyers will bear the larger share of the tax burden. If demand is relatively more elastic than supply, the larger share of the burden will fall on sellers. If the good is subject to prohibition rather than to a tax, elasticity of demand will determine how many resources are likely to be devoted to enforcement and evasion of the prohibition.

## Key Terms

| | Page # |
|---|---|
| Elasticity | 72 |
| Price elasticity of demand | 72 |
| Revenue | 72 |
| Elastic demand | 73 |
| Inelastic demand | 74 |
| Unit elastic demand | 74 |
| Perfectly inelastic demand | 74 |
| Perfectly elastic demand | 74 |
| Income elasticity of demand | 80 |
| Price elasticity of supply | 81 |
| Cross-elasticity of demand | 81 |
| Tax incidence | 83 |

## Problems and Topics for Discussion

1. **Time horizon and elasticity**   Suppose a virus infects the California lettuce crop, cutting production by half. Consider three time horizons: (a) The

"very short" run means a period that is too short to allow farmers to change the amount of lettuce that has been planted. No matter what happens to the price, the quantity supplied will be the amount already planted, less the amount destroyed by the virus. (b) The "intermediate" run means a period that is long enough to allow farmers to plant more fields in lettuce, but not long enough to permit them to develop new varieties of lettuce, introduce new methods of cultivation, or acquire new specialized equipment. (c) The "long" run means a period that is long enough to allow farmers to develop new varieties of virus-resistant lettuce and improve cultivation techniques. Discuss these three time horizons in terms of the price elasticity of supply. Sketch a figure showing supply curves for each of the time horizons.

2. **Calculating elasticity**   Draw a set of coordinate axes on a piece of graph paper. Label the horizontal axis from 0 to 50 units and the vertical axis from $0 to $20 per unit. Draw a demand curve that intersects the vertical axis at $10 and the horizontal axis at 40 units. Draw a supply curve that intersects the vertical axis at $4 and has a slope of 1. Make the following calculations for these curves, using the midpoint formula:

   a. What is the price elasticity of demand over the price range $5 to $7?

   b. What is the price elasticity of demand over the price range $1 to $3?

   c. What is the price elasticity of supply over the price range $10 to $15?

   d. What is the price elasticity of supply over the price range $15 to $17?

3. **Elasticity and revenue**   Look at the demand curve given in Figure 2.1 of the preceding chapter. Make a third column in the table that gives revenue for each price-quantity combination shown. Draw a set of axes on a piece of graph paper. Label the horizontal axis as in Figure 2.1, and label the vertical axis from 0 to $5 billion of revenue in increments of $1 billion. Graph the relationship between quantity and revenue using the column you added to the table. Discuss the relationship of your revenue graph to the demand curve, keeping in mind what you know about elasticity and revenue and about variation in elasticity along the demand curve.

4. **Elasticity of demand and revenue**   Assume that you are an officer of your campus theater club. You are at a meeting at which ticket prices are being discussed. One member says, "What I hate to see most of all is empty seats in the theater. We sell out every weekend performance, but there are always empty seats on Wednesdays. If we cut our Wednesday night prices by enough to fill up the theater, we'd bring in more money." Would this tactic really bring in more revenue? What would you need to know in order to be sure? Draw diagrams to illustrate some of the possibilities.

5. **Cross-elasticity of demand**   Between 1979 and 1981, the price of heating oil rose by 104 percent. Over the same period, use of fuel oil fell slightly while use of LP gas, another heating fuel, rose. Assuming that there was no change in the price of LP gas, what does this suggest about the cross-elasticity of demand for LP gas with respect to the price of fuel oil? Draw a pair of diagrams to illustrate these events. (Suggestion: Draw upward-sloping supply curves for both fuels. Then assume that the supply curve for heating oil shifts upward while the supply curve for LP gas stays the same.)

## Case for Discussion

*VP Asks Cigarette Firms for Sacrifice*

**Rendi A. Witular,** *The Jakarta Post,* Jakarta, Indonesia, June 1, 2005

The lower profits cigarette-makers are likely to experience when the government raises the retail price on cigarettes should be viewed as a sacrifice to the state, [Indonesian] Vice President Jusuf Kalla said on Tuesday.

"The tobacco industry is one of the most profitable sectors in [Indonesian] business. Raising the (retail) rate won't affect tobacco firms much since they will still be able to make a profit. Remember that cigarette prices here are still the lowest in the world," Kalla said.

By increasing the retail price of cigarettes, the government planned to make more money on the excise duty it charged manufacturers, which was calculated on the final retail price.

The amount of the increase has not been finalized, but last week the Minister of Finance Jusuf Anwar suggested it would be in the range of 15 to 20 percent. This extra revenue would help plug the state budget deficit that has increased in line with the rising costs of the government's fuel subsidy.

PT H. M. Sampoerna, the country's second-largest cigarette maker by sales, said that more than a 10 percent increase in the cigarette prices could hurt producers as it would affect sales.

Sampoerna is 98 percent owned by U.S. cigarette giant Philip Morris International.

"Less than a 10 percent increase in the price is likely to be OK, but more (than that) could disturb sales," Sampoerna director Angky Camaro said after meeting Kalla earlier in the day.

Angky said the industry had not yet fully recovered from the aggressive excise rate hikes in 2002 and 2003, which had resulted in declines in the volumes of cigarette produced and lower profits across the board.

Last year, local cigarette company profits rose on increased consumption spurred on by higher general economic growth and the absence of any increases in excise duty.

The Indonesian Cigarette Producer Union (Gappri) estimates that some 141 million of the country's 220 million people are smokers.

## QUESTIONS

1. On the basis of this article, do you think that price elasticity of demand for cigarettes in Indonesia is elastic, inelastic, unit elastic, perfectly elastic, or perfectly inelastic? Cite the specific passages supporting your conclusion, and note any apparent contradictions in the article.

2. According to the article, 64 percent of the people of Indonesia, where cigarette prices are among the lowest in the world, are smokers, compared to less than 25 percent in the United States, where prices are higher. What does this suggest about the price elasticity of demand for tobacco in the long run? Why might the long-run elasticity of demand for cigarettes be greater than the short-run elasticity?

3. According to Angky Camaro of Sampoerna, a tax increase that reduced quantity sold would hurt producers. Using a diagram similar to Figure 3.4, explain why this would be true even if the percentage decrease in quantity were less than the percentage increase in price.

4. According to the article, in 2004, cigarette sales increased as income increased, while taxes were unchanged. What does this tell you about the income elasticity of demand?

## End Notes

1. As we have said, the midpoint formula (also sometimes called *arc-elasticity*) is not the only one for calculating elasticity. A drawback of this formula is that it can give misleading elasticity values if applied over too wide a variation in price or quantity. Because of this limitation, the midpoint formula works best over fairly small ranges of variation in price or quantity. An even more

precise approach is to use an alternative formula that gives a value for elasticity for a single point on the demand curve. For a linear demand curve having the formula $q = a - bp$ (with $q$ representing quantity demanded, $p$ the price, and $a$ and $b$ being constants), the *point formula* for elasticity of demand (stated, as elsewhere, as a positive number) is

$$\text{Elasticity} = bp/(a - bp).$$

2. Jonq-Ying Lee, Mark G. Brown, and Brooke Schwartz, "The Demand for National Brand and Private Label Frozen Concentrated Orange Juice: A Switching Regression Analysis," *Western Journal of Agricultural Economics* (July 1986): 1–7.

# PART 2

# *An Overview of Macroeconomics*

# CHAPTER *4*

# In Search of Prosperity and Stability

**After reading this chapter, you will understand the following:**

1. The meaning and origins of economic growth
2. The nature of the business cycle
3. The meaning of unemployment and its importance for economic policy
4. The meaning of inflation and its impact on the economy

**Before reading this chapter, make sure you know the meaning of the concepts:**

1. Positive and normative economics
2. Production possibility frontier

MANY ECONOMISTS DATE the beginning of their discipline from the publication, in 1776, of Adam Smith's book *The Wealth of Nations*. (See *Who Said It? Who Did It? 1.2*). The question raised by Smith's book—why some nations prosper while others lag behind—remains a central focus of macroeconomic policy. In the early 2000s, prosperity was widespread. A booming financial sector powered growth and job creation in the United States, China's export-led economy grew by more than 10 percent per year, and energy-producers like Russia and the Persian Gulf States piled up large surpluses. Even in those years, some nations fell behind, especially where conflict and corruption undermined the economy. Then, beginning in 2007, things started to go wrong. A recession that began in the financial and construction sectors of the U.S. economy spread rapidly through much of the world. As the economies of the leading industrialized countries slowed down, demand for Chinese manufactured goods and Middle-Eastern oil collapsed. As output fell, unemployment rose; and gloom replaced the recent global euphoria.

This chapter begins the exploration of macroeconomics by looking both at the broad forces that shape the search for prosperity and stability in the long run and those that cause short-run cyclical disturbances like the recent global crisis.

# Macroeconomics in the Long Run: Economic Growth

No country becomes wealthy overnight. Nations that are prosperous have become so as the result of steady growth over periods of decades and even centuries. Countries that are poor rarely become so because of sudden catastrophe, but rather, due to long periods of gradual decline or slow growth that lags behind the leaders.

Figure 4.1 shows how widely growth rates have differed among major areas of the world. During the quarter century up to 2006, standards of living in much of Asia rose rapidly. At the same time, average incomes in many countries of Sub-Saharan Africa actually decreased. Economic growth theory seeks to explain the reasons for these differences in growth over time and among countries.

**FIGURE 4.1    MEAN ANNUAL GROWTH RATES OF REAL GDP 1981–2006**

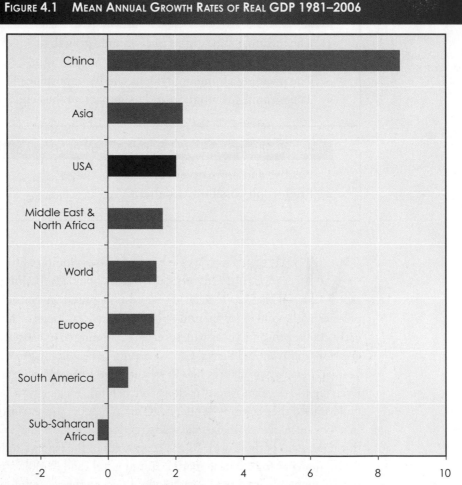

In the quarter century from 1981 to 2006, growth rates of real GDP varied widely. The United States grew somewhat faster than the world average and many formerly impoverished countries of Asia made rapid gains, but Sub-Saharan Africa became poorer.

SOURCE: World Resources Institute www.earthtrends.wri.org

## Measuring Economic Growth

Economic growth is most often expressed in terms of *Gross Domestic Product* (GDP), a measure of the value of total output of goods and services produced within a nation's borders during a period of time.[1] If GDP is to provide a meaningful measure of growth over time, it, like other economic quantities, must be expressed in **real** terms; that is, it must be adjusted for the effects of changes in the average price level. For example, from 1995 to 2005 U.S. **nominal** GDP (that is, GDP measured according to prices at which goods were actually sold in the given year) grew from $7,298 billion to $12,191 billion, or 68 percent. However, part of the increase in nominal GDP can be attributed to a 20 percent rise in the average price level during the period. Adjusted for inflation and expressed in constant 1995 dollars, real GDP increased over the decade by only about 40 percent. The term **real output** is frequently used as a synonym for real gross domestic product.

## Sources of Economic Growth

The sources of economic growth can be divided into two main components: the growth of total labor inputs, on the one hand, and the growth of output per unit of labor, or labor productivity, on the other.

The growth of total labor inputs tends to be determined by social and demographic factors that differ from one country to another, but that do not change rapidly within any one country. One source of growth of labor inputs is population growth. Population in the United States is now growing at about 1 percent per year or less, largely thanks to immigration. Population in most other advanced countries is stable or slowly declining. Another possible source of increased labor input is increased labor

**Real**

In economics, a term that refers to data that have been adjusted for the effects of inflation

**Nominal**

In economics, a term that refers to data that have not been adjusted for the effects of inflation

**Real output**

A synonym for real gross domestic product

Largely due to immigration, the population in the United States is growing about one percent a year.

force participation. In the United States, for example, from 1960 to 1989, labor force participation by women increased from 37 percent to 57 percent, more than offsetting a small decline in labor force participation among men. Since 1990, labor force participation trends of various groups have roughly balanced out so that the total rate has not changed much. Over the same period, both population growth and increased labor force participation have been offset, in part, by a decrease in average weekly hours worked from about 39 in 1960 to about 34 today. Taking all these trends together, total hours worked in the U.S. economy have grown moderately.

In contrast to the relatively steady growth of hours worked, productivity in the United States has increased erratically over the past 50 years, as shown in Figure 4.2. From the end of World War II up to the early 1970s, productivity grew at an average rate of about 2.8 percent per year. Then, from the mid-1970s to the early 1990s, productivity suffered a puzzling slowdown, falling to less than half its previous rate. In the 1990s, productivity growth recovered. From 1996 to 2004, U.S. productivity grew at its fastest rate for any comparable period since World War II.

Since hours worked per capita tend to decrease as countries get richer, productivity growth holds the key to prosperity in the long run. What determines whether productivity grows rapidly or slowly?

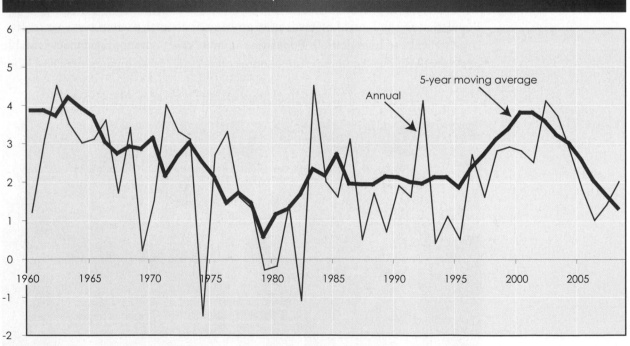

**FIGURE 4.2    U. S. ANNUAL PRODUCTIVITY GROWTH, NON-FARM BUSINESS SECTOR**

This chart shows the rate of increase of productivity in the non-farm business sector of the U.S. economy, measured as the annual increase in output per worker from 1960 to 2008. Productivity growth is highly variable from year to year. To make trends stand out more clearly, a 5-year moving average is plotted along with the annual data.

DATA SOURCE: President's Council of Economic Advisors, Economic Report of the President, 2009, Table B-50.

**Total factor productivity**

A measurement of improvements in technology and organization that allow increases in the output produced by given quantities of labor and capital

Increases in capital per worker are one important source of productivity growth. Capital includes industrial equipment like bulldozers and assembly robots, capital used in service jobs like hospital equipment and office information systems, and infrastructure capital like roads and communications systems. Any increase in output per worker not due to measured changes in capital per worker is attributed to **total factor productivity**.

Sources of growth in total factor productivity include technological innovation, better organization of production, better education of the labor force (sometimes called "human capital,"), and improvements in political institutions that reduce corruption and conflict. All of these play a role in year-to-year and longer-term variations in productivity growth. *Applying Economic Ideas 4.1* illustrates some

### Applying Economic Ideas 4.1
## THE U.S. PRODUCTIVITY SLOWDOWN OF THE 1970s AND 1980s

The productivity slowdown of the 1970s and 1980s was a source of great concern for observers of the U.S. economy. Productivity growth had been the driver of steadily rising living standards in the period after World War II. Suddenly, the productivity machine seemed to grind to a halt. Why did it happen? Did it signal a permanent change in the economy, or was it merely a pause? Here are some of the factors that are among those most often cited as contributing to the productivity slowdown:

• **Changes in the labor force**  Many analyses of the productivity slowdown pointed to the entry of millions of women and young people into the labor force during the 1970s. These new workers were, on the whole, capable and motivated; but they tended to have less experience than those who already held jobs. At the same time, by their sheer number they pulled down the ratio of capital to labor. By the 1990s, these demographic changes had worked their way through, allowing historic productivity trends to resume.

In the 1970s, an oil price shock, combined with price controls, led to long gas lines.

• **Supply shocks**  Some economists believe that the shock of sharply higher oil prices in the 1970s contributed to the productivity slowdown by rendering much of the economy's capital stock obsolete.

Many inefficient older trucks, planes, furnaces, generators, and so on had to be retired or placed on standby because high oil prices made them too costly to operate. The effect was almost the same as if the equipment had been destroyed by fire or flood. Moreover, it is argued, the oil price shocks made it necessary to re-channel much investment into finding ways to get by with less oil—either through the design of more energy-efficient equipment or through the production of substitute energy sources—rather than into other productivity-enhancing areas of research. By the end of the 1980s, the effects of these supply shocks had run their course, leaving a leaner, more efficient capital stock as a basis for further growth.

• **Research and technology**  During the 1970s, research and development spending fell from a high of 3 percent of GDP to a low of 2.2 percent in 1977. Some economists saw the R&D slowdown as a major culprit in the stagnation of productivity. In the 1980s and even more in the 1990s, these trends were reversed and replaced by a technology boom, as businesses made huge investments in computers and communications technology. At

*continues*

first the impact of these on economy-wide productivity was disappointing, but after a period of learning and organizational change the new technologies began to pay off in a big way. Some economists see the spurt of productivity in the early 2000s as a delayed result of technology investments of the preceding decade.

- **Inflation**  Inflation is an enemy of economic growth. The productivity slowdown of the 1970s occurred at the same time as a speedup of inflation. Inflation disrupted business planning and labor-management relations, and distorted the impact of taxes on business and investment income. This not only reduced total investment but also tended to channel investment toward uses that did little to enhance productivity, such as housing and tax shelters, and away from more productive projects. In the 1990s inflation returned to a more moderate range. Many economists think it is not coincidental that the moderation of inflation coincided with the revival of productivity growth.
- **Measurement problems**  One reason productivity trends are hard to explain is that productivity is hard

to measure accurately. Productivity is especially difficult to measure in sectors where the quality of goods changes rapidly. It makes much more sense to measure the number of tons of coal produced per worker in U.S. mines than to measure the number of computer chips produced per worker hour. If workers produce the same number of chips as the year before but the chips have double the computing power, has productivity doubled? Official data are believed to understate such quality changes. Also, productivity is notoriously difficult to measure in the service sector, which makes up an increasing part of the economy over time.

The productivity boom of the 1990s, which continued into the early 2000s, caused some economists to hope that a new era of technology-driven growth had arrived. The recession that began in late 2007 sent productivity growth lower again. Productivity normally falls during a recession. Employers, who try when possible to retain their best workers during a slump, tend to reduce output by more than their workforce. It will be several years before it will be possible to see whether the end of the recession brings a renewal of productivity growth, or whether the productivity boom around the turn of the century was a one-time event.

of the determinants of changes in productivity growth with the case of the U.S. productivity slowdown of the 1970s and 1980s.

## The Benefits and Costs of Economic Growth

Economic growth has many benefits. First and foremost, growth provides consumers with a higher standard of living in the form of more goods and services. Growth also provides people with greater opportunities to choose between work and leisure. If more people choose to work, as has recently been the case in the United States, economic growth makes possible the capital investment needed to create jobs for them. Over a longer span of U.S. history, however, people have opted for more leisure. As the economy grew during the nineteenth and early twentieth centuries, it was possible to shorten the average workweek at the same time that material living standards were rising. Finally, many people see economic growth as a necessary condition for reducing poverty and economic injustice. Whether a rising tide lifts all boats more or less automatically, as some people would have it or whether, at least in some periods, the rich benefit more from growth than the poor remains a source of controversy. However, there is little dispute that issues of social equality are even harder to resolve in countries where the tide is going out.[2]

Despite its obvious benefits, economic growth has had its critics. More than a century ago the English economist John Stuart Mill worried that growth might cause the loss of "a great portion of the earth's pleasantries" (see *Who Said It? Who Did It? 4.1*). This sentiment is shared in our own time by environmentalists, who worry that growth is accompanied by increased pollution, destruction of wilderness areas, and the possibility of a global climate disaster.

Criticisms of economic growth have their merits. We have only to look around us to see that the economic growth we have experienced has brought costs as well as benefits. However, some of the critics can be faulted for failing to distinguish between two issues: the *rate* of economic growth and its *direction*.

In Figure 4.3, a production possibility frontier is used to help separate the two issues. The diagram shows an economy in which resources can be devoted either to improving environmental quality or increasing per capita consumption of material goods. For an economy operating efficiently on its production possibility frontier, environmental quality can be improved only by diverting resources away from production of material goods, while producing more goods will harm the environment. Over-time, however, investment and innovation shift the production possibility frontier

## Who Said It? Who Did It? 4.1
## JOHN STUART MILL ON THE STATIONARY STATE

Economic growth was a major concern of the classical economists of the nineteenth century. Then, as now, most of the leading economists were inclined to view economic growth as a good thing. However, some of them feared that the pressure of growing populations on limited natural resources would sooner or later bring economic growth to a halt. Economists portrayed the "stationary state" toward which society was moving as one of poverty and overpopulation, causing one critic to dub economics the "dismal science."

John Stuart Mill thought otherwise. Mill was one of the most remarkable figures of the nineteenth century. Eldest son of the prominent economist James Mill, John Stuart Mill began studying Greek at age 3, was tutoring the younger members of his family in Latin at age 8, and first read Smith's *Wealth of Nations* at age 13. His *Principles of Political Economy*, published in 1848, was the standard text on the subject until Alfred Marshall transformed "political economy" into "economics" at the end of the century.

Mill agreed with earlier classical economists that the economy would sooner or later reach a stationary state, but he did not view the prospect as entirely gloomy:

John Stuart Mill

I cannot ... regard the stationary state of capital and wealth with the unaffected aversion so generally manifested towards it by political economists of the old school. I am inclined to believe that it would be, on the whole, a very considerable improvement on our present condition. I confess I am not charmed with the ideal of life held out by those who think that the normal state of human beings is that of struggling to get on; that the trampling, crushing, elbowing, and treading on each other's heels, which form the existing type of social life, are the most desirable lot of human kind, or anything but the disagreeable symptoms of one of the phases of our industrial progress ...
If the earth must lose that great portion of its pleasantries which it owes to things that the unlimited increase of wealth and population would extricate from it, for the mere purpose of enabling it to support a larger, but not a better or happier population, I sincerely hope, for the sake of posterity, that they will be content to be stationary long before necessity compels them to.

Today Mill's sentiments are echoed by writers who are concerned about problems of population, pollution, and resource depletion.

## FIGURE 4.3    ENVIRONMENTAL QUALITY AND ECONOMIC GROWTH

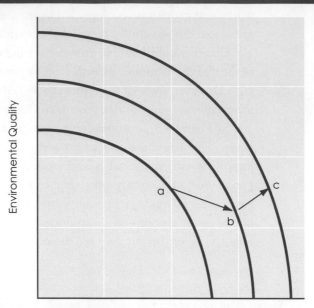

Per Capita Consumption of Material Goods

This figure shows a production possibility frontier for consumption of material goods, on the one hand, and environmental quality, on the other. At any given time there is a trade-off. For example, more power plants of an unchanged kind mean dirtier air; investing more to make power plants cleaner means that less total energy will be produced. Over time, investment and innovation shift the production possibility frontier outward. A choice can be made between two growth paths as the frontier expands. The path from A to B shows an increase in the output of goods and a decrease in environmental quality. Along the path from B to C, investment in cleaner production technologies allow environmental quality to improve while material output also increases.

outward. If, as it does so, the economy follows a growth path like that from point A to point B, people will complain that growth has led to a deterioration of environmental quality. It is not really growth itself that is to blame, however. Instead, the problem lies in the *direction* of growth. Further expansion of the production possibility frontier could make possible growth along a path from point B to point C. That growth path would be possible if more effort and expense were devoted to production of renewable energy and restoring wildlife habitats. Comparing the arrow from A to B with that from B to C, we see that growth can bring both more material output and improved environmental quality *if people choose to go that way*. As is often the case, our problems turn out to arise not from inescapable economic laws but from the choices we make.

Of these two possibilities, in which direction is the world actually headed? Many economists believe that the early stages of economic development move a country in a direction like that from A to B, and later development moves it from B to C. Among other evidence, they point to the fact that standard measures show better air and water quality in the wealthiest countries like the United States and Sweden than in middle-income countries like Mexico or China. Within the United States itself, some measurements of environmental quality, for example, quality of urban air, improved in recent decades after deteriorating through much of the nineteenth and early twentieth centuries.[3]

## Short-Run Macroeconomics and the Business Cycle

**Natural level of real output**

The trend of real GDP growth over time, also known as potential real output

**Output gap**

The economy's current level of real output minus its natural level of real output

The first section of this chapter focused on prosperity—economic growth and its causes in the long run. In this section we turn to issues of stability, that is, to short-run variations around the long run trends of real GDP, inflation, and employment.

Figure 4.4 shows growth of the U.S. economy since 1991. Because of increasing labor inputs, capital accumulation, and technological and organizational improvements, the economy's production capacity, known as its **natural** or **potential level of real output** (natural or potential real GDP) has risen steadily.

As the chart shows, real GDP has moved sometimes above and sometimes below the long-term trend line. At any point in time, the difference between the current level of real output and natural real output is known as the **output gap**. The output gap is stated as a percentage of natural real output. A positive output gap indicates that real output is above its natural level; a negative output that it is below the natural level. In some years real GDP has not just grown more slowly than the trend but has actually

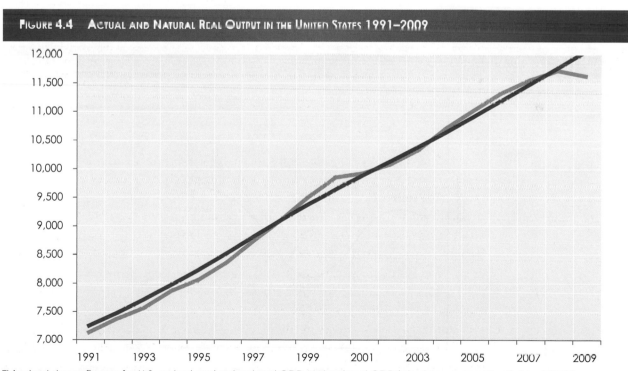

**FIGURE 4.4    ACTUAL AND NATURAL REAL OUTPUT IN THE UNITED STATES 1991–2009**

This chart shows figures for U.S. actual and natural real GDP. Natural real GDP (also known as potential real GDP) represents the long-term trend of growth for the economy. In any given year, actual real GDP may fall below or rise above the trend. The difference between actual and natural real GDP in any year is known as the output gap.

SOURCES: Author's calculations based on data from Federal Reserve Bank of St. Louis and OECD Economic Outlook.

**Business cycle**

A pattern of irregular but repeated expansion and contraction of aggregate economic activity

fallen. This pattern of irregular but repeated expansion and contraction of overall economic activity about its natural level is known as the **business cycle**.

## Phases of the Business Cycle

An idealized business cycle is shown in Figure 4.5. The cycle can be divided into four phases. The peak of the cycle is the point at which real output reaches a maximum. At that point there is a positive output gap. The period during which real output falls is known as the *contraction* phase. At the end of the contraction, real output reaches a minimum known as the *trough* of the cycle. At that point there is a negative output gap. After the trough, real output begins to grow again and the economy enters an *expansion* that lasts until a new peak is reached.

**Recession**

A cyclical economic contraction that lasts six months or more

According to a commonly used (although somewhat simplified) definition, a contraction lasting six months or more is a **recession**. The most recent recession, which began in late 2007, can be seen clearly in Figure 4.4.

The nineteenth and early twentieth centuries saw a number of cyclical contractions that were much more severe than any since World War II. These were called *depressions*. The most spectacular of these was the Great Depression of the 1930s, which actually consisted of two contractionary periods separated by an incomplete recovery. During this episode, real output fell by one-third, the price level fell by one-quarter, and the unemployment rate climbed to 24 percent of the labor force.

---

**FIGURE 4.5   AN IDEALIZED BUSINESS CYCLE**

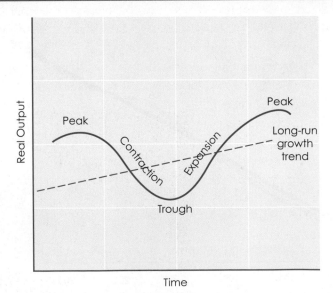

This figure shows an idealized business cycle. The cycle begins from a peak and then enters a contraction. A contraction lasting six months or more is called a recession. The low point of the cycle is known as its trough. Following the trough, the economy enters an expansion until a new peak is reached. Because real GDP varies about an upward trend, each cyclical peak tends to carry the economy to a higher level of real GDP than the previous one.

Because no succeeding contraction has come close to it in severity, the term *depression* has passed out of use in all but historical contexts.

## Employment and the Business Cycle

As real output rises and falls over the business cycle, employment also varies. Changes in employment tend to get even more public attention than changes in output. After all, real GDP is a very abstract concept, whereas the security of one's job, and the jobs of relatives and friends, has a far bigger personal impact than a percentage-point wiggle one way or the other in real output.

**MEASURING UNEMPLOYMENT TRENDS**    The most widely used measure of the national employment situation is the **unemployment rate,** which is the percentage of the labor force that is unemployed at a given time. Understanding this deceptively simple statistic requires some definitions of related terms and a discussion of measurement technique.

The U.S. Bureau of Labor Statistics, in conjunction with the Bureau of the Census, obtains the data used in calculating unemployment from a monthly sample of about 50,000 randomly selected households. Field agents go to those households and ask a series of questions about the job status of each member of the household. The questions include such things as: Did anyone work last week? Did anyone look for work? How long has the person been looking for work? How did the person go about looking?

On the basis of their answers to these questions, people are counted as employed or unemployed. A person is considered to be **employed** if he or she works at least one hour per week for pay or at least fifteen hours per week as an unpaid worker in a family business. A person who is not currently employed but is actively looking for work is said to be **unemployed**. The employed plus the unemployed—that is, those who are either working or looking for work—constitute the **labor force**.

If people are neither employed nor actively looking for work, they are not counted as members of the labor force. People out of the labor force include many people who could work but choose not to for one reason or another. For example, they may be full-time students or retired. The most commonly reported data for the labor force (the *civilian labor force*) and employment also exclude members of the armed forces.

Figure 4.6 presents unemployment data for the United States since 1960. The shaded band, labeled "low to moderate unemployment,"

**Unemployment rate**

The percentage of the labor force that is unemployed

**Employed**

A term used to refer to a person who is working at least one hour a week for pay or at least fifteen hours per week as an unpaid worker in a family business

**Unemployed**

A term used to refer to a person who is not employed but is actively looking for work

**Labor force**

The sum of all individuals who are employed and all individuals who are unemployed

The unemployment rate is the most widely used measure of the national employment situation.

## FIGURE 4.6    U.S. CIVILIAN UNEMPLOYMENT RATE (PERCENT OF LABOR FORCE)

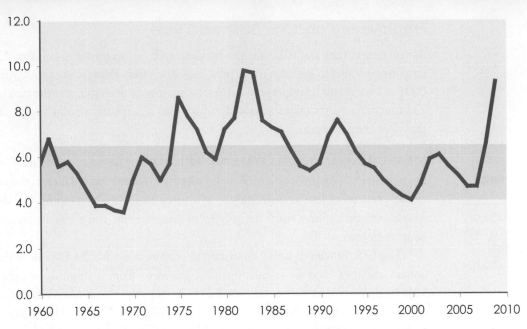

There is no one level of unemployment that is universally accepted as best for the economy. Some unemployment is always present as people change jobs or they enter the labor force in a normally functioning economy. This figure highlights a range of 4 to 6.5 percent unemployment that can be considered "low to moderate." Until 1975, unemployment stayed within that range, for the most part. The mid-1970s and early 1980s saw much higher rates. During the 1990s and early 2000s, unemployment returned to the low-to-moderate range, but it rose sharply again during the recession that began in late 2007.

SOURCE: Table B-43 ERP 05 Civilian unemployment rate. Economic Report of the President, 2009, Table B-42

reflects a range of views about reasonable economic performance. During the 1950s and 1960s, unemployment stayed within this range most of the time. In the 1970s and early 1980s, the unemployment rate took a turn for the worse. It jumped to 8.3 percent in 1975 and fell into the moderate range in only two of the next 12 years. The period from the early 1990s to the mid-2000s marked another extended period of low to moderate unemployment.

**GRAY AREAS IN THE MEASUREMENT OF UNEMPLOYMENT**    There are many gray areas in the measurement of unemployment. The official unemployment rate can be criticized for both understating and overstating the "true" number of unemployed adults. One way to understand these gray areas better is to compare the official definition of unemployment with two common-sense definitions, namely, "not working" and "can't find a job."

The official definitions of employment and unemployment differ greatly from the simple definitions of "working" and "not working." On the one hand, there are many people who work but are not officially employed. By far the largest such group consists of people who work full time at housekeeping and childcare. These occupations are counted as employment if they are performed for pay, but much of such work is done without pay. Also, children under 16 are not counted either as employed or as part of the labor force, even if they work for pay.

On the other hand, not everyone who does not work is counted as unemployed. In addition to those who are not looking for work and, therefore, are not counted in the labor force, people who have jobs but are absent from them because of illness, bad weather, or labor disputes are nonetheless counted as employed. Finally, there are those who work part time and are counted as employed but are actively seeking full-time employment and people who have full-time jobs that do not make full use of their skills and education. People in both of these situations are sometimes referred to as *underemployed*.

The second common-sense definition of unemployment, "can't find a job," also only loosely fits the official definition. In some ways, the official definition overstates the number of people who cannot find jobs. Some people who are counted as unemployed are on layoffs from jobs to which they expect to be recalled or have found jobs that they expect to start within 30 days. Other people who are counted as unemployed could easily find a job of some kind but prefer to take their time and find just the kind of job they want. (People who are not the sole income earners in their households, for example, may be in a position to look longer and be more selective than people in households with no other income.) Finally, there is some doubt as to whether the description "can't find a job" fits people who could have stayed on at their last job but quit to look for a better one.

In other ways, however, the official definition of unemployment understates the number of people who cannot find jobs. For example, it does not include **discouraged workers**—people who are not looking for work because they believe no suitable jobs are available. The Bureau of Labor Statistics officially counts as a discouraged worker anyone who has looked for work within the last six months but is no longer actively looking. The description "can't find a job" could also be applied to the underemployed—those who have part-time jobs but would take full-time jobs if they could find them.

Because the unemployment rate is an imperfect measure of the state of the labor market, the U.S. Bureau of Labor Statistics publishes several alternative measures of labor underutilization. For example, a measure known as "U-6" includes many discouraged and underemployed workers along with those who are officially unemployed. In December 2008, when the official unemployment rate was 7.2 percent, the U-6 index stood at 13.5 percent.

**THE NATURAL RATE OF UNEMPLOYMENT**    Figure 4.6 emphasized short-term swings in the unemployment rate associated with the business cycle. For a longer-term perspective, it is useful to look at trends in what economists call the **natural rate of unemployment**.[4] This is the rate of unemployment that prevails when real GDP is at its natural level. Another way to express it is to say that unemployment is at its natural rate when there is a zero output gap.

Figure 4.7 shows the trend of the natural rate of unemployment in the United States with comparison to that in major economies of European Union. As the figure shows, the natural rate of unemployment has fallen gradually in the United

**Discouraged worker**

A person who would work if a suitable job were available but has given up looking for such a job

**Natural rate of unemployment**

The rate of unemployment that prevails when real output is at its natural level

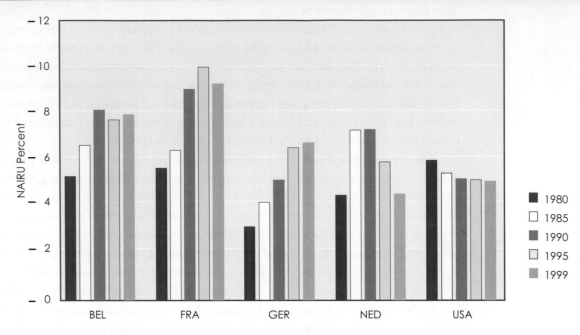

**FIGURE 4.7   NATURAL RATE OF UNEMPLOYMENT TRENDS IN THE UNITED STATES AND EUROPE**

This figure shows trends in the natural rate of unemployment for the United States and several European economies. While the natural rate of unemployment has fallen gradually in the United States since 1980, it has risen in France and Germany, Europe's largest economies. Unemployment rates, which were once much lower in France and Germany than in the United States, are now higher.

SOURCE: Achim Kemmerling et al., Regional Input: Labor Markets, Eurozoneplus Working Paper 6a, Jean Monnet Center of Excellence, Freie Univertaet Berlin, Sept. 2002, Chart 1

States since the 1980s. It is now lower than that in the largest European economies. Similar data for the United Kingdom and Ireland, where labor markets are structurally more similar to that of the United States than to those of Continental Europe, would show generally lower natural and actual unemployment rates than those of the two largest Continental European economies, France or Germany.

This divergence of unemployment trends within the EU has been a significant source of controversy. Some economists argue that the trends show a clear superiority of the so-called "Anglo-American" model of flexible labor markets with relatively few restrictions on hiring and firing workers and with a relatively modest social safety net for the unemployed. By comparison, according to these thinkers, the "Franco-German" model is fundamentally flawed. Although it intends to protect jobs by making layoffs difficult and making life easy for the unemployed, it has the unintended effect of providing too few incentives for employers to hire and workers to seek jobs. In reply, thinkers aligned with Europe's tradition of social democracy see the Anglo-American model as harsh and uncaring. Many social democratic thinkers in France and Germany believe their labor markets can be reformed without sacrificing their countries' traditional emphasis on generous social protection of workers.

**OTHER MEASURES OF UNEMPLOYMENT**   The unemployment rate is not the only measure of the state of the labor market. Quite aside from the problems of definition just discussed, the unemployment rate may give a misleading picture of what is happening in the labor market because it is sensitive both to changes in its numerator (the number of unemployed) and its denominator (the size of the labor force). During the early stages of recovery from a recession, the labor force often grows at the same time that the number of employed people grows, and the unemployment rate remains unchanged or even increases. This happens because news of possible new jobs draws discouraged workers back into the labor force, but the new workers do not immediately find work. Once a recovery is underway, the size of the labor force stabilizes and the unemployment rate may fall even though just a few new jobs are created.

Because month-to-month changes in the unemployment rate do not give a complete picture, news reports of short-term labor market developments often focus on the number of new payroll jobs created in a given month. The monthly figure for change in payroll jobs is based on a survey of employers that is entirely separate from the household survey used to calculate the unemployment rate. The sample size of the employer survey is larger, and some people consider it more reliable at times when unemployment data and payroll jobs data point in opposite directions. For example, in November 2006, the Bureau of Labor Statistics reported that the number of new jobs created was a larger-than-expected 132,000 but, at the same time, that the unemployment rate rose from 4.4 to 4.5 percent. The reason unemployment rose was that thousands of people streamed into the labor market to find temporary jobs for the holiday season, raising the denominator of the unemployment ratio at the same time the 132,000 new jobs increased the numerator.

Another job statistic that helps complete the picture of the labor market is the **employment-population ratio**. This ratio is the percentage of the noninstitutional adult population that is employed. The denominator of the employment-population ratio, which is governed by such demographic factors as birthrates and death rates, changes slowly and predictably. Hence, this ratio is less likely than the unemployment rate to stand still, while the economy moves ahead, or to give other misleading signals. In particular, during the early stages of an economic recovery when firms first start hiring new workers, the employment-population ratio will rise even though the unemployment rate may temporarily not change because of the return of discouraged workers to the labor force.[5]

**FRICTIONAL, STRUCTURAL, AND CYCLICAL UNEMPLOYMENT**   One final way to look at the state of the labor market is to ask how long people remain unemployed. During times of prosperity, many of the unemployed are out of work only briefly. For example, Figure 4.8 shows that as of the fourth quarter of 2006, when the job market was at its strongest, 38 percent of unemployed workers were out of a job for five weeks or less. By the first quarter of 2009, the job market had weakened significantly, but more than 30 percent of unemployed workers were still out for five weeks or less between jobs.

The term **frictional unemployment** is used to refer to short-term, largely voluntary unemployment spells needed to match jobs and workers. It represents people who quit old jobs to look for new ones, people who take a week or so to move or go on vacation before starting a newly found job, and people who enter occupations,

## Employment-population ratio

The percentage of the noninstitutional adult population that is employed

## Frictional unemployment

The portion of unemployment that is accounted for by the short periods of unemployment needed for matching jobs with job seekers

FIGURE 4.8    U.S. UNEMPLOYMENT BY DURATION

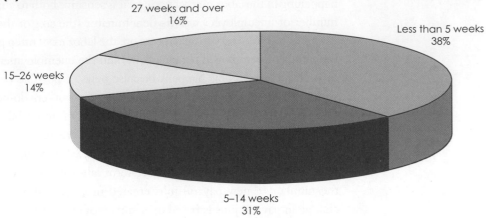

**(a) Fourth Quarter 2006**

27 weeks and over
16%

Less than 5 weeks
38%

15–26 weeks
14%

5–14 weeks
31%

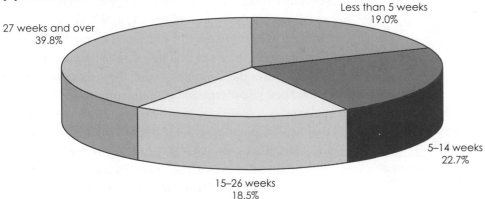

**(b) Fourth Quarter 2009**

27 weeks and over
39.8%

Less than 5 weeks
19.0%

5–14 weeks
22.7%

15–26 weeks
18.5%

As this chart shows, there is considerable variation in the length of time people are unemployed. When the job market is strong, as it was in 2006, frictional unemployment predominates. When the job market weakens, structural unemployment rises; but many people are still out of work for relatively short spells.

SOURCE: U.S. Department of Labor, Bureau of Labor Statistics

**Structural unemployment**

The portion of unemployment that is accounted for by people who are out of work for long periods because their skills do not match those required for available jobs

such as construction work, in which temporary layoffs are frequent but year-round earnings are good. Economists view a certain level of frictional unemployment as necessary in a labor market in which information is incomplete and the costs of job search are often high.

In contrast to frictional unemployment, the term **structural unemployment** is applied to people who spend long periods out of work, often with little prospect of finding adequate jobs. Figure 4.8 shows that as of late 2006, just 16 percent of unemployed workers were out of a job for half a year or more. By 2009, the percentage of structurally unemployed had risen as the economy fell into recession. Some workers who experience prolonged joblessness once held good jobs but lost them because the shifting structure of the economy has made their skills obsolete. This category of workers also includes people with few skills and work experience needed to find steady work. Workers without high-school education are particularly vulnerable to structural unemployment, and structural unemployment rates are higher for some minorities than for the population as a whole.

As Figure 4.8 shows, both frictional and structural unemployment are present in good years as well as bad ones. Frictional plus structural unemployment constitute the natural rate of unemployment, but unemployment is not always at its natural level. In some years, a vigorous economic expansion makes jobs so easy to find that the duration of unemployment falls below normal, reducing the number of unemployed below the number normally unemployed for frictional and structural reasons. Even many of the hard-core, structurally unemployed find jobs. In other years, business contractions cause unemployment to rise above its natural rate. At such times even workers who have worked a long time for their present employer and who have excellent skills may find themselves temporarily laid off. The average duration of unemployment rises above normal frictional plus structural levels. The difference between the actual unemployment rate in a particular month and the natural rate is known as **cyclical unemployment**. When the economy slows down, cyclical unemployment is added to frictional and structural unemployment. At the peak of an expansionary period, cyclical unemployment is negative.

## Price Stability

Up to this point, our discussion has focused on real variables—real output and the level of employment. However, changes in the prices at which goods and services are sold are also important. **Inflation**, which means a sustained increase in the average level of prices of all goods and services, is a potential disruptive force in the economic life of nations and individuals. **Price stability**—a situation in which the rate of inflation is low enough so that it is not a significant factor in business and individual decision making—can be considered another of the major goals of macroeconomic policy.

Figure 4.9 shows inflation trends in the U.S. economy and around the world. Before the 1970s, U.S. inflation was low. In fact, for the entire century from the Civil War to the mid-1960s, the U.S. peacetime inflation rate averaged only about 2 percent per year. Beginning in the 1970s, however, inflation rose and became highly variable. The struggle against inflation was a dominant theme in economic policy from the mid-1970s through the 1980s. By the late 1980s, inflation was again brought under control and has remained low since.

Figure 4.9b shows that the rise of inflation in the 1970s and its decline since the 1990s was part of a world-wide phenomenon. It also shows that the U.S. inflation experience was moderate by comparison with the average for other countries There was a brief spike in inflation throughout the world in early 2008 as a result of a surge in global food and energy prices, but inflation fell quickly again in the second half of the year as the world economy began to slow.

**Cyclical unemployment**

The difference between the observed rate of unemployment at a given point in the business cycle and the natural rate of unemployment

**Inflation**

A sustained increase in the average level of prices of all goods and services

**Price stability**

A situation in which the rate of inflation is low enough so that it is not a significant factor in business and individual decision making

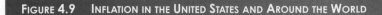

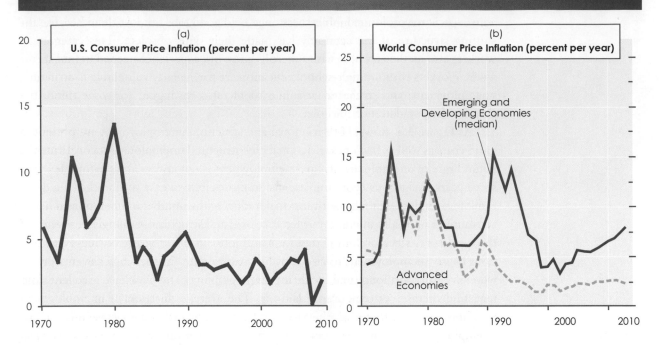

**FIGURE 4.9**    INFLATION IN THE UNITED STATES AND AROUND THE WORLD

Part a of this figure shows the trend of inflation in the United States since 1970, as measured by the annual percentage change in the Consumer Price Index. The 1970s and early 1980s were years of high and variable inflation; but by the late 1980s, inflation was brought under control. By late 2008, inflation had vanished, and many economists saw a possibility of deflation. Part b shows that what the U.S. experienced was shared by both developing and advanced economies around the world. An upturn in world inflation in the mid-2000s, fueled by higher energy and commodity prices, was reversed by the spreading global financial crisis.

SOURCE: Figure 4.9a, Economic Report of the President Table B-64. Figure 4.9b: IMF, World Economic Outlook October 2008, Fig 1.1.

## Short-Run Costs of Inflation

**Transfer payments**

Payments to individuals that are not made in return for work they currently perform

**Indexation**

A policy of automatically adjusting a value or payment in proportion to changes in the average price level

As can be seen in Figure 4.9, the rate of inflation varies over the business cycle. As the cycle approaches its peak, inflation accelerates. During recessions, inflation shows again. As inflation rises and falls over the business cycle, its costs are distributed unevenly across the population.

Most people receive the bulk of their income in the form of wages and salaries. Wage and salary earners often feel that they are badly hurt by inflation. They compare what their paychecks can buy each month at ever-higher prices with what they would be able to buy with the same paychecks if prices remained stable. However, measured over a period of several years, nominal wages and salaries tend to adjust to inflation. Real wage and salary earnings in the United States rose during the inflationary 1970s and 1980s and also during the low-inflation 1960s and 1990s. People who receive income in the form of social security, other government **transfer payments**, and some private pensions are protected from inflation by automatic adjustments that compensate for changes in consumer prices. The automatic adjustment for inflation of wages, benefits, or other payments is called **indexation**.

Inflation also affects the income of creditors, who receive interest from mortgage loans, corporate bonds, and the like, and that of debtors, who pay interest. The traditional view is that inflation injures creditors and aids debtors. Suppose, for example, that I borrow $100 from you today, promising to repay the $100 of principal plus $5 interest, or $105 in all, at the end of a year. If there is no inflation during the year, I get the use of the funds for the year; and you get $5 of real income in the form of the interest on the loan. Suppose, however, that during the year the price level goes up by 10 percent. In that case, I get the use of the funds for the year, and what is more, I pay you back in depreciated dollars. The $105 I give you at the end of the year will buy only about as much then as $95 will buy today. Your real income is negative because the real value of $105 a year from now is less than the real value today of the $100 that I borrow. I, the debtor, benefit from inflation; and you, the creditor, are hurt.

However, this view of the effects of inflation is incomplete in that it does not distinguish between *unexpected* and *expected* inflation. The example just given implicitly assumes that neither you nor I (the lender and borrower, respectively) expected any inflation at the time the loan was made. Suppose instead that we both had expected a 10 percent increase in the price level between the time the loan was made and the time it was repaid. In that case, you would not have loaned me the $100 in return for a promise to repay just $105 at the end of the year. Instead, you would have insisted on a repayment of $115—the $100 principal, plus $10 to compensate you for the decline in purchasing power of the principal plus $5 of real interest income. I, in turn, would have agreed to those terms, knowing that the $115 payment under conditions of 10 percent inflation would be no more burdensome than the $105 payment I would have agreed to if no inflation had been expected.

This example shows that we need to distinguish between two interest concepts: the **nominal interest rate**, which is the interest rate expressed in the ordinary way, in current dollars, and the **real interest rate**, which is the nominal rate minus the rate of inflation. In the example, a 15 percent nominal interest rate, given a 10 percent rate of inflation, corresponds to a 5 percent real interest rate.

The distinction between nominal and real interest rates helps us to understand the impact of expected and unexpected inflation on debtors and creditors. Expected inflation, it turns out, is neutral between debtors and creditors because the parties will adjust the nominal interest rate to take the expected inflation into account. If they would agree to a 5 percent nominal interest rate given no expected inflation, they would agree to a 15 percent nominal rate given 10 percent expected inflation, a 20 percent nominal rate given 15 percent expected inflation, and so on. All of these adjusted rates correspond to a 5 percent real rate. Unexpected inflation is not neutral, however. Unexpected inflation harms creditors and benefits debtors. If you lend me $100 at a 5 percent nominal rate of interest, and the price level unexpectedly rises by 10 percent over the year before I repay the loan, the real rate of interest that you receive is minus 5 percent.

## Long-Run Costs of Inflation

In the short run, unexpected inflation helps some people while it hurts others. In the long run, however, inflation, whether expected or unexpected, has other costs that harm the economy as a whole without producing offsetting benefits.

**Nominal interest rate**

The interest rate expressed in the usual way: in terms of current dollars without adjustment for inflation

**Real interest rate**

The nominal interest rate minus the rate of inflation

One problem arises from the way inflation upsets economic calculations. When the rate of inflation is high and variable, as it was in the United States in the 1970s and early 1980s, business planning becomes difficult. The outcomes of investment projects that require firms to incur costs now in the hope of making profits later come to depend less on manufacturing and marketing skills than on the ups and downs of wages, interest rates, and the prices of key raw materials. As the investment environment becomes riskier, firms may avoid projects with long-term payoffs and gamble instead on strategies that promise short-term financial gains. Similarly, households, facing more uncertainty about future price trends, may reduce their long-term saving in favor of increased current consumption. These effects are hard to measure, but many economists think that they are substantial.

Other costs arise from the effort to rid the economy of inflation once it has become established. The experiences of many countries suggest that bringing inflation under control has a cost in terms of higher unemployment and lower real output. For example, the slowdown in inflation in the United States in the early 1980s coincided with back-to-back recessions during which the unemployment rate that reached a peak of more than 10 percent, the worst in half a century.

International comparisons, which include countries that have experienced much more rapid inflation than the United States, show the negative effects of inflation even more clearly. Figure 4.10 shows data on the relationship between growth and inflation from a sample of 103 countries over a 30-year period. There is a clear tendency for inflation to undermine economic growth. Countries that experienced inflation of more than 100 percent per year (that is, a doubling or more of the price level each year) on average experienced decreases in real GDP.

## Deflation

Sometimes a country experiences a period in which the price level falls for a sustained period. Such an episode is known as **deflation**. Superficially, one might think that if inflation is bad, deflation must be good; but that turns out not to be the case. Deflation can be as harmful to the economy, or even more so, than inflation. For example, from 1929 to 1933, at the beginning of the Great Depression, the price level in the United States fell by more than 25 percent. Real output fell by a third during this period, and the unemployment rate rose to a record high of 25 percent. More recently, from 1998 to 2005, Japan experienced more gradual deflation of about one

---

**Deflation**

An episode during which the price level falls for a sustained period

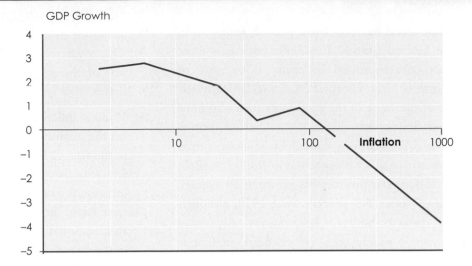

**FIGURE 4.10   INFLATION GDP GROWTH, 103-COUNTRY AVERAGE**

GDP Growth

On average, inflation higher than a very moderate rate is harmful to economic growth. This chart, based on a sample of 103 countries over a period of thirty years, shows a clear inverse relationship between growth and inflation. Countries with inflation over 100 percent per year tend to have negative economic growth.

SOURCE: Based on data from Atish Gosh and Steven Phillips, Inflation, Disinflation, and Growth, IMF Working Paper 98/68, May 1998

percent per year. Even this relatively gentle deflation led to stagnation of real output and rising unemployment, an episode that became known as Japan's "lost decade."

Because both inflation, if rapid, and deflation, even if moderate, are harmful to the economy, policy makers in most countries aim for a low, but positive, inflation rate. When we speak of price stability as a goal of macroeconomic policy, then, we do not mean a measured rate of inflation of zero. Instead, policy makers in most countries aim to hold the rate of inflation at a rate of something like 2 percent on average over a time horizon of a few years. In later chapters we will look in detail at strategies for steering the economy between the dangers of excessive inflation and deflation.

# Summary

1. **What trend has economic growth followed in the United States?** Economic growth is most commonly expressed in terms of the rate of growth of *Gross Domestic Product (GDP)*, a measure of the value of the economy's total output of goods and services during a given period of time. To avoid distortions caused by inflation, gross domestic product is expressed in real terms. Real gross domestic product has grown at an average rate of about 2–3 percent since 1950, although that growth has not been steady. Economic growth is widely seen as beneficial, in that it makes possible higher living standards, jobs for those who want them, and more leisure for those who want it. Some people criticize growth as damaging to the environment. In evaluating such damage, the composition of real domestic product as it grows must be considered as well as its rate of growth.

2. **What is the business cycle?** Over time, the economy undergoes a pattern of irregular but repeated expansion and contraction of aggregate economic activity that is known as the *business cycle*. The point at which output reaches a maximum is known as the peak of the cycle. A contraction, a trough, an expansion, and a new peak follow this. A contraction lasting six months or more is known as a recession. Over the course of the business cycle, the economy sometimes rises above its *natural level of real output*, resulting in a positive *output gap*, and sometimes falls below the natural level, resulting in a negative output gap.

3. **What is unemployment and why is it important for economic policy?** A person who works at least one hour a week for pay or fifteen hours per week as an unpaid worker in a family business is considered to be *employed*. A person who is not currently employed but is actively looking for work is *unemployed*. The *unemployment rate* is the percentage of the *labor force* that is not employed. Unemployment may be classified as *frictional*, *structural*, or *cyclical*, depending on its cause. Structural plus frictional unemployment is known as the *natural rate of unemployment*. The *employment-population ratio* is the percentage of the adult non-institutional population that is employed.

4. **What is inflation and what impact does it have on the economy?** *Inflation* is a sustained increase in the average level of prices of all goods and services. *Price stability* is a situation in which the rate of inflation is low enough so that it is not a significant factor in business and individual decision making. Inflation is frequently measured in terms of the rate of change in the *consumer price index*. In measuring economic quantities, a distinction must be made between *real* values, or values adjusted for inflation, and *nominal* values, or values expressed in the ordinary way, in current dollars. Applying these concepts to interest rates, we can say that the *real interest rate* is equal to the *nominal interest rate* minus the rate of inflation. Inflation disrupts the economy in two ways. First, it harms or benefits individuals according to their source of income. Second, it disrupts economic calculation, thereby discouraging saving and investment. In addition, the effort to stop inflation once it has begun often entails substantial costs. Sustained periods during which the price level falls are known as deflation. Deflation is also harmful to the economy.

# Key Terms

## Problems and Topics for Discussion

1. **Your personal labor force status** What is your current labor force status? Are you a member of the labor force? Are you employed? Unemployed? Explain the basis for your answers. When was the last time your labor force status changed? Do you expect it to change soon? Give details.

2. **Employment hardship** It has been suggested that the unemployment rate should be replaced with an "employment hardship index" that tries to measure the percentage of people who suffer hardship because of their labor force status. What kinds of people who are not now counted as unemployed might fit into this category? What kinds of people who are now counted as unemployed would not suffer hardship? Discuss.

3. **Real and nominal interest rates** Check with your local bank to find out what interest rates currently apply to (a) one-year savings certificates and (b) three-year automobile loans. Compare these nominal interest rates with the current rate of inflation as measured by the most recently announced rate of change in the consumer price index. (You can get this statistic from the web site of the Bureau of Labor Statistics, www.bls.gov.) If the current rate of inflation were to continue unchanged, what real rate of interest would you earn on the saving certificate? What real rate of interest would you pay on the loan?

4. **Economic growth and the environment** The pace of economic growth varies from one area of the United States to another. Some regions are growing rapidly with people moving in, much new construction, rising incomes, and so on. Other areas are stagnant or declining with little new construction and people moving away. Which type of area do you live in? Can you identify any environmental problems in your area that seem to be caused by economic growth? Can you identify any environmental problems that seem to be caused by economic decline? What policies could you suggest that would permit growth in your area to take place with less environmental disruption?

5. **The current state of the business cycle** Unemployment and inflation data are announced monthly, and data on economic growth is announced on a quarterly basis. Watch your local newspaper, The *Wall Street Journal*, or business magazines such as *Business Week* for discussions of the most recent data. What changes have there been? What is happening to the employment rate? Are the employment and unemployment rates moving in the same direction or in opposite directions? What is the current rate of inflation? Is it increasing, decreasing, or staying the same? Judging from available data, in which phase of the business cycle does the economy appear to be at the moment?

## Case for Discussion

### *Unemployment and Politics*

What did the elections of Presidents Truman, Johnson, Nixon, and Clinton have in common? Those of

Presidents Kennedy, Reagan, and Obama? The answer, for the first four, is that they all held the presidency for their parties in election years when the unemployment rate was falling. The other three achieved a change of party in years when the unemployment rate was stagnant or rising.

The election of 1982, in which incumbent President George H. W. Bush faced challenger Bill Clinton, provides a particularly interesting example. In the spring of that year, the economy was just beginning recovery from a recession although its end had not yet been officially announced. Although the economy was growing, it was doing so at a rate of only about 2 percent per year. That was well below the average rate of growth of 4.6 percent per year for the six post–World War II elections in which the incumbent party retained power. In June, employers slashed 117,000 jobs from their payrolls, and the unemployment rate hit an 8-year high. The jobs data made every news broadcast, and the news was bad.

Moreover, although the first President Bush could hope for good news between early summer and election time, history suggests that such news would be too little, too late. Economists like Ray Fair of Yale, who have studied the economics-politics link in detail, say that last-minute improvements are not enough. The economy's performance during the spring and summer is more important in an election year.

As it turns out, the economic numbers did improve later in the year. Unemployment fell again. An early estimate of the rate of economic growth in the third quarter, announced just before the election, turned out to be 2.7 percent, higher than forecasters had anticipated. Three weeks after the election, this was revised upward to 3.9 percent; but the third-quarter improvement was indeed too little, too late. Challenger Clinton sailed through the election by a wide margin. What is more, by the time of the next presidential election in 1996, the economy was moving strongly forward again. Thanks in part to the favorable economic climate, Clinton was re-elected for a second term.

## QUESTIONS

1. If the economy was growing at a rate of 2 percent or better in mid-1992, how is it possible that the unemployment rate was rising?

2. The unemployment rate rose by only 2.7 percentage points from its low of 5.1 percent in March 1989, to its peak in June 1992. A loss of 2.7 percent of voters would not have been nearly enough to defeat the incumbent president. However, his actual vote total fell far more than that. This implies that a rise in unemployment affects the voting behavior not just of those who are actually unemployed, but of many more people as well. Why do you think this is the case?

3. Use your Internet research talents to compare the role of employment as an issue in the 1992 presidential election with that in the 2008 election. What were the beginning and end dates of the recessions that preceded those elections? Based on past experience, how much longer would the "Bush boom" have had to continue to give the Republicans a good chance of holding the White House in 2008?

## End Notes

1. Chapter 6 will give a formal definition of GDP and explain the methods used to measure it.

2. Chapter 16 in the companion volume, *Introduction to Microeconomics*, explores the issues of poverty and equality in the United States and around the world in detail.

3. For a thorough discussion of these issues, see Susmita Dasgupta et al., "Confronting the Environmental Kuznets Curve," *Journal of Economic Literature*, Vol. 16 No. 1 (Winter 2002), pp. 147–168.

4. The natural rate of unemployment tends to be associated with periods during which the rate of inflation is neither accelerating nor decelerating. For that reason, another name for it is the *non-accelerating-inflation rate of unemployment*, or NAIRU. The relationship between inflation

and changes in real output and unemployment will be explored in detail in later chapters.

5. All three measures of the U.S. labor market situation can be obtained from the Employment Situation Summary released monthly by the Bureau of Labor Statistics, available on line at www.bls.gov.

# CHAPTER 5

# The Circular Flow of Income and Expenditure

THE PREVIOUS CHAPTER took a long-term perspective on growth of GDP. Sources of output growth were broken down into growth of labor inputs, increases in capital per worker, and improvements in technology and organization. Discussions of changes in GDP in the short run typically take a different perspective. For example, in January 2009 the government reported that U.S. real GDP fell at a 3.8 percent annual rate in the fourth quarter of 2008, the sharpest drop since 1982. News reports said nothing about growth of population, capital, or total factor productivity. Instead, they focused on the behavior of individual components of GDP. Consumption expenditures, especially for durable goods like cars, led the decline in total GDP. Exports, also, decreased as U.S. trading partners also slipped into recession. Federal government purchases rose moderately, counter to the trend of other GDP components, but the rise was partially offset by weakness of spending by state and local governments.

The data on investment received special attention. Overall, investment was down; but one category, increases in inventory, was up. While inventory investment helped moderate the total drop in GDP for the fourth quarter, it was taken as a bad sign for the future. At this point in the business cycle, the increase in business inventories did not reflect an optimistic stocking up by businesses to meet growing consumer demand. Instead, it was an unplanned buildup resulting from disappointing sales. Business firms were expected to cut back their orders for goods in the new year until the unwanted inventory buildup was worked off.

This chapter will adopt the same focus on GDP components as that used in news reports. It begins by introducing the **circular flow of income and product**, dividing the economy into five major sectors, and showing important linkages among them. In the second part of the chapter, the circular flow is used to develop the important concept of planned expenditure, which serves as a first step in building a general theory of macroeconomics.

## The Circular Flow

Figure 5.1 divides the economy into five main sectors: firms, households, government, financial markets, and the rest of the world. Arrows indicate flows of payments among the sectors. We can begin with the largest and most important set of flows, those representing the incomes that households receive from business firms and the expenditures they make in purchasing goods and services from those same firms.

### *Gross Domestic Product, Domestic Income, and Consumption*

At the top of Figure 5.1 we encounter **gross domestic product (GDP),** a measure of a country's total output of goods and services. The production of goods and services by business firms generates income for the country's households.[1] The bulk of this income consists of wages and salaries. Some is also paid out in interest, rents, and royalties on capital and natural resources owned by households and loaned or sold to firms. Whatever firms have left over, after they have paid all wages and other costs of production, is profit. Profit is earned by the firm's owners, who are a subset of households.[2]

The sum of income received in the form of wages, rents, interest, and profit by all households is known as **gross domestic income**, or for short, simply **domestic income**. From the way the circular flow is drawn, it is clear that domestic income and domestic product must be equal, since payments equal to the value of what is produced and sold are paid out to households—either as elements of costs (wages, interest, rents) or as profit (what is left over when cost is subtracted from the value of output).[3]

In Figure 5.1, which shows the simplest imaginable economy, households immediately spend all the income they receive to purchase goods and services from the firms that

---

**Circular flow of income and product**

The flow of goods and services between households and firms, balanced by the flow of payments made in exchange for goods and services

**Gross domestic product (GDP)**

The value at current market prices of all final goods and services produced annually in a given country

**Gross domestic income (domestic income)**

The total income of all types, including wages, rents, interest payments, and profits, paid in return for factors of production used in producing domestic product

**FIGURE 5.1    THE BASIC CIRCULAR FLOW OF INCOME AND EXPENDITURE**

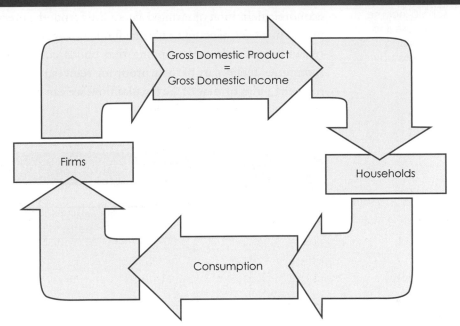

This figure shows flows of income and expenditure for the simplest possible economy. Production, carried out by firms, generates incomes for households in the form of wages, interest, rents, and profits. Households, in turn, immediately spend all of their income on consumption.

**Consumption**

All purchases of goods and services by households for the purpose of immediate use

**Closed economy**

An economy that has no links to the rest of the world

**Leakages**

The saving, net tax, and import components of the circular flow.

**Net taxes**

Tax revenue minus transfer payments

**Tax revenue**

The total value of all taxes collected by government

**Transfer payments**

Payments by government to individuals not made in return for services currently performed, for example, unemployment compensation and pensions

pay them their incomes. The corresponding arrow is labeled **consumption**, which includes all purchases of goods and services for immediate use. (Purchases by households of long-lasting items like houses and apartments are discussed in the next section.)

## Leakages and Injections in a Closed Economy

The economy shown in Figure 5.1 is called a **closed economy** because it has no connection with the rest of the world. Even in a closed economy, however, the circular flow is not really so watertight as shown in that diagram. Instead of spending all of their income immediately on consumption, part of household income "leaks out" of the basic circular flow as shown in Figure 5.2. Two types of **leakages** are shown there.

The first leakage is labeled **net taxes**. These consist of **tax revenues** paid by households to government minus **transfer payments** received by households. Transfer payments mean government payments like pensions, retirement benefits, disability payments, temporary aid to needy families, and so on. In everyday life, we tend to think of retirement benefits or disability payments as another form of income, so we might expect to see them added to the domestic income component of the circular flow. For reasons that will become clear in the following chapters, however, economists prefer to think of them more as a sort of "tax rebate" that partially offsets the revenue received by government from households in the form of income taxes, sales taxes, property taxes, and so on.

## Saving

The part of household income that is not used to buy goods and services or to pay taxes

The second leakage shown in Figure 5.2 is **saving**. Saving is the part of domestic income that is not used by households to purchase consumer goods or pay taxes. This economic definition of saving differs a little from the everyday idea of saving as money placed in a bank account or mutual fund. Saving, in the economic sense, also includes repayment of debt and spending that builds equity in a home. Also, corporations sometimes retain part of their profit for reinvestment in their operations. Looked at from the point of view of the circular flow, we can consider the retained earnings to be

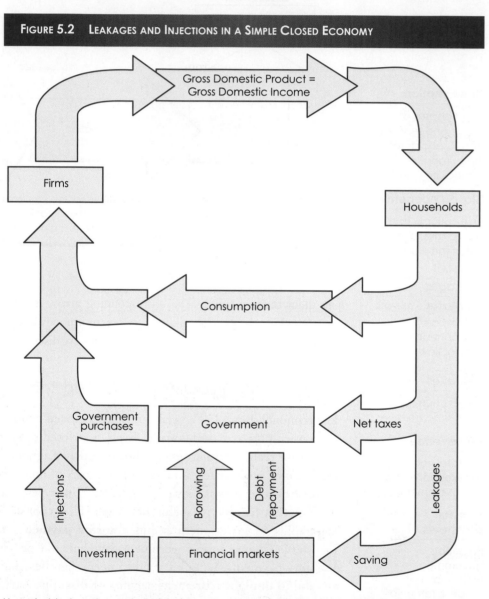

**FIGURE 5.2  LEAKAGES AND INJECTIONS IN A SIMPLE CLOSED ECONOMY**

Households do not spend all of their income on consumption. Part of it "leaks out" of the basic circular flow of income and consumption through payments of taxes and through saving. These two leakages are balanced by "injections" of expenditure into the basic circular flow in the form of government purchases and investment. Total leakages (S + T) must equal total injections (I + G) for this simple closed economy.

first "earned" by the households who own the firm and then "saved" by those households in the sense that they, as shareholders, approve the idea of using the retained profits for reinvestment.

To match the leakages, Figure 5.2 also shows two **injections**. Injections are types of expenditure on goods and services that have any origin other than the household consumption that was shown as part of the basic circular flow in Figure 5.1.

The first injection is **government purchases of goods and services** or, more simply, **government purchases**. These include all purchases of goods made by all levels of government (national, regional and local) plus services purchased from contractors and the wages paid to all government employees. Government purchases do not include transfer payments like social security, disability payments, or unemployment compensation. As explained earlier, those items, which are not payments for currently performed services, are subtracted from tax revenue to get the leakage "net taxes." The sum of government purchases of goods and services plus transfer payments is called **government expenditures** or, sometimes, **government outlays**.

The second injection is **investment**. Investment, as the term is understood in macroeconomics, is made up of two components. The first, **fixed investment**, means purchases of newly produced capital goods—machinery, office equipment, software, farm equipment, construction of buildings used for business purposes, including construction of rental housing, and so on. The second component, **inventory investment**, means changes in stocks of finished goods ready for sale, stocks of raw materials, and stocks of partially completed goods in process of production. Inventory investment has a negative value if stocks of goods decrease in a given period.

The term *investment* as used in macroeconomic models is sometimes called *economic investment* to emphasize that it means expenditures on real productive assets and inventories. Economic investment should not be confused with *financial investment*, which means purchases of corporate stocks, bonds, and other securities. The latter are

### Injections

The government purchase, investment, and net export components of the circular flow

### Government purchases of goods and services (government purchases)

Purchases of goods by all levels of government plus purchases of services from contractors and wages of government employees

### Government expenditures (government outlays)

Government purchases of goods and services plus transfer payments

### Investment

The sum of fixed investment and inventory investment

### Fixed investment

Purchases of newly produced capital goods

### Inventory investment

Changes in stocks of finished goods ready for sale, raw materials, and partially completed goods in process of production

Farm equipment is a large part of farming fixed investments.

not included in GDP because they do not represent new production, but rather are changes in ownership of assets that already exist. When the term investment is used without modifier, it is usually clear from context whether economic or financial investment is meant.

## The Role of the Financial Sector

In addition to the leakages and injections that have been mentioned, Figure 5.2 includes an important box that represents the economy's financial sector. This sector includes banks, mutual funds, insurance companies, and a host of other financial institutions, some of which will be discussed in detail in later chapters. As an element of the circular flow, the financial sector performs two functions.

First, it acts as an intermediary in transmitting flows of funds from savers to investors. In most cases, savers do not directly purchase productive assets like machine tools or office buildings. Instead, they make bank deposits, which are used by banks to make loans, buy securities like stocks and bonds, or in other ways indirectly finance the expenditures on capital goods that make up the "investment" arrow in the circular flow diagram.

Second, the financial sector plays a key role in redirecting flows of funds between the private and government sectors of the economy. Without the financial sector, the government would always have to balance its budget, exactly, every year. In terms of the diagram, the amount of funds flowing through the "net taxes" arrow would have to be exactly equal to the flow through the "government purchases" arrow. With the help of the financial sector, the government budget does not have to be balanced.

If government purchases exceed net taxes, the government has a budget deficit. To cover the deficit, the government must then borrow from the private financial sector. In most cases, it does this by selling bonds to private investors through the financial markets. The resulting flow of government borrowing is shown as an arrow running from the financial sector to the government.

On the other hand, the government sometimes collects more in net taxes than it spends on purchases of goods and services. In that case, the budget is in surplus. The surplus funds are used to repay past debt. The result is an arrow from the government sector to the private financial sector. In practice, since there are many units of government—federal, state, and local—at any given time some of them may have budget deficits and others budget surpluses; thus, funds are usually flowing in both ways at once between the financial and government sectors.[4]

Before moving on, it is worth pointing out one more feature of the circular flow. In a closed economy like that of Figure 5.2, which has no links to the rest of the world, the sum of saving plus net taxes must equal the sum of investment plus government purchases, even though the individual leakage and injection items do not have to balance. This fact has important implications for economic policy. If the government runs too large a deficit, borrowing too much from financial markets, not enough saving may be left over to meet the country's investment needs. That can result in a condition of high interest rates and slow growth for the economy as a whole. On the other hand, if the government has a budget surplus, additional funds flow into financial markets that can help keep interest rates low and stimulate private investment. This link between the government budget and private investment does not mean that it is always a mistake for the government to run a deficit. Circumstances when it can prudently do so will be discussed in detail in chapter 11. However, we can see even from the simple circular flow that the way the government's budget is managed has important implications for the health of the economy as a whole.

## The Open Economy

**Open economy**

An economy that is linked to the outside world by imports, exports, and financial transactions

**Imports**

A leakage from the circular flow consisting of payments made for goods and services purchased from the rest of the world

**Exports**

An injection into the circular flow that consists of payments received for goods and services sold to the rest of the world

**Net exports**

Payments received for exports minus payments made for imports

**Financial inflow**

Purchases of domestic assets by foreign buyers and borrowing from foreign lenders; also often called *capital inflows*

**Financial outflow**

Purchases of foreign assets by domestic residents or loans by domestic lenders to foreign borrowers— also often called *capital outflows*

We do not live in a closed economy. Our economy has many links, both real and financial, with the rest of the world. By adding these links, Figure 5.3 represents the circular flow model for an **open economy**.

The first link that is added to the circular flow for an open economy is another leakage, **imports**. In everyday life, we are used to thinking of imports as goods flowing into the economy, so it might seem surprising to see imports represented as a leakage, not an injection. However, there is a simple explanation. Remember, the circular low represents flows of money, not flows of physical objects. The leakage represented by the "imports" arrow could perhaps more accurately be labeled "payments for imports of goods and services." Then it would be more clearly seen as what it is: The part of household income that is devoted to purchase of goods and services produced in the rest of the world, rather than in the domestic economy.[5]

Figure 5.3 also adds a new injection, **exports**, to match the import leakage. Again, we could more fully describe this item as "payments from the rest of the world for goods and services exported from the domestic economy." It would then be apparent why an arrow representing an injection of funds into the domestic economy represents "exports".

The final detail added to Figure 5.3 is a pair of arrows linking the rest of the world to domestic financial markets. Just as government purchases do not always exactly equal net taxes, resulting in a government surplus or deficit, imports do not always exactly equal imports, resulting in a surplus or deficit of payments with the rest of the world. In the context of the circular flow, we call this external surplus or deficit **net exports**, which means exports of goods and services minus imports. In everyday discussions, the term net exports is instead called the *trade surplus* (or the *trade deficit* if imports exceed exports).[6]

If imports exceed exports, where do domestic purchases get the funds they need to buy all the imports? Only part of the imports can be financed by funds received from exports. The balance must come in the form of **financial inflows** from the rest of the world, shown in the diagram by an arrow from the rest of the world to domestic financial markets. The most common forms of financial inflows are borrowing from foreign banks or other lenders, and sales of domestic securities like stocks or bonds to foreign investors. Financial inflows are also often called *capital inflows*.

On the other hand, if exports exceed imports, the opposite question arises: How do foreign buyers afford the exports, since only part of them can be paid for by the payments they receive through the "imports" arrow of the circular flow? The answer is that an export surplus must be financed by **financial outflows**. The most common forms of financial outflows are lending by domestic banks and other financial institutions to foreign borrowers, and purchases of foreign securities like stocks or bonds by domestic investors.

## FIGURE 5.3 CIRCULAR FLOW IN AN OPEN ECONOMY

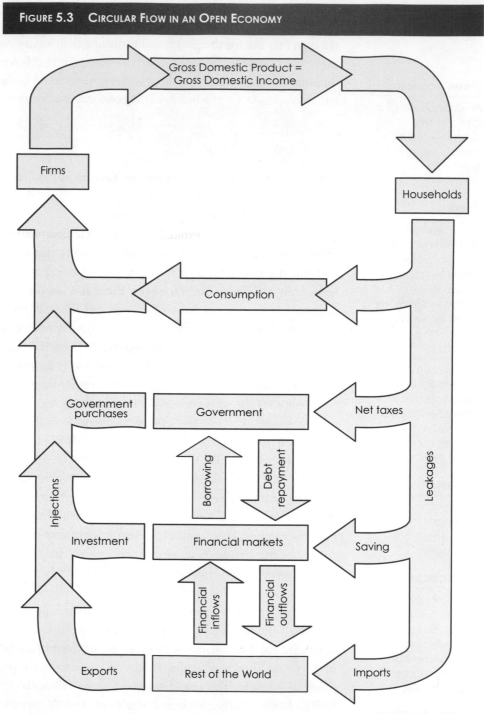

This version of the circular flow represents an open economy that is linked to the rest of the world through imports (a leakage) and exports (an injection). If imports exceed exports, the excess imports must be financed by a financial inflow from the rest of the world. If exports exceed imports, the resulting trade surplus will be balanced by a financial outflow. As was the case in a closed economy, total injections must equal total leakages (S + T + Im = I + G + Ex).

As is the case with government deficits, a country can have financial inflows from some trading partners and financial outflows to others at the same time; thus, both arrows can be in action. From the point of view of the economy as a whole, there will be a net financial inflow whenever net exports are positive, and a net financial outflow whenever net exports are negative.

## The Balance of Leakages and Injections in an Open Economy

As was the case with a closed economy, individual pairs of leakages and injections do not have to be equal, but total leakages must equal total injections. In equation form,

$$S + T + Im = I + G + Ex$$

It is not possible to explore every possible combination of the way leakages and injections balance, but some important variants are worth mentioning. One possibility is that a country can use a net financial inflow to finance a greater level of domestic investment than would be possible on the basis of domestic saving alone. For example, during much of the nineteenth century, the United States had a persistent trade deficit with Europe and, at the same time, a steady financial inflow that made possible the construction of canals, railroads, and other industrial infrastructure that underpinned the country's rapidly developing economy. More recently, many of the new member states of the European Union are in the same position, with trade deficits and corresponding financial inflows that help finance their economies as they catch up with their wealthier Western European neighbors. In these cases, an external deficit can be a sign of strength, rather than weakness, for an economy.

Another possibility is that a country may use borrowing from abroad not to finance domestic investment but rather to finance a government budget deficit. In terms of the circular flow diagram, such a country would see funds flowing along the arrow from the rest of the world to financial markets, and from there, flowing directly along to the government through sale of government bonds to foreign buyers. A country in this position is said to suffer from the "twin deficit" syndrome. The United States has been in this position, with both government budget deficits and trade deficits, for much of the recent past. The twin deficit issue is examined in more detail in *Applying Economic Ideas 5.1*.

## The Determinants of Planned Expenditure

Up to now, we have focused on definitions and relationships, but economic theory is concerned with more than that. To really understand the economy, we need to be able to explain why GDP or other variables have one value rather than another and why they change over time. In order to do that, we need to look at the choices made by consumers, business managers, and other decision makers. This section provides an overview of the choices that affect the various components of GDP. The appendix to this chapter supplements the overview with an optional formal model of planned expenditures.

## Applying Economic Ideas 5.1
# UNDERSTANDING THE TWIN DEFICITS

Over the past 20 years, the government budget and trade deficits of the United States have inspired a great amount of comment and controversy. To understand the many issues raised by these "twin deficits," it is helpful to interpret them in terms of the equality of leakages and injections. The needed data are shown in the chart.

The upper part of the chart is based on a classification of leakages and injections into three components corresponding to a rearrangement of the terms of the leakages-injection equation in the form $(Ex - Im) + (G - T) + (I - S) = 0$. $G - T$ represents the consolidated federal, state, and local budget deficit, stated as a positive number when government purchases exceed net taxes. $Ex - Im$ is the trade surplus (net exports), which becomes a negative number when there is a trade deficit. The $I - S$ component is positive if domestic investment exceeds domestic saving and negative if there is more domestic saving than investment. The lower part of the chart shows saving and investment separately.

Looking at the chart, we see that the trade deficit grew steadily, from less than 1 percent of GDP in 1991 to over 6 percent of GDP by 2005. As we know from our discussion of the circular flow, a trade deficit must be matched by a financial inflow from the rest of the world. This financial inflow can be used either to finance the government budget deficit, to finance extra private investment beyond what can be financed by domestic saving, or some of both. Looking at the chart, we see three periods representing different relationships among the various leakages and injections.

In the early 1990s, there was more domestic saving than investment. The extra saving was enough to finance both

domestic investment and part of the government budget deficit so that the needed financial inflow from the rest of the world, and the associated trade deficit, were small.

During the later 1990s, the government budget swung into surplus. Other things being equal, this could have allowed the United States to finance all of its own investment—and the trade balance could have moved into surplus; but this did not happen. Instead, as the lower part of the chart shows, just at this time the U.S. economy experienced an investment boom, especially in information technology. Simultaneously, private saving fell. The government surplus helped to finance the investment boom but was unable to do so in full, so financial inflows from abroad were still needed.

At the end of the 1990s, the high-tech investment boom collapsed; and the economy fell into recession. With incomes falling and transfer payments for unemployment compensation rising, the government budget swung back into deficit. The administration of President George W. Bush decided to use tax cuts to stimulate spending in order to speed recovery from the recession. Perhaps in part because of the tax cuts, the recession did prove to be a short one, but the economic recovery did not restore the government budget to surplus. Instead, the continued effect of tax cuts, spending to finance the war in Iraq, and other factors pushed the government budget far into deficit. At the same time, investment was rising again—this time with an emphasis on housing rather than information technology. Where was the country to find the funds to finance all of this? Not from domestic saving. Although business saving in the form of retained corporate profits grew strongly, household saving fell to record lows. Total saving thus grew only weakly, not enough even to finance domestic investment let alone the growing budget deficit. That meant that financial inflows from abroad had to finance both the budget deficit and large part of the housing boom.

At the end of 2007, the housing bubble burst; and the U.S. economy moved into a severe recession. Investment fell, closing the gap between investment and domestic saving, but the government budget deficit increased to a record high. By 2008, the economy found itself in the classic "twin deficit" situation in which the government was wholly dependent on financial inflows from the rest of the world to finance its borrowing.

The bursting of the housing bubble sent the economy into a severe recession

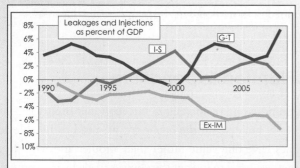

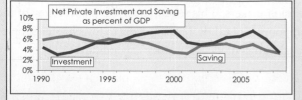

SOURCE: Data from *The Economic Report of the President*, 2009. Table B-32. Net government investment included in G – T. Statistical discrepancy included in X – M.

## The Components of GDP

Our starting point is the circular flow of income and product shown in Figure 5.3. This time our focus is on the total flow of expenditures on goods and services produced by the economy's business firms. These expenditures consist of consumption (by far the largest component) plus purchases of goods and services by government, purchases of investment goods, and expenditures on exported goods and services. Together, these equal gross domestic product, which in turn, equals gross domestic income.

In moving from the circular flow diagram to our macroeconomic model, however, we need to be careful about one detail. The consumption arrow in the diagram represents consumption expenditures on domestically produced goods. A separate arrow representing the "imports" leakage shows consumption of imported goods. In practice, as we will see in the next chapter, government statisticians do not measure consumption in this way. Instead, the number that they give us in the official national income accounts includes consumption of both domestic and imported consumer goods. The same applies to purchases of imported investment goods by business firms and imported goods used by government. Without adjustment, then, the sum of consumption, investment, government purchases, and exports would overstate expenditures on domestically produced goods and services and, hence, would overstate domestic GDP.

The needed adjustment is, fortunately, very simple. To get an accurate measure of GDP, we simply need to subtract total imports from total measured expenditures. That gives us the following key equation from which we begin construction of our model, in which Q stands for the total quantity of output, that is, GDP, and the final component, Ex-IM, represents net exports:

$$Q = C + I + G + (Ex - Im)$$

## Planned Versus Unplanned Expenditure

Earlier in the chapter, we pointed out that investment could be broken down into *fixed investment* and *inventory investment*. Our next step is to divide inventory investment, in turn, into planned and unplanned components. Inventory investment is considered **planned** if the level of inventories is increased (or reduced) on purpose as part of a firm's business plan. For example, a retail store might increase inventories in response to growth in the number of customers it serves or the number of branch stores in constructs. Inventory investment is considered **unplanned** if goods accumulate contrary to a firm's business plan. This happens whenever demand is less than expected so that some goods the firm bought or produced with the intention to sell them, in fact, remain unsold. If demand is greater than expected, so that inventories unexpectedly decrease (or increase at a rate less than scheduled in the business plan), there is negative unplanned inventory investment (disinvestment).

All fixed investment is treated as planned. Total **planned investment**, then, means fixed investment plus planned inventory investment. All other types of expenditure—consumption, government purchases, and net exports—are also considered to be planned. For that reason, we use the term **planned expenditure** to mean the sum of

**Planned inventory investment**

Changes in the level of inventory, made on purpose, as part of a firm's business plan

**Unplanned inventory investment**

Changes in the level of inventory arising from a difference between planned and actual sales

**Planned investment**

The sum of fixed investment and planned inventory investment

**Planned expenditure**

The sum of consumption, government purchases, net exports, and planned investment

consumption, government purchases, net exports, and planned investment. That is shown as the following equation form:

$$E_p = C + I_p + G + (Ex - Im)$$

We can explain the level of planned expenditure, as a whole, by looking at the choices that lie behind each of its components.

## Consumption Expenditure

Choices made by consumers have a more powerful effect on the economy than those made by any other group. Consumer expenditure accounts for about two-thirds of GDP in the United States. In some other countries it is a little more, in some a little less; but everywhere consumption is the largest single component of expenditure. What determines the amount of consumer spending?

Among the first economists to pose this question was John Maynard Keynes (*Who Said It? Who Did It? 5.1*). In his path-breaking book *The General Theory of Employment, Interest, and Money*, he put it this way: "The fundamental psychological law, upon which we are entitled to depend with great confidence … is that men are disposed, as a rule and on the average, to increase their consumption as their income increases, but not by as much as the increase in their income."[7] He called the amount of additional consumption, resulting from a one-dollar increase in income, the **marginal propensity to consume**. For example, if your marginal propensity to consume is .75, you will tend to increase your spending by $750 if your income goes up by $1,000.

This "psychological law" regarding consumption needs a few qualifications if it is to be stated exactly. First, in place of "income," we really should say **disposable income**. That means the amount of income left after taxes. If a person in one state earns $40,000 and pays $5,000 in taxes, while a person in another state earns $50,000 and pays taxes of $15,000, both would have the same disposable income of $35,000. Other things being equal, we would expect them to spend the same amount on consumption.

Second, the relationship between consumption and disposable income is properly stated in real terms. If both prices and nominal disposable income rise in exact proportion, there is no change in real income; so we would expect no change in real consumption expenditure, other things being equal.

Third, the marginal propensity to consume is not equal to the average obtained by dividing total consumption by total income. Instead, there is a minimum level of consumption that people would like to maintain even if their income were zero. Keynes called this "autonomous consumption." Intuitively, you can think of the case of a college student who has no income but maintains a minimum level of consumption by borrowing against future income, or an unemployed person who has no income but maintains a minimum level of consumption by drawing on past saving. The appendix to this chapter states the relationship between consumption spending and income in mathematical terms, taking into account both autonomous consumption and the marginal propensity to consume.

**Marginal propensity to consume**

The proportion of each added dollar of real disposable income that households devote to consumption

**Disposable income**

Income minus taxes

## Who Said It? Who Did It? 5.1
## JOHN MAYNARD KEYNES: THE GENERAL THEORY

John Maynard Keynes was born into economics. His father, John Neville Keynes, was a lecturer in economics and logic at Cambridge University. John Maynard Keynes began his own studies at Cambridge in mathematics and philosophy. However, his abilities so impressed Alfred Marshall that the distinguished teacher urged him to concentrate on economics. In 1908, after Keynes had finished his studies and done a brief stint in the civil service, Marshall offered him a lectureship in economics at Cambridge; Keynes accepted.

John Manynard Keynes

Keynes is best remembered for his 1936 work, *The General Theory of Employment, Interest, and Money*, a book that many still see as the foundation of what is today called macroeconomics. Although this was by no means Keynes's first major work, it was the basis for his reputation as the outstanding economist of his generation. Its major features are a bold theory based on broad macroeconomic aggregates and a strong argument for activist and interventionist policies.

Keynes was interested in more than economics. He was an honored member not only of Britain's academic upper class but also of the nation's highest financial, political, diplomatic, administrative, and even artistic circles. He had close ties to the colorful "Bloomsbury set" of London's literary world. He was a friend of Virginia Woolf, E. M. Forster, and Lytton Strachey; and in 1925 he married ballerina Lydia Lopokovia. He was a dazzling success at whatever he turned his hand to, from mountain climbing to financial speculation. As a speculator, he made a huge fortune for himself; and as bursar of Kings College, he built an endowment of 30,000 pounds into one of over 380,000 pounds.

In *The General Theory*, Keynes wrote:

*The ideas of economists and political philosophers, both when they are right and when they are wrong, are more powerful than is commonly understood. Indeed the world is ruled by little else. Practical men, who believe themselves to be quite exempt from any intellectual influences, are usually the slaves of some defunct economist. Madmen in authority, who hear voices in the air, are distilling their frenzy from some academic scribbler of a few years back. ... There are not many who are influenced by new theories after they are 25 or 30 years of age, so that the ideas which civil servants and politicians and even agitators apply to current events are not likely to be the newest.*

Was Keynes issuing a warning here? Whether or not he had any such thing in mind, his words are ironic because he himself has become one of those economists whose ideas remain influential long after they were first articulated.

Although income is the principal factor that determines consumption spending, there are certain other factors that also can have an effect. Among them are the following:

- Changes in net taxes (either taxes paid or transfer payments received), which act by changing the amount of disposable income associated with a given total income

- Changes in consumer wealth, that is, the accumulated value of assets a person owns, considered apart from current income—One very important example concerns the value of housing, since a home is the biggest asset for many households. In a period when housing prices rise more rapidly than income, as happened in the United States in the early 2000s, consumer spending rises more in proportion to income than it otherwise would.

- Interest rates—If interest rates fall, people can borrow more cheaply and may buy more goods and services on credit. Also, the amount they have to pay in interest on credit cards, mortgages, and other debt decreases, leaving more to buy consumer goods.

- Consumer confidence—In periods when consumers feel secure about their jobs and expect their incomes to rise in line with general prosperity, they tend to spend more for any given level of income. In times of pessimism and insecurity, people tend to be cautious and increase their saving as protection against the expected rainy day.

## Planned Investment

The second component of planned expenditure is planned investment. It depends on two principal factors.

First, planned investment depends on interest rates (more specifically, on real interest rates, that is, interest rates adjusted for inflation, as explained in chapter 4). The relationship between interest rates and investment is easiest to understand in the case of a business that needs to borrow in order to invest. Suppose you run a construction business, and you are thinking about improving the productivity of your workers by buying a new backhoe, which costs $50,000. Your banker is willing to lend you the money, but you will have to pay 6 percent per year interest, equivalent to $250 per month on the loan of $50,000. If the bank charged 12 percent interest, your monthly interest payments would rise to $500; and you would be less likely to buy the new machine. If the interest rate was just 3 percent, monthly interest payments would be only $125; and you would be more likely to make the investment.

Although it is not so obvious, interest rates also play a role in investment decisions for a company that plans to finance investment from its own retained profits. Suppose that as a result of good profits in the previous year, your construction company had put aside $100,000 in cash. You would not then have to borrow from the bank to buy the backhoe. However, using half of your cash reserves to buy the backhoe still has an opportunity cost that depends on interest rates. For example, if the rate of interest on government bonds is 6 percent, your company could earn $250 per month by using $50,000 of your cash reserves to buy bonds instead of buying the backhoe.[8] That is an opportunity cost. If the interest rate were 12 percent per year, your monthly income from the bonds would be $500—a greater opportunity cost—and you would be more tempted to buy the bonds instead of the backhoe.

Interest rates influence investment decisions by consumers as well as business. Residential construction accounts for about a third of all private fixed investment in the United States. When mortgage interest rates are low, as they were in the early 2000s, housing construction booms.

The importance of interest rates for investment spending is one of the reasons that we will spend several chapters in this book talking about banking, financial markets, and related topics.

Interest rates are not the only factor influencing investment decisions. The psychological factor of *business confidence* is also important. By this, we mean the whole complex of expectations and hopes on which firms make their plans for the future. If you expect a boom in the housing market in your area, your construction company is more likely than otherwise to buy that backhoe. If you expect doom and gloom ahead, you'll play it safe by buying the government bonds. Keynes referred to business confidence using the colorful term "animal spirits." In doing so, he wanted to emphasize the fact that business confidence can change quickly for reasons that are hard for economists to measure exactly.

On a global scale, the decision of how much to invest in a given country depends on the country's *investment climate*, as well as interest rates. Among the conditions that make up a country's investment climate are its tax laws, the amount of "red tape" imposed by the country's bureaucracy, the likelihood that profits will be drained away by criminal gangs or corrupt officials, and the stability of macroeconomic conditions. In countries where the investment climate is good, domestic firms are willing to put profits into expansion of their operations, and international firms are willing to bring in new capital and know-how. In countries where the investment climate is bad, domestic firms send their profits abroad for safekeeping rather than investing them at home, and global business stays away.

## Government Purchases

**Exogenous**

Term applied to any variable that is determined by noneconomic considerations, or by economic considerations that lie outside the scope of a given model

**Endogenous**

Term applied to any variable that is determined by other variables included in an economic model

Government purchases are considered to be **exogenous** in most simple macroeconomic models, including the one outlined in the appendix to this chapter. This means that they are determined by politics or other considerations that lie outside the model rather than by any variables that are included in the model. Transfer payments and tax revenues, on the other hand, are **endogenous** in that they depend on the level of real GDP, a variable that is included in the model. During the expansion phase of the business cycle, tax revenues rise and transfer payments, especially for unemployment benefits, fall. During a recession, tax collections fall and transfer payments rise.

Chapter 11 will take a closer look at the determination of government purchases and net taxes.

## Net Exports

The variable *net exports* is endogenous because it also depends on real GDP. As real GDP increases, both consumers and businesses spend some of their increased income on imported goods. For this reason, net exports tend to fall, and a country's trade deficit tends to widen during the expansion phase of the business cycle.

The exchange rate of a country's currency relative to the currencies of its trading partners is another factor that affects net exports. For example, during the early 2000s, the U.S. dollar weakened relative to the euro, the currency used by the country's major European trading partners. As the dollar weakened, it became easier for U.S. firms to sell their exports in Europe; and, at the same time, imports from Europe became more expensive for U.S. buyers. Consequently, net exports to Europe strengthened. Exchange rates, in turn, are influenced by many factors, including changes in real GDP, inflation, and interest rates. The complex interaction between net exports and other economic variables will be explored in several coming chapters.

# Equilibrium in the Circular Flow

In chapter 2, we introduced the concept of market equilibrium. The market for any single good, say chicken, is said to be in equilibrium when the amount buyers plan to purchase equals the amount that producers supply for sale. When the market for chicken is in equilibrium, there will be no tendency for accumulation or decrease of inventories and no immediate pressure for market participants to change their plans.

The idea of equilibrium as a situation in which there is no unplanned change in inventories can be extended to the circular flow of income and expenditure. When total planned expenditures (consumption plus planned investment plus government purchases plus net exports) equal GDP, total planned purchases will equal total production; and there will be no unplanned inventory change for the economy as a whole. As a result, there will be no pressure from unplanned inventory change to cause changes in production plans. If something happens to increase or decrease total planned expenditures, the equilibrium will be disrupted. Let's see how this process works out as the economy expands and contracts over the business cycle.

## An Expansion of Planned Expenditure

Suppose that the circular flow is initially in equilibrium with total planned expenditure exactly equal to GDP. Since goods are being produced at just the rate they are being sold, the level of inventories remains constant from one month to the next. Now suppose that something happens to disturb this equilibrium. For example, suppose that development of new energy-efficient technologies causes an upturn in investment as firms replace obsolete, energy-wasting equipment. As equipment makers increase their output of goods to satisfy the increased investment demand, they will take on more workers. The wage component of national income will increase. Profits of equipment makers are also likely to increase, further adding to the expansion of national income.

From our earlier discussion, we know that when incomes rise, households will increase their consumption expenditure. So far there has been no change in the output of consumer goods; so as consumption expenditure begins to increase, the first effect will be an unplanned decrease in inventories. Only then, when makers of consumer goods see inventories falling, will they modify their production plans to meet the new demand. As they do so, they too will need to hire new workers; and incomes will rise further.

In this way, the original economic stimulus, which began in the industrial equipment sector, spreads through the economy. GDP and domestic income continue to rise, but not without limit. According to the principle of the marginal propensity to consume, people spend only a part of any increase in income on consumer goods, and each round of the cycle of more-production-more-income-more-spending is smaller than the previous one. Before long, GDP reaches a new equilibrium where production and planned expenditure balance, and there are no further unplanned changes in inventories.

Recall that the whole process began with an assumed increase in planned investment. By the time the new equilibrium is reached, the total change in GDP will be greater than the original increase in planned investment because it will also include production of additional consumer goods. The principle that a given initial change in planned expenditure changes equilibrium GDP by a greater amount is known as the multiplier effect. The appendix to this chapter explains the multiplier effect in more detail.

## A Contraction of Planned Expenditure

The same process operates in reverse if equilibrium is disturbed by a decrease in some category of planned expenditure. For example, suppose a crisis in the Mexican economy reduces U.S. exports to that country. The first effect will be that U.S. makers of export goods will find inventories rising because Mexican importers are not buying as much as they had planned before the crisis. To bring inventories in line with reduced sales, U.S. makers of export goods cut their output. Workers are laid off or work shorter hours, and their incomes fall. As a result, they cut back on consumption expenditures, following the principle of the marginal propensity to consume. When this happens, makers of consumer goods also find that their inventories unexpectedly increase. They, too, cut back on output, and incomes of their workers fall.

As this process continues, GDP and domestic income decrease. They do not decrease without limit, however. Before long a new equilibrium is reached. In the new equilibrium, real GDP will have decreased by a greater amount than the original change in exports. This is an example of the multiplier effect operating in reverse.

## The Multiplier Effect and the Business Cycle

**Multiplier effect**

The tendency of a given exogenous change in planned expenditure to increase equilibrium GDP by a greater amount

The **multiplier effect** was one of the key ideas in Keynes' *General Theory*. Coming at the height of the Great Depression, the multiplier effect was immediately seized upon as an explanation for the business cycle.

Reduced to its simplest form, the Keynesian explanation of the Great Depression went something like this. During the 1920s, the U.S. economy entered a boom due to the multiplier effect of huge investment expenditures, especially expansion of automobile production and road building. Then, in 1929, came the Black Friday stock market crash. The crash destroyed business confidence, and investment fell. This time the multiplier effect operated in reverse to produce the Great Depression.

At the same time the multiplier effect seemed to give an explanation of the causes of the Great Depression, it also seemed to suggest a cure. What if the government increased its purchases of goods and services by enough to offset the drop in private investment? Wouldn't this send equilibrium GDP back to its original level? This reasoning gave rise to various attempts to spend the country back to prosperity, for example, by hiring thousands of unemployed workers for service in national parks. The nation did not fully recover from the Great Depression until the start of World War II brought on a further surge in government purchases.

Modern macroeconomics makes a place for the multiplier effect and recognizes that there is an element of truth in the simple Keynesian view of the business cycle. However, the simple multiplier theory is seriously incomplete. One shortcoming concerns changes in the price level over the business cycle. When producers respond to an unexpected decrease in inventories, do they increase real output without changing prices, do they raise prices to take advantage of unexpectedly strong demand, or do they do a little of both? Another problem is that the simple multiplier theory does not consider capacity constraints related to labor inputs, capital, and technology. Does real output respond in the same way to a change in planned expenditure when the economy is operating above its natural level of real output as below it? Still another limitation is that the theory pays too little attention to the role of money and the financial sector. Later chapters will deal with all of these issues in order to give a more complete picture.

## Summary

1. **How are households and firms linked by incomes and expenditures?** In order to produce goods and services, firms pay wages and salaries to obtain labor inputs, interest to obtain capital, and rents and royalties to obtain natural resources. If sales exceed costs, firms earn profits. The sum of wages, salaries, interest, rents, royalties, and profits constitute domestic income.

2. **What are the relationships between injections and leakages in the circular flow?** Saving, net taxes (tax revenues minus transfer payments), and imports are leakages from the circular flow. Investment, government purchases, and exports are injections. The total of leakages must always equal the total of injections; however, the individual pairs (saving and investment, net taxes and government purchases, imports and exports) do not need to balance. Any imbalance in the individual pairs is balanced by flows of funds through the financial sector.

3. **How is expenditure divided into consumption, investment, government purchases, and net exports?** The largest part of domestic income is used to purchase consumer goods and services. Some also is used to buy newly produced capital goods or add to inventories (investment), to pay for goods and services purchased by government, or to buy imported goods. Foreign buyers also make some expenditure. The term net exports refers to exports minus imports.

4. **Why is some investment planned and other unplanned?** *Planned investment* means fixed investment (purchases of newly produced capital goods) plus *planned inventory investment* (changes in inventory made on purpose as part of a business plan). In addition, inventories may change unexpectedly in ways not called for by firms' business plans. These changes are called *unplanned inventory investment*.

5. **How can the concept of equilibrium be applied to the circular flow of income and expenditure?** The *circular flow of income and product* is in equilibrium when total planned expenditure equals GDP. If *planned expenditure* exceeds GDP, so that more goods and services are being bought than are being produced, there will be unplanned decreases in inventories. In reaction, firms will increase output, and GDP will tend to rise. If total planned expenditure falls short of GDP, there will be unplanned increases in inventories. In response, firms will tend to decrease their output and GDP will fall.

6. **What is the multiplier effect and how is it related to the business cycle?** According to the multiplier effect, a given change in one type of expenditure (say, planned investment) will produce a larger change in equilibrium GDP.

The multiplier effect helps explain how relatively small disturbances in expenditure can cause relatively larger changes in GDP over the course of the business cycle.

## Key Terms

## Problems and Topics for Discussion

1. **Your personal expenditures** What was your income last month (or last year) from all current resources, including wages and salaries plus any interest earned or other investment income? Do not count money that you received as transfer payments, such as government benefits, gifts from family, scholarship grants, and so on. How much was your saving? Did you add to your savings or draw down on past savings? How much did you spend on consumer goods or services? Of your spending, approximately how much do you think was spent on imported goods or services purchased while on foreign travel? Identify where the answer to each of these questions appears in the circular flow diagram, Figure 5.3.

2. **Planned versus unplanned inventory changes.** Suppose your school bookstore manager learns from the admissions office that enrollment of students will rise by 10 percent next year. What planned inventory investments would the bookstore manager make? Suppose that a storm delays the departure of 100 students from another university who have visited your campus for a hockey game. While waiting for their buses to leave, they decide to browse your school bookstore and buy some items that catch their eye. How would this affect the store's inventories?

3. **Injections and leakages in the Russian economy** In recent years, Russia has benefited from high world prices for the large amount of oil it produces for export. As a result, Russia has had positive net exports. Because oil is partly state owned and heavily taxed where privately owned, government tax revenues have increased so that the Russian government budget is in surplus. How would these differences between the Russian and U.S. economies affect the direction of the arrows in the circular flow diagram of Figure 5.3? Explain any changes that would need to be made.

4. **Unplanned inventory change and disequilibrium**   Suppose that you read in the news that inventories in retail stores fell last month, to the surprise of analysts. Would interpret this as a sign of equilibrium or disequilibrium in the circular flow? Which do you think would be more likely in the coming months, an increase or a decrease in GDP? Why?

5. **Adjustment to change in planned expenditure.**   Starting from a state of equilibrium, trace the effects of each of the following. What happens to inventories? How do firms react? What happens to incomes? To consumption expenditure? To GDP?

   a.   Business managers, anticipating future profit opportunities in consumer electronics, increase orders for production equipment in order to prepare for the expected increase in demand.

   b.   The federal government reduces income tax rates.

   c.   Good harvests in Africa reduce the demand for exports of U.S. farm products.

## Case for Discussion

*Excerpts from the Annual Report of the President's Council of Economic Advisers, 2007*

The expansion of the U.S economy continued for the fifth consecutive year in 2006. Economic growth was strong, with real gross domestic product (GDP) growing at 3.4 percent during the four quarters of 2006.

Consumer spending sustained its strong growth during the four quarters of 2006 (rising 3.7 percent in real terms), continuing its 15-year pattern of rising faster than disposable income. As a result, the personal saving rate fell to a negative 1.0 percent for the year as a whole—its lowest annual level during the post-World War II era. Corporate net saving rose to 3.8 percent of gross domestic income (GDI) during the first three quarters of 2006, its highest level since the 1960s.

During 2006, real business investment in equipment and software grew 5 percent, slower than the 7 percent average pace during the 3 previous years. Its fastest-growing components included computers, as well as machinery in the agricultural and service sectors. Investment in mining and oil field machinery was also strong, likely in response to elevated crude oil prices and to the need to replace Gulf of Mexico facilities damaged by the 2005 hurricanes.

Inventory investment was fairly steady during 2006 and had only a minor influence on quarter-to-quarter fluctuations. Real nonfarm inventories grew at an average $44 billion annual pace during 2006, a 3.0 percent rate of growth that is roughly in line with the pace of real GDP growth over the same period

Real Federal purchases of goods and services grew 2.4 percent during 2006. This was the third consecutive year of growth at roughly 2 percent. Defense spending accounted for all of the increase during the four-quarter period, while non-defense purchases fell. Nominal Federal revenues grew 15 percent in FY 2005 and 12 percent in FY 2006. These rapid growth rates exceeded growth in outlays and GDP as a whole; and the U.S. fiscal deficit, as a share of GDP, shrank from 3.6 percent in FY 2004 to 2.6 percent in FY 2005 to 1.9 percent in FY 2006.

The current account deficit (the excess of imports and income flows to foreigners over exports and foreign income of Americans) jumped to 7.0 percent of GDP in the fourth quarter of 2005, partly due to petroleum imports that replaced lost Gulf of Mexico production. The current account deficit then retraced some of its earlier increase in the first three quarters of 2006, when oil imports declined.

## QUESTIONS

*The following questions may be answered on the basis of information in the main text of the chapter. However, if you have read the appendix, use what you learned there to give additional detail to your answers.*

1. Why is growth of consumer spending considered a positive factor for expansion of GDP, even when personal saving is falling to a negative level? Are the long-term and short-term effects of a negative personal saving rate both favorable to economic growth? Discussed, based on concepts from this chapter and the preceding one.

2. According to the report, inventories grew at about the same rate as the economy as a whole. Taken in isolation from other things going on in the macroeconomy, would you expect this behavior of inventories to bias the economy toward faster expansion in the near future, bias it toward a slowdown in the near future, or to be roughly neutral in its effect?

3. According to the report, exports grew faster than imports during the first part of the year. Would you expect this to have a positive or a negative effect on future economic growth? Why?

4. The government budget remained in deficit during 2006. What information given here helps understand how the deficit was financed?

## End Notes

1. Economists use the term *households* to refer to families who live together and make economic decisions together about issues of work and spending, as well as to individuals living alone who make such decisions independently.

2. Some minor qualifications of this statement will be made in the next chapter.

3. There are two different ways to represent the government surplus or deficit in equation form. For purposes of the macroeconomic models in this text, we usually write the government's budget equation this way: surplus = net taxes − government purchases. If the budget is in deficit "surplus" has a negative value. In other contexts, the surplus or deficit may be represented this way: surplus = tax revenue − government expenditure. Because the item "transfer payments" is subtracted from tax revenue to give net taxes, and is added to government purchases to give government expenditure, it is clear that the two ways of representing the surplus or deficit always give the same result.

4. Figure 5.3 is drawn as if the only imports were imports of consumer goods purchased by households. In practice, business firms purchase some imported capital goods as part of their investment spending, and the government also purchases some imported goods and services. At the risk of making the circular flow diagram too complex to read easily, we could, in principle, draw in additional small arrows to represent flows of payments for imported capital goods and government purchases.

5. The term *trade deficit* as popularly used does not always correspond exactly to our term *net exports*. The next chapter will discuss concepts related to imports, exports, and the balance of payments in more detail.

6. The economy's financial sector, including banks, securities markets, insurance companies, and other institutions will be discussed in more detail in chapter 7.

7. John Maynard Keynes, *The General Theory of Employment, Interest, and Money* (New York: Harcourt, Brace and World, 1936), 96.

8. To understand this example, it is important to remember that buying the backhoe is a purchase of newly produced capital goods, that is, part of the fixed investment component of planned expenditure. Buying the government bond is a financial investment, a purchase of the right to receive future payments from the government. The bonds are not newly produced capital goods and do not count as part of GDP.

# Appendix to Chapter 5:
# THE PLANNED EXPENDITURE MODEL

### The Elements of Planned Expenditure

The object of this appendix is to present a simple graphical and mathematical model that shows how the equilibrium level of planned expenditure and GDP is determined. Our starting point is the planned expenditure equation given in the chapter:

$$E_p = C + I_p + G + (Ex - Im)$$

Our next step is to look one by one at the main components of planned expenditure. In doing so, we will in each case distinguish between two types of expenditures—those that are a function of the level of income, and those that are not. The former can be referred to as *income-dependent* components of planned expenditure and the latter as *autonomous* components.

Consumption   The level of consumption, other things being equal, depends on the level of disposable income, that is, on the level of gross domestic income minus net taxes. In equation form

$$C = \alpha + \beta(Q - T)$$

In this equation, which is known as the *consumption function,* $\alpha$ represents *autonomous consumption* (that is, the part of consumption that does not depend on the level of income), $\beta$ the marginal propensity to consume, and Q the level of real GDP, which, as we know, is equal to the level of domestic income.

Many kinds of taxes, for example, income and profits taxes, are income-dependent. Other taxes, known as *autonomous net taxes,* do not depend on the level of income—for example, taxes based on the value of real estate. Taking both kinds of taxes into account, the level of net taxes, T, can be represented by the following equation:

$$T = t_0 + t_1 \times Q$$

where $t_0$ represents autonomous net taxes and $t_1$ represents the share of each added dollar of real GDP that goes to net taxes. This variable is called the *marginal tax rate.*

If the tax equation is substituted into the consumption function, the latter can be restated in terms of GDP rather than in terms of disposable income:

$$C = a + bQ$$

The parameter a, which is equal to $\alpha - \beta t_0$, is the level of autonomous consumption corresponding to zero real GDP, and the parameter b, which is equal to $\beta(1 - t_1)$ could be called the marginal propensity to consume from GDP.

**Investment**    As explained earlier, the main factors that determine planned investment are interest rates, which determine the cost of financing purchases of inventories and capital goods, and business confidence. For accuracy, our model must use real interest rates. (As explained in chapter 4, The real interest rate is the nominal interest rate minus the rate of inflation. Using r to represent the real interest rate, the level of planned investment can be stated as

$$I_p = i_0 - i_1 \times r$$

where $i_0$ stands for business confidence and $i_1$ represents the sensitivity of planned investment to the real interest rate. Because it is not a represented in our model as a function of the level of GDP, planned investment is considered a type of autonomous expenditure.

**Government Purchases and Net Exports**    In simple macroeconomic models, government purchases are considered to be *exogenous,* that is, not determined by variables included in the model. Because government purchases are not a function of GDP, they are considered a form of autonomous expenditure.

Net exports are an endogenous variable determined in part by exchange rates and in part by the level of GDP. As mentioned earlier in the chapter, when GDP rises, consumers and businesses tend to spend more on imports. This affects the value of the parameter b, which we have called the marginal propensity to consume from GDP. In an economy open to international trade, this variable should be interpreted as referring to the consumption of domestically produced consumer goods. As a result, the value of b in an open economy is somewhat less than it would be in a closed economy, that is, one with no international trade. Export demand is not dependent on domestic GDP, so it is treated as a type of autonomous expenditure.

Putting consumption, planned investment, and government purchases together, the level of planned expenditure can be represented by the equation

$$E_p = A + bQ$$

where A stands for *autonomous expenditure,* that is, the total of autonomous consumption, planned investment, government purchases, and the autonomous component of net exports, and the parameter b is the marginal propensity to consume from GDP. The value of A must be greater than zero, and the value of b between zero and 1.

## The Equilibrium Level of Real Output

As explained earlier in the chapter, the circular flow as a whole is in equilibrium when planned expenditure equals real output, that is, $E_p = Q$. Figure 5A.1 provides a graphical representation of the concept of equilibrium.

Because autonomous expenditure is positive and the value of the marginal propensity to consume from GDP is between zero and 1, the planned expenditure schedule $E_p = A + bQ$ is a line with a positive intercept and a slope less than 1. (For the diagram, the equation $E_p = 200 + .5Q$ is used.) Equilibrium occurs where this schedule intersects the line $E_p = Q$, which represents the equilibrium condition.

FIGURE 5A.1  EQUILIBRIUM OF PLANNED EXPENDITURE AND REAL
OUTPUT IN THE CIRCULAR FLOW

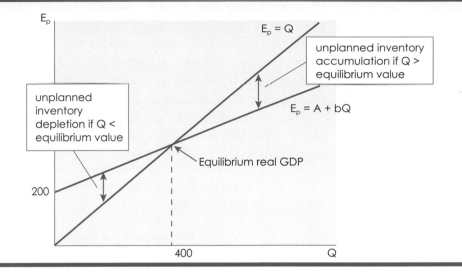

For any level of real output greater than the equilibrium level, planned expenditure is less than real output. That means that consumers, investors, government and exporters are planning to buy a smaller volume of goods and services than is being produced. Goods that are produced but not purchased do not vanish into thin air. Instead, they accumulate in inventory, even though this was not part of the producers' original business plans. We can see, then, that whenever real output is greater than the equilibrium level, there must be unplanned inventory accumulation. Businesses tend to react to unplanned inventory accumulation by reducing output. When they do so, real GDP will move downward toward its equilibrium level.

Similarly, when real output is below its equilibrium level, total planned expenditure will exceed production. If more goods are being purchased than are being produced, there will be an unplanned depletion of inventories. To correct the unplanned depletion of inventories, businesses will tend to increase their level of output, and real GDP will move upward toward its equilibrium level.

We can express the same equilibrium condition in algebraic terms by substituting the planned expenditure equation $E_p = A + bQ$ into the equilibrium condition $E_p = Q$. The result is an equation for the equilibrium level of GDP:

$$Q = A \times 1/(1 - b)$$

## The Multiplier Effect

The term $1/(1 - b)$ is known as the *expenditure multiplier* because a $1 increase in autonomous expenditure will cause equilibrium real GDP to increase by $1 times the multiplier. For example, in Figure 5A.1, autonomous expenditure is 200, and the marginal propensity to consume from GDP is 0.5; so equilibrium GDP is 400. The value of the expenditure multiplier is 2, so a $1 increase in autonomous consumption would produce a $2 increase in the equilibrium level of real GDP.

A change for any reason in any component of autonomous expenditure can cause a change in the equilibrium level of real output. As an example, Figure 5A.2 considers the effect of a change in planned investment resulting from a change in the real interest rate. In that figure, an increase in the interest rate r from $r_0$ to a higher value of $r_1$ reduces the planned investment component of autonomous expenditure by 50 units. Graphically, this is shown as a downward shift of the planned expenditure schedule to a position where the vertical intercept is 150 rather than 200. Through the operation of the multiplier effect, the equilibrium value of real output is reduced from 400 to 300.

The value of 2 given for the expenditure multiplier in our example is arbitrary. In practice, the value of the expenditure multiplier for a given economy depends on several considerations. Other things being equal:

- The greater the marginal propensity to consume (from disposable income) is, the greater the multiplier.

- The greater the marginal tax rate is, the lower the expenditure multiplier. The reason is that when the marginal tax rate is high, a given change in GDP will result in a smaller change in disposable income.

- The greater the share of consumption devoted to imported goods is, the less the expenditure multiplier is. As a result, we expect the multiplier effect to be stronger for large, relatively closed economies where most consumer goods are domestically produced than for small, open economies where more consumer goods are imported.

**FIGURE 5A.2   EFFECT OF AN INCREASE IN INTEREST RATES**

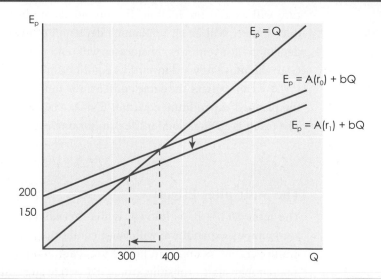

# CHAPTER *6*

# Measuring Economic Activity

### After reading this chapter, you will understand the following:

1. How gross domestic product is officially defined and measured
2. How the measurement of domestic income differs from the measurement of gross domestic product
3. The major types of international transactions
4. How changes in the average level of prices are measured
5. The limitations of official economic statistics

### Before reading this chapter, make sure you know the meaning of the concepts:

1. Real and nominal values
2. Indexation
3. Transfer payments
4. Domestic income and product

**National income accounts**

A set of official government statistics on aggregate economic activity

IN THE INTERNET age, government reports of GDP and related data are available, and acted on, instantly throughout the world. For example, in January 2009, when the Commerce Department reported that the U.S. trade deficit rose by more than expected in the preceding quarter, the euro immediately rose in value relative to the dollar. An index of economic expectations in Germany moved upward. Evidently, German investors thought that U.S. demand for Audis and BMWs would remain strong. Just having instant access to the numbers, however, is not enough. To use the latest data intelligently, you must know what they mean and where they come from. That means not only knowing the theoretical relationships among GDP components, as discussed in the previous chapter, but also how they are measured. That is the subject of this chapter.

Together, the data on aggregate economic activity published by the government are known as the **national income accounts**. The economists and statisticians whose job it is to

149

make these measurements for the U.S. economy are widely held to be the best such team in the world. Yet, as this chapter will show, they face many problems. There are technical problems posed by sampling errors and survey methods. There are conceptual problems that arise when real-world institutions do not match the theoretical categories of economic models. Finally, there is a tradeoff between accuracy and timeliness of data. All of these issues will be addressed in this chapter.

## The National Income Accounts in Nominal Terms

We begin with an examination of the national income accounts in nominal terms—that is, in terms of the prices at which goods and services are actually sold. Nominal measures do not tell the whole story because they are not adjusted to reflect the effects of inflation; but they do provide a starting point. Data are first collected in nominal form; and only after a set of nominal accounts has been assembled, can the process of adjusting for price changes begin.

### Gross Domestic Product

**Gross domestic product (GDP)**

The value, at current market prices, of all final goods and services produced annually in a given country

The most widely publicized number in the national income accounts is gross domestic product. We have mentioned this important term before; now we can give it a formal definition. **Gross domestic product (GDP)** is the value at current market prices (that is, the nominal value) of all final goods and services produced annually in a given country.

The term **final goods and services** is a key part of the definition of gross domestic product. GDP attempts to measure the sum of the economic contributions of each firm and industry without missing anything or counting anything twice. To do this, care must be taken to count only goods sold to *final users*—parties that will use them for domestic consumption, government purchases, investment, or export. *Intermediate goods*—those that are purchased for use as inputs in producing other goods or services—are excluded.

**Final goods and services**

Goods and services that are sold to or ready for sale to parties that will use them for consumption, investment, government purchases, or export

Table 6.1 shows why counting both final and intermediate goods would overstate total production. The table traces the process of producing a kitchen table with a retail price of $100. The final stage of production takes place in a furniture factory, but the factory does not do $100 worth of work. Instead, it produces the table by taking $40 worth of lumber and adding $60 worth of inputs in the form of the labor of factory workers, capital in the form of woodworking machines, and other factors. The $40 worth of lumber is an intermediate good; the $60 contribution made by the manufacturer is the **value added** to the product at its final stage. (In practice, other intermediate goods, such as paint and fuel for heating the plant, are used in making the table. To simplify the example we assume that the table is made solely from lumber plus the manufacturer's effort.)

**Value added**

The dollar value of an industry's sales less the value of intermediate goods purchased for use in production

The second section of Table 6.1 shows the next-to-last stage of production: making the lumber. The sawmill buys $15 worth of logs, adds $25 worth of labor and capital, and produces lumber worth $40. The value added at the sawmill stage is thus $25.

Going still further back, we come to the stage at which the logs were produced. To produce $15 worth of logs, a forest products company bought $5 worth of fuel,

**TABLE 6.1　VALUE ADDED AND THE USE OF FINAL PRODUCTS IN GDP**

| | | |
|---|---:|---:|
| Final stage—manufacturing: | | |
|     Value of one table | $ 100 | |
|     Less value of lumber | −40 | |
|     Equals value added in manufacturing | 60 ⟶ | $ 60 |
| Next to final stage—sawmill: | | |
|     Value of lumber | $ 40 | |
|     Less value of logs | −15 | |
|     Equals value added at sawmill | 25 ⟶ | 25 |
| Second to final stage—timber farming: | | |
|     Value of logs | $ 15 | |
|     Less value of fuel, equipment, etc. | −5 | |
|     Equals value added in timber farming | 10 ⟶ | 10 |
| All previous stages: | | |
|     Value added in fuel, equipment, etc. | $ 5 ⟶ | 5 |
| **Total value added** | | **$ 100** |

This table shows why GDP must include only the value of final goods and services if it is to measure total production without double counting. The value of sales at each stage of production can be divided into the value added at that stage and the value of purchased inputs. The selling price of the final product (a $100 table, in this case) equals the sum of the values added at all stages of production.

equipment, and so on, and added $10 in exchange for the effort involved in tending the trees and harvesting the logs. That is an additional $10 of value added.

Clearly, the process of making the table could be traced back indefinitely. The last section of the exhibit sums up the value added at all stages of production prior to timber farming—the fuel and equipment suppliers, their own suppliers, and so on. If production were traced back far enough, every penny could be attributed to the value added to the final product somewhere in the chain of production.

Now compare the first and last lines of the table. The value of the final goods turns out to be exactly equal to the sum of the values added at each stage of production. This is why only final goods are counted in GDP. Adding together the $100 value of the finished table, the $40 value of the lumber, the $15 value of the timber, and so on would far overstate the true rate of productive activity (the true total value added) in the economy.

## The Expenditure Approach to Measuring GDP

In principle, GDP can be measured by adding together the value of each good or service sold and adjusting for the cost of inputs to get the value added at each stage of production, as shown in Table 6.1. However, the approach that gets the greatest attention makes use of the equality of domestic product and total expenditure. It is easier to gather data on the total amount spent by households, investors, governments, and buyers of exports on final goods produced in the domestic economy than it is to stand at factory gates and count goods as they roll off assembly lines. This method of measuring GDP is known as the *expenditure approach*. Table 6.2 shows how it works, using 2006 data for the U.S. economy.

**CONSUMPTION** The first line of Table 6.2 gives total household consumption of both domestically produced and imported goods and services. The national income accounts divide consumption into three categories: durable goods like cars and appliances, nondurable goods like food and clothing, and services like medical care and banking.

All three components of consumption contain some items that do

Medical care is included in the services section of the national income accounts.

**TABLE 6.2  NOMINAL GROSS DOMESTIC PRODUCT BY TYPE OF EXPENDITURE, 2008 (DOLLARS IN BILLIONS)**

| | | |
|---|---:|---:|
| Personal consumption expenditure | | $ 10,058.5 |
| Durable goods | $ 1,022.7 | |
| Nondurable goods | 2,966.9 | |
| Services | 6,068.9 | |
| Plus gross private domestic investment | | 2,004.1 |
| Fixed investment | 2,044.0 | |
| Change in private inventories | −39.9 | |
| Plus government purchases of goods and services | | 2,883.3 |
| Federal | 1,071.2 | |
| State and local | 1,812.1 | |
| Plus net exports of goods and services | | −665.1 |
| Exports | 1,867.8 | |
| Less imports | −2,533.0 | |
| Equals gross domestic product (GDP) | | $ 14,280.8 |
| Less allowance for consumption of fixed capital | | −1,623.9 |
| Equals net domestic product (NDP) | | $ 12,656.9 |

Gross domestic product is estimated using the expenditure approach. This involves adding together the values of expenditures on newly produced final goods and services made by all economic units to get a measure of aggregate economic activity. Net domestic product is derived from gross domestic product by excluding the value of expenditures made to replace worn-out or obsolete capital equipment.

SOURCE: *Bureau of Economic Analysis, News Release: Gross Domestic Product, Jan. 30, 2009.*

not pass through markets on their way to consumers. One such item is an estimate of the quantity of food produced and consumed on farms; another is an estimate of the rental value of owner-occupied homes. However, many non-market goods and services—for example, unpaid childcare and housework—are not captured in the national income accounts.

**INVESTMENT** The item termed *gross private domestic investment* is the sum of all purchases of newly produced capital goods (fixed investment) plus changes in business inventories (inventory investment). The fixed-investment component includes both business fixed investment—all new equipment and structures bought by firms—and the value of newly constructed residential housing. In the national income accounts, then, a home-owning household is treated like a small firm. When the house is bought, it is counted as an investment. Then, as we saw earlier, the firm's "product"—the rental value of its shelter services—is counted as part of consumption each year.

The gross private domestic investment item does not include investment in structures, software, and equipment that are made by federal, state, and local governments. These amounted to some $503 billion in 2008, adding about 25 percent to the total. From the point of view of short-run business cycle theory, it makes sense to treat government and private investment differently since the motives for the investment are different. However, from the point of long-term growth theory, government investment, like private investment, adds to a country's stock of capital and increases future natural real GDP.

**GOVERNMENT PURCHASES** The item called "government purchases" in macroeconomic models is titled "Government Consumption Expenditures and Gross Investment" in the official national income accounts. Whether consumption-like or investment-like, government purchases are valued at cost in the national income accounts. No attempt is made to measure the value added by government because most government outputs—primary and secondary education, defense services, and police protection, to name a few—are financed by taxes and provided to the public without charge rather than sold. Transfer payments are not included in the expenditure approach to GDP because they do not represent purchases of newly produced final goods and services.

**NET EXPORTS** The last item in the GDP account is *net exports*—exports minus imports. In calculating GDP, imports must be subtracted from exports to avoid double counting. Some of the goods bought by consumers, investors, and government and included in their expenditures are not produced in the domestic economy. For example, a consumer might buy a Japanese television set, an insurance company might buy Korean computers for use in its offices, and a city government might buy a Swedish-built police car. The figures for consumption, investment, and government purchases, therefore, overstate the final use of domestically produced goods and services to the extent that some of those goods and services were produced abroad. To correct for the overstatement in earlier lines in Table 6.2, imports are subtracted from exports at the bottom. Adding total consumption plus total investment plus total government purchases plus exports less imports yields the same sum as would be obtained by adding domestic consumption of domestically produced goods, domestic purchases of domestically produced capital goods, domestic government purchases of domestically produced goods, and total exports.

**GROSS VERSUS NET DOMESTIC PRODUCT**   What makes gross domestic product "gross"? It is the fact that gross private domestic investment measures total additions to the nation's capital stock without adjusting for losses through wear and tear or obsolescence. For example, gross private domestic investment includes the value of new homes and factories built each year without subtracting the value of old homes and factories that are torn down. Gross private domestic investment minus an allowance for depreciation and obsolescence yields net private domestic investment, a measure of the actual net addition to the nation's capital stock each year. Only net investment adds to the capital stock, thereby helping to expand the economy's natural real output over time. The part of gross investment that covers depreciation and obsolescence is needed just to keep the capital stock from shrinking. Although depreciation and obsolescence are hard to measure accurately, national income accountants use an approximate measure called the *allowance for consumption of fixed capital*. Gross domestic product minus this allowance equals *net domestic product (NDP)*.

## The Income Approach to Measuring Aggregate Economic Activity

In the previous chapter, we looked at the economy in terms of a circular flow of income and expenditure. There are several points in the circular flow where aggregate economic activity can be measured. The GDP accounts displayed in Table 6.2 use an expenditure approach, adding together consumption, investment, government, and net export components as expenditures flow into the markets where firms sell their products. Instead, the circular flow can also be measured by an income approach— observing wages, rents, interest, and profits as they flow into the household sector. This approach is summarized in Table 6.3.

*Compensation of employees* consists of wages and salaries plus certain supplements. The most important supplement is employer contributions to social insurance (social security). As the social security tax law is written, employees are legally required to pay only half of the tax; employers must pay the other half. Because both halves contribute to employees' retirement benefits, both are counted as part of employee compensation. The supplements line also includes health insurance and contributions to 401k and other private pension plans.

*Rental income of persons* consists of all income in the form of rent and royalties received by property owners. *Net interest* includes interest income received by households less interest payments made by consumers.

*Corporate profits* encompass all income earned by the shareholders of corporations. Dividends are the part of corporate income that are actually paid out to stockholders. Another part of corporate profits goes to pay taxes. Corporations hold a third part, undistributed corporate profits, back for reinvestment. Because

| TABLE 6.3    NOMINAL DOMESTIC INCOME, 2008 (*DOLLARS IN BILLIONS*) | | |
|---|---:|---:|
| Compensation of employees | | $ 8,055.1 |
|    Wages and salaries | $ 6,543.2 | |
|    Supplements | 1,504.4 | |
| Plus rental income of persons | | 64.4 |
| Plus net interest | | 682.7 |
| Plus corporate profits | | 1,476.5 |
| | | |
| Plus proprietors' income | | 1,072.4 |
| Plus indirect business taxes, business transfers, etc. | | 1,078.6 |
| Equals national income | | 12,429.7 |
|    Less receipts of factor income from rest of world | | – 798.3 |
|    Plus payments of factor income to rest of world | | 665.1 |
| Equals domestic income | | $ 12,296.5 |

National and domestic incomes are measured using the income approach. This involves adding together the values of all forms of income earned by a country's residents. U.S. national income includes some income received in return for factors of production used abroad, and excludes payments to foreign residents for the use of factors owned by them but located in the United States. Domestic income is derived from national income by subtracting receipts of factor income from the rest of the world and adding factor income paid to the rest of the world.

SOURCE: Bureau of Economic Analysis

reinvestment of profits adds to shareholder wealth, it is counted as a part of household income. In the income approach, corporate profits are also adjusted for changes in the value of inventories and for consumption of fixed capital, that is, depreciation. *Proprietors' income* lumps together all forms of income earned by self-employed professionals and owners of unincorporated business. The final item includes certain items, like business property taxes, that are expenses to firms, but are not paid out as income to individuals.

**National income**

The total income earned by a country's residents, including wages, rents, interest payments, and profits

The total of these items is **national income**, the total income received by a country's residents. The term *national* is used because the income items listed in the table are those earned by a country's residents, regardless of whether their productive activities take place in the home country or another country. For example, corporate profits shown in the table would include the profits earned by capital the Ford Motor Company has invested in the UK, but they would not include profits earned by Honda Motors that is invested in a plant in the United States. In contrast, *domestic* income and product are geographical concepts that measure activity that takes place on the territory of a country, regardless of who owns the factors of production involved. We can

**Domestic income**

The total income of all types, including wages, rents, interest payments, and profits, paid in return for factors of production used in producing domestic product

obtain a geographical measure of income, **domestic income**, by subtracting factor income received by U.S. residents from the rest of the world and adding factor income paid to foreign residents.[1]

**RECONCILING THE INCOME AND EXPENDITURE APPROACHES** In the official accounts, gross and net domestic product are measured by the expenditure approach using one set of data, and domestic and national income are measured by the income approach using a different set of data. No matter how carefully the work is done, there will be some errors and omissions; therefore, the two sets of figures will not quite fit together. The difference between net domestic product and domestic income is called the *statistical discrepancy*. Most of the time this error is very small—well below 1 percent of GDP. Theoretical models, including those in this book, treat domestic income and domestic product as equal by definition.

Profits earned by Ford Motor Company from its UK operations are included in US Gross National Product, but not US Gross Domestic Product.

## Measuring International Linkages

The item "net exports" in the national income accounts gives a glimpse of the linkage between the domestic economy and the rest of the world. These ties have grown over time. In 1960, U.S. exports amounted to only 6 percent of GDP and imports to less than 5 percent. By 2008, exports had grown to 13.6 percent of a much larger GDP. Imports grew even more rapidly over the same period, reaching 18.6 percent of GDP. In view of the growing importance of the foreign sector, then, it is worth taking a closer look at the international ties of the U.S. economy.

Any discussion of an economy's balance of international payments is complicated by the fact that thousands of different kinds of international payments are made every day. Payments for the goods and services that are exported and imported come to mind first, but there are many others. Equally important are long- and short-term international loans and international financial transactions linked to purchases and sales of securities and direct investments in foreign businesses. In addition, governments and private individuals make many kinds of transfer payments to residents of other countries, including outright gifts, pension payments, and official foreign aid. Finally, the U.S. Federal Reserve System and foreign central banks engage in many kinds of official transactions. Table 6.4 shows a simplified version of the accounts used to keep track of these international transactions for the United States.

**TABLE 6.4  U.S. INTERNATIONAL ACCOUNTS FOR 2008 (*DOLLARS IN BILLIONS*)**

### Current Account

| | | |
|---|---|---|
| 1. Balance on goods | | −821.6 |
| 2. Exports of goods | 1,291.3 | |
| 3. Imports of goods | −2,112.9 | |
| 4. Services, net | | 139.7 |
| 5. Exports of services | 544.4 | |
| 6. Imports of services | −404.7 | |
| 7. Net receipts of factor income | | 127.6 |
| 8. Income receipts from abroad | 755.4 | |
| 9. Income payments by the United States | −627.8 | |
| 10. Transfers, net | | −119.7 |
| 11. Current account balance (lines 1 + 4 + 7 + 10) | | −674.0 |

### Capital and Financial Account

| | | |
|---|---|---|
| 12. Net change in U.S. assets abroad (− indicates increase in U.S. assets abroad, that is, a financial outflow) | | −52.4 |
| 13. U.S. private assets | 481.8 | |
| 14. U.S. official reserve assets | −4.8 | |
| 15. Other U.S. government assets | −529.5 | |
| 16. Net change in foreign assets in the United States (+ indicates increase in foreign assets in the United States, that is, a financial inflow) | | 599.0 |
| 17. Capital account transactions, net | | −2.6 |
| 18. Capital and financial account balance (lines 12 + 16 + 17) | | 544.0 |
| 19. Statistical discrepancy | | 130.0 |

This table gives details of U.S. international transactions for 2008. The first section shows current account transactions, consisting of imports and exports of goods and services, together with international flows of factor income and transfer payments. The second section shows capital and financial account transactions, consisting of international borrowing and lending, securities transactions, direct investment, and official reserve transactions. If all amounts were measured completely and accurately, the current account and financial account balances would be equal and opposite in sign. In practice, there is a statistical discrepancy indicating errors and omissions in measurement.

SOURCE: U.S. Department of Commerce, Bureau of Economic Analysis

## The Current Account

The first section of the international accounts shown in Table 6.4 is called the *current account*. This section includes imports and exports of goods and services, payments of factor income between countries, and international transfer payments.

Imports and exports of merchandise (goods) are the most widely publicized items in the international accounts. During much of the nineteenth century the United States was a net importer of merchandise. From 1894 to 1970 it was a net exporter. Since 1970, it has again become a net importer, as shown by the negative **merchandise balance** in Table 6.4.

**Merchandise balance**

The value of a country's merchandise exports minus the value of its merchandise imports

In addition to trade in merchandise, there is a large international trade in services. Travel expenditures, airline passenger fares, and other transportation services account for somewhat more than half of these services. Other services include insurance, royalties, and license fees. In recent years, the United States has been a net exporter of services in 2006.

Earlier, in drawing the distinction between domestic and national product, we noted that U.S. residents receive substantial flows of factor income (wages, profits, interest, and so on) from U.S. residents and financial assets located abroad. These are treated as exports and enter the current account with a positive sign. At the same time, payments of factor income are made to residents of other countries as a result of production carried on in the United States. These are treated as imports and enter the current account with a negative sign. The United States typically receives more factor income from abroad than it pays.

The final item on the current account consists of net transfer receipts. This typically is a negative item in the U.S. international accounts because transfers to other countries exceed transfers received from them. This item takes into account both government transfers (for example, foreign aid and social security payments to retired workers living abroad) and private transfers (for example, remittances sent to relatives abroad by U.S. residents and private charitable contributions to beneficiaries overseas.)

**Current account balance**

The value of a country's exports of goods and services minus the value of its imports of goods and services plus its net transfer receipts from foreign sources

The sum of merchandise trade, services, factor income, and net transfers is called the country's **current account balance**. The United States has had a current account deficit every year since 1981.

Sometimes the official term "current account balance" is used in news reports and other popular discussions, but not everyone is careful in their use of terminology. Sometimes the terms "balance of payments" or "balance of trade" are used when discussing the current account balance. To add to the confusion, the term "balance of trade" is sometimes used when referring to the merchandise balance and sometimes to the sum of trade in goods and services. The current account balance is closely related to the concept "net exports" used in macroeconomic models; although for certain reasons related to the methodology of national income accounting, the correspondence is not quite exact.

## The Capital and Financial Account

Current account transactions are not the only ones that take place among residents of different countries. The international lending and borrowing and international sales and purchases of assets mentioned in an earlier chapter also account for an enormous volume of daily transactions. A U.S. company, for example, might obtain a short-term loan from a London bank to finance the purchase of a shipload of beer for import to the United States. The Brazilian government might get a long-term loan from Bank of America to help finance a hydroelectric project. A wealthy U.S. resident might open an account in a Swiss bank. All of these transactions are recorded in the capital and financial account section of Table 6.4. In this book, we will use the shorter term "financial account" to refer to this section. Some writers, instead, use the term "capital account" as shorthand to refer to the entire capital and financial account.

**Financial inflow**

Purchases of domestic assets by foreign buyers and borrowing from foreign lenders, also often called capital inflows

**Financial outflow**

Purchases of foreign assets by domestic residents or loans by domestic lenders to foreign borrowers, also often called capital outflows

Purchases of U.S. assets by foreign residents and borrowing from foreign financial intermediaries by U.S. firms and individuals create flows of funds into the United States. These are called **financial inflows**. (Many writers instead use the term *capital inflows.*) Purchases of foreign assets by U.S. residents or loans by U.S. financial intermediaries to foreigners create flows of funds out of the United States that are termed **financial outflows**. (Many writers use the term *capital outflows.*)

Table 6.4 lists several types of capital and financial account transactions. Changes in U.S. private assets include *direct investments*—for example, construction of foreign plants by U.S. firms and portfolio investments (for example, purchases of foreign securities). Accumulation of short-term foreign assets, like foreign bank balances and foreign currency, are also included on this line. Changes in U.S. official reserve assets include foreign currency and other foreign assets acquired by the Federal Reserve System and the U.S. Treasury. Changes in other U.S. government assets relate to short- and long-term credits and other assets by government agencies other than the Federal Reserve System and U.S. Treasury.

Changes in foreign assets in the United States include both private and government transactions. Construction of U.S. plants by foreign firms, purchases of U.S. securities by foreign financial institutions, accumulation of U.S. currency by foreign residents, and purchases of U.S. securities as official reserve assets by foreign central banks are all included on this line.

The "capital account"—in the narrow sense in which the term is officially used—is a small item that refers to transactions in non-financial assets, such as ownership of patents and copyrights, and also includes private and governmental debt forgiveness and defaults on debt.

## Relationship of the Accounts

The balance on the capital and financial account is logically related to the current account surplus or deficit. If, as shown in Figure 6.4, the United States runs a current account deficit, its earnings from the sales of exports will not be enough to pay for all of its imports. The additional funds needed to finance the excess imports must be obtained through net financial inflows, that is, through net U.S. borrowing from abroad or net sales of U.S. assets to foreign residents. In this case, the country shows a positive balance on the capital and financial account that offsets the current account deficit. On the other hand, countries like Japan or China that usually have current account surpluses must do something with the extra export earnings not used to buy imports. These earnings can be used to make net loans to foreign borrowers or to accumulate foreign assets through direct foreign investment, portfolio investment, or accumulation of foreign currency and bank balances. For that reason, countries with current account surpluses have negative balances on their capital and financial accounts.

In principle, the balances of the current and financial accounts should be equal and opposite in sign. If there is a current account surplus of $100 billion (entered with a plus sign in the accounts), there should be a net financial outflow of $100 billion (entered with a minus sign in the accounts). If there is a current account deficit of $500 billion, there should be a net financial inflow of $500 billion. The reason for this symmetry is that the two account components taken together include all the sources and uses of the funds that change hands in international transactions. Every dollar used in international transactions must have a source; thus, when the sources (+) and the uses (–) are added together, the sum should be zero.

In practice, however, government statisticians always miss some items when they tally up imports, exports, and financial flows. As a result, the numbers do not quite add up. The difference between the current and financial account balances is called the *statistical discrepancy*. Much of the discrepancy is believed to reflect unrecorded financial flows, for example, investments made in the United States by residents of other countries, but never officially reported. Part of it also reflects a tendency for U.S. exports, especially to Canada, to be reported less fully than U.S. imports. A small part of the statistical discrepancy is presumably accounted for by criminal activity, including drug smuggling (unrecorded current account activity) and money laundering (unrecorded financial account activity).

## Measuring Real Income and the Price Level

Between 1994 and 2008, the nominal value of U.S. gross domestic product approximately doubled, rising from $7.1 trillion to $14.2 trillion. However, even though nominal GDP doubled over this period, the real output of goods and services that determined people's standard of living did not. A good part of the increase in the dollar value of GDP reflected an increase in the prices at which goods and services were sold; adjusted for changing prices, real GDP increased by only about a third. Clearly, to understand what really happens in the economy over time, we must adjust the growth of nominal GDP and its components to account for inflation.

**GDP deflator**

A weighted average of the prices of all final goods and services produced in the economy

### Real Gross Domestic Product and the Deflator

To adjust nominal GDP for the effects of inflation, we need a measure of the change in the average prices of goods and services. The most broadly based measure of price changes for the U.S. economy is the **GDP deflator**. The appendix to this chapter explains how it is calculated. For now, we will simply define the GDP deflator as a weighted average of the prices of all the final goods and services that make up GDP.

**Base year**

The year that is chosen as a basis for comparison in calculating a price index or price level

**Price level**

A weighted average of the prices of goods and services expressed in relation to a base year value of 1.0

**Price index**

A weighted average of the prices of goods and services expressed in relation to a base year value of 100

**BASE YEAR**   When we speak of price changes, the first question that comes to mind is: Change from what? We can answer this question by choosing a convenient **base year** as a benchmark against which to measure change. The U.S. Department of Commerce currently uses 2000 as a base year for calculating the GDP deflator. The government uses two methods of calculating the GDP deflator: fixed and chained. Here, we will focus on the first method of computing GDP using fixed, or "constant," dollars.

The base year can be used in one of two ways in stating a weighted average of prices. One way is to let the base year value equal 1.0. A statement of average prices relative to a base year value of 1.0 is called a statement of the **price level;** for example, the 2008 price level, relative to the 2000 base year, was 1.23. The other way is to let the base year value equal 100. A statement of average prices relative to a base year value of 100 is known as a **price index.** Thus, using 2000 as a base year, we could say that the 2006 price index was 123. The price level and price index are two different ways of stating the same information. In news reports the index form is used most frequently, whereas in building economic models the price level form is more convenient.

To convert nominal GDP for any year to real GDP stated in constant 2000 dollars, we simply divide nominal GDP by the price level for that year. For convenience, we can refer to the year for which we are making the adjustment as the current year. In equation form, then, the rule for adjustment can be stated as follows:

Current-year real GDP = Current-year nominal GDP/Current-year price level.

For example, 2008 nominal GDP was $14,280 billion. Dividing this by the current year GDP deflator of 1.19 gives the 2008 real GDP, stated in constant 2000 dollars, of $11,609 billion. If one looks at a year earlier than the base year, the price level has a value less than one. For example, the GDP deflator for 1994, using the 2000 base year, was 0.9. Nominal GDP in 1994 was $7.1 trillion. Dividing this by .9 gives a value for 1994 real GDP of $7.8 trillion.

**Consumer price index (CPI)**

A price index based on the market basket of goods and services purchased by a typical urban household

**THE CONSUMER PRICE INDEX**   Although the GDP deflator is the most broadly based price index for the U.S. economy, it is not the best-known one. That honor belongs to the consumer price index. Rather than taking into account the prices of all final goods and services produced in the economy, as the GDP deflator does, the **consumer price index (CPI)** considers only the goods and services that make up the "market basket" purchased by a typical urban household. For example, the CPI market basket includes cars, but not railway locomotives.

The CPI currently uses the period 1982–1984 rather than a single year as its base year. The appendix to this chapter explains how the CPI is calculated.

The CPI plays a key role in the economy partly because it is widely used to index wages, government transfers, and many other payments. As explained in Chapter 4, indexation of a payment means automatically adjusting it on a regular schedule for changes in the price index involved. Millions of workers whose contracts include *cost-of-living-adjustment* (COLA) clauses receive automatic raises as a result of increases in the CPI.

## Producer Price Indexes

**Producer price index (PPI)**

A price index based on a sample of goods and services bought by business firms

Another widely publicized set of price indexes consists of **producer price indexes**. These are price averages for three classes of goods that are traded among business firms. The most widely publicized is the producer price index for *finished goods*—investment goods sold to businesses plus other goods that are ready for final use but have not yet been sold to consumers—for example, wholesale sales of clothing to clothing stores. Other producer price indexes cover intermediate goods and crude materials ready for further processing. The producer price indexes currently use a base year of 1982. Because producer price indexes measure prices at early stages in the production process, they are often studied for hints of trends in consumer prices. They are also frequently used to index payments that firms agree to make to one another.

Table 6.5 shows data for the GDP deflator, the consumer price index, and the producer price index for finished goods. To make comparison easier, the CPI and PPI figures have been restated using the same 2000 base year as the GDP deflator. As can be seen from the table, although the indexes tend to move in the same direction, the amount of inflation recorded by the various indexes differs. This is not surprising, inasmuch as they are based on different baskets of goods and services.

## How Good Are the National Income Accounts?

This chapter began by stressing the importance of the national income accounts to economics, while warning that they are less than perfect. Now that we have surveyed the main components of the nominal and real national income accounts, it is time to try to answer the question of how good those accounts are. We will focus on four possible problem areas: the accuracy and timeliness of the data, the underground sector of the economy, bias in price indexes, and nonmaterial aspects of the standard of living.

**ACCURACY VERSUS TIMELINESS**[2]   As this chapter has made clear, the measurement of GDP involves an enormous amount of data collection. Both government and private decision makers want the data they use to be timely and accurate; however, in practice, there is a trade-off. It is not feasible to station a monitor at every factory gate and supermarket checkout counter in the country to record real-time data on all production and expenditures. Instead, national income accountants rely on detailed data that are collected at relatively infrequent intervals and update these with less complete samples that are collected more frequently.

The most detailed data are those in the "benchmark" estimates that are compiled every five years on the basis of an economic census that covers about 95 percent of all expenditures in GDP. Between the benchmarks, annual surveys are conducted for about 150,000 reporting units and monthly surveys for about 35,000 units. The quarterly GDP estimates are based on a combination of the benchmark, annual, and quarterly surveys, supplemented by estimates based on past trends in cases where complete data is not yet available. The first estimate of GDP for each quarter, called the "advance" estimate, is released about three months after the end of the quarter (for example, about January 21 for the fourth quarter of the preceding year.) The advance estimate incorporates actual

**TABLE 6.5   U.S. PRICE INDEXES, 1980–2008**

| Year | GDP deflator | CPI | PPI |
|------|------|------|------|
| 1980 | 54.0 | 47.9 | 63.8 |
| 1981 | 59.1 | 52.8 | 69.6 |
| 1982 | 62.7 | 56.0 | 72.5 |
| 1983 | 65.2 | 57.8 | 73.6 |
| 1984 | 67.7 | 60.3 | 75.1 |
| 1985 | 69.7 | 62.5 | 75.9 |
| 1986 | 71.3 | 63.6 | 74.8 |
| 1987 | 73.2 | 66.0 | 76.4 |
| 1988 | 75.7 | 68.7 | 78.3 |
| 1989 | 78.6 | 72.0 | 82.3 |
| 1990 | 81.6 | 75.9 | 86.4 |
| 1991 | 84.4 | 79.1 | 88.2 |
| 1992 | 86.4 | 81.5 | 89.3 |
| 1993 | 88.4 | 83.9 | 90.4 |
| 1994 | 90.3 | 86.1 | 90.9 |
| 1995 | 92.1 | 88.5 | 92.7 |
| 1996 | 93.9 | 91.1 | 95.1 |
| 1997 | 95.4 | 93.2 | 95.5 |
| 1998 | 96.5 | 94.7 | 94.7 |
| 1999 | 97.9 | 96.7 | 96.4 |
| 2000 | 100.0 | 100.0 | 100.0 |
| 2001 | 102.4 | 102.8 | 102.0 |
| 2002 | 104.1 | 104.5 | 100.7 |
| 2003 | 106.0 | 106.9 | 103.8 |
| 2004 | 109.0 | 109.7 | 107.6 |
| 2005 | 112.5 | 113.4 | 112.8 |
| 2006 | 115 | 117.1 | 116.2 |
| 2007 | 119.8 | 120.4 | 120.4 |
| 2008 | 122 | 125.5 | 125.5 |

This table compares the trends of the GDP deflator, the consumer price index, and the producer price index for finished goods from 1980 to 2008 for the United States. For ease of comparison, all three indexes have been restated to use the same base year, 2000.

SOURCE: *Economic Report of the President,* 2008, Tables B-3, B-60, and B-65.

data for about 45 percent of expenditures, with the rest based on partial monthly data and trends. A month later the "preliminary" estimate is released, and a month after that, the "final" estimate. About 85 percent of the final estimate is based on actual data collected in the quarter, with the remaining 15 percent based on trends for data that are still missing. In this case, "final" is a misnomer since the quarterly data are subject to a still more complete annual revision and to further revisions as much as several years later.

Not surprisingly, the advance estimates, which give a first look at activity for a given quarter, are not perfectly accurate. On average, the advance estimate of real GDP is revised up or down by six tenths of one percent by the time of the "final" quarterly estimate, and on average by a little over one full percentage point by the time all eventual revisions are made. For example, the advance estimate for the fourth-quarter of 2008, released in January 2009, showed a 3.8 percent decrease in real GDP. If the final estimate released in March 2009 had shown an average revision, it would have shown a decrease in the range of 3.2 to 4.4 percent. In fact, the revision was much larger than average. The final estimate released in March actually showed a decrease of 6.3 percent for fourth quarter, 2008 GDP.

**THE UNDERGROUND ECONOMY**  The economic activity that is measured in the national income accounts constitutes the observed sector of the economy; however, a considerable amount of production, consumption, and investment is never officially measured. The national income accounts try to take the unobserved sector into account when they include estimates of the rental value of owner-occupied housing and the value of food produced and consumed on farms, but those items are only the tip of the iceberg.

Some have estimated that organized crime produces some $150 billion a year in illegal goods and services in the form of drugs, gambling, pornography, and so on. If this estimate is correct, it makes organized crime the second-largest industry in the United States after the oil industry. However, organized crime is probably not the largest sector of the so-called underground economy. The unreported income of businesses and self-employed people may add as much as $250 billion. This includes cash income that goes unreported to escape payment of taxes (for example, a concert pianist failing to report income from occasional piano lessons) and barter transactions that involve no cash at all (for example, the pianist gets her teeth straightened in exchange for giving piano lessons to her orthodontist's child).

Even if the U.S. underground economy amounts to as much as 10 percent of officially measured GDP, that proportion is moderate by world standards. The French underground economy is thought to equal one-third of that country's GDP; in Italy, the figure may be 40 percent; and in some third-world countries, the official GDP data bear only the haziest relationship to what is actually going on in the economy.

**PRICE INDEX BIASES**  A third problem with the official statistics is that of price index biases. The accuracy with which changes in price levels are measured became a matter of growing concern as inflation increased in the late 1970s and indexing and automatic cost-of-living adjustments became more widespread. If the official price indexes are found to understate inflation, policy makers should perhaps make a greater effort to restore price stability. On the other hand, if price indexes overstate inflation, contracts that provide automatic adjustments for inflation may be too generous.

The problem of price index biases has been closely studied, and the results are far from reassuring. The consumer price index has been criticized for two built-in biases that have caused it to overstate inflation: substitution bias and quality bias.

***Substitution Bias***   The first reason that the consumer price index tends to overstate the true rate of increase in the cost of living is the so-called substitution bias. As the appendix to this chapter explains, the CPI is a weighted average of the prices of goods that are typically purchased by urban consumers. Because the weights used to calculate the index remain constant, they always reflect patterns of consumption at some point in the past. However, because patterns change over time, the weights typically are not those of the most recent year being observed.

If changes in buying patterns were random, an obsolete set of weights would cause only random errors, not an upward bias, in the CPI. The bias results from the fact that consumer demand is influenced by changes in relative prices. As time passes, consumers tend to buy less of the goods whose prices have risen most and more of those whose prices have lagged behind the average or have actually fallen. Thus, the CPI tends to overstate the increase in the cost of living because it assigns unrealistically large weights to products whose prices have increased but that are consumed in relatively smaller amounts than formerly. For example, if large increases in gasoline prices lead consumers to purchase more fuel-efficient cars, and thus to consume less gasoline, the weight given to gasoline will be too high. As a result, the CPI will exaggerate the impact of gas prices on the cost of living. The market basket on which the CPI is based is periodically adjusted to reflect such changes, but the adjustments are not frequent enough to remove the bias altogether.

***Quality Bias***   A second source of bias in the consumer price index is the failure to adjust product prices for changes in quality. It would be highly misleading, for example, to say that a 2009 model car costs three times as much as a 1979 model without considering the facts that the 2009 model can be driven longer between servicing and is much safer than the 1979 model. In terms of dollars per unit of transportation service, the newer model clearly would be less than three times as expensive.

For automobiles, computers, and a few other major goods, the Bureau of Labor Statistics does try to make quality adjustments. As recently as the late 1960s, it cost over $1,000 to buy a desk-size electromechanical calculator that would add, subtract, multiply, and divide. Today half of that sum will buy a basic laptop computer, and a calculator equivalent to the 1960 model can be purchased for less than $5. Studies of changes in computer quality have led to significant adjustments in price indexes. However, government statisticians do not have the resources to make such detailed studies of all items that enter into GDP.

Taken together, the substitution bias and quality bias are substantial. At one time, they may have added 1 to $1\frac{1}{2}$ percent per year to the stated rate of inflation as measured by the CPI. Recent changes in methodology are thought to have reduced the bias, but it is still probably in the range of $\frac{1}{2}$ to 1 percent per year.

Today's basic laptop costs about half of what an electromechanical calculator went for in the 1960s.

**NONMATERIAL SOURCES OF WELFARE**    The final problem with GDP is that it measures only material sources of welfare (which, after all, is all it tries to do). Sometimes per capita GDP is used as an indication of living standards; but when one is comparing living standards over time and across countries, nonmaterial sources of welfare are important, too.

One key nonmaterial component of the standard of living is the quality of the environment. This not only varies widely from one place to another but also has changed greatly over time. Problems of global warming and toxic wastes are "bads" that, in principle, should be subtracted from GDP just as "goods" are added to it. In the same spirit, Robert Repetto of the World Resources Institute in Washington, D.C., recommends that depletion of such natural resources as oil fields and tropical forests should be subtracted along with the capital consumption allowance when calculating net domestic product. For countries such as Indonesia and Brazil, which have used huge quantities of natural resources, the effect of this adjustment could cut measured rates of economic growth nearly in half.

A second nonmaterial source of welfare is the state of human health. By broad measures, especially life expectancy, standards of health in the United States appear to be improving. For example, since World War II the life expectancy of a typical 45-year-old American has increased from 72 years to 77, and a 65-year-old American can now expect to live to the age of 81. This increase clearly improves human welfare even for people who add nothing to measured GDP after they retire from their jobs. If the improvement in health could be measured, it would add to the growth of U.S. GDP. On the other hand, such an adjustment would make the economic picture look even bleaker in a country like Russia, where health indicators such as life expectancy and infant mortality have gotten worse in recent years.

Education and literacy also contribute to human welfare, independently of income level. The United Nations Development Program publishes an index called the Human Development Index (HDI) that combines information on health, education, and literacy with real GDP. According to the HDI for 2008, Iceland, Norway, and Canada had the world's best standard of living. The United States ranked fifteenth out of 179 countries studied. Mostly countries of Sub-Saharan Africa populate the bottom of the list.

The HDI is hardly the last word in alternative measures of welfare. It contains no environmental component, except to the extent environmental quality has an impact on health. The HDI also pays no attention to human rights, political freedom, or corruption—all of which are arguably important for human welfare. In short, despite all of its defects, GDP remains the most widely used measure for international comparisons of economic achievement.

# Summary

1. **How is gross domestic product officially defined and measured?** Two domestic product concepts are featured in the official accounts of the United States. *Gross domestic product (GDP)* is defined as the value at current market prices of all *final goods and services* produced annually in a given country. *Gross national product* is the product produced by a country's factors of production, regardless of what country they are located in. *Net domestic product* is derived from GDP by subtracting an allowance for consumption of fixed capital that reflects the value of capital goods worn out during the year.

2. **How does the measurement of domestic income differ from the measurement of gross domestic product?** *Domestic income* is the sum of wages and supplements, rental income of persons, corporate profits, and proprietors' income earned in a country. In principle, domestic income and gross domestic product should be equal but in the official accounts, they differ because of the capital consumption allowance, indirect business taxes, and a statistical discrepancy that results from the use of different data sources for income and product measurements.

3. **What are the major types of international transactions?** Many types of transactions appear in the nation's international accounts. Exports less imports of goods constitute the *merchandise balance*. Adding services yields net exports of goods and services. Adding net international transfers (normally a negative number for the United States) yields the most widely publicized measure, the *current account balance*. In addition, the international accounts record financial inflows and outflows resulting from private financial transactions and official reserve transactions by the Federal Reserve and foreign central banks.

4. **How are changes in the average level of prices measured?** The *GDP deflator* is the most broadly based measure of the *price level*. It can be viewed as a weighted average of the prices of all final goods and services that go into GDP. The *consumer price index (CPI)* includes only the market basket of goods purchased by a typical urban household. The *producer price index (PPI)* is based on goods that are typically bought and sold by business firms.

5. **What are the limitations of official economic statistics?** The national income statistics of the United States are considered to be among the best in the world. However, they have some limitations. Potential problem areas include timeliness of data, the unobserved sector of the economy, price index biases, and nonmaterial aspects of the standard of living.

## Key Terms

## Problems and Topics for Discussion

1. **Updating the national income accounts** Data on national income accounts and international transactions for the United States are available from several sources on the Internet. Two of the easiest to use are the tables attached to each year's *Economic Report of the President* (http://www.gpoaccess.gov/eop) and those given by the Commerce Department's Bureau of Economic Analysis (http://www.bea.gov) Using one of these sources, update the tables in this chapter to the most recent year or quarter. If you do not live in the United States, search the Internet for similar data for your home country and compare them to the U.S. data given in this chapter.

2. **Inventory in the national income accounts** Suppose that a firm sells $10,000 worth of shoes that it has held in inventory for several years. What happens to GDP as a result? Which of its components are affected, and how?

3. **International accounts** Following the pattern in Table 6.4, show how the international accounts might look for a year in which there was a $50 billion surplus on current account, no official reserve transactions, and no statistical discrepancy. What would the capital and financial account balance have to be?

4. **The current account deficit** "A current account deficit is a very healthy thing. If we can get foreigners to give us real goods and services and talk them into taking pieces of paper in return, why should we want anything different?" Do you agree or disagree with this statement? Discuss.

5. **Real and nominal quantities** From 1982 to 1984, the base period used for the consumer price index, the average earnings of construction workers were $442.74 per week. By 1989 the earnings of construction workers had reached $506.72 per week, but the consumer price index had risen to 124.0. What were construction workers' real earnings in 1989 stated in 1982–1984 dollars?

6. **Changes in prices and qualities** Try to find a mail-order catalog or similar price list of common consumer items that is at least 10 years old. By how much has the price of each item changed? What changes in quality have occurred? Assuming that you could buy at list price from either the old list or the new one, which old items would you buy and which new items?

## Case for Discussion

*Laid-Off Steel Workers Join the Underground Economy*

**HOMESTEAD, PA** A half-dozen men lounge on metal folding chairs outside a storefront on Ann Street, sweating in the muggy afternoon air and talking baseball. A pay phone rings inside, and a young man runs to answer it. Moments later, he speeds off in a long, beat-up sedan.

The man is about to cheat the government. He and the other men drive people around town for a fee, but they don't pay any taxes on the fares they receive. What's more, they don't see why they should.

Most of the men used to work at the sprawling Homestead Works a half block away. Now that the steel mill has closed, their car service allows them to make a living. "It ain't bothering anyone. It ain't stealing," says Earl Jones, who was laid off last December after 36 years at the mill. How much does he make? "Ain't saying," he replies with a smile.

The men are part of a vast underground economy made up of people who work "off the books" for cash. From the tired mill towns of the Midwest to the oil patches dotting the Southwest, the underground thrives. In communities that have suddenly lost a major employer, it helps those who were laid off make ends meet, and it helps keep towns like Homestead alive.

The number of Homestead residents with off-the-books livelihoods began to increase in the early 1980s when USX Corporation's Homestead Works, which employed about 15,000 at its peak, started to lay off workers in droves. The mill's few remaining workers lost their jobs early in 1986. For most residents here, where only half the people have their high-school diplomas, the mill was all there was.

After they were laid off, many older workers retired and some of the younger ones withdrew their savings and migrated south, chasing dreams of work in more prosperous states. However, many others stayed, bound by their unmarketable homes, their families, or a strong sense of community. Unable to find legitimate jobs, they have parlayed their handyman skills underground.

One former mill worker says that half the people he knows are working off the books. For the most part, they are intensely proud people who hang the American flag from their neat front porches on holidays and respect the law, believing strongly in right and wrong. They definitely don't like the underground's seamy side—thefts and drugs; but their changed circumstances have altered the way many of them think.

"You tell me. Your kids go to bed crying at night because they're hungry. Is 'off the books' going to bother you?" asks a former steelworker.

SOURCE: Clare Ansberry, "Laid-Off Steelworkers Find That Tax Evasion Helps Make Ends Meet," *The Wall Street Journal,* October 1, 1986, 1. Reprinted by permission of *The Wall Street Journal,* © Dow Jones & Company, Inc., 1986. All Rights Reserved Worldwide.

## QUESTIONS

1. What are the advantages of working "off the books" from the viewpoint of the people involved?
2. How might the failure to measure off-the-books activity affect economic policy decisions?
3. How might off-the-books work affect the statistical discrepancy in the national income accounts?

## End Notes

1. Following the same logic, it is also possible to calculate *Gross National Product (GNP),* a measure of goods and services produced by factors of production owned by a country's residents, including factors of production physically located in another country. Until the early 1990s, U.S. accounts emphasized GNP rather than GDP. In practice, the difference between GDP and GNP is small for the United States.
2. The source for much of the material in this section is J. Steven Landefeld, Eugene P. Seskin, and Barbara Fraumeni, "Taking the Pulse of the Economy: Measuring GDP," *Journal of Economic Perspectives* (Spring 2008): 193–216.

# Appendix to Chapter 6:
# COMPUTATION OF PRICE INDEXES

This appendix provides further details on how price indexes are calculated. An understanding of these details will make it easier to see the differences among various price indexes and to understand the source of the substitution bias, which affects each index differently.

## The GDP Deflator for a Simple Economy

A much simpler economy than that of the United States will serve to illustrate the computation of price indexes. Table 6A.1 shows price and quantity data for two years for an economy in which only three goods are produced: movies, apples, and shirts. The exhibit shows that nominal GDP grew from $1,000 in 2000 to $1,700 in 2010. What do these figures indicate? Do they mean that people really had more of the things they wanted in 2010 than in 2000? More precisely, do they mean that people had 1.7 times as much? These questions cannot be easily answered by looking at the exhibit in its present form.

A line-by-line comparison of the two years shows that the figures on nominal product do not tell the whole story. The prices of movies, apples, and shirts all went up sharply between 2000 and 2010. The amounts of goods produced have also changed. Twice as many movies and shirts were produced in 2010 as in 2000, but only half as many apples.

If we wish to know how much better off people were in 2010 than in 2000, we need a way to separate the quantity changes that have taken place from the price changes. One way to do this is to ask how much the total value of output would have changed

| TABLE 6A.1 | NOMINAL GDP FOR A SIMPLE ECONOMY | | |
|---|---|---|---|
| **2000** | **Quantity** | **Price** | **Value** |
| Movies | 50 | $ 5.00 | $ 250 |
| Apples | 1,000 | .60 | 600 |
| Shirts | 10 | 15.00 | 150 |
| 2000 nominal GDP | | | $ 1,000 |
| **2010** | | | |
| Movies | 100 | $ 6.00 | $ 600 |
| Apples | 500 | 1.20 | 600 |
| Shirts | 20 | 20.00 | 400 |
| 2010 nominal GDP | | | $1,600 |

In this simple economy in which only three goods are produced, nominal domestic product grew from $1,000 in 2000 to $1600 in 2010. Because prices also went up during that time, people did not really have 1.6 times as many goods in 2010 as they did in 2000.

from 2000 to 2010 if prices had not changed. This approach gives the results shown in Table 6A.2. There we see that the 2010 output of 100 movies, 500 apples, and 20 shirts, which had a value of $1,600 in terms of the prices at which the goods were actually sold, would have had a value of only $1,100 in terms of the prices that prevailed in 2000. This figure of $1,100 is a measure of real GDP for 2010, which can be compared with the 2000 GDP of $1,000 to give a clearer idea of what happened to output between the two years. Instead of having 180 percent as much output in 2010 as in 2000, as indicated by the change in nominal GDP from $1,000 to $1,600, the people in this simple economy really had only about 110 percent as much, as indicated by the change in real GDP from $1,000 to $1,100.

In computing real GDP for 2010, we have not explicitly used a price index, but we have created one implicitly. This implicit index, or implicit GDP deflator, is the ratio of current-year nominal GDP to current-year real GDP times 100, as expressed in index form by the following formula:

$$\text{GDP deflator} = \frac{\text{Current-year output valued at current-year prices}}{\text{Current-year output valued at base-year prices}} \times 100.$$

Applying the formula to the data in Tables 6A.1 and 6A.2 gives a value of 145 for the deflator.

## The Consumer Price Index for a Simple Economy

The consumer price index differs from the GDP deflator in two ways. First, it takes into account only the prices of goods and services purchased by consumers. Second, it is calculated according to a formula that uses base-year rather than current-year quantities.

### TABLE 6A.2    NOMINAL AND REAL GDP FOR A SIMPLE ECONOMY

| Good | 2010 Quantity | 2010 Price | Value of 2010 Quantity at 2010 Price | 2000 Price | Value of 2010 Quantity at 2000 Price |
|------|------|------|------|------|------|
| Movies | 100 | $ 6.00 | 600 | $ 5.00 | $ 500 |
| Apples | 500 | 1.20 | 600 | .60 | 300 |
| Shirts | 20 | 20.00 | 400 | 15.00 | 300 |
| Totals | | | $ 1,600 | | $ 1,100 |

**2010 nominal GDP = $1,600; 2010 real GDP = $1,100**

This table shows how the figures from Table 6A.1 can be adjusted to take changing prices into account. The 2010 quantities are multiplied by 2000 prices to get the value of 2010 GDP that would have existed had prices not changed. The total of 2010 quantities valued at 2000 prices is a measure of real GDP for 2010 stated in constant 2000 dollars. The implicit GDP deflator for 2010, calculated as the ratio of 2010 nominal GDP to 2000 real GDP, has a value of 145.

The first difference does not matter for this simple economy in which all goods are consumer goods; but the second one does, as Table 6A.3 shows.

To calculate the CPI for this economy, instead of asking how much current-year output would have cost at base-year prices, we begin by asking how much base-year output would have cost at current-year prices. We then calculate the index as the ratio of the two different valuations of base-year quantities:

$$\text{Consumer price index} = \frac{\text{Base-year market basket valued at current-year prices}}{\text{Base-year market basket valued at base-year prices}} \times 100.$$

The CPI is calculated using base-year quantities partly because data on current prices are easier to collect than data on current output. This index, therefore, can be announced each month with little delay.

## Comparing the CPI and the GDP Deflator

As Table 6A.3 shows, the CPI for 2010 in our simple economy had a value of 145.0, whereas the GDP deflator for 2010 was 154.5. Both indexes were calculated using the same data, and both used 2000 as a base year. Which, if either, is the true measure of the change in prices between the two years?

The answer is that neither the CPI nor the GDP deflator is a "true" measure of change in the price level; instead, each answers a different question. The GDP deflator answers the question, "How much more did the 2010 output cost at the prices at which it was actually sold than it would have cost had it been sold at 2000 prices?" The CPI, in contrast, answers the question, "How much more would the 2000 output have cost had it been sold at 2010 prices instead of at 2000 prices?"

---

**TABLE 6A.3   A CONSUMER PRICE INDEX FOR A SIMPLE ECONOMY**

| Good | 2000 Quantity | 2000 Price | Value of 2000 Quantity at 2000 Price | 2010 Price | Value of 2000 Quantity at 2010 Price |
|------|---------------|------------|--------------------------------------|------------|--------------------------------------|
| Movies | 50 | $ 5.00 | 250 | $ 6.00 | $ 300 |
| Apples | 1,000 | .60 | 600 | 1.20 | 1,200 |
| Shirts | 10 | 15.00 | 150 | 20.00 | 200 |
| Totals | | | $ 1,000 | | $ 1,700 |

$$\text{CPI} = \frac{\$1,700}{\$1,000} \times 100 = 170.0$$

The consumer price index can be calculated as the base-year market basket of goods valued at current-year prices divided by the base-year market basket valued at base-year prices multiplied by 100. This table shows how such an index can be calculated for a simple economy. The 2000 output cost $1,000 at the prices at which it was actually sold. Had it been sold at 2010 prices, it would have cost $1700. The CPI for 2010 is 170.

A close look at the data shows why the answers to the two questions differ. In 2000, lots of apples were produced compared with 2010, while fewer shirts and movies were produced. Between the two years the price of apples doubled while the price of shirts increased by just 25 percent and that of movies by just 20 percent. Because the CPI uses base-year quantities, it gives a heavy weight to apples, which showed the largest relative price increase, and a lower weight to shirts and movies, which showed smaller price increases. In contrast, the GDP deflator uses current-year quantities, thereby decreasing the importance of apples and increasing that of movies and shirts.

Because people will tend to substitute purchases away from items with faster growth in prices, the CPI tends to have an upward substitution bias relative to the GDP deflator, as is the case in our example. However, that does not make the GDP deflator a true measure of change in the cost of living. It could just as easily be said that the GDP deflator has a downward substitution bias relative to the CPI. There are still other ways of calculating price indexes that give a value between those shown. The bottom line is that there is no "true" measure of the cost of living. In practice, the methods shown here, despite their inherent biases, are the most commonly used.

# PART 3

## Banking, Money, and the Financial System

# CHAPTER 7

# The Banking System and Regulation

**After reading this chapter, you will understand the following:**

1. What banks and their key financial tasks are
2. The main items on a bank's balance sheet
3. The traditional originate-to-hold model of banking
4. The risks of banking
5. The originate-to-distribute model of banking
6. Policies that aim to maintain the safety and stability of the banking system
7. The meaning of systemic failure of the banking system

**Before reading this chapter, make sure you know the meaning of the concepts:**

1. Circular flow of income and expenditure
2. Financial markets
3. Price level

THE FINANCIAL SECTOR occupies a strategic position at the very heart of the circular flow of income and product. It gathers savings from households and directs those savings to investments in new capital, without which long-term growth of the economy is impossible. The financial sector, also, has an important short-term function in redirecting the surpluses and deficits of the government, household, and foreign sectors in a way that keeps the circular flow in balance. This chapter and the following focus on the financial sector. We begin this chapter with an examination of the banking system. Chapter 8 introduces the concept of money and explains the instruments used to conduct monetary policy. The ideas presented in these chapters will form the basis for the further exploration of macroeconomic policy in the rest of the book.

# The Banking System

For most of us, the banking system is our first point of contact with the financial system. Banks help us with three important financial needs. First, they assist in making payments by check, debit card, and Internet banking transfers; and they also facilitate cash payments by supplying currency through ATMs and over the counter in bank branches. Second, they help us manage cash flows over time by accepting deposits of funds that we want to set aside for later use. Third, they help us manage risks when they make loans for promising, but less-than-certain, business ventures.

In this book, we use the term **bank,** in a general sense, to refer to all financial institutions that accept deposits and make loans. A more detailed discussion of banking in the United States would distinguish between several kinds of depository institutions. The largest and most important are *commercial banks*. These usually include the word bank in their names. Historically, they specialized in business loans and deposits. *Thrift institutions*, which include *savings and loan associations* and *mutual savings banks*, historically specialized in consumer saving deposits and home mortgage lending. *Credit unions* are small financial intermediaries organized as cooperative enterprises by employee groups, union members, or certain other groups with shared work or community ties.

Since the 1980s, the historical distinctions among these four types of institutions have become blurred. We will use the simple term *bank* to refer to all of them except when there is a particular reason to single out one type of institution. In fact, at times we will find it difficult to confine our focus to banks even in the broad sense. Increasingly, commercial banks, investment banks, mutual funds, hedge funds, pension funds, and even insurance companies have spread out and overlapped to the point that they share in the core functions of the financial system.

In addition to the private banks and related financial institutions that serve the needs of firms and households, every country also has a **central bank**, which is a government agency responsible for regulating the banking system and carrying out monetary policy. In the United States, the central bank is called the **Federal Reserve System** or, for short, simply **the Fed**. The Federal Reserve System consists of twelve regional Federal Reserve Banks whose policies are controlled by a Board of Governors located in Washington, D.C. The regulatory functions of the Fed will be discussed later in this chapter, and its monetary policy functions in later chapters.

## The Banking Balance Sheet

The operations of a commercial bank can best be understood by reference to its balance sheet. A firm's or household's **balance sheet** is a financial statement showing what it owns and what it owes or, to use more technical language, its *assets, liabilities*, and *net worth*. **Assets**, which are listed on the left-hand side of the balance sheet, are all the things that the firm or household owns or to which it holds a legal

---

**Bank**

A financial institution whose principal business consists of accepting deposits and making loans

**Central bank**

A government agency responsible for carrying out monetary policy and often, also, for regulating the country's banking system

**Federal Reserve System (the Fed)**

The central bank of the United States, consisting of twelve regional Federal Reserve Banks and a Board of Governors in Washington, D.C.

**Balance sheet**

A financial statement showing what a firm or household owns and what it owes

**Assets**

All the things that the firm or household owns or to which it holds a legal claim

## Liabilities

All the legal claims against a firm by nonowners or against a household by nonmembers

## Net worth

A firm's or household's assets minus its liabilities, also called *equity* or *capital*

## Vault cash

Paper currency and coins that are held by banks as part of their reserves of liquid assets

## Transaction deposit

A deposit from which funds can be freely withdrawn by check or electronic transfer to make payments to third parties

claim. **Liabilities**, which are listed on the right-hand side of the balance sheet, are all the legal claims against a firm by nonowners or against a household by nonmembers. **Net worth**, also listed on the right-hand side of the balance sheet, is equal to the firm's or household's assets minus its liabilities. In a business firm, net worth represents the owners' claims against the business. *Equity* is another term that is often used to refer to net worth. In banking circles, net worth is often referred to as *capital.*

The balance sheet gets its name from the fact that the totals of the two sides always balance. This follows from the definition of net worth because net worth is defined as assets minus liabilities; liabilities plus net worth must equal assets. In equation form, this basic rule of accounting reads as follows:

$$\text{Assets} = \text{Liabilities} + \text{Net worth}$$

Table 7.1 shows a total balance sheet for U.S. commercial banks. On the assets side of the balance sheet, the first line, cash items, includes deposits that individual banks maintain with the Federal Reserve System, as well as paper currency and coins that banks keep in their own vaults. Paper currency and coins held by banks are known as **vault cash**. The next two items on the asset side of the balance sheet show the bank's main income-earning assets. The largest item is loans made to firms and households. In addition, commercial banks hold a substantial quantity of securities, including private securities and those issued by federal, state, and local governments. The final asset item includes some smaller income-earning items plus the value of the bank's buildings and equipment.

The first two items on the liabilities side of the bank balance sheet include various kinds of deposits. **Transaction deposits** are deposits from which funds can be withdrawn freely by check or electronic transfer to make payments to other parties.

### TABLE 7.1  TOTAL BALANCE SHEET FOR U.S. COMMERCIAL BANKS, JANUARY 2009 (BILLIONS OF DOLLARS)

| Assets | | Liabilities | |
|---|---|---|---|
| Cash items | $ 976.2 | Transaction deposits | $ 703.4 |
| Securities | $ 2,736.4 | Nontransaction deposits | $ 6,656.8 |
| Loans | $ 7,116.4 | Bank borrowing | $ 2,443.9 |
| Other assets | $ 1,397.2 | Other liabilities | $ 1,244.2 |
| | | | |
| Total assets | $12,226.2 | Total liabilities | $11,048.3 |
| | | Net worth (capital) | $ 1,177.9 |
| | | Total liabilities plus net worth | $12,226.2 |

This table shows the total balance sheet for all U.S. commercial banks as of January 2009. Assets of banks include cash, securities, and loans. Liabilities include deposits of all kinds and other borrowings. Net worth (capital) equals assets minus liabilities.

SOURCE: Board of Governors of the Federal Reserve System, *H.8 Statistical Release*, Feb. 20, 2009.

Transaction deposits sometimes go by other names, as well. In the United States, they are often known as checking deposits or demand deposits. In some countries, they are called current accounts. Nontransaction deposits include saving deposits, certificates of deposits, and others deposits which may be subject to some restrictions on the timing of withdrawals or on the use of funds for making payments. Banks also borrow money from other banks and non-bank institutions, and in relatively small amounts from the Fed. Because the banks' total liabilities are less than their assets, they have a positive net worth. This sum represents the claim of the banks' owners against the banks' assets.

## Traditional Banking: Originate to Hold

Banks, as private institutions, are in business to make a profit. Their traditional business model emphasizes profits earned by charging interest rates on loans that are higher than those paid on deposits. Furthermore, it was the traditional practice of banks to *originate* loans (banking terminology for lending money to someone) and then to hold those loans to maturity, that is, until all principal and interest payments were made in full. This traditional business model has come to be known as the **originate-to-hold model of banking**.

**Originate-to-hold model**

A model of banking that emphasized making loans, and then holding the loans until maturity

One reason for the prevalence of the originate-to-hold model in traditional banking was the difficulty of selling individual loans. When a bank first makes a loan, it investigates the creditworthiness of the borrower, including the borrower's reputation, income available for repayment, availability of collateral, and exposure to risk. Over time, the bank learns more about the borrower. Perhaps it finds out that the borrower is even more reliable than first thought, or perhaps unforeseen difficulties make it harder than first thought for the borrower to meet the terms of the loans. Some of this knowledge may be easily expressed in hard facts and numbers, while other knowledge may be based more on intuition and experience. As this knowledge accumulates, banks are able to classify loans as being of higher or lower quality.

This situation can create problems when a bank tries to sell a loan to another bank or an outside investor. Suppose that two years ago, your bank made a five-year loan for $100,000 to Ace Co.; and now you offer to sell this loan to my bank. I can easily calculate the mathematical value of the three years' worth of interest and principal payments remaining on the loan, but something bothers me. Why is it, I ask myself, that you want to sell *that particular* loan? Maybe you know something about Ace Co. and its ability to make payments that I do not. After all, if Ace were an exceptionally good customer, why would you want to sell its loan? Maybe the reason you are selling the Ace loan is that it is a "lemon"—a loan that looks good on paper but is really at risk of going sour. To guard against the risk that the Ace loan is a lemon, I must offer you a price that is a substantial discount from what the paperwork indicates the loan's value to be. Anticipating my caution, your bank, as originator, would be reluctant to put any good loans up for sale, knowing that they could only be sold at a deep discount. This "lemons problem," as it has come to be called, hampered the development of an active secondary market for loans and left banks with little choice but to hold loans to maturity.

## The Risks of Banking

While banking can be a very profitable business, it is also risky. Three of the risks faced by banks are particularly important for understanding the problems that banks and other financial institutions have encountered in recent years.

**CREDIT RISK**  The first major risk faced by banks is *credit risk*—the possibility that borrowers will not be able to repay their loans on time or in full. Banks' first line of defense against credit risk is to carefully evaluate the creditworthiness of borrowers before they make a loan. However, banks would not be doing their job if they made loans only to customers who were 100 percent sure to repay. For household loans, there is always some risk that loss of a job, illness, or some other expected event will make repayment impossible. For businesses, a downturn in the business cycle, introduction of a superior product by competitors, or rising prices of inputs may make a seemingly sound project turn out to be unprofitable and prevent repayment of the loan used to finance it. Even in good times, then, banks do not expect every single loan to be paid on time and in full.

As shown in Table 7.1, banks list loans as assets on their balance sheets, based on the assumption that they will be repaid. If a borrower falls behind or defaults completely, the value of that loan as an asset decreases, possibly all the way to zero. According to the basic equation of accounting, capital is equal to assets minus liabilities; so if the value of a bank's assets falls, while its liabilities (deposits and others) remains the same, its capital will decrease. When a bank's capital falls to zero, it is said to be **insolvent**; and it must cease operation.

**Insolvency**

A state of affairs in which the net worth (capital) of a bank or other business falls to zero

To guard against insolvency, banks must be sure they have an adequate cushion of capital, so that borrowers' default on one or a few loans does not push their capital too close to the line of insolvency. Table 7.1 shows that as of January 2009, U.S. commercial banks had capital equal to about 9 percent of their total assets. That level was considered adequate, on average, although some individual banks were closer to the danger level, or even below it. In fact, several banks had become insolvent, or dangerously close to it, during the previous year and had either been closed by regulators or had to merge with other, healthier banks.

**MARKET RISK**  The second major risk of banking is *market risk*. Market risk refers to any change in market conditions that causes a loss of value of assets or an increase in the burden of liabilities. Changes in interest rates are one among several kinds of market risk. An unexpected increase in interest rates can lower the market value of bonds or other securities that a bank holds as assets, thereby reducing the bank's capital. An increase in interest rates can also increase the burden of liabilities, for example, by increasing the interest a bank must pay on deposits and thereby undermining profitability.

Banks have a number of tactics that they can use to manage market risk, for example, by making variable rate loans that automatically adjust to changing market conditions. None of the available management methods completely free banks from market risk, however. Market risk is thus a second reason why banks must be careful to maintain an adequate cushion of capital.

**Liquidity**

An asset's ability to be used directly as a means of payment, or to be readily converted into one, while retaining a fixed nominal value

**LIQUIDITY RISK**    The third major risk that banks face is called *liquidity risk*. In finance, an asset is said to be **liquid** if it can be used directly as a means of payment or easily converted to cash without loss of nominal value. Currency and bank deposits are example of liquid assets. The special deposits that banks hold with the Fed are also completely liquid. Bonds and other securities that banks own are not completely liquid because their market price changes from day to day, and also because it may be hard to find a buyer for them under distressed market conditions. Loans that banks hold as assets also are not fully liquid. As explained above, the lemons problem and other considerations often make it difficult for a bank to sell loans at a realistic value.

Liquidity risk arises when circumstances force banks to sell illiquid assets, like bonds or loans, at a price lower than their value as stated on the balance sheet. One kind of circumstance that can cause liquidity problems is a loss of deposits. Depositors have the right to pull funds out of a bank on short notice; and, if they do so, the bank can be forced to sell illiquid assets at a loss. Another possible source of liquidity problems for a bank is the refusal of other banks, or non-bank lenders, to continue supplying the borrowed funds that, in addition to deposits, appear on the balance sheet as liabilities. Still another source of liquidity problems is the possibility that a bank may quickly need to raise funds to make a new loan to a valued customer or meet some other contractual commitment to make loans or buy assets.

**Reserves**

Cash in bank vaults and banks' deposits with the Federal Reserve System

As in the case of other risks, banks have several tools they can use to manage liquidity risks. One of the most basic is to hold a certain level of **reserves** in the form of vault cash or deposits with the Fed. The entry "cash items" in Table 7.1 represents banks' liquid reserves. There is an opportunity cost to this line of defense, however. Vault cash and reserve deposits at the Fed pay either no interest at all or low rates relative to other market interest rates. An alternative to cash reserves is for banks to hold

Vault cash and deposits with the Fed are among the tools banks use to manage liquidity risk.

government securities like Treasury bills which pay a little more interest than cash and can be sold quickly if the need arises. Still another defense against liquidity risk is to maintain good relations with other banks and non-bank lenders from which cash can quickly be borrowed when the need arises, or even to borrow directly from the Fed itself. None of these defenses against liquidity risk is foolproof, however. If, despite its best defenses, a bank is forced to sell assets at a cut-rate price, the bank's capital will fall and it can be threatened with insolvency.

## Modern Banking: Originate to Distribute

In one form or another, banks have been a part of economic life for hundreds of years. In some ways, the basic business of banking has remained the same. Today, as in the past, the main business of banking remains that of accepting deposits and making loans. In other ways, however, banking is constantly changing. For example, at one time banks held most of their reserves in the form of gold coin. They issued their own paper banknotes as liabilities, which their customers used instead of the government-issued paper currency we are familiar with today. The kinds of assets and liabilities that appear on bank balance sheets have changed in many other ways, as well.

**Originate-to-distribute model**

A model of banking that emphasizes the sale of loans soon after they are made, and use of the proceeds from the sale to make new loans

One of the most significant changes of recent years has been a move away from the traditional originate-to-hold model of banking to a new model in which banks are able to sell many kinds of loans soon after they are made and use the cash raised from those sales to make new loans. This new business model is called **originate-to-distribute**. The originate-to-distribute model has several potential benefits, both for banks and their customers.

First, because banks can turn over money faster, they can originate more loans. As a result, they can earn more income from fees to supplement their traditional income from the spread between interest rates on loans and those on deposits. Some of the new income comes from up-front fees charged to borrowers when loans are first made. For home mortgages, these fees are popularly called "points," and often amount to 1 percent or more of the amount loaned. For some kinds of business loans, the fees are even greater. Sometimes after banks sell loans to third parties, they continue to do the work of "servicing" the loans, that is, sending out statements, maintaining tax and insurance escrows, and dealing with delinquent borrowers. They are paid a separate servicing fee for doing this work even if some new owner of the loan receives the principal and interest payments. For many banks, fees from loan originations, loan servicing, and other financial services are now more important than interest income.

Second, the originate-to-distribute model gives banks a new tool for managing credit risk. Once a loan has been sold, the new owner bears the risk of default, which frees the originating bank from the need to maintain capital to guard against the credit risk. From the point of view of the financial system as a whole, originate-to-distribute banking has the potential to move credit risk to parties who are best able to bear it.

Third, the originate-to-distribute model benefits bank customers by making a much larger volume of credit available. Under the traditional originate-to-hold model, a bank's ability to expand its assets by making new loans was limited by the need to maintain a cushion of capital to guard against risk. Once a bank's assets increased to the maximum allowed by its available capital, it was "loaned up" and could only make new loans as old ones were paid off. Instead, under the originate-to-distribute model, banks can make as many loans as they can find creditworthy borrowers. Because the loans are quickly moved off their books, less capital is tied up and total lending expands.

## Securitization

In order for the originate-to-distribute model of banking to become widespread, a way had to be found to overcome the lemons problem, which had traditionally hampered the sale of loans by the originating bank. The tool developed to do this was **securitization**. The basic concept of securitization is easy to understand, although refinements and variations can make things very complex.

The first step in securitization is to form a specialized financial intermediary whose job is to act as a go-between to facilitate the sale of the loan to potential investors. The best known of these specialized intermediaries are Fannie Mae and Freddie Mac, which specialize in home mortgage loans. The roots of these organizations go all the way back to the 1930s. They are called **Government Sponsored Enterprises (GSEs)**, which means they are privately owned but backed and partially controlled by the government. In addition to the GSEs, private intermediaries that have the legal form of trusts and are sponsored by banks or other financial institutions carry out many securitizations.

The second step in securitization is the purchase by the intermediary of a pool of assets. For example, the pool of assets might consist of 10,000 home mortgage loans worth a total of $1,000 million, which the intermediary buys from the banks that have originated them. This pool of loans provides a stream of income to the intermediary in the form of the principal and interest payments that borrowers make on the loans.

The third step in securitization is for the intermediary to issue securities, backed by the income from the pool of mortgages, which are then sold to investors. The simplest way to do this is to issue *pass-through bonds*, which give each bondholder an equal share in all of the interest and principal payments received from the pool of mortgages. For example, if 1 million pass-through bonds are sold, and the original pool of loans produces total income of $100 million per year, each bond will pay $100 per year to the investor who buys it. The income will continue until all of the original mortgages are paid off. If any of the borrowers default on their mortgages, less income will be available; and the loss will be distributed evenly among all investors. The even distribution of income and losses goes a long way to overcoming the lemons problem because now no single investor runs the risk of being stuck with a "lemon" mortgage and suffering a total loss. Instead, all investors share both the good and the bad.

As securitization developed over the years, intermediaries found many ways to improve on the original idea of simple pass-through bonds. One widely used technique is to issue several different kinds of securities that appeal to the preferences for risk versus return of different kinds of investors. Each type of security issued is called a *tranche*. Securities in senior tranches give the investors who buy them the first right to receive payments of interest and principal on the pool of mortgages and place them

## Securitization

A process in which a specialized financial intermediary assembles a large pool of loans (or other assets) and uses those loans as a basis for issuing its own securities for sale to investors

## Government Sponsored Enterprises (GSEs)

Privately owned but government-sponsored specialized intermediaries that engage in the business of securitizing home mortgage loans and, sometimes, other loans

last in line to bear losses from defaults. Investors in tranches are first in line to bear losses and last in line to receive income. Obviously, the tranches have to be sold at a deep discount in order to attract buyers, but some buyers with a high tolerance for risk will be willing to buy them if the price is low enough. The senior tranches, in contrast, appeal to investors with low tolerance for risk, who are willing to accept a lower return if the investment is relatively safe. This technique is so successful that some securitizations have involved the issue of thirty or more different tranches, each tailored to the risk preferences of specific kinds of investors.

Another way for intermediaries to improve the marketability of the securities they issue is to obtain a *rating* from a nationally recognized, statistical rating organization like Standard and Poor's, Moody's Investor Services, or Fitch Ratings. The rating agencies analyze the likely risks and rewards of each tranche of securities, giving them ratings like AAA, B, or C that show them to be of low, medium, or high risk. Investors who rely on the analysis done by the ratings agencies save costs of hiring their own analysts to do the complex work of judging the risk associated with any given security.

**Credit default swap**

An arrangement in which one party buys protection against the risk of default on a bond by paying an agreed premium to another party, the seller of protection, in return for which the protection seller agrees to compensate the protection buyer if the bond is not paid in full and on time

Still another financial innovation of recent years, **credit default swaps**, give investors a different kind of tool to protect themselves against the risk of owning securities, including both ordinary corporate bonds and financial instruments issued as a result of securitization. In a credit default swap, one party, the buyer of protection, pays an agreed premium to another party, the seller of protection. In return, the protection seller agrees to compensate the protection buyer if the bond is not paid in full and on time. If the bond turns out to be good, the protection seller profits from the premium received. If the bond defaults, compensation is paid to the protection buyer and the loss is borne by the protection seller. Credit default swaps are, in effect, a kind of insurance against the risk of default on a bond.

A schematic representation of the securitization process is given in Figure 7.1. The figure is somewhat simplified in that it shows the securities issued by intermediaries as being sold directly to investors. In practice, the process can be more complicated. Sometimes the securities issued by one intermediary are purchased by another intermediary that uses them as a basis for further securitizations. Sometimes the "investor" who purchases the securities is itself another kind of intermediary, like an insurance company, a mutual fund, or a hedge fund, that gets its money from other investors still further down the line.

## New Types of Mortgages

Securitization was one important innovation that allowed rapid expansion of credit markets during the early 2000s, but it was not the only one. New types of mortgages were also developed that made it possible to extend credit to families who had previously not found it possible to borrow.

As long ago as the early 1970s, people who studied housing policy became concerned that the market worked well only for middle- and upper-income families. For the most part, lower-income families were frozen out of the mortgage market. Some of the problem appeared to arise from "redlining"—a term applied to discrimination based on race or

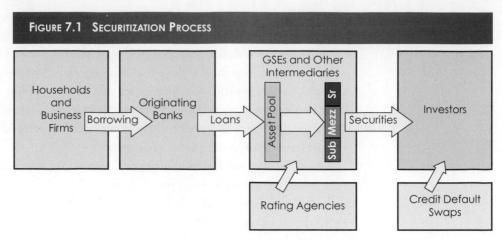

**FIGURE 7.1  SECURITIZATION PROCESS**

In this simplified presentation, the securitization process begins when households and firms borrow from originating banks. The banks then sell the loans to Government Sponsored Enterprises and other specialized intermediaries, who issue securities based on pools of loans or other assets that they buy. The securities are divided in "tranches" of senior (low risk), mezzanine (medium risk), and subordinate (high risk) securities. Each type of security is given a rating by an independent rating agency. The securities are sold to investors, who buy the type of security that best fits their appetite for return versus risk. Investors can further protect themselves against risk by means of credit default swaps.

neighborhood of residence. However, even after the 1977 Community Reinvestment Act restricted redlining, it remained difficult for low-income families to get a mortgage.

When bankers were confronted with this fact, they had a simple explanation. They did not make mortgage loans to low-income families because such loans were too risky to be profitable. Low-income families could not afford the fixed interest rates and high down payments that "prime" borrowers paid. If down payments and interest rates were cut by enough to make them affordable to low-income families, the risk of default would rise; and then the loans would be unprofitable.

In the late 1990s, a combination of pressure from policymakers and innovations by lenders led to the development of new types of loans that could make home ownership both affordable for low-income families and profitable for banks. The new loans were called **subprime mortgages**. Subprime mortgages typically had three major features. First, they required low down payments, usually less than 10 percent, and sometimes no down payment at all. Second, they had variable interest rates that kept mortgage payments affordably low for the first two or three years of the mortgage and, then, increased to higher rates after the owner had had a chance to accumulate some equity. Third, they included prepayment penalties to discourage borrowers from taking advantage of low "teaser" interest rates and then reselling the house before the more profitable "step-up" interest rates came into force.

As long as house prices were rising, sub-prime mortgages were profitable both to borrowers and lenders. Borrowers were able to buy houses they could not possibly have afforded using a conventional mortgage. By the time the 2 or 3 years of low introductory interest rates expired, rising prices would allow them to accumulate equity in their homes. At that point, they could refinance with a conventional mortgage offering better

**Subprime mortgage**

Mortgages with features like low down payments, variable interest rates, and prepayment penalties that make them attractive to low-income borrowers

terms or, alternatively, sell the house and buy a better one using a new subprime mortgage. By offering low introductory interest rates, banks lost some potential income in the early years of the mortgage; but they were able to gain this back with prepayment fees, points, and other loan origination fees when the property was sold or the mortgage was refinanced. In the worst case, if the borrower defaulted, rising property values would allow banks to recover the full amount they had loaned through foreclosure.

It was obvious to everyone that subprime mortgages would be risky if house prices ever began to fall. In that case, the frequency of default on subprime mortgages would surely be higher than on prime mortgages; and what is more, lenders would not be able to recover fully through foreclosure in a falling market. However, one comforting fact kept this worry in the background: From the time the government first started collecting statistics in 1975 through 2006, there had never been a single year during which the average value of American houses decreased. It seemed to be a market that could only go up.

Subprime loans, like other kinds of loans, were sold through securitization, as described in the preceding section. By 2006, some 40 percent of all mortgage-backed securities were based on subprime mortgages or a closely related type of mortgage called "Alt-A." Together, subprime lending and securitization transformed the business of banking during the 1990s and early 2000s. They allowed originating banks to sell more than half of all the mortgage loans they made, making it possible to recycle the proceeds from securitization to make more loans. Securitization worked so well for mortgages that it was extended to other kinds of loans, too, including credit card loans, auto loans, and student loans. The result, as shown in Figure 7.2, was an astonishing expansion of household debt that, by 2006, reached 100 percent of GDP. In fact, consumer credit—in the form of mortgages, credit cards, and home equity loans—became so easy to get that households stopped saving altogether. By 2006, total household consumption spending rose to more than 100 percent of after-tax income. Truly, it was a golden age of finance.

## Regulating the Banking System

Banks play a vital role in our economy, yet we often take them for granted until they experience problems. Unfortunately, the U.S. banking system has had serious problems at several times in the nation's history. A banking panic in 1907 led to the founding of the Federal Reserve. During the 1930s, a wave of bank failures helped plunge the economy into the Great Depression. In the 1980s, another wave of failures shook the banking world. More recently, beginning in 2007, the banking system of the whole world has again fallen into crisis with the United States leading the way. This section looks at regulations that are intended to reduce the frequency and severity of bank failures. The final section of the chapter will then look at the reasons these regulations failed to prevent the current global banking crisis.

### Do Banks Take Excessive Risks?

Earlier in the chapter, we looked at three kinds of risks that are inherent in banking—credit risk, market risk, and liquidity risk. Singly or in combination, these can cause a

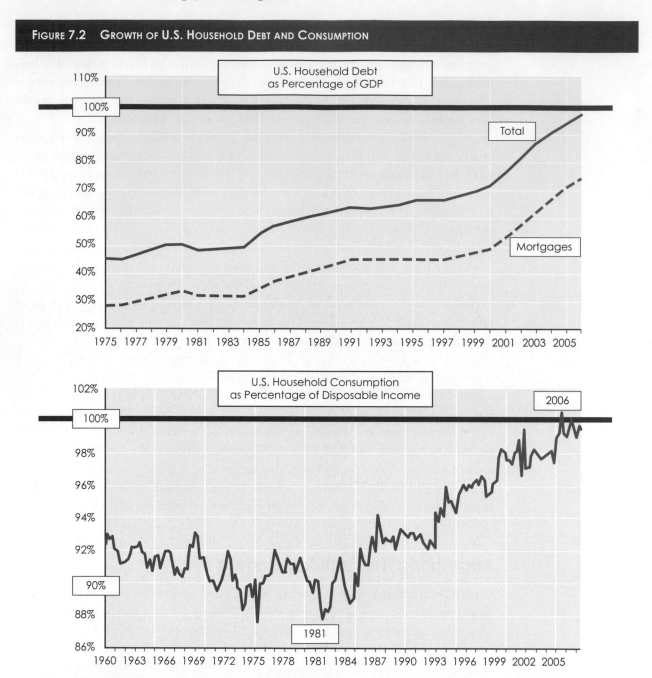

**FIGURE 7.2   GROWTH OF U.S. HOUSEHOLD DEBT AND CONSUMPTION**

Easy availability of credit and changing social attitudes toward debt and saving led to fundamental changes in the behavior of U.S. consumers during the late 1990s and early 2000s. Household debt, including mortgage debt, credit card debt, and other forms of debt, rose to 100 percent of GDP. Saving essentially disappeared as household consumption rose to 100 percent of disposable income (income after taxes).

SOURCE: Barry Z. Cynamon and Steven M. Mazzari, "Household Debt in the Consumer Age: Source of Growth—Risk of Collapse," *Journal of Capitalism and Society*, 2008.

bank to fall into insolvency and force it to cease operation. The risk of insolvency does not in itself make banking unique, however. Any business runs a risk of going broke if things start going wrong. Even in times of prosperity, business failures are common whether they involve a new pizza restaurant that was built in a poorly selected location or a huge venture like the Iridium satellite phone system, which was a technological success, but at the cost of huge financial losses for its original investors.

The government does not maintain any comprehensive regulatory system to prevent business failures of pizza restaurants or innovative telecommunications firms. It leaves the task of balancing risk against profit to the companies and their shareholders. So the first question to ask about banking regulation is, why are banks different? Why is there reason to fear that banks and other financial institutions, left to their own devices, would take risks that are excessive from the point of view of public policy?

**SPILLOVER EFFECTS**   There are two main reasons to think that banks may take excessive risks. The first has to do with the spillover effects of bank failures. If a pizza restaurant or telecommunication company fails, most of the loss is born by its owners, perhaps shared by banks or others who made loans to the firm. Competing restaurants or phone companies are likely to gain from the failure since they will divide the business of the failed firm's customers.

Things are different when a bank fails. One problem is that the failure of one bank tends not to strengthen other banks but to weaken them. Rather than dividing the business of the customers of the failed bank, other banks may also lose customers because news of a bank failure makes people distrustful of the banking system as a whole. In the worst case, as happened in the 1930s, there can be a *run* on the banking system, with people lining up to be the first to withdraw their money from all banks before additional failures occur.

Another problem is that the failure of one or several banks weakens the rest of the economy. When some banks fail and others have to reduce lending because they lose deposits, small businesses cannot get the loans they need to finance inventory or meet payrolls. Farmers cannot get loans to plant crops. Home builders cannot get construction loans, and home buyers cannot get mortgages to buy homes if they do get built. The whole economy slows down. Preventing these cascading spillover effects, then, is the first reason to think that without special regulation, banks might take risks that are reasonable from the banks' own point of view, but excessive from the point of view of the economy as a whole.

**GAMBLING WITH OTHER PEOPLE'S MONEY**   The second reason to worry that banks may take excessive risks has to do with the potential for conflicts of interest within a bank—between management and shareholders, between traders and managers, or at other points. Economists call these conflicts of interest *principal-agent problems* because one party, the agent, fails to fulfill a duty to act in the interest of another party, the principal. In everyday language, we use a simpler expression: Gambling with other people's money.

When people gamble with their own money, the most popular games are ones that do not win often but which have limited losses when they lose and very large payoffs when they win. Lotteries, like Powerball, are an example. In contrast, when people gamble with someone else's money, they look for a different pattern of gains and losses. The most attractive strategies are those that win at least a moderate amount most of the time and lose rarely. It does not matter if the losses, when they do occur, are catastrophically large because the gambler (the agent) keeps the upside winnings and someone else (the principal) is stuck with the downside.

Opportunities to gamble with other people's money can occur in any complex business organization, but they are especially widespread in the world of finance. One of the most common situations is that of an executive of a bank or other financial institution with a bonus-based compensation plan that is based on a percentage of the company's quarterly or annual earnings. *Applying Economic Ideas 7.1* gives the example of a hypothetical bank executive who has a choice between a relatively low-risk strategy that produces the greatest profit for shareholders, and a riskier strategy that produces the greatest bonus for the executive.

By law, corporate executives, as agents, have an obligation—*a fiduciary duty*—to choose the strategy that maximizes profit for their principals, the shareholders. In practice, if they are given bonus-based compensation plans like the one in the example, they are tempted to gamble with shareholders' money, pocketing the bonus money in good times, and when their luck finally runs out, keeping their accumulated

### Applying Economic Ideas 7.1
### PRINCIPAL-AGENT PROBLEMS IN THE WORLD OF FINANCE

Opportunities to gamble with other peoples' money (principal-agent problems) can arise in many business situations, but they are especially common in the world of finance. One reason is the widespread use of executive compensation schemes that emphasize bonuses based on quarterly or annual profits. Typically, there are no "clawback" provisions to recapture past bonuses if risky strategies result in short-run profits followed later by catastrophic losses.

The table gives a hypothetical example. If a bank executive chooses the relatively conservative Strategy A, the bank will make a good profit half the time and a small loss half the time. Averaged over 10 good and bad quarters, shareholders earn a solid net profit; and

the executive earns a respectable, but not spectacular, bonus. If the more aggressive Strategy B is chosen, the bank earns a larger profit in 9 quarters out of 10; and in those quarters, the executive earns a larger bonus. The problem is that when Strategy B eventually fails, it produces a catastrophic loss for the bank. The shareholders bear all of the loss. With no clawback provision in the compensation scheme, the manager gets to keep bonuses based on past profits.

Under such compensation schemes, risky strategies can generate such high bonuses that executives will be tempted to choose them even if they know they will lose their jobs when the strategies finally fail.

| Payoffs from Two Business Strategies, Assuming Executive Bonus of 0.1% of Company's Net Profit Each Calendar Quarter | |
|---|---|
| **Strategy A** | **Strategy B** |
| • 5 quarter of $100 million profit | • 9 quarters of $200 million profit |
| • 5 quarters of $10 million loss | • 1 quarter of $2,000 million loss |
| • 10 quarter net profit for shareholders of $449.5 million | • 10 quarter net loss for shareholders of $201.8 million |
| • 10 quarter total bonus for executive of $500,000 | • 10 quarter total bonus for executive of $1,800,000 |

wealth even if they lose their jobs. Meanwhile, during their years of leadership, they have pursued strategies that are excessively risky both from the point of view of their own shareholders and from that of public policy.

Top executives are not the only people in the financial industry who have opportunities to gamble with other people's money. On a smaller scale, department heads, team leaders, and even ordinary traders frequently work under bonus-based compensation schemes that tempt them to take excessive risks at the expense of the shareholders' companies that employ them. Shareholders themselves can be in a position of gambling with other people's money to the extent that, in case of insolvency, part of the bank's losses will be borne by bondholders, other creditors, or taxpayers who may be called on to clean up the financial mess.

## Policies to Ensure Safety and Soundness of Banks

There is nothing new about the idea that banks may be tempted to take excessive risk. Already in the nineteenth century, governments began to introduce measures to restrain excessive risk taking by banks. In the 1930s, many additional regulatory tools were introduced during the Great Depression. The resulting system for protecting the safety and soundness of the banking system is based on three main tools: bank supervision and regulation, loans to troubled banks, and deposit insurance.

**SUPERVISION AND REGULATION**   Bank examinations are the oldest tool for ensuring the safety and soundness of the banking system. These examinations, conducted by state or federal officials, are intended to ensure that banks do not make unduly risky loans, that they value their assets honestly, that they maintain adequate levels of capital and liquid reserves, and that they have competent management. Honest bookkeeping, prudent lending, and adequate reserves and net worth help banks to survive business downturns without becoming insolvent. In the United States, a variety of federal and state agencies—including the Federal Reserve System, the Federal Deposit Insurance Corporation (FDIC), and the Office of the Comptroller of the Currency (part of the Treasury Department)—share responsibility for supervision and regulation.

Supervision and regulation do not always ensure sound banking practices. Examinations do not always spot danger signals. Sometimes, fraudulent operators of banks and thrifts deceive examiners; in other cases, they do no better than bank managers in spotting bad loans or other risk factors. Sometimes the standards that examiners are asked to enforce are themselves too weak. In the wake of the recent financial crisis, a comprehensive review is being made of bank supervision and regulation.

**LENDER OF LAST RESORT**   Bank examinations, introduced more than a century ago, were not, by themselves, enough to prevent banking panics. In 1907 an especially severe panic took place, which eventually led to the establishment of the Federal Reserve System (the Fed) in 1913. Among other duties, the Fed has the power to aid the banking system in times of trouble by acting as a *lender of last resort*. For example, when the stock market experienced a record 22.6 percent loss on October 19, 1987, the Fed quickly announced that it stood ready to lend extra funds to any banks that needed additional cash because of customer losses. In another case, discussed in *Economics in the News 7.1*, the Fed played an essential role in maintaining the soundness of the U.S. banking system following the 9/11 terrorist attacks in 2001. However, useful though the lender-of-last resort concept has proved in some crises, when the health of the whole financial system is threatened, this tool alone is not enough.

**DEPOSIT INSURANCE**   Even with its power as a lender of last resort, the Fed failed to prevent a major bank panic in 1933 during the Great Depression. In 1934, in response to that crisis, Congress established the Federal Deposit Insurance Corporation (FDIC). Since the Monetary Control Act of 1980, all deposits are insured up to $100,000 per account, a limit that was increased to $250,000 in 2008.

The idea of deposit insurance is to short-circuit runs on banks. If deposits are insured, depositors need not run to the bank to withdraw their funds; even if the bank fails, the government will pay them their money or arrange for the transfer of their deposits to a solvent bank. Also, if runs can be avoided, the problems of one or a few banks will not touch off a panic that threatens the whole system. Depository institutions are supposed to bear the cost of deposit insurance through premiums charged by

### Economics in the News 7.1
## 9/11: THE FED AS A LENDER OF LAST RESORT

The September 11, 2001 attacks on the World Trade Center in New York and the Pentagon in Washington, D.C. caused severe disruptions in the financial system that left banks short on funds. The Fed's actions during the crisis highlight its importance not only as a lender of last resort but also as a central authority in the payments system.

At 11:45 a.m., just three hours after the attacks, the Federal Reserve issued the following press statement: "The Federal Reserve System is open and operating. (The discount window is available to meet liquidity needs." (The discount window is a facility that banks may use to take out loans from the Fed. Once such transactions were carried out face-to-face through an actual window; today, loan disbursements are made electronically.) In addition, the Federal Reserve's staff contacted banks in the days surrounding the attacks to promote borrowing from the Fed as banks faced difficulty in honoring payments and extending lines of credit to their customers.

A series of events prevented timely payments both in the business and banking sectors. The physical damage to communications, computers, and general operations in New York slowed payments dramatically. The Federal

William Poole, former president of the Federal Reserve Bank of St. Louis.

Aviation Administration (FAA) halted air traffic, preventing the delivery of checks to banks by air. As a result, the volume of interbank transfers, essential in the bank payments system, fell 43 percent between September 10 and 11, 2001.

The Federal Reserve System responded by acting in its original role as a lender of last resort, providing large sums in the form of loans to the banking system. Between September 5 and September 12, Fed loans to banks increased from $195 million to $45.6 billion. As the president of the Federal Reserve Bank of St. Louis, William Poole, stated: "In the absence of Fed intervention, we would have seen a cascade of defaults as firms due funds that were not arriving would be unable to meet their obligations."

SOURCES: Kristin Van Gaasbeck, "Circling the Wagons: The Fed's Response to 9/11," presented at the *Western Economics Association International 78th Annual Meeting*, Denver, CO, July 12, 2003; William Poole, "The Role of Government in U.S. Capital Markets," lecture presented at the Institute of Governmental Affairs, University of California, Davis, October 18, 2001.

the insurance funds—although sometimes premiums have fallen short of costs and taxpayers have had to make up the difference.

There is a downside to deposit insurance, however. Without deposit insurance, banks are subject to market discipline from their depositors, who, other things being equal, will be reluctant to put their money in banks that pursue risky strategies. With deposit insurance in force, depositors themselves are given an opportunity to gamble with other people's money. They can search the Internet for banks that pay the highest available interest on certificates of deposit. As long as the bank's website carries the magic words "Deposits protected by the FDIC," depositors do not have to wonder what reckless strategies make the high CD rates possible. They know that if the bank fails, federal taxpayers will cover their losses.

## Systemic Failure and the Global Financial Crisis

Occasional bank failures that occur due to poor management or bad luck do not threaten the health of the economy as a whole. Rather than removing all risk of failure, government policies to ensure the safety and soundness of banking are intended to prevent systemic failure, meaning a situation in which simultaneous failure of many banks threatens the ability of the whole banking system to perform its functions—those of facilitating payments, helping households and firms to manage money over time, and managing financial risk. Unfortunately, measures to prevent systemic failure do not always work. Many countries and regions have experienced systemic banking failures in recent decades.

The global financial crisis that began in the United States in 2007 has been the most widespread of these since the 1930s. Economists will be debating the causes of this crisis for many years. Without attempting to be at all complete, this section looks at some of the main factors that triggered the crisis and made it so severe, and then, briefly, at possible remedies.

### The Housing Bubble and Subprime Loans

The U.S. housing market must be the starting point for any discussion of the global financial crisis. During the 1970s, 1980s, and early 1990s, the median nominal price of houses in the United States rose gradually along a trend that reflected rising household incomes and general inflation of consumer prices, as shown in Figure 7.3. There were no significant periods of declining prices. In the late 1990s, the rate of increase of house prices accelerated sharply. The rapid rise in house prices in this period was not driven by household incomes or other prices, which continued to increase only moderately. Instead, two factors seem to have pushed house prices upward. One was the easy availability of loans that, in turn, was made possible by the spread of subprime mortgages and securitization. The other factor was the emergence of a "bubble psychology," meaning that each acceleration of the upward trend in prices was taken as evidence that future price increases would be even greater. There appeared to be no limit to profit opportunities in the housing market both for lenders and home buyers.

**FIGURE 7.3    U.S. NOMINAL MEDIAN HOME PRICE**

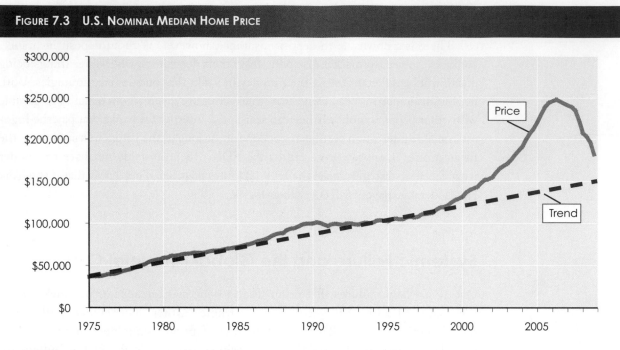

From 1975 to 2006, nominal home prices in the United States increased gradually, following a trend line that reflected rising median family income and inflation of the general price level. Beginning in the late 1990s, the rate of increase in home prices began to outstrip household income and the prices of other goods and services. By the peak of the housing bubble, in mid-2006, home prices were more than 50% higher than the trend and had still not returned to the historical trend by the end of 2008.

SOURCE: Data from http://mysite.verizon.net/vzeqrguz/housingbubble/, compiled using data from National Association of Realtors, U.S. Office of Federal Housing Enterprise Oversight, and Case-Schiller HPI.

Eventually the bubble burst, and the law of gravity took over. By the end of 2008, house prices were approaching their historical relationship with other prices and household incomes. Many lenders and homeowners, who had gambled with their own money in the mistaken belief that prices could go nowhere but up, suffered devastating losses. This was especially true of banks that had made subprime loans and their low- and middle-income borrowers. As explained earlier, subprime loans are profitable both to borrowers and lenders when prices are rising, but are much more vulnerable to foreclosures when prices fall. However, many traders, mortgage brokers, and financial executives—those who had been in a position to gamble with other people's money—walked away from the crash with millions of dollars in untouchable bonus money that had been paid out during the years of illusory profits.

## Ratings Failures and Vanishing Liquidity

A second major factor that contributed to the financial crisis was a failure of the rating function that, together with other failures, led to a destruction of liquidity in securities markets. As explained earlier, ratings are an essential part of the process of securitization of loans. Neither in the case of traditional corporate bonds nor in that of complex mortgage-backed securities is it practical for every investor to carry out all the steps needed to estimate the riskiness of a security. Instead, ratings agencies do this work once, assigning a rating like AAA or B; and buyers rely on the honesty and accuracy of the ratings to select securities that fit their appetite for risk versus return.

During the mid-2000s, the rating process suffered a serious failure as applied to mortgage-backed securities. In particular, it turned out that senior tranches of mortgage-backed securities, including those with the highest AAA ratings, were far riskier than their ratings implied. Potential buyers, no longer able to rely on the work of the nationally recognized statistical rating agencies, began to avoid buying mortgage backed securities and other complex financial instruments altogether. Liquidity—the ability to sell a security easily at a price reflecting its true value—disappeared. Institutions that were left holding these securities were able to sell them only at unrealistically low "fire-sale" prices, if at all. In a short period, highly rated senior tranches of securities became "toxic waste."

Why did the ratings process, which had operated tolerably well for decades, suddenly fall apart? Observers disagree on many details, but at least three things appear to have gone wrong. First, it appears that technical errors were made. The new types of securities were not only complex but also were not standardized, so that no one security was exactly like any other. The technical staffs and statistical models used by the ratings agencies were overloaded; and as a result, their work was not up to the standard that investors had come to expect. Second, there were failures to control conflicts of interest within the ratings agencies. To protect their reputation for objectivity, ratings agencies are supposed to isolate the technical specialists who assign ratings from front-office staff, who might be tempted to offer "easy" ratings in order to attract business and earn commissions. Unfortunately, these isolation mechanisms did not always work. Third, there may have been cases in which banks and other financial institutions, knowing that they were gambling with other people's money, willingly bought securities that they knew were too highly rated.

## Regulatory Failures

Failures in the prudential regulations that were supposed to safeguard the safety and soundness of banks and other financial institutions are a third factor that helped bring about the financial crisis. There were so many failures, or at least allegations of failure, it is impossible to list more than a few of the most important.

One problem was the fragmentation of regulation. In the United States, prudential regulation of banks is split among several competing agencies, including the Fed, the Treasury, the FDIC, and the Office of Thrift Supervision. Investment banks, brokers, mutual funds, and other institutions fall under the authority of the Securities and Exchange Commission. State insurance regulators and other agencies also have a role. The work of these agencies is not always adequately coordinated; and, in some cases, financial firms were able to engage in "regulatory arbitrage," a fancy term for shifting their activities around so that they came under the authority of the regulatory agency thought to be most lenient.

International regulation is even more fragmented, a serious problem in a world where banks increasingly operate across national borders. Fearing a "race to the bottom," in which banks move their activities to the least regulated countries, financial regulators around the world have attempted to agree on minimum standards. These attempts led to the Basel Accords, named after the Swiss city where an international body called the Bank for International Settlements maintains its headquarters. Unfortunately, despite many years of hard work to improve them, the Basel Accords proved inadequate to contain the crisis. Among other problems, international regulations relied too heavily on the banks' own assessments of the risks of complex securities and on the work of ratings agencies.

Credit default swaps are another area in which the regulatory process failed. Credit default swaps, which protect investors against the risk of default on bonds, are often compared to insurance; however, they were not subjected to the same regulations as ordinary insurance. For example, regulations do not permit you to buy insurance on property that you do not own. Buying fire insurance on your neighbor's house would at best be viewed as gambling on the possibility that the house would burn down, and at worst, as an arrangement that gave you an incentive to set the fire. However, people were freely allowed to speculate on bond defaults by buying credit default swap protection on bonds that they did not own. Some market observers view this speculation as inherently destabilizing. In addition, regulations require sellers of fire or auto insurance to maintain large reserves that guarantee their ability to pay claims in case of losses. In contrast, no such reserves were required for sellers of credit default swaps. The loose regulation of credit default swaps was a major factor in the failure of insurance giant American International Group (AIG), described in *Economics in the News 7.2*.

## Rehabilitating Failed Banks

By the fall of 2008, the combination of the housing bubble, failures of ratings and liquidity, and failures of prudential regulation had brought on the worst banking crisis in the United States since the Great Depression. In these circumstances, it would hardly have been enough for the government agencies involved to say, "Sorry, we messed up. We'll try not to do it again." Instead, like the governments of other countries that had experienced systemic banking failure in the past, Congress, the Federal Reserve, the Treasury, and other agencies were expected to do something to rehabilitate the banking system, that is, to restore its ability to perform its essential functions of facilitating payments, lending, and managing risk. As this is written, the job of rehabilitation is by no means complete, despite Congressional approval of the Treasury's $700-billion Troubled Asset Relief Program (TARP) in October 2008, and additional billions in funds from the Fed and other sources. In some respects the process of rehabilitation is hardly started. Nevertheless, it will be worth looking briefly at some of the main decisions and challenges that must be faced to restore the banking system to health.

## Economics in the News 7.2
## AIG—TOO BIG TO FAIL?

Among all the events of the global financial crisis, none has been more spectacular or more costly to U.S. taxpayers than the failure of the insurance giant American International Group (AIG). Until 2008, AIG was known to most people as a very large, very safe, and highly respected seller of insurance. Founded by Western investors in Hong Kong in 1919, AIG grew to become the world's 18th largest public corporation. Its insurance activities were closely regulated wherever it operated, and it held the coveted AAA rating that allowed it to borrow and to sell bonds on the very best of terms.

Unfortunately, AIG did not limit itself to the conservative and closely regulated types of insurance on which its reputation was built. Instead, in the early 2000s, a London-based division of the company became a major player in the market for credit default swaps (CDSs). Because of AIG's AAA rating and its reputation in other areas of insurance, buyers of credit default protection looked on the company as the ideal counterparty. AIG was able to sell CDSs on very good terms without posting any reserves against losses. As long as there were no defaults on the bonds it insured, the business was incredibly profitable. AIG raked in billions in premiums without having to pay out anything in return.

One reason that AIG's CDS business grew so rapidly was the big European banks' use of a form of regulatory arbitrage. Banking regulations allow banks to operate with less capital if they hold only very safe assets. Less capital means more opportunity for profit; but there is a downside to a banking strategy based on safe assets because the safest assets are also those with the lowest rates of return. Credit default swaps created a loophole in the regulations that allowed banks to have their cake and eat it, too. They could buy relatively risky but high-yielding assets, like mortgage backed securities, and then insure them against loss with CDSs from AIG. Because AIG itself was AAA rated, its guarantees allowed the banks to count their mortgage-backed securities as also being AAA rated. If something went wrong, AIG, not the bank, would bear the loss.

Or so it seemed. The problem was that AIG sold too many CDSs, some $450 billion in all, and did not charge a high enough premium to cover all the losses that eventually occurred. When the underlying securitization deals began to go bad, even this largest of all insurance companies did not have enough reserves to meet its obliga-

tions. In September 2008, it was forced to turn to the U.S. government for a bailout in the form of an $85 billion loan. In January 2009, it announced further losses of $60 billion for the fourth quarter of 2008, forcing the government to increase its stake in AIG to $150 billion. Some of this will no doubt be paid back, but some analysts think that the bailout of AIG will eventually cost the U.S. taxpayer as much as $100 billion. Meanwhile, much to the disgust of those same taxpayers, the very AIG executives who had gambled with other peoples' money continued to pay themselves tens of millions of dollars in bonuses.

So, why not simply let AIG fail? Alas, AIG was judged "too big to fail." By the end of 2008, its shareholders had already lost nearly all of their investment; the share price fell from $70 in October to less than a dollar by the end of the year. That meant that in case of bankruptcy, its remaining losses would have to be borne by its creditors, including all of those big European banks that bought credit default protection. That could easily be enough to push those banks, already suffering from many other woes, into outright insolvency. In the minds of the U.S. Treasury and Federal Reserve, the failure of one or more large European banks would have catastrophic effects on the world financial system.

Make you mad? You're not the only one. Testifying before Congress, Fed Chairman Ben Bernanke said, "If there is a single episode [of the financial crisis] that has made me more angry, I can't think of one." Neither can anyone else.

Large bonuses awarded by AIG, after it received a huge government bailout, provoked public protests.

**WHO SHOULD BE HELPED?** The first decision to be made is which banks should receive government help. A traditional view is to practice *triage*. This term, borrowed from battlefield medicine, means that scarce resources should be used to help only those who would not survive without aid and should not be wasted on hopeless cases. However, during the first phase of TARP, in the fall of 2008, the Treasury provided assistance to many healthy banks as well as to those close to failure. The rationale was that unless all banks were pressured to accept funds, those banks that received government aid would be stigmatized as weak. Clients would shun them, and they would fail even faster.

A related issue is whether to help only commercial banks, or to extend government aid to all financial institutions whose failure might pose risks for the system as a whole. In this regard, the U.S. government's policy during the chaotic fall of 2008 was uneven. In an early test case, Bear Stearns—an investment bank, not a commercial bank—was given generous funding to help it find a merger partner. Soon after that, however, the government stood by and allowed the failure of Lehman Brothers, another large investment bank. The failure of Lehman Brothers was such a shock to financial markets that only days later, the government reversed course again and rescued AIG, which was not a bank at all but an insurance company. Of course, judging which institutions really pose "systemic risk" is inherently subjective; but even allowing for that fact, many observers found it hard to see a consistent pattern in these three cases.

**WHO SHOULD BEAR THE LOSSES?** Banks fail when their losses mount to the point that their liabilities exceed their assets. It is rarely possible to recover what has been lost. Instead, a decision must be made as to who should bear the losses.

Here, the traditional view is that the bank's shareholders should stand first in line to absorb the losses. If there are excess losses even after shareholders are fully wiped out, other uninsured parties the bank has done business with—its *counterparties*, to use financial jargon—should be the next to suffer. Ordinary depositors, on the other hand, are shielded from loss by deposit insurance. If the deposit insurance

The government allowed Lehman Brothers, a large investment bank, to fail; then, reversed course two weeks later and bailed out AIG, an insurance company.

funds run out of money (as they did during the U.S. banking crisis of the 1980s), taxpayers have to pick up the tab.

This traditional procedure was not fully followed by U.S. federal authorities in 2008 and 2009, however. Instead, federal aid from TARP, from the Fed, and from other sources was provided to many banks and other financial institutions that had not yet become fully insolvent. As a result, although share prices in most banks fell sharply, they did not fall to zero and shareholders were not completely wiped out. The policy of intervening before banks became fully insolvent also had the effect of protecting uninsured bank counterparties (including investment banks, pension funds, hedge funds, and foreign banks) from losses they would have suffered if the banks had been liquidated. Defenders justified the policy on a "too big to fail" theory—allowing large banks to become fully insolvent was seen as risking a "complete meltdown" of the world financial system. Others, more critical, saw the policy as a way of shifting losses to taxpayers while some of those who were protected from loss were the very individuals and institutions whose excessive risk taking had caused the crisis in the first place. There is no reason to think the debate over this issue will end soon.

**HOW SHOULD AID BE PROVIDED?**   Once it is decided who should be helped, a final issue is the form in which the aid should be given. There are two main alternatives.

The first is called a *capital injection*. In this approach, the government provides fresh capital to a troubled bank in order to strengthen its balance sheet while other assets and liabilities of the bank are left unchanged, at least initially. One way to inject capital is through a government purchase of common stock. In this case, the government becomes a part owner, perhaps even a majority owner, of the bank, meaning that the bank is effectively nationalized. Instead, to avoid political controversy over nationalization of private companies, capital can be injected in the form of preferred stock, which does not give the government full voting rights.

The second alternative is called a *carve-out*. This approach begins by identifying the specific bank assets that have suffered the largest losses, for example, tranches of securities backed by subprime mortgages. These are popularly known as "toxic assets" because, although they might someday turn out to be worth something, no one wants to buy them. In a carve-out, the government acts like a surgeon making an organ transplant. It removes the bad assets from the bank balance sheet and replaces them with good assets—for example, government bonds. If the terms of the exchange are set properly, the value of the bank's assets increases and it escapes the threat of insolvency.

During late 2008 and early 2009, the U.S. government tried a mix of both approaches. The Treasury's original plan, presented in October 2008, was to use $700 billion in TARP funds to conduct a massive carve-out. There were immediate protests that doing so would expose U.S. taxpayers to huge immediate losses with no promise of sharing in the gains when the financial system eventually recovered. Treasury Secretary Henry Paulson, the chief architect of TARP, quickly backed down and instead used a large part of the funds for a capital injection in the form of preferred stock. Later, in the spring of 2008, a new Treasury Secretary, Timothy Geithner, revived the carve-out idea in a modified form.

It is hard to draw a hard and fast conclusion as to which method of bank rescue is more likely to be successful. Precedents of successful use of each alternative can be found in the experience of other countries in the past, although capital injections seem to have been used somewhat more often and more successfully. All that can be said with certainty at this point is that the controversy is likely to continue for years.

These comments about the housing bubble, liquidity problems, regulatory failures, and bank rehabilitation touch on only a few of the many aspects of the global financial crisis. In the following chapters, we will add additional details regarding the causes of the crisis and measures being taken to recover from it. However, at the time of writing, global economic activity was still on the downward slope of the most widespread recession since World War II. Many features of the crisis and the full scope of its impact remain unknown.

## Summary

1. **What are banks and what do they do?** *Banks* are financial institutions that accept deposits and make loans. Their key tasks are facilitating payments, assisting customers with management of money over time, and helping with the management of risk. In addition to private banks, each country also has a *central bank*, which is a government institution responsible for regulating the banking system and conducting monetary policy.

2. **What are the main items on a bank's balance sheet?** A *balance sheet* is a financial statement that shows the *assets*, *liabilities*, and *net worth* (*capital*) of a bank or other financial unit. A balance sheet must always conform to the principle that assets are equal to liabilities plus net worth. The principal assets of banks are cash reserves, securities, and loans. Its principal liabilities are deposits and borrowings.

3. **What is meant by the traditional originate-to-hold model of banking?** In the traditional *originate-to-hold model* of banking, banks made loans to customers (that is, "originated" the loans) and then held the loans until they were paid in full.

Their profit came from the difference between interest on the loan and interest paid on deposits and other liabilities. The reason for holding loans until they matured was partly that it was traditionally difficult to sell loans to another bank because the purchasing bank might fear that any loans offered for sale would be "lemons."

4. **What are the risks of banking?** *Credit risk* is the risk that borrowers may not repay their loans in full or on time. *Market risk* is the risk that changes in market conditions (for example, changes in interest rates) will lower the value of assets or increase the burden of liabilities. *Liquidity risk* is the risk that the bank may be forced to raise cash by selling illiquid assets below their value as indicated on the bank's books. Banks protect themselves against these risks by holding adequate levels of capital and liquid reserves.

5. **What is the originate-to-distribute model of banking?** In the *originate-to-distribute model*, banks do not hold loans to maturity, but instead, sell them soon after the loans are made. The process through which loans are packaged for sale to investors is known as *securitization*. Many

kinds of loans can be securitized, including traditional mortgages, subprime mortgages, credit card loans, auto loans, student loans, and others.

6. **What policies aim to maintain the safety and security of the banking system?** Because of spillover effects and the temptation to gamble with other peoples' money, banks may take risks that are excessive from the point of view of the economy as a whole. Several kinds of government policy attempt to contain excessive risk taking. One is a system of supervision and regulation that requires banks to maintain certain standards of safety and soundness. Another is the Federal Reserve's role as lender of last resort in times of crisis. A third is a system of deposit insurance that discourages bank runs by protecting depositors in case of bank failures.

7. **What does "systemic failure" mean for the banking system?** Systemic failure means the failure of so many banks that the financial system can no longer do its job of underpinning the rest of the economy. The crisis that began in 2007 is not the first instance of systemic banking failure, but it is the worst—at least since the Great Depression. Among the many factors that led to the crisis, at least three stand out. One was the housing bubble in the United States and some other countries. A second was the failure of the ratings process, which resulted in an evaporation of liquidity throughout the financial system. A third was the failure of several parts of the regulatory system that is supposed to ensure safety and soundness of the financial system.

## Key Terms

## Problems and Topics For Discussion

1. **Your bank** Go to the web site for the bank where you have an account, and look for information on the bank's assets and liabilities. The information may be contained in the bank's annual report. What are the bank's main assets and liabilities? Is your bank solvent? Are there any reasons to be concerned about its financial conditions? (If you cannot find this information for your own bank, do the same for a major bank like Bank of America.)

2. **The lemons problem** "Loans are just like used cars. If you see an ad in the paper for a used car, you have to wonder, why is the owner selling it? Maybe there is something wrong with the car that is hard to see. As a result, when you approach the seller, you will want to offer a very low price to make up for any hidden defects. Instead, you could buy the used car from a dealer. The dealer offers a warranty on the car to protect its reputation. It is safer to buy from the dealer. In this regard, selling a used car through a dealer rather than directly is just like selling loans through securitization rather than one by one." Do you agree, disagree, or agree in part with this statement?

What similarities and differences do you see between securitization and selling used cars?

3. **Your mortgage**   Do you own a home that is financed by a mortgage? If so, how large a down payment did you make? Is the interest rate fixed or variable? If you pay the mortgage off early, are there prepayment penalties? Based on the answers to this question, would you classify your mortgage as prime, subprime, or somewhere in between? (If you do not have a home of your own, base your answers to these questions on an interview with a friend or relative who is a homeowner.)

4. **Recent bank failures**   The FDIC maintains a list of recently failed banks online at http://www.fdic.gov/bank/. How many banks have failed so far in the year when you are reading this chapter? How many failed in the previous year? Go to this list and download the information for the most recently failed bank. Why did the institution fail? How did federal authorities respond to the failure?

## Case for Discussion

### Bank Run at Northern Rock

The United States has not been the only country affected by the global financial crisis that began in 2007. In fact, one of the very first large bank failures occurred not in the United States, but in the United Kingdom.

The failed bank in question was the Northern Rock Building Society, a large mortgage lender located in North East England. Northern Rock had been formed in 1965 from the merger of two traditional mutual building societies. After its merger, it became a shareholder-owned corporation and grew rapidly. Its specialty was home loans, many of which required low down payments. In some cases Northern Rock even made loans that exceeded the value of the property in question.

Like many banks throughout the world, Northern Rock relied on a mixture of deposits and borrowing as a source of funds with which to make loans. Compared with other banks, however, Northern Rock's deposit base was fairly small—just 25 percent of assets. Borrowing, mostly short-term, was correspondingly a larger share of its liabilities. The bank's business strategy depended critically on its ability to roll over those short-term loans, that is, to borrow more short-term money on a continual basis as it paid off old borrowing.

In the summer of 2007, it became apparent to many people that all was not well in the U.K. housing market. A bubble mentality had pushed home prices unrealistically high, and some homeowners were facing foreclosure. The rising prospect of defaults and foreclosures cast doubt on Northern Rock's business strategy. Lenders who had supplied short-term funds to Northern Rock began to refuse to roll over their loans, and the bank almost immediately found itself in serious trouble.

At this point, another factor came into play. The U.K., like the United States, has a system of deposit insurance to protect ordinary depositors from loss if a bank fails. However, the British scheme does not operate as smoothly as the American one. Only the first £2,000 of deposits (about $4,000 at the time) were fully guaranteed, with another £33,000 (about $66,000) covered by a 90 percent guarantee. Furthermore, whereas U.S. depositors usually have immediate access to money deposited in failed banks, British depositors can find their money tied up for months before it is paid out. Knowing of these flaws in the deposit insurance scheme, worried depositors of Northern Rock lined up at bank offices and began withdrawing funds in large amounts.

By September, the Bank of England, as the central bank of the U.K., was forced to step in with a huge loan to replace lost deposits and short-term borrowing. The loan was not enough to stabilize

Northern Rock, however. After months of searching for a private buyer, the British government gave up and fully nationalized Northern Rock. Although larger banks later failed as well, the Northern Rock episode is viewed as one of the critical triggers that set off the European phase of the global financial crisis.

## QUESTIONS

1. Which of the major risks of banking (credit risk, market risk, and liquidity risk) were involved in the failure of Northern Rock? Explain how each type of risk does or does not apply, based on information in the case.

2. Of the major tools used by governments to ensure the safety and stability of the banking system, which are illustrated by this case? Give specific examples.

3. Why do you think the British government stepped in to save Northern Rock, first using its lender-of-last resort powers and later nationalizing the bank? Why not just let the bank fail, and let the bank's shareholders, depositors, and creditors pick up the pieces?

# CHAPTER 8

# Money and Central Banking

**After reading this chapter, you will understand the following:**

1. What money is and why money matters
2. How banks create money
3. Limits to the size of the money stock
4. Instruments of monetary policy available to the central bank

**Before reading this chapter, make sure you know the meaning of the concepts:**

1. Balance sheets
2. Liquidity
3. Vault cash
4. Central bank
5. Federal Reserve System
6. Bank reserves
7. Current account and financial account transactions in the balance of payments.

I F WE THINK of the circular flow of income and expenditure as a giant system of pipes connected by pumps and valves, then we can think of money as the fluid that moves through the pipes. In this chapter, we will provide a formal definition of money and explain why money is so important for macroeconomics. Next we explain how money is created by the banking system. Finally, we look at the instruments of monetary policy used by central banks.

# Money: What It Is and What It Does

**Money**

An asset that serves as a means of payment, a store of purchasing power, and a unit of account

**Money** is best defined in terms of what it does. It serves as a means of payment, a store of purchasing power, and a unit of account. Regardless of its name—U.S. dollars, Japanese yen, or the European euro—the monies of all countries function in all three ways.

As a means of payment, money reduces the costs of exchange, which would otherwise have to take the form of barter. Imagine a market in which farmers meet to trade produce of various kinds. Apples will get you peppers, cauliflower will get you beets, and turnips will get you garlic. However, what if you want garlic and have only potatoes? What you need is a universal means of exchange—one that all sellers will accept because they know that others will also accept it, one that is in limited supply so that you know its exchange value will remain constant, and one that is easily recognized and hard to counterfeit. In times past, gold and silver coins served these purposes. In a modern economy, coins and paper currency serve for many small transactions. Transferring funds from one bank deposit to another by check, debit card, electronic transfer, or other means usually makes larger payments.

As a store of purchasing power, money makes it possible to arrange economic activities in a convenient manner over time. Income-producing activities and spending decisions need not occur simultaneously. Instead, we can accept money as payment for our work and keep the money handy until we want to spend it. The U.S. dollar is a good store of purchasing power—so good, in fact, that billions of dollars of U.S. currency are held by citizens of other countries who trust it more than their own currencies.

Finally, as a unit of account, money makes it possible to measure and record economic stocks and flows. Your own daily spending on food, transportation, and entertainment can be expressed in terms of money. So can an entire country's output of goods and services. Without money as a unit of account, private and public economic planning would be virtually impossible.

## Money as a Liquid Asset

Anything of value can serve as a store of purchasing power if it can be sold and the proceeds can be used to buy something else. Money, however, has two important traits that no other asset has to the same extent. One is that money itself can be used as a means of payment without first having to be exchanged for something else. A house, a corporate bond, or a steel mill may have great value, but they cannot usually be used to buy anything without first being exchanged for an equivalent amount of money. The other trait is that money can neither gain nor lose in nominal value; this is necessarily so because money is the unit of account in which nominal values are stated. Where a house, a bond, or a steel mill may be worth more or fewer dollars next year than this year, the nominal value of a dollar is always a dollar—no more and no less.

As we learned in the previous chapter, an asset that can be used as or readily converted into a means of payment and is protected against gain or loss in nominal value is said to be liquid. No other asset is as liquid as money. In fact, a comparison of the definitions of money and liquidity suggests that any perfectly liquid asset is, by definition, a form of money.

## Measuring the Stock of Money

For purposes of economic theory and policy, we need to know not only what money is but also how it can be measured. Control of the money stock is an important function of government. Without measurement, control is impossible.

A narrow approach to measurement views money as consisting of just two types of assets: currency and transaction deposits. **Currency** means coins and paper money. Transaction deposits, as explained in the previous chapter, are deposits from which money can be withdrawn by check or electronic transfer without advance notice and used to make payments. Economists refer to this narrow concept of money as **M1**. Table 8.1 shows M1 and its components. Note that travelers checks, a very small item by comparison with other forms of money, are included in M1 along with currency and transaction deposits.

The narrow approach to the money stock, M1, focuses on the function of money as a means of payment because almost all transactions are made with either currency or transaction deposits. If we choose instead to focus on the function of money as a store of value, we need a broader approach to money that includes several other liquid assets. This broader definition is known as **M2**.

Shares in money market mutual funds are one of the additional items included in M2. A *money market mutual fund* is a financial intermediary that sells shares to the public. The proceeds of these sales are used to buy short-term, fixed-interest securities such as Treasury bills. The fund passes along almost all the interest earned on those securities to its shareholders, after charging a small fee for management services. Shareholders can redeem their shares in a number of ways—by writing checks, by debit card, by electronic transfer to a merchant, or by transfer to another fund. Because the proceeds from sales of shares are invested in very safe short-term assets, a money market mutual fund is able to promise its shareholders a fixed nominal value of $1 per share, although the interest paid on the shares varies with market rates. For all practical purposes, money market mutual fund balances are almost as liquid as those of ordinary transaction accounts.

### Currency

Coins and paper money

### M1 *printed*

A measure of the money supply that includes currency and transaction deposits

### M2

A measure of the money supply that includes M1 plus retail money market mutual fund shares, money market deposit accounts, and saving deposits

**TABLE 8.1  COMPONENTS OF THE U.S. MONEY STOCK, MARCH 2009 (BILLIONS OF DOLLARS, SEASONALLY ADJUSTED)**

| | | |
|---|---:|---:|
| Currency | | $ 841.3 |
| + Travelers checks | | $ 5.5 |
| + Transactions deposits | | $ 778.2 |
| = **M1** | | **$ 1,625.0** |
| + Savings deposits (including MMDAs) | $ 4,379.8 | |
| + Small-denomination time deposits | $ 354.2 | |
| + Retail money market fund shares | $ 1,076.6 | |
| = **M2** | | **$ 7,435.6** |

This table breaks down the U.S. money supply into its components as of March 2009. It gives two of the most commonly used money supply measures. M1 is the total of currency and transaction deposits; M2 includes M1 plus other highly liquid assets.

SOURCE: Board of Governors of the Federal Reserve System, *H.6 Statistical Release*, March 26, 2009.

Savings deposits serve as a liquid store of purchasing power.

**Savings deposit**

A deposit at a bank
that can be fully
redeemed at any
time, but from
which checks
cannot be written

**Time deposit**

A deposit at a bank
or thrift institution
from which funds
can be withdrawn
without payment of
a penalty only at
the end of an
agreed-upon
period

**Equation of
exchange**

An equation that
shows the relation-
ship among the
money stock (M),
the income
velocity of money
(V), the price level
(P), and real
domestic product
(Q); written as
MV = PQ

**Velocity
(income velocity
of money)**

The ratio of nominal
GDP to the money
stock; a measure of
the average
number of times
each dollar of the
money stock is used
each year to
purchase final
goods and services

Banks compete with money market funds by offering several kinds of accounts that serve as liquid stores of purchasing power while, also, offering higher interest rates than transaction deposits. **Savings deposits** are one example. Savings accounts have limited, if any, checking privileges; but they are fully protected against loss in nominal value and can be redeemed at any time at a bank branch, at ATMs, or by using Internet banking. **Time deposits** differ from savings deposits in that the account holder agrees in advance to leave funds on deposit for a specified period of time, perhaps for as little as three months or as long as five years. Time deposits (popularly known as Certificates of Deposit or CDs) pay higher interest rates than either transaction deposits or savings deposits. They are slightly less liquid than other bank deposits in that there may be a small penalty if funds are withdrawn before the agreed period is up. However, they are liquid enough to be included in M2.[1]

## Why Money Matters

How is money, as measured either by M1 or M2, related to the macroeconomic themes of real output growth, price stability, and employment? It will take several chapters to explore the relationship in detail, but a preliminary overview can be given in the form of an equation known as the **equation of exchange**:

$$MV = PQ$$

In this equation, M stands for a measure of the money stock, P for the price level, and Q for real GDP. The remaining variable, V, stands for **velocity** or, more fully, the **income velocity of money**. Velocity can be thought of as the average number of times each dollar of the money stock is spent each year to purchase final goods and services of the kind that enter into GDP. It can also be thought of as the ratio of nominal GDP to the money stock. For example, if a country had a money stock of $200 billion and a real GDP of $1,000 billion, velocity would be 5, indicating that each dollar of the money stock changed hands about 5 times a year for purchases of final goods and services.

The equation of exchange shows that any change in the money stock must affect the price level, real output, velocity, or some combination of these variables. Thus, control over the money stock gives the government a powerful policy instrument with which to influence key macroeconomic variables. Later chapters will show in detail the means by which policymakers can influence the money stock. They will also discuss the effects of changes in the money stock on other variables.

Which "M" is best used in the equation of exchange? As we have seen, different measures of the money stock are based on different cutoff points along a range of financial assets with varying degrees of liquidity, from currency at one end to long-term securities at the other. No hard-and-fast answer can be given to the question of which M is "best" without also asking, "Best for what?"
For purposes of macroeconomic modeling and policy, the best money stock measure would be the one with the most predictable velocity and, hence, the most predictable relationship to the variables lying on the right-hand side of the equation of exchange (real output and the price level). At one time economists considered M1 to be the best available measure in this regard. In the 1980s, as banking institutions and ways of doing business changed, M1 began to lose its close relationship to other economic variables; and M2 came to be regarded as a better measure. In this book, unless we specify otherwise, the term *money* can be understood to refer to M2.

## Determining the Quantity of Money

As shown in Table 8.1, the bulk of the U.S. money stock (M2) consists of paper currency issued by the Federal Reserve System and deposits at commercial banks and thrift institutions. Other forms of money—travelers checks and money market mutual fund shares—form a smaller part of the money stock. We will leave them out of the picture altogether in this chapter.

### A Balance-Sheet View of Money

Money in the form of currency and bank deposits appears on three important balance sheets, as shown in Figure 8.1. The first balance sheet is that of the Federal Reserve System, the central bank of the United States. The second balance sheet shows the total assets, liabilities, and net worth of all the country's commercial banks and thrift institutions. The third balance sheet includes the total assets, liabilities, and net worth of everyone else in the economy, that is, all households and all business firms except banks.

We can begin by looking at where currency appears on these three balance sheets. As we saw in the previous chapter, currency is a liability of the Federal Reserve System; it appears on the right-hand side of the Fed's balance sheet. Commercial banks and thrifts keep currency on hand for their tellers to hand out over the counter and to fill their ATM machines. This currency held by banks—called vault cash—counts as part of the bank's reserves. Because vault cash is an asset, it appears on the left-hand side of the banks' balance sheet. The rest of the currency issued by the Fed appears as an asset on the balance sheets of households and firms, which use it as a means of payment and a store of value. Only this currency—called *currency in circulation*—is included in the official measures of the money stock (M1 and M2). Vault cash does not count as part of the nation's money stock.

## FIGURE 8.1  BALANCE SHEETS

| Federal Reserve System | |
|---|---|
| Government securities<br>Other net assets | Monetary base<br>  *includes*<br>  Currency<br>  Reserve deposits |
| **Commercial Banks and Thrifts** | |
| Reserves<br>  *includes*<br>  Reserve deposits (at Fed)<br>  Currency (vault cash)<br>Loans<br>Other assets | Bank deposits<br>Other liabilities<br><br><br><br>Net worth |
| **Households and Firms** | |
| Currency<br>Bank deposits<br>Other assets | Bank loans<br>Other liabilities<br>Net worth |

Money, consisting of currency and bank deposits, appears on three balance sheets. Currency in the hands of the public is an asset of households and non-bank firms and a liability of the Fed. Currency held as vault cash by banks is not part of the money stock. The remainder of the money stock consists of bank deposits, which are an asset of households and firms and a liability of banks. Currency plus banks' reserve deposits constitute the monetary base.

The second component of the money stock consists of funds on deposit at the nation's commercial banks and thrift institutions. These are assets of households and firms and liabilities of banks. They are used by the public as a means of payment and a store of value.

One last item links the balance sheet of commercial banks and thrifts with that of the Fed. This item consists of reserves that banks deposit with the Fed in somewhat the same way that businesses and households keep money on deposit in commercial banks. These reserve deposits, together with vault cash, are used to help customers meet their payment needs and to help protect banks against liquidity risk. The total reserves of the banking system thus consist of reserve deposits at the Fed plus currency held as vault cash.

### The Monetary Base

**Monetary base**

The sum of currency and reserve deposits, the monetary liabilities of the central bank

Let's look more closely now at the Fed's balance sheet. This balance sheet is arranged in such a way that only the Fed's monetary liabilities—currency and the reserve deposits of commercial banks and thrifts—appear on the right-hand side of the balance sheet.[2] The sum of currency and reserve deposits is called the **monetary base**. Notice that the monetary base includes both currency in circulation, which appears on the balance sheet of households and firms, and vault cash, shown on the commercial bank balance sheet. As we will see, the monetary base plays an important role in the conduct of monetary policy.

## A Closer Look at Bank Reserves

In Chapter 7, we saw that banks hold a certain quantity of liquid reserves in order to serve the needs of their customers for payment services and to guard against liquidity risk. In this section we take a closer look at bank reserves. First we will see how banks distribute reserves between currency and reserve deposits and, then, how they determine the total amount of reserves they will hold.

**RESERVE DEPOSITS VERSUS CURRENCY**   From the banks' point of view, reserve deposits and currency held as vault cash are close substitutes. Reserve deposits are used in the process of clearing checks, which are written on one bank and deposited in another, and for other kinds of interbank transactions. Currency is distributed to customers over the counter by a bank's tellers and through Automatic Teller Machines (ATMs) located at the bank or in other convenient locations.

Banks have complete flexibility in deciding how much of their reserves to hold as currency and how much as reserve deposits. Some banks, depending on their location, their customers' needs, and the time of year, tend to receive more currency each day from their customers' deposits than they supply to customers through their branches and ATMs. When that is the case, they have the right to send the excess currency to the Fed, which records the amount received as an increase in the bank's reserve deposit. Other banks may find that they are paying out more currency to their customers than they receive as deposits. To replenish their tellers' drawers and their ATM machines, they ask the Fed to send them additional currency. The Fed loads the requested amount of currency on an armored truck and sends it to the bank. As it does so, it reduces the bank's reserve deposit by the same amount.

Whether banks send excess currency to the Fed or request additional currency from it, there is no change in total bank reserves (reserve deposits plus vault cash) and no change in the monetary base (total currency plus reserve deposits). Only the relative proportion of these items held in currency or non-currency form changes.

**DETERMINING THE AMOUNT OF RESERVES**   In addition to deciding how to divide reserves between currency and reserve deposits, banks must also decide what total quantity of reserves to hold. The quantity of reserves is most conveniently stated as a ratio of reserves to deposits, which we will call the **reserve ratio**. Two major factors influence the quantity of reserves banks choose to hold.

The first factor influencing reserves is a trade-off between liquidity and income. On the one hand, holding a greater quantity of liquid reserves makes life easier for a bank. It has greater flexibility in meeting its customers' needs, and it also avoids liquidity risk. The risk comes partly from the possibility that unanticipated withdrawals of funds by depositors will drain away liquid assets, and partly from the need to immediately fulfill promises to supply regular customers with short term loans as they need them. For either of these reasons, a bank could have to borrow more reserves or sell other assets like loans or bonds. If market conditions are unfavorable, it may be costly to borrow additional reserves, and the prices it gets for selling other assets may be disappointingly low. In either case, the bank will suffer a loss. In extreme cases, the bank might not be able to

### Reserve ratio

The ratio of a bank's reserves (reserve deposits at the central bank plus vault cash) to its own deposit liabilities

obtain the needed liquid reserves at any price and would not be able to fulfill its promise that customers can withdraw funds on demand. In that case, the bank would fail.

On the other hand, despite the convenience and reduced risk of holding a large amount of liquid reserves, there is an opportunity cost of doing so. The opportunity cost comes from the fact that assets held in the form of currency or reserve deposits at the Fed earn little or no interest. Until October 2008, the Fed did not pay any interest at all on reserve deposits. As part of the Emergency Economic Stabilization Act of 2008, the Fed received the authority to pay interest on reserve deposits and began to do so. However, as the economy fell into recession and interest rates in general reached low levels, the Fed lowered the rate of interest on reserves to just one quarter of one percent. It is likely that when the economy recovers, the rate paid on reserves will be raised again; but it is expected that it will remain low compared to other market interest rates. As long as that is true, banks will experience an opportunity cost for holding liquid reserves.

Reserve regulations are the second factor influencing the quantity of reserves a bank holds. The degree of regulation varies. In the past, the Federal Reserve, like most other central banks, tended to regulate reserves rather strictly. It did so by setting a minimum ratio of reserves to deposits. In recent decades, central banks have tended to back away from strict regulation of reserves. In some countries, including the United Kingdom, Canada, and New Zealand, the ratio of reserves to deposits is not regulated at all. The Fed has not gone quite so far, but it has moved more cautiously in the same direction. In 1990, it eliminated reserve requirements on saving and time deposits, which constitute nearly 90 percent of all deposits. In 1992, reserve requirements on transactions deposits were cut to 10 percent. As a result, reserve requirements, as a percent of all bank deposits, are at a historically low level.

Banks must take both central bank regulations and considerations of safe banking practice into account when choosing the amount of reserves to hold. If they hold too many reserves, they will forego an opportunity to invest in more profitable assets like loans and securities. If they hold too few, they increase their liquidity risk and they may be subject to central bank penalties for insufficient reserves. We will call the minimum quantity of reserves that banks desire to hold consistent with opportunity costs, regulations, and safe banking practices the **target reserve ratio**. The difference between the amounts of reserves a bank actually holds at any given time and the minimum required by regulations are called **excess reserves**. In the United States, a bank's target reserve ratio has normally been only slightly greater than the minimum required by Federal Reserve regulations. However, as the financial crisis deepened during 2008, banks began to hold much higher levels of excess reserves than usual.

**Target reserve ratio**

The minimum amount of reserves a bank needs to hold that is consistent with regulations and safe banking practices

**Excess reserves**

The difference between the amounts of reserve a bank actually holds and the minimum required by regulations

## How Banks Create Money

Where does money come from? There is no mystery about the creation of the part of the money stock that consists of currency. As explained in the previous section, paper money is printed by the government and distributed through the banking system whenever banks ask for it; and coins, which are minted by the Treasury, are distributed in a similar way. However, the origin of the bulk of the money stock, which consists of bank deposits, is less well understood. Lending by commercial banks is the most important mechanism through which the deposit component of the money stock is created. The following, simple example will show how a bank creates new money by making a loan.

Suppose that I am a banker and you are a consumer. You have found a nice new car at a local dealer and have agreed on a price of $25,000. You go to your laptop to check the balance in your account at my bank and see that you have $10,000 on deposit, more than enough for a down payment but not enough to buy the car for cash. You come into the bank and apply for a loan of $20,000. I check your credit history and approve the loan. You sign a promissory note, promising to repay the $20,000 with interest over a three-year period. I give you the $20,000 by crediting that amount to your account. The next morning, you go online and check your account balance once again. Sure enough, you now have $30,000—the $10,000 you started with plus the $20,000 loan proceeds that the bank credited to your account. You go to the dealer, write out a check for $25,000, and drive off in your new car. You have $5,000 left over to pay for groceries and rent for the rest of the month. Later in the day, the dealership deposits the check in its account at whatever bank it does business with—maybe my bank, but more likely, another one.

Figure 8.2 shows how these transactions affect the three key players in the monetary system: the Fed, the banking system, and the rest of the private sector, consisting of firms and households. Unlike Figure 8.1, this time we do not show the complete balance sheets for the three key players. Instead, the figure shows **T-accounts**, which are simplified versions of the balance sheets that show only the items that change as a result of a given set of transactions.

First, look at the T-account for the banking system. When you signed the promissory note for the loan, my bank gained a new asset worth $20,000. This is shown as an entry of +20,000 under loans. At the same time, when I credited the $20,000 of loan proceeds to your account, my bank gained a new liability. This is shown as an entry of ¡20,000 under deposits. Later, when you bought the car, the deposit moved from my bank to the bank where the car dealer maintains an account. That transaction does not

**T-account**

A simplified version of a balance sheet that shows only items that change as a result of a given set of transactions

## FIGURE 8.2  T-ACCOUNTS

| Federal Reserve System | |
|---|---|
| *no changes* | *no changes* |

| Commercial Banks and Thrifts | | | |
|---|---|---|---|
| Reserves | *no change* | Bank deposits | +20,000 |
| Loans | +20,000 | | |

| Households and Firms | | | |
|---|---|---|---|
| Bank deposits | +20,000 | Bank loans | +20,000 |

This diagram shows how the money stock is affected when a bank makes a loan. Instead of complete balance sheets, T-accounts are used, which show only items that change as the result of the loan. The loan results in an increase in bank assets and consumer liabilities; at the same time, it produces an increase in bank deposits, which are consumer assets and bank liabilities.

show up on this T-account, which shows only the total balance sheet for all banks. Just moving funds from an account at one bank to an account at another does not affect total bank assets or liabilities.

Next, look at the T-account for firms and households. The increase in deposits when my bank credited your deposit with the proceeds of the loan shows up on the asset side of the T-account as an entry of +20,000. Your obligation to repay the loan according to the terms of the promissory note shows up on the liability side as an entry of +20,000. Later, you used the $20,000 to pay for the car, but that part of the transaction does not show up here because this is the total balance sheet for all firms and households. Just moving the funds from your account to that of the car dealer does not affect the totals.

While all this goes on, the balance sheet of the Fed is unaffected.

Now look at the three T-accounts together to see what has happened to the money stock. No new currency has been issued, so that part of the money stock is unchanged. However, the total amount of deposits in the economy has increased by $20,000. That is a net addition to the money stock. The lesson to be learned from this example is: *Whenever a bank makes a loan, the immediate effect is to increase the money stock by the amount of the loan.*

## Limits to Banks' Ability to Create Money

Wait a minute, you say. I know bankers are rich, but this looks *too* easy! If banks can create money whenever they want, what keeps them from creating *unlimited* amounts of money? Why don't bankers create enough to buy up everyone and everything there is?

These are good questions, and they deserve a careful answer. Although banks do create money when they make loans, they can't create unlimited amounts of money. There are two principal constraints on banks' powers of money creation.

**THE RESERVES CONSTRAINT**    The first constraint arises from the need for banks to hold reserves of liquid assets in the form of currency or reserve deposits at the central bank. As explained in the previous section, banks try to maintain a target reserve ratio, taking into account central bank regulations and safe banking practices. Banks forego too many profitable lending opportunities if reserves are above the target ratio, and they face excessive liquidity risk and possible administrative penalties if the reserve ratio falls below the target.

A close look at Figure 8.2 shows that when a bank creates new deposits by making a loan, the amount of total reserves in the banking system does not change. However, since deposits increase and reserves do not, that means the *ratio* of reserves to deposits decreases. As banks make more and more loans, at some point the reserve ratio will fall to the target level, as determined by regulations or safe banking practices. Once this minimum is reached, banks cannot safely make more loans until the banking system receives more reserves.

Sometimes, banks may find that their reserves have temporarily fallen below the target level. If so, they can restore reserves to their target ratio by reducing the volume of loans. They do this mainly by allowing old loans to be repaid without making new loans to replace them. Similarly, banks will not allow the reserve ratio to rise above its target for long. Whenever the reserve ratio is higher than the target, they will pursue new lending opportunities more aggressively, lowering interest rates or easing other loan terms if that is necessary to attract borrowers.

Although the target reserve ratio places a constraint on lending for the banking system as a whole, the target ratio is not a strict constraint for any individual bank. For one thing, the Fed enforces its reserve requirements, on average, over a two-week period, not on a day-to-day basis. More importantly, although at first glance, it might seem that a bank must wait until it has excess reserves before it can make new loans, that is not really true. Suppose some bank is already operating at its target reserve ratio when a customer comes in the door with an attractive proposal to borrow several million dollars for a new wind farm. The bank has several ways of obtaining the reserves it needs to make the loan while still meeting its target reserve ratio. One option is to sell some other asset, for example, short-term, easily marketable securities. Another option is to borrow reserves from some other bank that temporarily has more reserves than it needs. There are other options as well. None of these tactics by which a single bank can get the reserves it needs changes the total reserves of the banking system. However, they do mean that no single bank has to wait passively for reserves to arrive before it can take advantage of new loan opportunities.

**THE DEPOSIT MULTIPLIER**   In a simplified banking system where deposits were the only form of money, the constraint on deposit creation imposed by the reserve ratio would imply a simple relationship between the total amount of deposit-money and total reserves. We can state this relationship as follows:

$$\text{Total deposits} = \text{Total reserves} \times (1/\text{Reserve ratio})$$

The term 1/Reserve ratio on the right-hand side of this equation can be called the **deposit multiplier**. The deposit multiplier shows the amount of deposits that can be created for each dollar of total reserves in a simple banking system where deposits are the only form of money.

**THE CURRENCY CONSTRAINT**   The preceding examples leave out an important aspect of the monetary system—currency. In an economy where people choose to use currency for part of their transactions, the picture changes. Bank lending still causes the money stock to increase, but not by as much. A modification of our earlier example will make this clear.

Suppose that this time instead of borrowing money from my bank to buy a car, you want to borrow $2,000 to go on vacation. As before, you sign the papers for a loan, and my bank credits $2,000 to your account. This time, however, as soon as you verify that the funds are on deposit in your account, you go to the nearest ATM and withdraw $1,000 in currency to take with you on your trip. You will use this money on occasions when you need to pay cash, and you leave the rest on deposit to cover parts of your vacation that you plan to pay for by check or debit card.

Figure 8.3 shows the T-accounts for this set of transactions. As before, the loan appears as an increase in bank assets and an increase in household liabilities. Also, as before, the loan produces an equal increase in the money stock, this time consisting of

**Deposit multiplier**

The quantity of total deposits that can be created for each dollar of total reserves in a simple banking system where deposits are the only form of money, equal to 1/Reserve ratio

## FIGURE 8.3   T-ACCOUNT EFFECTS OF A LOAN

| Federal Reserve System | | | |
|---|---|---|---|
| no changes | | no changes | |
| **Commercial Banks and Thrifts** | | | |
| Reserves (vault cash) | -1,000 | Bank deposits | +1,000 |
| Loans | +2,000 | | |
| **Households and Firms** | | | |
| Bank deposits | +1,000 | Bank loans | +2,000 |
| Currency | +1,000 | | |

This figure shows the T-account effects of a loan, when part of the loan proceeds are withdrawn as cash. The end result is an increase in the money stock (bank deposits plus currency in circulation) and a decrease in total bank reserves.

$1,000 of additional deposits and $1,000 of currency in circulation.[3] The big difference between Figure 8.3 and Figure 8.2 lies in what happens to bank reserves. When you withdraw $1,000 from the bank's ATM, the vault cash portion of the banking system's reserves decreases by $1,000, in contrast to the earlier example, where total bank reserves remained unchanged.

On average, the fraction of each increase in the money stock that will be withdrawn from the banking system as currency is predictable. These cash withdrawals put an added constraint on banks' ability to make loans. Now lending not only causes deposits to increase, it also causes total reserves to fall through withdrawals of currency. Starting from any given amount of reserves, the ratio of reserves to deposits will approach the target reserve ratio faster than would be the case if deposits were the only form of money. The total amount of money that banks can create is accordingly less.

**THE MONEY MULTIPLIER**   For an economy where deposits were the only form of money, we were able to state the money stock as a multiple of bank reserves. We can do something similar for an economy that includes currency, except that now reserves are a variable, not a constant, so they no longer make a suitable reference point. Instead, the best reference point for the size of the money stock is the monetary base—the sum of bank reserve deposits and currency issued by the Federal Reserve. Although total bank reserves change when currency moves from banks into the hands of the public, the monetary base does not. The monetary base includes all currency, regardless of whether it is held by banks, households, or firms.

In equation form, we can state the relationship between the money stock (currency in circulation plus bank deposits) and the monetary base (total currency plus bank reserve deposits at the central bank) as follows:

$$\text{Money stock} = \text{Monetary base} \times [(1+CUR)/(RES+CUR)]$$

In this equation, we use the symbol RES to stand for the target reserve ratio. The symbol CUR stands for the amount of currency that the public chooses to hold per dollar of bank deposits. The expression (1+CUR)/(RES+CUR) on the right-hand side of the equation is known as the **money multiplier**. The money multiplier gives the total quantity of money that can be created for each dollar of the monetary base.[4]

**Money multiplier**

The total quantity of money that can be created for each dollar of the monetary base

For example, suppose that banks want to hold $1 in reserves for each $10 in deposits, so that the variable RES equals 0.1. (It does not matter whether banks decide to hold this quantity of reserves because it is required by central bank regulations or whether they decide on their own that they need that quantity of reserves in order to safely serve their customers.) Suppose also that the public decides to hold $2 in currency for each $10 in deposits, so that the variable CUR equals 0.2. In that case, the money multiplier will be (1+.2)/(.1+.2) = 1.2/.3 = 4. A maximum of $4 of money can be created for each $1 of the monetary base.

The money multiplier differs from one country to another depending on regulations, payment habits of the public, and the degree of development of the banking system. In the United States, the money multiplier for M2 is approximately 8. By comparison, in Russia, the money multiplier is only a little over 3. The main reason for the smaller money multiplier in Russia is that currency accounts for a much larger portion of the total money stock. That, in turn, reflects the fact that the commercial banking system in Russia is less developed and less trusted by the public than in the United States.

# Central Banking and the Instruments of Monetary Policy

As we learned in Chapter 7, the Fed, like the central banks of many other countries, has a major role in ensuring safety and stability. Now we turn to an even more important function of central banks—the monetary policies by which central banks control the money stock and interest rates. These provide the single most important means by which governments can influence short-run macroeconomic variables like unemployment, inflation, and real output.

## Open Market Operations

The most important instruments of monetary policy for the Fed and many other central banks are the purchase and sale of government securities. For the Fed, these are usually short-term securities issued by the U.S. Treasury in order to finance the government's budget deficit. The U.S. Treasury sells newly issued securities to the public through frequently scheduled auctions, but the Fed is not allowed to participate directly in those auctions. Instead, it buys and sells government securities that have been previously issued by the treasury through securities dealers that operate in public financial markets. Because the Fed normally buys securities in public markets that are open to traders of all kinds, rather than buying them directly from the Treasury, the Fed's purchases and sales of government securities are called *open market operations*.

**EFFECTS OF AN OPEN MARKET PURCHASE**   Figure 8.4 shows the immediate impact of an open market purchase of $1,000,000 of securities by the Fed. The purchase appears on the Fed's T-account as a $1,000,000 increase in assets. The securities dealer from whom the securities are purchased is part of the "households and firms" sector, so the asset side of that T-account shows a decrease of government securities. The Fed pays the dealer by issuing a payment order to the commercial bank where the dealer's firm maintains a deposit. When the payment order is carried out, the dealer's deposit increases by $1,000,000, as shown by an entry on the left-hand side of the firms and households T-account and a corresponding entry on the right-hand side of the banking sector's T-account. At the same time, the bank's reserve deposit account at the Fed is credited with an increase of $1,000,000. The increase in reserve deposits is shown on the left-hand side of the banking sector's T-account and the right-hand side of the Fed's T-account.

Looking at Figure 8.4 as a whole, we see that the immediate impact of the open market operation is an increase of $1,000,000 in bank reserves, bank deposits and the money stock. That is not the end of the story, however. To trace the full impact of the open market operation on the money stock, we have to look at how banks adjust their operations in response to the increase in reserves.

Suppose that before the open market operations, banks were operating at their target reserve ratio. If so, an equal increase in total reserves and deposits, as shown in Figure 8.4, raises the ratio of total bank reserves to deposits above its target. Banks will take advantage of the new reserves to make additional loans, and the money stock will expand further, following the process illustrated earlier in Figures 8.2 and 8.3.

As the banks create additional deposits through lending, the reserve ratio decreases. When borrowers withdraw part of the loan proceeds as currency, total bank reserves decrease and the reserve ratio falls further. When the reserve ratio reaches its target, expansion of the money stock ceases. At that point, the total change in the money stock will be equal to the money multiplier times the change in the monetary base. For example, suppose the reserve ratio is .1 and the public's desired ratio of currency to deposits is .2, as in our earlier example. In that case, the money multiplier is 4, so the $1,000,000

---

**FIGURE 8.4   IMMEDIATE IMPACT OF AN OPEN MARKET PURCHASE**

| Federal Reserve System | | | |
|---|---|---|---|
| Government securities | +1,000,000 | Reserve deposits | +1,000,000 |

| Commercial Banks and Thrifts | | | |
|---|---|---|---|
| Reserve deposits | +1,000,000 | Bank deposits | +1,000,000 |

| Households and Firms | | | |
|---|---|---|---|
| Bank deposits | +1,000,000 | | |
| Government securities | −1,000,000 | | |

This figure shows the T-account effects of a $1,000,000 open market purchase of securities by the Fed. The immediate result is an increase in commercial bank reserves, bank deposits, and the money stock. Later (not shown here), banks can use the new reserves as a basis for new loans, leading to further expansion of the money stock.

open market purchase of securities and the resulting $1,000,000 increase in the monetary base will cause the total money stock to expand by $4,000,000. Part of the newly created money will be deposits and part will be currency.

The example just given assumes that the Fed makes an outright purchase of securities from a dealer. In that case, the effect on the monetary base and the money stock will be permanent. Instead of buying securities outright, the Fed often buys them subject to a *repurchase agreement*. Under a repurchase agreement, the Fed agrees to sell the securities back to the dealer, for an agreed price, at some specific date in the future, often as soon as the next day. The effects of an open market purchase subject to a repurchase agreement are only temporary because the change in the monetary base lasts only until the repurchase is completed. Repurchase agreements are routinely used by the Fed to make small, day-to-day adjustments in the monetary base.

In addition to buying and selling short-term Treasury securities, the Fed also has the power to buy many other kinds of assets. In normal times, it does not need to do so; but as the U.S. financial system came under increasing strain in 2008 and 2009, the Fed began to buy a much broader range of assets—including long-term Treasury securities, bonds issued by government sponsored enterprises like Fannie Mae and Freddie Mac, and certain kinds of private securities. The effects of such purchases on the balance sheets of the Fed, commercial banks, and the public are exactly the same as those shown in Figure 8.4.

**EFFECTS OF AN OPEN MARKET SALE**   If the Fed sells securities instead of buying them, the entire process just described is reversed. When the Fed sells securities, the securities dealers who buy them pay by drawing on their accounts at commercial banks. Deposits, bank reserves, the monetary base, and the money stock—all fall. The immediate impact on reserves and the monetary base would be shown by a set of T-accounts identical to Figure 8.4, except that all the plus and minus signs would be reversed.

The immediate impact of an open market sale by the Fed is to decrease reserves and deposits by an equal amount, so the ratio of reserves to deposits will fall below the target reserve ratio. Given the reduced quantity of reserves, the only way banks can restore the reserve ratio to its proper level is to reduce the total amount of outstanding loans, which they can do by allowing old loans to be repaid without making enough new loans to replace them. As repayments exceed new loans, total deposits and the total money stock decrease. The process will come to an end when the reserve ratio once again reaches its target level. Assuming a money multiplier of 4, a $4,000,000 decrease in the money stock would be required to restore the target reserve ratio following a $1,000,000 open market sale of securities.

## Interest Rates

In addition to open market purchases and sales of securities, changes in interest rates provide the Fed with a second important instrument of monetary policy. The interest rates in question are the rate that the Fed charges banks for reserves that they borrow and the rate it pays to banks for the reserves they keep on deposit.

Let's look first at the rate charged for borrowed reserves. As mentioned earlier, when individual banks see profitable lending opportunities, they do not need to wait passively for new reserves to arrive. Instead, they can borrow the reserves they need. One way to do this is to borrow them from another bank. The market in which banks make short-term loans of reserves to other banks is known in the United States as the **federal funds market**. (A more general term is the interbank loan market. All countries have interbank loan markets although the local names of these markets differ.) The interest rate charged on such loans is called the **federal funds rate**. Transactions in this market, in which the usual loan term is overnight, total billions of dollars per day.

The borrowing and lending of reserves through the federal funds market has no effect on total bank reserves; this type of borrowing just moves reserves around from one bank to another. However, banks also have the option of borrowing funds directly from the Fed through the so-called **discount window**. Funds that banks borrow from the Fed through the discount window are a net addition to total bank reserves. They affect the money stock in exactly the same way as do additional reserves provided through open market operations.

Banks borrow from the Fed in two kinds of situations. The most frequent kind of borrowing, called *primary credit*, is done by banks that are fundamentally healthy but which find themselves temporarily short of reserves because of unexpected withdrawals. They are charged an interest rate called the **discount rate**. To discourage banks from borrowing too often or too much through the discount window, the Fed sets the discount rate above the prevailing level of the federal funds rate at which banks can borrow from one another.

In addition to such lending, the Fed sometimes makes loans to troubled banks to give them time to get their affairs in order. Since these banks are less creditworthy, they must pay a higher interest rate. Typically, their interest rate is one-half of a percentage point above the discount rate charged on primary credit loans.

The discount rate gives the Fed a second instrument of monetary policy, although a less powerful one than open market operations. If the Fed wants to encourage more borrowing of reserves, it lowers the discount rate. As the discount rate falls relative to the federal funds rate, the cost of discount borrowing falls relative to the cost of borrowing from other banks and the volume of discount borrowing expands. If the Fed wants to reduce borrowing from the discount window, it raises the discount rate.

Since passage of the Emergency Economic Stabilization Act of 2008, the Fed has acquired an additional instrument of monetary policy, the power to pay interest on reserves that banks keep on deposit with the Fed. An increase in the interest rate paid on reserves decreases the opportunity cost to banks of holding excess reserves. Other things being equal, that would tend to increase banks' desired holdings of excess reserves and, hence, to increase their target ratio of reserves to deposits. That, in turn, would tend to reduce the money multiplier, so that banks would tend to create less money for each dollar of the monetary base. This new power was introduced at a time when the U.S. financial system was under extraordinary stress, so it is uncertain exactly how the Fed will exercise its power to pay interest on reserves in normal times. However, it appears likely that it will adopt a practice used by other central banks around the world, namely, that of charging a discount rate for borrowed reserves that is slightly higher than the rate for pri-

## Federal funds market

A market in which banks lend reserves to one another for periods as short as 24 hours

## Federal funds rate

The interest rate on overnight loans of reserves from one bank to another

## Discount window

The department through which the Federal Reserve lends reserves to banks

## Discount rate

The interest rate charged by the Fed on loans of reserves to banks

vate interbank borrowing (the federal funds rate in the United States) and, at the same time, paying a rate on deposited reserves that is slightly below the interbank rate.

## Changes in Required-Reserve Ratios

Changes in required-reserve ratios are a third potential policy instrument that central banks can use to control the money stock. Earlier in the chapter we showed that the total volume of money is equal to the monetary base times the money multiplier:

$$\text{Money stock} = \text{Monetary base} \times [(1+\text{CUR})/(\text{RES}+\text{CUR})]$$

The term RES in this equation stands for the target reserve ratio, which in the United States depends, in part, on the minimum level of reserves required by the Fed for transaction deposits. An increase in the required reserve ratio increases the term RES, which appears in the denominator of the money multiplier. Accordingly, the money multiplier as a whole decreases when RES increases. That, in turn, will cause the money stock to decrease for any given level of the monetary base. Similarly, a decrease in reserve requirements will cause the money multiplier and the money stock to increase.

Changes in reserve requirements have never been used for day-to-day control over the money supply, but there have been times in the past when the Fed changed the ratios in order to make a strong move toward expansion or contraction of the money supply. For example, in late 1990, the Fed eliminated a 3 percent reserve requirement on non-personal saving and time deposits. In April 1992, it reduced the required reserve ratio on transaction deposits from 12 percent to 10 percent. These changes were made, in part, to speed recovery from the 1990–1991 recession although they also reflected a belief that lower reserve requirements would reduce bank's costs, encourage bank lending, and strengthen the role of banks in the financial system. Since that time, the Fed has not used the reserve requirement as an instrument to control the money supply. Changes in reserve requirements pose difficulties for bank balance sheet management, and high reserve requirements make banks less competitive with other financial institutions.

Occasionally, the central banks of other countries use changes in required reserves as an instrument of monetary policy; but on the whole, this instrument is not of great importance. It is not available at all in countries like the UK and Canada, where central banks leave the determination of the reserve ratio up to the business judgment of individual banks.

## Purchases and Sales of Foreign Reserves

In addition to holding large amounts of securities issued by the U.S. Treasury and other domestic institutions, the Fed, working together with the Treasury, also has the power to buy and sell assets denominated in foreign currency—for example, bonds issued by the governments of Germany, denominated in euros, or Japan, denominated in yen. Such purchases would not be made directly from the foreign governments but instead from private securities dealers, much in the same way that open market purchases of domestic securities are made. The effects on the monetary base of a purchase or sale of foreign assets are exactly the same as domestic open market purchases, as illustrated in Figure 8.4.

The Fed, working with the Treasury, has the power to buy and sell assets dominated in foreign currency.

In addition to their effects on the money stock, purchases and sales of foreign assets also tend to affect the exchange rates between currencies. For example, if the Fed were to buy German bonds denominated in euros, the exchange rate of the euro would tend to strengthen relative to the dollar. If the Fed sold euro-denominated bonds, the dollar would tend to strengthen.

In recent decades, the Fed has not used this instrument of monetary policy although there have been times in the past when it did so. In contrast, purchases and sales of foreign assets are the single most important instrument of monetary policy for the central banks of many countries. We will return to this instrument of monetary policy and the subject of exchange rates in later chapters.

## Other Factors Affecting the Money Multiplier

We have already seen that the money multiplier is subject to change as a result of changes in reserve requirements. In addition, even if central bank policy remains unchanged, changing market conditions can cause the money multiplier to vary through effects on the currency ratio (CUR) or the target reserve ratio (RES).

The amount of currency that firms and households want to hold per dollar of deposits varies, among other reasons, according to the season of the year. During the Christmas shopping season, consumers withdraw additional money from their bank accounts to buy gifts, and retailers also stock the cash drawers in their stores with extra currency. Accordingly, the variable CUR increases and the money multiplier decreases.[5] The same thing happens during the summer vacation season, when consumers withdraw extra cash for their travels.

The target reserve ratio can also be affected by changing conditions in financial markets. When market interest rates increase, it becomes more expensive for firms to borrow liquid reserves. They tighten their liquidity management practices in order to get by with the lowest amount of reserves they can, consistent with central bank regulations and safe banking practices. Accordingly, an increase in market interest rates, other things being equal, tends to decrease the target reserve ratio and increase the money multiplier. Similarly, when interest rates fall, the opportunity cost of holding excess reserves falls. The target reserve ratio then increases, raising the money multiplier.

Such market-driven changes in the money multiplier pose a challenge to the Fed. When the money multiplier increases, the Fed must offset the increase with open market sales of securities or an increase in the discount rate. When the money multiplier decreases, the Fed must buy securities on the open market or lower the discount rate. Normally, central banks can make such adjustments smoothly enough to maintain reasonably close control over the money stock. For example, the Fed can anticipate seasonal changes in currency demand fairly accurately. Still, because the money multiplier is not a constant, central banks cannot control the money stock precisely. In extreme cases, changes in the money multiplier may cause serious problems. For example, during Japan's long period of deflation in the late 1990s and early 2000s, that country's commercial banks became very reluctant to make new loans. As banks accumulated unused reserves, the money multiplier fell to levels far below normal; and the Bank of Japan found it very difficult to provide the amount of monetary policy stimulus it needed to speed economic recovery. As discussed further in Chapter 10, a similar problem developed in the U.S. economy during 2008 and 2009.

⌒

## Summary

1. **What is money, and why does money matter?** *Money* is an asset that serves as a means of payment, a store of purchasing power, and a unit of account. A narrow measure of the money stock, *M1*, includes *currency* (coins and paper money) plus *transaction deposits* (deposits on which checks can be freely written). A broader and more widely used measure, *M2*, includes the components of M1 plus money market mutual fund shares, *savings deposits*, small-denomination *time deposits*, and certain other liquid assets. The relationship between money and other economic variables can be stated as the *equation of exchange:* MV = PQ, in which M stands for the money stock, V for *velocity*, P for the price level, and Q for real domestic product.

2. **How do banks create money?** Banks create money, in the form of deposits, by making loans. When a bank makes a loan, it credits the proceeds to the borrower's account. This increase in total bank deposits adds to the money stock. The borrower will probably spend the borrowed funds, rather than leaving them in the bank from which they were borrowed. As long as the funds are spent in a way that just moves them from one bank to another (for example, by writing a check on one bank that is deposited in another), lending adds to the money stock without changing the total quantity of reserves in the banking system.

3. **What limits the size of the money stock?** The reserve ratio is the bank reserves to bank deposits. When banks lend money, other things being equal,

the reserve ratio falls. When it reaches the *target reserve ratio* consistent with regulations and safe banking practices, the banking system cannot further increase its total lending; the money stock will cease growing. In addition, when banks make loans, bank customers may withdraw part of borrowed funds in the form of currency. Such withdrawals reduce the total level of bank reserves and constitute a second limit on the ability of banks to expand the money stock by lending. Taking both limits into account, the size of the money stock is determined by the *monetary base* times the *money multiplier.*

4. **What instruments are available to the Fed for controlling the money stock?** *Open market operations*, in which the Fed affects the banking system's reserves through purchases or sales of government securities, are the Fed's principal instrument of monetary control. An open market purchase injects reserves into the banking system and allows the money stock to expand; an open market sale drains reserves and causes the money stock to contract. Changes in the discount rate charged by the Fed on loans of reserves to banks or the interest rate paid by the Fed on deposits of reserves are a second instrument of monetary control. Changes in required-reserve ratios are potentially a third means of controlling the money stock. A decrease in the required-reserve ratio creates excess reserves and allows the money stock to expand; an increase in the ratio causes the money stock to contract. In practice, the Fed no longer uses changes in reserve ratios as a policy instrument. Purchases and sales of foreign assets are a fourth potential instrument of monetary control. Although the Fed does not actively use this instrument, it is important for many foreign central banks.

## Key Terms

## Problems and Topics for Discussion

1. **Barter in the modern economy** For most purposes, money lowers the cost of making transactions relative to barter—the direct exchange of one good or service for another. However, barter has not disappeared, even in an advanced economy such as that of the United States. Can you give an example of the use of barter in the U.S. economy today? Why is barter used instead of money in this case?

2. **Current monetary data** Every Thursday the Federal Reserve reports certain key data on money and the banking system. These reports are available from the Board of Governors of the Federal Reserve System's *H.6 Statistical Release*. Obtain the most recent H.6 release online at http://www.federalreserve.gov/releases/ and answer the following questions:

    a. What items are included in M2 that are not included in M1? What was the total of such items in the most recent month for which data are reported? Which of these money measures grew most quickly in the most recent month for which data are reported?

b. Demand and other transaction deposits at these banks account for about what percentage of M1? What percentage of M1 is held in the form of currency and travelers checks?

3. **Repayment of a loan** Suppose that you maintain a checking account at Best National Bank and that you also have a loan from Best National. The remaining balance on the loan is $1,000. You have more than that amount in your checking account, so you write a check to the bank to pay off the loan in full. Using the T-accounts of Figure 8.2 as an example, show what happens to total bank reserves, total loans, total deposits, and the total money stock as a result of your loan repayment.

4. **Deposit of currency** Begin with a blank set of T-accounts for the Fed, commercial banks and thrifts, and households and firms. Now suppose that you deposit $500 of currency in your checking account at your commercial bank. Show the immediate effects of this transaction using the T-accounts. How does the deposit affect your total assets? How does it affect the monetary base? The money stock? How does it affect the total assets and total reserves of the banking system? How does it affect the ratio of reserves to deposits in the banking system? Suppose that before your deposit of currency, the banking system had reached the target reserve ratio, so that it was not able to make additional loans. Now, after your deposit, will the banking system be able to make new loans?

5. **The deposit multiplier** What is the value of the deposit multiplier if the target reserve ratio is (a) .2. (b) .25. and (c) .05? For each of these cases, what would the equilibrium quantity of deposits be, assuming total bank reserves of $1 trillion? (For this problem, assume that deposits are the only form of money in the economy.)

6. **The money multiplier** What is the value of the money multiplier given each of the following sets of values for CUR and RES? (a) CUR=.5 and RES = .25 (b) CUR = .15 and RES = .25 (c) CUR = 1 and RES = .25. For each of these cases, what would be the equilibrium value of the total money stock assuming a monetary base of $10 trillion?

## Case for Discussion

### Makeshift Money in the French Colonial Period

*Governor de Meulle of the French province of Quebec wrote the following letter in September 1685:*

My Lord—

I have found myself this year in great straits with regard to the subsistence of the soldiers. You did not provide for funds, My Lord, until January last. I have, notwithstanding, kept them in provisions until September, which makes eight full months. I have drawn from my own funds and from those of my friends, all I have been able to get, but at last finding them without means to render me further assistance, and not knowing to what saint to pay my vows, money being extremely scarce, having distributed considerable sums on every side for the pay of the soldiers, it occurred to me to issue, instead of money, notes on [playing] cards, which I have had cut in quarters. I send you My Lord, the three kinds, one is for four francs, another for forty sols, and the third for fifteen sols, because with these three kinds, I was able to make their exact pay for one month. I have issued an ordinance by which I have obliged all the inhabitants to receive this money in payments, and to give it circulation, at the same time pledging myself, in my own name, to redeem the said notes. No person has refused them, and so good has been the effect that by this means the troops have lived as usual. There were some merchants who, privately, had offered me money at the local rate on condition that I would repay them in money at the local rate in France, to which I could not consent as the King would have lost a third; that is, for 10,000 he would have paid 40,000 livres; thus personally, by my credit and by my management, I have saved His Majesty 13,000 livres.

[Signed] de Meulle

Quebec, 24th September, 1685

SOURCE: From *Canadian Currency, Exchange and Finance During the French Period,* vol. 1, ed. Adam Shortt (New York: Burt Franklin, Research Source Works Series no. 235, 1968).

## QUESTIONS

1. What indication do you find that the playing-card notes issued by the governor served as a means of payment? Why were they accepted as such?
2. What indicates that the notes served as a store of value? What made them acceptable as such?
3. Did the invention of playing-card money change the unit of account in the local economy?

## End Notes

1. Care must be used in international comparisons because different countries measure money somewhat differently. For example, the U.S. M2 measure is close to, but not identical with, the M3 measure of money used by the European Central Bank.
2. To construct this version of the Fed's balance sheet, non-monetary liabilities and net worth, which would normally appear on the right-hand side, are moved to the left-hand side, with the sign reversed, and are included in the item *other net assets*.
3. Remember that only currency in circulation outside banks counts as part of the money stock. The $1,000 of currency that you withdraw in our example does not count as part of the money stock while it is stored in the ATM waiting for you to come by with your card. Until you withdraw it, the currency is recorded on the bank's balance sheet as vault cash, a part of bank reserves.
4. The formula for the money multiplier can be derived as follows:

    *Eq1* $\quad$ TR = DEP*RES (TR is total reserves held by banks, including reserve deposits and vault cash; DEP is total deposits held by firms and households in commercial banks; and RES is the target reserve ratio. This equation is an equilibrium condition for banks, indicating that reserves are at their target level.)

    *Eq2* $\quad$ CC = DEP * CUR (CC is currency in circulation, and CUR is the public's desired ratio of currency to deposits. This is an equilibrium condition for public distribution of money holdings between currency and deposits.)

    *Eq3* $\quad$ B = CC + TR (B is the monetary base, which can be stated either as reserve deposits plus total currency or as total reserves plus currency in circulation.)

    *Eq4* $\quad$ M = CC + DEP (Definition of money stock)

    Substitute *Eq2* into *Eq4* to get

    *Eq5* $\quad$ M = DEP*CUR + DEP

    Simplify this to get

    *Eq5a* M = (1+CUR) * DEP

    Substitute *Eq1* into *Eq3* to get

    *Eq6* $\quad$ B = CC + DEP*RES

    Substitute *Eq2* into *Eq6* to get

    *Eq7* $\quad$ B = DEP*CUR + DEP*RES

    Solve this for DEP to get

    *Eq7a* $\quad$ DEP = B/(CUR+RES)

    Substitute *Eq7a* into *Eq5a* to get

    *Eq8* $\quad$ M = (1+CUR)*[B/(CUR+RES)]

    Restate this to get

    *Eq8a* M = [(1+CUR)/(RES+CUR)]*B (The term in brackets [ ] is the money multiplier.)

5. For example, suppose that initially the currency ratio CUR is .2 and the reserve ratio is .1. As in our previous examples, the money multiplier will be (1.2)/(.3)=4. If CUR increases to .4 while RES remains at .1, the money multiplier will decrease to (1.4)/(.5) = 2.8.

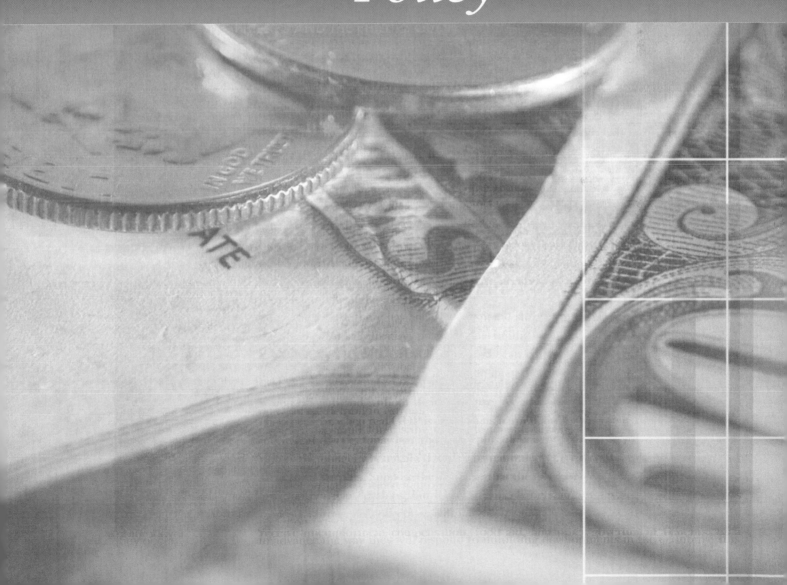

# PART 4

## Macroeconomic Policy

# CHAPTER 9

# Prices and Real Output in the Short Run

---

**After reading this chapter, you will understand the following:**

1. The conditions that determine the slope of the aggregate demand curve
2. The sources of shifts in the aggregate demand curve
3. The conditions that determine the slopes of short- and long-run aggregate supply curves
4. The sources of shifts in the aggregate supply curves
5. How prices, real output, and unemployment behave as the economy responds to a change in aggregate demand

---

**Before reading this chapter, make sure you know the meaning of the concepts:**

1. Supply and demand
2. Real and nominal values
3. Natural level of real output
4. Money
5. Planned expenditure
6. The multiplier effect
7. Final goods
8. Price level
9. Output gap

---

THIS CHAPTER RETURNS to the search for prosperity and stability, first introduced in Chapter 4. We saw there that macroeconomics is dominated by two great sets of questions. One set of questions is associated with Adam Smith's book *The Wealth of Nations:* What are the sources of economic growth in the long run? Why are some countries rich and others poor? The other set of questions is associated with John Maynard Keynes' book *The General Theory of Employment, Interest, and Money:* Why does the economy not grow steadily in the short run? Why does the economy sometimes drop below its long run trend of growth and fall into recession? Why do increases in planned expenditure sometimes cause inflation as well as, or instead of, increases in real output? What, if anything, can government do to tame the business cycle?

We posed these questions in Chapter 4, but we were able to answer them only in a very preliminary way. Since that time we have acquired a number of useful tools and concepts. We know how the parts of the economy fit together in the circular flow. We know how prices and real output are measured. We, also, know the banking system and the instruments of monetary policy. This chapter will pull together these ideas to formulate a model of the macroeconomy for which we will find many applications in the remaining chapters of this book.

## The Aggregate Demand Curve

Our first step will be to develop a new type of supply and demand model. We call it the aggregate supply and demand model because it shows supply and demand relationships not for individual goods, but for the economy as a whole. **Aggregate demand** means total real planned expenditure. **Aggregate supply** means total real output of final goods and services, a synonym for real GDP.

### Aggregate and Market Demand Curves

**Aggregate demand**

Total real planned expenditure

**Aggregate supply**

Total real output of final goods and services (real GDP)

**Aggregate demand curve**

A graph showing the relationship between aggregate demand and the aggregate price level

Figure 9.1 shows a typical **aggregate demand curve**. In some ways, the aggregate demand curve is similar to the demand curves for individual markets, like the market for chicken, which we introduced in Chapter 2. Both kinds of curves represent inverse relationships between price and quantity variables. Both summarize the market choices made by many individual buyers. Both show a price variable on the vertical axis. In addition, as we will show, both kinds of curves interact with other curves representing supply to determine equilibrium conditions. However, there are some important differences between the aggregate demand curve and market demand curves. Two of those differences concern the "other things being equal" conditions that lie behind the curves:

- The market demand curve for a good such as chicken shows the price of chicken on the vertical axis. It is drawn on the assumption that the prices of all other goods remain constant as the price of chicken varies. In the case of the aggregate demand curve, the variable on the vertical axis is an index showing the average prices of all final goods and services, as discussed in chapter 6. As the economy moves upward along the aggregate demand curve, the average level of prices increases; but the prices of particular individual goods may increase, stay the same, or even decrease.

- A market demand curve is drawn on the assumption that consumers' incomes remain constant at all points along the demand curve. The same is not true of

**FIGURE 9.1   AN AGGREGATE DEMAND CURVE**

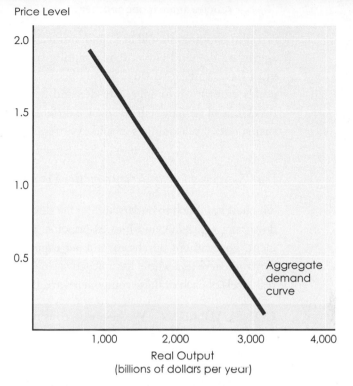

The aggregate demand curve shows the relationship between total real planned expenditure on final goods and the average price level of final goods. The curve has a negative slope because each of the major components of real aggregate demand—consumption, planned investment, government purchases, and net exports—varies inversely with the price level of final goods.

total income in relation to the aggregate demand curve. In Chapter 5, we learned that within the circular flow of income and expenditure, any change in real output necessarily brings with it a change in real income. As we will see shortly, changes in the price level along the aggregate demand curve are also associated with changes in real output, and hence real domestic income.

If prices of other goods and incomes are not held constant as we move along the aggregate demand curve, what are the "other things being equal" conditions for this curve? We will discuss several of them in detail as we develop our model, but we can give a quick preview by noting that a given aggregate demand curve assumes constant values for the following:

- Expectation-related determinants of planned expenditure, for example, consumer confidence and business confidence

- Policy-related variables, including both policies related to government purchases and net taxes, and monetary policy as determined by the central bank

- Economic conditions in the rest of the world, in particular, the levels of real GDP and interest rates in other countries and exchange rates of various currencies against one another

These points should be kept in mind as we address the question of the slope of the aggregate demand curve. It is tempting to reason that the aggregate demand curve must have a negative slope simply because the individual demand curves for all the goods entering into aggregate demand have negative slopes. However, because the two kinds of demand curves involve different "other things being equal" assumptions, such a line of reasoning is invalid. A different approach must be taken instead.

## The Slope of the Aggregate Demand Curve

The best approach to understanding the slope of the aggregate demand curve is to break down aggregate demand into its principal components: consumption, planned investment, government purchases, and net exports. We can understand why the aggregate demand curve as a whole has a negative slope by looking at how decisions regarding the real levels of each of these components are affected by changes in the price level.

**CONSUMPTION**   We begin by considering how the real demand for consumer goods is affected by an increase in the average level of prices. When the price level rises, firms' revenues from sales of a given quantity of goods and services rise by the same proportion. As those revenues are passed along to households in the form of wages, profits, and other factor payments, consumers' nominal incomes also rise. This shields them, in part, from the effects of inflation.

However, even if consumer incomes in nominal terms keep up with the increase in the price level, consumers are not protected in all respects from the effects of inflation. In particular, the money that they hold in currency and bank balances has a fixed nominal value. As the price level increases, the real purchasing power of those nominal money balances falls. For example, $100 in twenty-dollar bills might be enough to buy yourself a week's worth of groceries today; but if you hold onto those five twenties for a year while the average price level rises 15 percent, the same money will buy only enough groceries to last about six days. Because of the falling real value of nominal money balances, then, consumers become less wealthy in terms of real purchasing power when the price level rises. They will correspondingly tend to buy less real output than they would have if the price level had not risen.

Similar reasoning would apply to a period during which the price level fell. The effect of such a drop would be to increase the real value of consumers' nominal holdings of money. As the purchasing power of each dollar in circulation increased, real wealth would rise, real consumption would be stimulated, and real aggregate demand would increase. Taking both increases and decreases in the price level into account, then, we conclude that the real consumption expenditure tends to vary inversely with the price level. That is the first reason for the negative slope of the aggregate demand curve.

**INVESTMENT**   Real planned investment will also be affected by changes in the price level. The reason is that a change in the price level, other things being equal, will change interest rates; and, as we know, interest rates are a key determinant of planned investment.

Suppose that the average price level of all final goods and services increases. If real output remained the same, the nominal sales volume of business firms and nominal incomes of households would also increase. With sales revenues and incomes both rising, firms and households would both want to increase their borrowing from the banking system. However, unless the Fed took some action to increase bank reserves, banks would not be able fully to meet the rising demand for loans at existing interest rates. Increased demand for loans would tend to drive up interest rates. As this happened, businesses and households would revise their plans. Firms would tighten up their cash management practices and cut back or postpone long-term investment projects. Households would find it more difficult to borrow to buy houses, and construction activity would fall.

**GOVERNMENT PURCHASES** The effect of a change in the price level on real government purchases is not the same for all budget items or for all levels of government. Many government purchase decisions are made in real terms. For example, Congress might decide to authorize the Pentagon to buy 100 jet fighters. If the price per plane goes up, more dollars will be added to the defense department budget to purchase the authorized number of planes. However, other government purchase decisions are made in nominal terms. For example, the Virginia Department of Transportation may be given a budget of $50 million for road improvements. If the price of asphalt goes up, the department, constrained by its $50 million budget, will be unable to pave as many miles of roads as it had planned. Perhaps it will be able to persuade the legislature to increase it budget next year, but in the meantime the price increase results in less spending in real terms.

If Congress decides to authorize the purchase of 100 jet fighters and the price per plane goes up, more dollars will need to be added to the defense department budget to complete the purchase.

Generalizing from this example, we conclude that to the extent that some elements of government budgets (federal, state, and local) are set in nominal terms, the government purchases component of aggregate demand will tend to fall in real terms as the price level rises, at least in the short run. Over a longer period, to the extent that inflation raises tax revenues, the government purchases component of planned expenditure is less sensitive to changes in the price level.

**NET EXPORTS**   Prices can rise in one country and remain the same in others. Suppose, for example, that the United States experiences higher prices while prices in Japan stay the same. With a given exchange rate between the dollar and the Japanese yen, U.S. goods will become more expensive for Japanese buyers and Japanese goods will become relatively cheaper for U.S. buyers. As U.S. buyers switch from domestic goods to imports and U.S. exports become harder to sell abroad, the real net export component of aggregate demand falls.

The tendency of real net exports to decrease when a country's price level rises, other things being equal, is another reason for the negative slope of the aggregate demand curve.

## Shifts in the Aggregate Demand Curve

As in the case of individual demand curves, a change in market conditions other than the price level will cause the aggregate demand curve to shift to the left or right. However, because of differences in the "other things being equal" assumptions underlying the two kinds of demand curves, the sources of the shifts are different. Among the sources of shifts in aggregate demand curves are expectations, changes in government policy, and changes in the world economy.

**EXPECTATIONS**   Expectation is one of the conditions held constant in drawing an aggregate demand curve. Chapter 5 emphasized the importance of consumer and investor confidence as determinants of planned expenditure. If consumers become more optimistic about the future, they may increase their real planned expenditures at any given price level. Similarly, an increase in firms' optimism about future profit opportunities may increase real planned investment at any given price level. In either case, the aggregate demand curve shifts to the right, as illustrated by the shift from $AD_1$ to $AD_2$ in Figure 9.2. A swing toward pessimistic expectations by consumers or firms would shift the aggregate demand curve to the left.

**CHANGES IN GOVERNMENT POLICY**   Changes in government policy can also affect aggregate demand. This is true both of **fiscal policy**, meaning policy related to government spending and taxes, and monetary policy, meaning central bank policy toward interest rates and the money stock.

**Fiscal policy**

Policy that is concerned with government purchases, taxes, and transfer payments

First consider an increase in government purchases. Because government purchases are a component of planned expenditure, an increase shifts the aggregate demand curve to the right. Similarly, a decrease in government purchases shifts it to the left. As explained in Chapter 5, the multiplier effect operates to increase the impact of a change

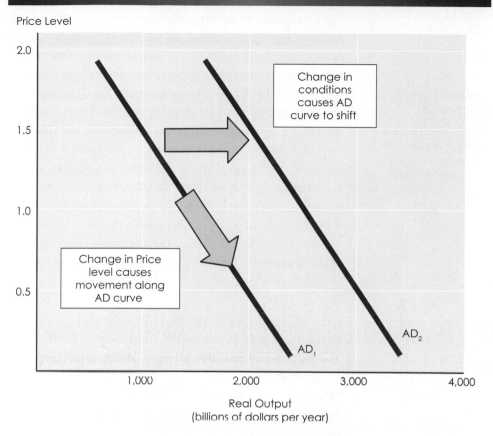

**FIGURE 9.2   SHIFTS IN THE AGGREGATE DEMAND CURVE**

Price Level

Change in conditions causes AD curve to shift

Change in Price level causes movement along AD curve

AD₁

AD₂

Real Output
(billions of dollars per year)

A change in the price level causes a movement along a given aggregate demand curve, other things being equal. A change in economic conditions other than the price level can cause the quantity of real planned expenditure associated with a given price level to change. In that case, the aggregate demand curve will shift, as shown in this diagram. Among the sources of shifts are changes in consumer or business expectations; changes in policies regarding government purchases, taxes, or money; and changes in the world economy.

in government purchases on aggregate demand. For example, suppose the government of the state of Montana hires 100 previously unemployed people as maintenance workers for state parks at a total cost of $250,000 per month. When these workers receive their paychecks, they spend much of their new income on consumer goods, in accordance with the marginal propensity to consume, thereby further adding to planned expenditure. The added expenditures stimulate hiring by consumer goods producers, continuing the multiplier process. In the end, the total addition to planned expenditure is greater than the initial $250,000 addition to government purchases.

Decreases in net taxes also cause aggregate demand to increase. If marginal tax rates are reduced, consumers have more disposable income left for any given total income. They use the extra income to buy consumer goods, adding to planned expenditure. The same is true of a reduction in net taxes taking the form of an increase in transfer payments. For example, an increase in unemployment benefits adds to demand by allowing people who are out of work to maintain a basic level of consumption expenditure.

Changes in monetary policy are another way that the government can increase or decrease aggregate demand. As we saw in Chapter 8, expansionary monetary policy can increase bank reserves, ease credit market conditions, and lead to lower interest rates. Expansionary monetary policy affects the economy via several channels, which together are known as the **transmission mechanism**. The most important aspect of the transmission mechanism is the effect of lower interest rates on increased planned investment in business equipment and housing and changes in exchange rates. In some countries (but not, in recent years, in the United States), the central bank may also stimulate aggregate demand by actions in foreign exchange markets that cause a depreciation of the currency, thereby stimulating net exports. Just as expansionary monetary policy can be used to shift the aggregate demand curve to the right, contractionary monetary policy can be used to shift it to the left.

Both fiscal and monetary policies play important roles in short-run stabilization of the economy. Chapter 10 will provide more detail on monetary policy, and chapter 11 will discuss fiscal policy.

**CHANGES IN THE WORLD ECONOMY**   Events in foreign countries have an impact on aggregate demand in the United States via the net exports component of planned expenditure. For example, suppose that the rate of real economic growth increases in the economy of a major U.S. trading partner—say, Canada. When this happens, Canadian firms and consumers will tend to buy more imported goods, thereby boosting the real net exports component of U.S. planned expenditure and shifting the aggregate demand curve to the right. Also, changes in price levels in foreign countries will affect U.S. net exports by changing the relative prices of imported and exported goods. The effects of price-level changes may be felt, in part, through changes in the exchange rates. The whole set of variables related to events in the world economy is held equal in drawing a given aggregate demand curve.

## The Aggregate Supply Curve

We turn now to the supply side of our aggregate supply-and-demand model. An **aggregate supply curve** shows the quantity of real domestic product supplied by the economy at various price levels. The aggregate supply curve can be used to show how the economy's equilibrium real output and price level change when there is a shift in the aggregate demand curve.

### The Importance of Input Prices

As we did for the aggregate demand curve, we must pay careful attention to the "other things being equal" assumptions that underlie the aggregate supply curve. In Chapter 2, where we dealt with individual goods like chicken and cars, one of our key assumptions

---

**Transmission mechanism**

The set of channels through which monetary policy affects aggregate demand

**Aggregate supply curve**

A graph showing the relationship between real output (real domestic product) and the average price level of final goods

**Input prices**

A measure of the average prices of labor, raw materials, and other inputs that firms use to produce goods and services

was that **input prices** remained unchanged as firms moved along the supply curve. By input prices, we mean the average prices of labor, raw materials, and other inputs that firms use to produce goods and services. For example, the input prices for a car maker would include the wages of production workers, the price of steel, and rates paid for electric power, along with prices of many other inputs.

Although it is reasonable to assume that input prices for an individual firm remain unchanged as it varies prices and output along its own individual supply curve, the assumption makes less sense for aggregate supply. It is not reasonable to assume that input prices remain unchanged as *all* firms in the economy vary prices and outputs. There are two reasons for this.

The first reason is that some firms' outputs are other firms' inputs. If an electric utility increases its rates, that not only increases the cost of electricity for homeowners who consume electricity as a final good but also for a car maker that uses electricity as an intermediate good. At the same time, the electric utility must buy cars and trucks for its own corporate fleet. An increase in output prices by the car maker is thus an increase in input prices for the electric utility. It follows that an increase in the average price level of all goods in the economy, reflected in a move along the economy's aggregate supply curve, can hardly fail to have an effect on input prices, as well.

The second reason why a change in the average price level for final goods must affect input prices has to do with the impact on wages of changes in the cost of living. Suppose there is a 10 percent increase in the average price of all final goods, including all consumer goods. If workers' nominal wages remain unchanged, they will experience a decline in their standard of living. Some workers will react by demanding raises from their bosses to make up for the higher cost of living. If their employers are getting higher prices for the goods they produce, they may well be willing to grant the wages. Other workers will react to the decline in living standards by looking for better jobs. If some employers resist demands for wage increases while others grant them, workers will move from lower-paying to higher-paying jobs. In one way or another, then, it is reasonable to expect that for the economy as a whole an increase in output prices will be reflected in upward pressure on the wage component of input prices.

For these two reasons, the simple "other things being equal" assumption that input prices are independent of output prices will not work for the aggregate supply curve. That leaves us with another question: How rapidly and completely will input prices adjust when there are changes in aggregate demand and supply? The answer depends on the amount of time allowed for the economy to adjust to changed conditions.

## Long-Run and Short-Run Aggregate Supply Curves

First, let's take a long-run perspective. The long run, in this case, means a period of time long enough for all markets in the economy to adjust fully to changes in conditions of aggregate supply and demand. Given enough time to adjust, it is reasonable for firms to expect input prices to adjust fully in proportion to any change in output prices. For example, suppose there is a 10 percent across-the-board increase in the prices of final goods, as measured by the GDP deflator. If you are, say, a chicken farmer, you expect the price you get for a broiler to go up by 10 percent; and you expect the prices of feed, fuel to heat your buildings, and the wages of your employees to increase by 10 percent, as well.

When input and output prices change in the same proportion, your profit per unit of output, adjusted for inflation, will not change at all. As a result, you have no incentive either to increase or decrease your output. If all firms in the economy behave the same way, there will be no change in real GDP as the economy moves along its aggregate supply curve. Consequently, the long-run aggregate supply curve will be a vertical line, as shown in Figure 9.3a. The intercept of the long-run aggregate supply curve with the horizontal axis coincides with the economy's natural level of real output.

Next we consider a short-run perspective. Even if we can expect input prices to move proportionately to output prices in the long run, that does not mean they do so immediately. In the short run, it is reasonable for firms to expect some, if not all, input prices to adjust only gradually when aggregate demand increases. In that case, there will be a chance for firms to take advantage of strong demand to improve profits by raising prices or increasing output during the interval while costs have not increased fully in proportion to revenues. If we assume that in the short run some firms respond to an increase in aggregate demand by increasing output, others by increasing prices, and others by doing a little of both, the economy's average price

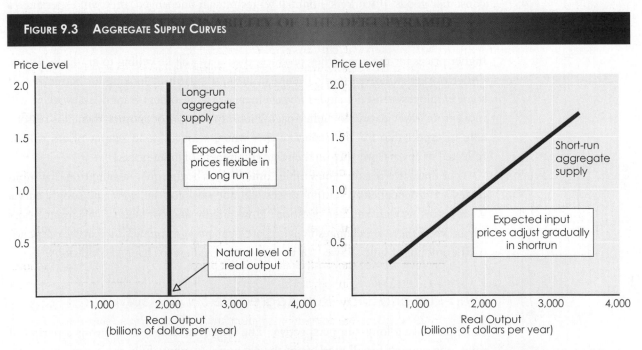

**FIGURE 9.3**    **AGGREGATE SUPPLY CURVES**

An aggregate supply curve shows the relationship between the level of final-goods prices and the level of real output (real domestic product). The slope of the aggregate supply curve depends on the way input prices are assumed to change when the prices of final goods change. In the long run, input prices can reasonably be expected to change in proportion to changes in the prices of final goods. The long-run aggregate supply curve therefore is a vertical line drawn at the economy's natural level of real output, as shown in part (a). In the short run, input prices can reasonably be assumed to adjust more slowly than the prices of final goods. Thus, the short-run aggregate supply curve has a positive slope, as shown in part (b).

level and total output will both increase. As a result, the short-run aggregate supply curve will have a positive slope, like that shown in Figure 9.3b.

There are several reasons to expect that input prices will not adjust fully and immediately to changes in aggregate demand in the short run.

1. *Long-term contracts* The prices of some inputs are fixed by long-term contracts. Union labor contracts are one example. Some firms may also rent buildings, buy fuel, or hire transportation services under long-term contracts. When the price level of final goods rises, the prices of these inputs cannot rise until it is time to renegotiate the contracts.

2. *Inventories* Inventories tend to have a cushioning effect on input prices. For example, suppose that a bakery experiences an increase in demand for its bread. At first it may gladly bake and sell more bread, using up its inventories of flour in the process. If prices have been rising throughout the economy, the bakery may have to pay more for the next batch of flour it orders. This change in input prices will cause it to revise its output and pricing plans, but by then a certain amount of time will have passed. Economists have sometimes argued that rational managers should adjust output prices immediately to reflect the expected replacement cost of inputs used from inventory, but in fact, many firms do not follow this practice.

3. *Incomplete knowledge* Firms may mistakenly interpret broad changes in demand as local changes affecting only their own market. For example, a bakery might think that an increased demand for bread is limited to the city it serves. Such a change would not be expected to have a perceptible effect on the price of flour, which is determined in a nationwide market. Only later will the bakery find out that the increase in demand for its bread is part of a broad increase in aggregate demand, so that it will affect the price of flour and other inputs.

4. *Cost of changing prices* When input prices change by small amounts, some firms may find it too costly to make immediate changes in the prices of the goods they produce. For example, suppose the owner of an independent pizza restaurant visits the market one morning and finds that the price of onions has increased from $.20 per pound to $.25 per pound. That will increase the cost of producing one of her special onion pizzas by one cent. Should she reprint her menu to show a price of $2.96 for an onion pizza instead of the previous $2.95? Probably not. The cost of printing the menu is greater than the gain from fine-tuning the product price to the small change in input prices. It would take a larger and more persistent change in input prices to trigger a change in the price of pizza as stated on the menu. Many firms other than restaurants experience costs of changing prices and therefore do not change them immediately in response to small or transitory changes in input prices. Although this phenomenon is seen far more widely than in the restaurant business alone, economists use the term *menu costs* to refer to the costs of changing prices regardless of the product involved. *Applying Economic Ideas 9.1* reports a specific example of menu costs in action.

Just how short is this short run, and how gradual is the gradual adjustment of prices? There is no simple answer. In reality, the rate at which input prices adjust

**Applying Economic Ideas 9.1**
## MENU COSTS AND THE INTRODUCTION OF THE EURO

In January 2002, twelve European countries made a historic policy change. Hoping to encourage further integration of their economies, they abandoned their long-established national currencies—the French franc, the German mark, the Spanish peseta, and others—in favor of a brand new currency, the euro.

The introduction of the euro was carefully planned. Long before paper euro notes were put into circulation, the euro had already been introduced in electronic form in banking and financial markets. The ratio at which each currency was converted to the euro was exactly calculated. For example, the German mark was converted at a rate of 1.95583 marks per euro, rather than rounding off to a more convenient 2-to-1 ratio. One of the aims of the planning was to avoid any unpleasant jump in inflation when the euro went into circulation. The European Commission, which planned the change, was rightly worried that any such burst of price increases would undermine public confidence in the new currency.

By and large, the careful planning paid off. On average, prices in the twelve euro area countries increased by just twelve-hundredths of one percent in January 2002, a barely measurable amount. In one sector, however, there was a big surprise: Restaurant prices increased by 15 percent on average for the twelve countries. In Germany the increase was 28 percent. Consumers were angry and the European Commission was put on the defensive. What went wrong?

According to a study by economists Bart Hobijn, Frederico Ravenna, and Andrea Tambalotti, the sudden jump in restaurant prices can be explained by menu costs. In their view, menu costs interacted with the introduction of the euro in two ways.

First, introduction of the euro affected the timing of menu revisions. Without the euro, each month a few restaurants would have decided that cost increases had accumulated to the point where it was worth printing new menus. The increases would have been staggered over time, so that the average increase in restaurant prices would have been gradual, in line with the general rate of inflation for all goods and services. However, introduction of the euro meant that all restaurants knew they would have to print new menus for January 2002. Restaurants that might normally have raised their prices in, say, September would think, why bother—wait until January. Restaurants that might normally have waited until June 2002 to revise prices would decide to do so early since they had to print new menus denominated in euros whether they raised prices or not. As a result, a higher than normal percentage of restaurants raised prices at the moment the new currency was introduced.

The other mechanism acting on menu costs has to do with the time horizon taken into account by restaurants when they print new menus. Normally, when setting prices, they would take into account cost increases that they expect to occur for many months ahead. However, restaurants that printed new menus in the last months before the end of 2001 would have had a shorter time horizon. They would have taken into account only cost increases up to January 2002, because they would have known they would have to print new menus again at that time. For that reason, part of the price increases normally expected in 2001 would be shifted forward to 2002.

Using a mathematical model that incorporates the ideas of timing and horizon effects, the authors compared the behavior of restaurant prices in the twelve countries that adopted the euro with those in other European countries, like the U.K. and Sweden, which did not do so. Their conclusion: menu costs explain most, if not all, of the unusual jump in restaurant prices.

SOURCE: Bart Hobijn, Frederico Ravenna, and Andrea Tambalotti, "Menu Costs at Work: Restaurant Prices and the Introduction of the Euro," Federal Reserve Bank of New York Staff Report No. 195, October 2004.

will depend on a variety of circumstances and will vary from one input to another. In what follows, we will make a simplifying assumption: When prices of final goods change, we will assume that firms expect the prices of all inputs to remain unchanged for a specific period of time (for the sake of discussion, we will assume one year) and then move up or down all at once in accordance with the preceding change in the prices of final goods. This stepwise adjustment of input prices is, of course, only a convenient approximation to the more complex adjustment process that takes place in the real world.

## Shifts in the Short-Run Aggregate Supply Curve

The distinctions between input and output prices and between long-run and short-run adjustments provide a basis for understanding shifts in the aggregate supply curves. We begin with shifts in the short-run curve.

When the economy is in long-run equilibrium at its natural level of real output, markets for individual goods, services, and factors of production are also in equilibrium. In that situation, the prices of final goods and services that firms sell and the prices of the inputs they use must be related in certain consistent ways:

1. In equilibrium, the prices of final goods must be at levels that will bring in sufficient revenue for firms to cover the costs of all inputs, given the prices of those inputs, and obtain a normal profit.

2. In equilibrium, the prices of labor inputs must be sufficient to balance supply and demand in labor markets. This means that, given the cost of living as determined by the prices of consumer goods, wages and salaries must be high enough to make it worthwhile for workers to acquire the skills they need for each kind of job and to show up for work each day. It also means that unemployment will be at its natural rate, which corresponds to the natural level of real output.

Suppose that we choose as a base year one in which the economy is in long-run equilibrium. In that year the prices of inputs and final goods will be related in the ways just described. We can assign a value of 1.0 to both the average level of input prices and the average level of prices of final goods for that year. We can then measure changes relative to those base year levels.

In graphical terms, the situation in such a base year is represented by point A in Figure 9.4. Real output is equal to its natural level, which is also its long-run equilibrium level. Point A thus is on the long-run aggregate supply curve, which is a vertical line at the natural level of real output. The short-run aggregate supply curve $AS_1$ that passes through point A shows the way firms will react to changes in aggregate demand during the interval before they expect any change in the prevailing level of input prices, 1.0.

Over a longer period, however, firms will expect input prices to adjust in response to an increase in demand. Suppose, for example, that after a number of years, the average price level of final goods rises to 2.0, and input prices have time to adjust fully so that they too rise to an average level of 2.0. Such a situation is shown as point B in Figure 9.4. In that situation, input prices and the prices of final goods will once again be in an equilibrium relationship. Firms will be selling their outputs for twice as much, enabling them to pay for their inputs, which also cost twice as much. Workers will be earning double the nominal wages and salaries they earned previously, which is just enough to allow them to maintain their original standard of living, given the doubled level of price level of consumer goods.

**FIGURE 9.4    A SHIFT IN THE SHORT-RUN AGGREGATE SUPPLY CURVE**

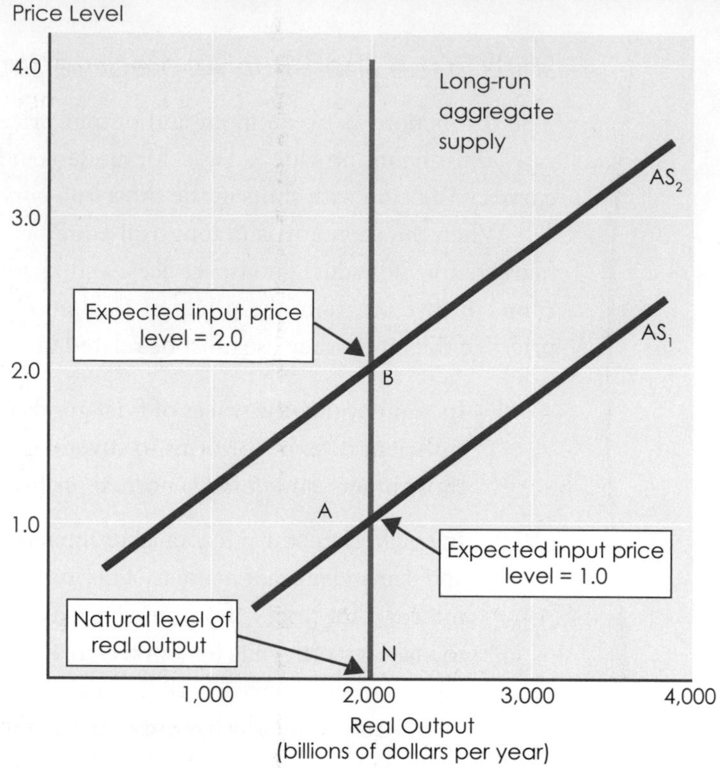

Price Level

The short-run aggregate supply curve is drawn so that it intersects the long-run aggregate supply curve at the expected level of input prices. Here, the short-run aggregate supply curve $AS_1$, which intersects the long-run aggregate supply curve at point A, is based on an expected input price level of 1.0. If the expected level of input prices later increases to 2.0, the aggregate supply curve will shift upward to the position $AS_2$.

Given this new equilibrium situation, a new short-run aggregate supply curve, $AS_2$, can be drawn through point B. This new aggregate supply curve shows how firms will react to changes in aggregate demand if they expect input prices to remain at the new level of 2.0 for the short run. The short-run aggregate supply has shifted upward because the level of input prices that firms expect to prevail when they make short-run production plans has increased.

To summarize:

1. The short-run aggregate supply curve intersects the long-run aggregate supply curve at a height corresponding to the level of input prices that firms expect to prevail in the short run. The expected level of input prices, thus, is the key "other things being equal" assumption underlying the short-run aggregate supply curve.

2. Over a longer period of time, a change in the expected level of input prices will cause the short-run aggregate supply curve to shift upward or downward to a new intersection with the long-run aggregate supply curve.

## Shifts in the Long-Run Aggregate Supply Curve

The key "other things being equal" assumption that underlies the long-run aggregate supply curve and determines its position is the economy's natural level of real output—the level of real output that can be produced with given technology and productive resources when unemployment is at its natural rate. As we first saw in Chapter 4, over time, the economy can expand its production potential through development of new technologies, growth of the labor force, investment in new capital, and development of new natural resources. Such long-run growth was represented in Chapter 4 as an outward expansion of the economy's production possibility frontier. Using the model presented in this chapter, the same kind of expansion can be represented by a rightward shift in the long-run aggregate supply curve.

The remainder of this chapter and the next three will focus on the short run. During this part of the discussion, we will assume that the position of the economy's long-run aggregate supply curve remains fixed. Chapter 12 will return to the question of long-run growth and shifts in the long-run aggregate supply curve.

# The Interaction of Aggregate Supply and Demand in the Short Run

Now that we have reviewed the conditions that determine the slopes of the aggregate supply and demand curves and shifts in those curves, we can put the curves together to form a complete model of short-run changes in prices and real output. This model will be applied to several issues of theory and policy in coming chapters. In this section, we illustrate its basic principles by showing how the economy responds to an increase in aggregate demand, beginning from a position of long-run equilibrium.

## Characteristics of Short- and Long-Run Equilibrium

The story begins at point $E_0$ in Figure 9.5, where the economy is in a position of both short- and long-run equilibrium. This situation is characterized by the intersection of three curves: the aggregate demand curve $AD_0$, the short-run aggregate supply curve $AS_0$, and the long-run aggregate supply curve. The significance of each of the intersections is as follows:

1. Expected input prices and prices of final goods are in their long-run equilibrium relationship at the intersection of the short-run aggregate supply curve $AS_0$ with the long-run aggregate supply curve. *The height of the intersection of the long- and short-run aggregate supply curves indicates the expected level of input prices.*

2. The intersection of $AS_0$ with $AD_0$ indicates the level of final-goods prices and real domestic product for which aggregate supply equals aggregate demand, given the expected level of input prices used in drawing $AS_0$. T*he intersection of*

**FIGURE 9.5   SHORT-RUN AND LONG-RUN EQUILIBRIUM**

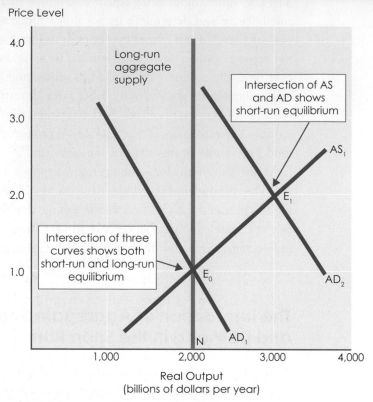

The economy is in short-run equilibrium at the point where the aggregate demand curve intersects the short-run aggregate supply curve. It can be in long-run equilibrium only at a point where the aggregate demand curve intersects the long-run aggregate supply curve. In this diagram, point $E_0$ is a point of both long- and short-run equilibrium, assuming that the aggregate demand curve is in the position $AD_0$. If the aggregate demand curve shifts to the position $AD_1$, the short-run equilibrium point moves to $E_1$, where there is a positive output gap. $E_1$ is not a point of long-run equilibrium because it is not on the long-run aggregate supply curve.

the short-run aggregate supply curve with the aggregate demand curve is always the economy's point of short-run equilibrium.

3.  The intersection of $AD_0$ with the long-run aggregate supply curve indicates the price level at which total real planned expenditures are equal to the economy's natural level of real output. *The economy can be in long-run equilibrium only at a point where the aggregate demand curve intersects the long-run aggregate supply curve.*

4.  The intersection of all three curves at $E_0$ indicates a price level and real domestic product that meet *both* the short-run and the long-run equilibrium conditions.

These four characteristics of short- and long-run equilibrium are essential to understanding the aggregate supply and demand model. Along with an understanding of the sources of shifts in each of the curves, they provide a set of basic working rules that can be applied to solve any problem that falls within the scope of the model.

## Short-Run Effects of an Increase in Aggregate Demand

Now suppose that, beginning from point $E_0$ in Figure 9.5, something causes an increase in total real planned expenditure so that the aggregate demand curve shifts to the right from $AD_0$ to $AD_1$. For the moment it does not matter just what causes the shift. It could be a change in government policy, a spontaneous increase in real consumption spending, an increase in real planned investment resulting from greater business confidence, a boom in demand for U.S. exports, or some combination of these factors.

Whatever the cause, the immediate effect of the increase in planned expenditure will be an unplanned decrease in inventories. Seeing that their products are being bought up faster than they can be produced, firms will alter their plans accordingly. As explained earlier, their short-run reactions to the change in demand will be based on the assumption that input prices will not immediately adjust to the change in demand for final goods. Given that assumption, firms will react to the increase in demand partly by increasing output and partly by raising prices. In graphical terms, these reactions are shown by a movement up and to the right along the short-run aggregate supply curve $AS_0$, which is drawn on the assumption that input prices are expected to remain at their initial level of 1.0 for the time being. As the economy moves along the aggregate supply curve, real output increases and the unemployment rate falls. Using a term introduced in chapter 4, we can say that a *positive output gap* develops as real GDP rises above its natural level.

When the economy reaches point $E_1$, where $AS_0$ and $AD_1$ intersect, planned expenditure and real output will be back in balance and the unplanned inventory depletion will cease. This is a new position of short-run equilibrium for the economy that is applicable as long as the aggregate demand and short-run aggregate supply curves remain in the positions shown.

## Transition to a New Long-Run Equilibrium

The point at which curves $AS_0$ and $AD_1$ intersect is a point of short-run equilibrium for the economy, but it is not a point of long-run equilibrium. Whenever there is a positive output gap, as there is at $E_1$, the price level of final goods will be greater than the expected level of input prices at that point. Expected input prices are still at level 1.0, shown by the intersection of $AS_0$ with the long-run aggregate supply curve. Prices of final goods, however, have risen to a level of 2.0 at $E_1$. This situation cannot be maintained indefinitely. Over time, input prices will gradually adjust to the change that has taken place in final-goods prices.

Figure 9.6 shows what happens as this adjustment takes place. Suppose that after a certain period (say, one year), input prices increase to a level of 2.0, catching up with the increase in prices of final goods that took place as the economy moved from $E_0$ to $E_1$. This new level of input prices will become the basis for business expectations in the subsequent year. Graphically, the increase in the expected level of input prices is shown as an

FIGURE 9.6   SHORT-RUN AND LONG-RUN ADJUSTMENT TO AN INCREASE IN AGGREGATE DEMAND

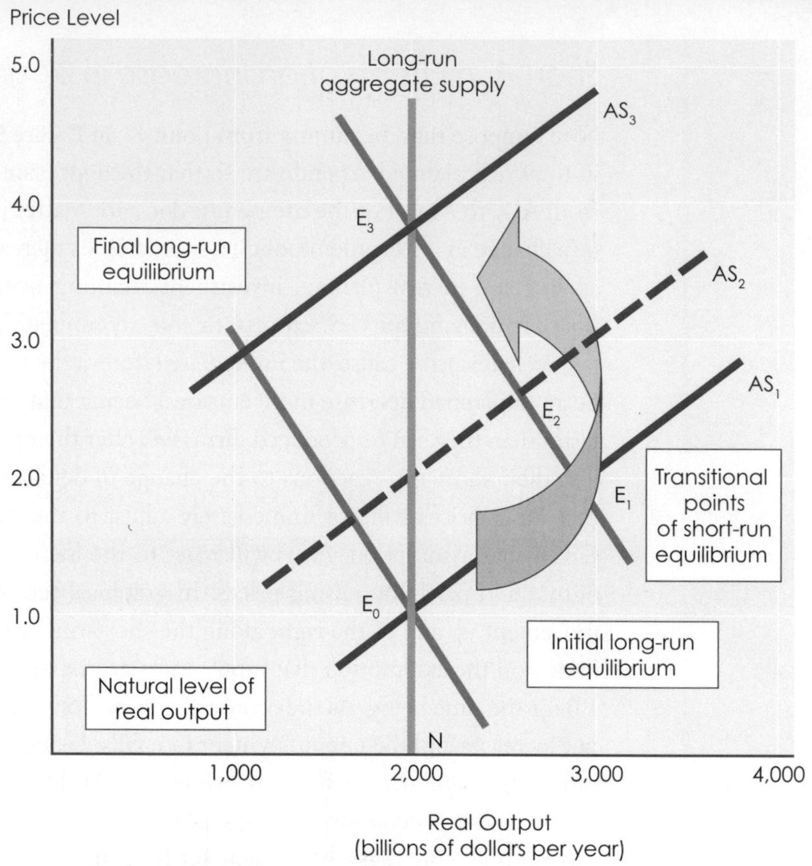

Beginning from an initial long-run equilibrium at $E_0$, a shift in the aggregate demand curve to $AD_1$ will cause the economy to move to a new short-run equilibrium at $E_1$. As it does so, real output will rise above its natural level, the price level of final goods will rise, a positive output gap will develop, and unemployment will fall below its natural rate. After a time, the expected level of input prices will begin to move upward in response to the increase that has taken place in the prices of final goods. As this happens, the short-run aggregate supply curve will shift upward, and the economy will move up and to the left along $AD_1$. Eventually it will reach a new equilibrium at $E_3$. As the economy moves from $E_1$ to $E_3$, the price level of final goods will continue to rise, the output gap will decrease until real output returns to its natural level, and unemployment will rise back to its natural rate.

upward shift in the short-run aggregate supply curve, from $AS_0$ to $AS_1$. $AS_1$ now intersects the long-run aggregate supply curve at the new expected level of input prices, 2.0.

Assuming that no further change takes place in planned expenditures, the aggregate demand curve will remain at $AD_1$. Given an unchanged level of aggregate demand, firms will react to the new, higher, expected level of input prices by raising their prices and reducing their output. As they do so, the economy will move along the aggregate demand curve from $E_1$ to $E_2$, where $AS_1$ and $AD_1$ intersect. Because the output gap is decreasing, the unemployment rate begins to rise.

However, like $E_1$, $E_2$ is not a point of long-run equilibrium. In the process of moving to $E_2$, the prices of final goods have increased again, reaching a level of about 2.7.

They are again out of balance with the expected level of input prices, which is now 2.0. Whenever the price level of final goods is above the expected level of input prices, input prices will tend to increase. Input prices thus will continue their gradual upward adjustment. As they do so, the short-run aggregate supply curve will continue to shift upward.

A succession of further intermediate positions could be shown as the aggregate supply curve shifts upward along the aggregate demand curve. To make a long story short, however, we will jump ahead to the point at which it has shifted all the way up to the position $AS_2$. When it reaches that position, its intersection with the aggregate demand curve $AD_1$ is at point $E_3$, which is also where $AD_1$ intersects the long-run aggregate supply curve. At $E_3$, then, all three curves again intersect at a common point. The economy is once again in both short-run and long-run equilibrium. The gradual process through which expected input prices catch up to the prices of final goods is complete. Both input prices and output prices have reached the level of 4.0 and are in a consistent relationship to one another. Real output is back to its natural level, the output gap is zero, and unemployment is back to its natural rate. If there is no further shift in aggregate demand, the economy can remain at $E_3$ indefinitely.

## Effects of a Decrease in Aggregate Demand

After a time, events may sooner or later cause aggregate demand to change again. Beginning from the long-run equilibrium point $E_3$, let's see what will happen if the aggregate demand curve shifts all the way back to its initial position, $AD_0$. Again, it does not matter for the moment whether the decrease in demand takes the form of a decrease in consumption, planned investment, government purchases, or net exports. Nor does it matter whether the change originates with a change in government policy or with a change in the choices made by households, firms, or buyers of exports.

Figure 9.7 shows how the firm will react to the leftward shift of the aggregate demand curve. Firms will notice a reduction in planned expenditure through an unplanned increase in their inventories. At first, they may not know whether the decrease in demand is local or is occurring throughout the economy. In any event, some will react by cutting output, some by reducing their prices, and many by doing some of both. The economy will move down and to the left along the aggregate supply curve $AS_2$ to a short-run equilibrium at $E_4$. There, the price level will have fallen to 3.0, and real output to $1,000 billion. Unemployment will also have increased, and a negative output gap will have developed. The economy will have experienced a recession.

As in the case of an increase in aggregate demand, point $E_4$ is not a possible long-run equilibrium because final-goods prices are out of line with the expected level of input prices. The negative output gap will soon begin to

Reducing prices is one alternative to the decrease in demand.

**FIGURE 9.7 SHORT-RUN AND LONG-RUN ADJUSTMENT TO A DECREASE IN AGGREGATE DEMAND**

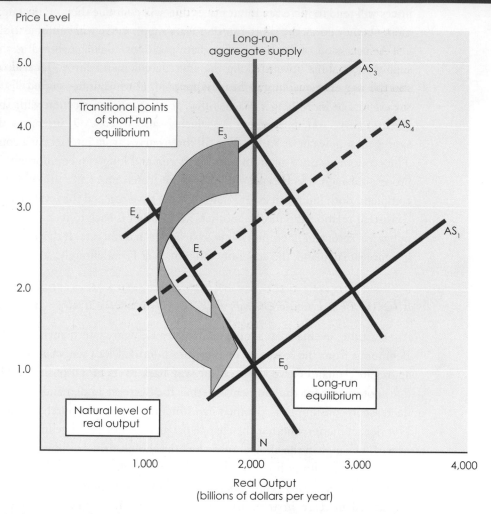

This figure begins from point $E_3$, the end point of the sequence of events described in Figure 9.6. From this point, aggregate demand is assumed to shift back to the position $AD_0$. At first, firms respond to falling demand and unexpected inventory accumulation by cutting back output and reducing prices. As the economy moves to a short-run equilibrium at $E_4$, the unemployment rate rises and final-goods prices fall. When expected input prices also begin to fall, the aggregate supply curve begins to shift downward. As it does so, the economy moves along $AD_0$, through the intermediate point $E_5$, and on down to $E_0$. If there is no further change in aggregate demand, the economy will remain in equilibrium at that point.

exert a downward pull on the expected and actual levels of input prices. Firms that produce intermediate goods, such as energy and semi-finished products, will find that demand for those goods is weak and will react by cutting prices (although perhaps only when long-term contracts are up for renewal). Unemployed workers will accept lower nominal wages in order to find some work. Even workers who have kept their jobs may be willing to accept lower nominal wages when their contracts are renewed, if they realize that lower final-goods prices mean that it costs less to maintain a given standard of living.

In response to the drop in input prices, and the expectation that they will fall still more, the aggregate supply curve shifts downward. $AS_3$ is an intermediate position corresponding to an expected input price level of 3.0. However, $E_5$, at the intersection of $AD_0$ and $AS_3$, is still not a long-run equilibrium because the level of final-goods prices there is less than 3.0. Long-run equilibrium will not be restored until the economy moves all the way back to its natural level of real output at $E_0$ and the negative output gap has disappeared. During the transition from $E_4$ to $E_0$, output will be increasing and unemployment decreasing, even while the price level of final goods continues to fall.

## Aggregate Supply, Demand, and the Business Cycle

If we look at the entire sequence of events shown in Figures 10.6 and 10.7, we can see that the economy has traced out something that looks very much like the business cycles discussed in Chapter 4:

1. Beginning from the natural level of real output, the economy expands. A positive output gap develops as domestic product rises above its natural level, unemployment falls below its natural rate, and the price level begins to rise.

2. After a time, a peak of real output is reached after which real output, although still above its natural level, begins to decrease and unemployment begins to increase.

3. If aggregate demand shifts to the left again after real output returns to its natural level, the economy will continue to contract, a negative output gap will develop, and unemployment will rise above its natural rate. During this phase of the cycle, the price level begins to decrease.

4. Eventually real output reaches a minimum, the trough of the recession. As real output moves back toward its natural level, unemployment again decreases. In principle, the economy could come to rest at the natural level of real output. If aggregate demand increases once more, however, a new cycle will begin.

This is not yet a complete theory of the business cycle, but it is a step forward over the simple Keynesian multiplier model. One big improvement over the simple multiplier model is that we now can show clearly how a given change in nominal planned expenditure is divided, in the short run and the long run, between changes in real output and changes in the price level. The other is that we now understand the role played by monetary conditions and interest rates in determining changes in planned expenditure, and, consequently, aggregate demand. We will build further on this model in the next three chapters.

## Summary

1. **What are the conditions that determine the slope of the aggregate demand curve?** The *aggregate demand curve* shows the relationship between real planned expenditure on final goods and the average price level of final goods. The curve has a negative slope because each of the components of real aggregate demand—consumption, planned investment, government purchases, and net exports—varies inversely with the price level. The aggregate demand curve is inelastic. As a result, the nominal value of planned expenditure (real planned expenditure times the price level) increases as one moves up and to the left along the curve.

2. **What are some sources of shifts in the aggregate demand curve?** Movements along the aggregate demand curve are associated with changes in the price level of final goods. Changes in other conditions can cause shifts in the curve. Among the sources of shifts are changes in consumer or business expectations; changes in policy regarding government purchases, taxes, and money; and changes in the world economy. Because of the *multiplier effect*, an initial $1 change in any of the components will cause the curve to shift to the right or left by more than $1.

3. **What are the conditions that determine the slopes of the short- and long-run aggregate supply curves?** An *aggregate supply curve* shows the relationship between the quantity of real output supplied (that is, real domestic product) and the average price level of final goods. The slope of the curve depends on what assumption is made about the way firms expect input prices to be affected by changes in the prices of final goods. In the long run, it is reasonable to expect input prices to adjust proportionately to changes in the prices of final goods. In that case, firms have no incentive to increase or decrease output, so the long-run aggregate supply curve is a vertical line drawn at the economy's natural level of real output. In

the short run, actual and expected input prices adjust only gradually to changes in the prices of final goods. Thus, in the short run, firms find it worthwhile to increase both output and prices in response to an increase in demand.

4. **What are the sources of shifts in the aggregate supply curves?** At the intersection of the long- and short-run aggregate supply curves, the price level of final goods and the expected level of input prices are equal. An increase (or decrease) in the expected level of input prices thus will cause the short-run aggregate supply curve to shift up (or down) along the long-run aggregate supply curve. The location of the long-run aggregate supply curve is determined by the natural level of real output. An increase in natural real output resulting from improved technology or greater availability of productive resources will cause a rightward shift in the long-run aggregate supply curve.

5. **How do prices, real output, and unemployment behave as the economy responds to a change in aggregate demand?** Beginning from a state of long-run equilibrium, an increase in real aggregate demand will, in the short run, cause the economy to move up and to the right along its short-run aggregate supply curve. As it does so, the prices of final goods will rise, a positive output gap will develop as real output rises above its natural level, and unemployment will fall below its natural rate. After a time, the expected level of input prices will begin to rise as a result of the increases that have taken place in the prices of final goods. As that happens, the economy will move up and to the left along the aggregate demand curve, assuming no further shift in that curve. The price level of final goods will continue to rise, real output will fall back toward its natural level, and unemployment will rise back toward its natural rate. If, after the new equilibrium is reached, aggregate demand shifts to the left again, a negative output gap will develop as real output drops below its natural level, and unemployment will rise above its natural

rate. The level of final goods prices will fall below the expected level of input prices. Soon, the expected level of input prices, too, will begin to fall. If there is no further change in aggregate demand, the economy will return to equilibrium at the natural level of real output.

## Key Terms

## Problems and Topics for Discussion

1. **Elasticity of aggregate demand**  Turn to the aggregate demand curve $AD_2$ in Figure 9.2. Along that curve, as the price level rises from 0.5 to 1.5, the quantity of real output demanded declines from $3,000 billion to $2,000 billion. What happens to the aggregate quantity demanded in nominal terms over this interval? Using the formula for price elasticity of demand (the ratio of the percentage change in the quantity of a good demanded to a given percentage change in its price), what is the elasticity of aggregate demand over this interval?

2. **The multiplier effect**  Suppose that a newly released popular hit by a U.S. rock group causes fans in Asia to order $50,000 worth of T-shirts with the band's picture. The T-shirts are entirely made in the United States. Other things being equal, would this tend to increase planned expenditure in the United States by exactly, more than, or less than $50,000? Would it shift the aggregate demand curve to the right, the left, or not at all? Explain in detail.

3. **Long- and short-run aggregate supply curves**  On a piece of graph paper draw a set of axes, such as those in Figure 9.4, but do not draw the supply curves shown there. Instead, draw a long-run aggregate supply curve based on the assumption that the natural level of real output is $3,000 billion. What is the slope of the curve? At what point does it intersect the horizontal axis? Next draw a short-run aggregate supply curve based on the assumption that the expected level of input prices is 1.5. Where does this short-run aggregate supply curve intersect the long-run aggregate supply curve that you drew?

4. **Final goods prices and expected input prices**  Given an aggregate demand curve and a short-run aggregate supply curve, how can you determine the short-run equilibrium price level of final goods? Given a long-run aggregate supply curve and a short-run aggregate supply curve, how can you determine the expected level of input prices? Turn to Figure 9.6. Give the short-run equilibrium price level of final goods and the expected level of input prices for each of the points $E_0$, $E_1$, $E_2$, and $E_3$.

5. **Long- and short-run equilibriums**  On a piece of graph paper draw a set of axes identical to those in Figure 9.6. Draw a long-run aggregate supply curve based on the assumption that a natural level of real output is $2,500 billion. Draw a short-run aggregate supply curve that passes through the points (2,500, 1.0) and (3,500, 2.0). Label it $AS_1$. What is the expected level of input prices indicated by this supply curve? Draw an aggregate demand curve that passes through the points (2,000, 2.0) and (2,500, 1.0). Label it $AD_2$. Given these three curves, where is the economy's point of short-run equilibrium? Where is its point of long-run equilibrium? Now draw another aggregate demand curve that passes through the points (2,500, 4.0) and (4,000, 1.0). Label it $AD_2$. Given

AD$_2$ and the aggregate supply curves on your diagram, where is the economy's point of short-run equilibrium? What is the relationship between the short-run equilibrium price level of final goods and the expected level of input prices? Is there a possible point of long-run equilibrium for the economy, given AD$_2$ and the long-run aggregate supply curve? If so, explain how the economy can reach that point starting from the short-run equilibrium just described.

## Case for Discussion

### We Weren't Talking Revolution; We Were Talking Jobs

Ed Paulsen's family was from South Dakota. He finished high school in 1930, as the country was sliding toward the Great Depression. He went west to pick apples in Washington state and then worked on road gangs. In 1931, he ended up in San Francisco. These are his words.

> I tried to get a job on the docks. I was a big husky athlete, but there just wasn't any work. Already by that time, if you were looking for a job at a Standard Oil service station you had to have a college degree. It was that kind of market …
>
> I'd get up at five in the morning and head for the waterfront. Outside the Spreckles Sugar Refinery, outside the gates, there would be a thousand men. You know dang well there's only three or four jobs. The guy would come out with two little Pinkerton cops: "I need two guys for the bull gang. Two guys to go into the hole." A thousand men would fight like a pack of Alaskan dogs to get through there. Only four of us would get through.
>
> These were fathers, 80 percent of them. They had held jobs and didn't want to kick society to pieces. They just wanted to go to

work and they just couldn't understand. There was a mysterious thing. You watched the papers, you listened to rumors, you'd get word somebody's going to build a building.

> So the next morning you get up at five o'clock and you dash over there. You got a big tip. There's three thousand men there, carpenters, cement men, guys who knew machinery and everything else. These fellas always had faith that the job was going to mature somehow. More and more men were after fewer and fewer jobs. …
>
> We weren't greatly agitated in terms of society. Ours was a bewilderment, not an anger. Not a sense of being particularly put upon. We weren't talking revolution; we were talking jobs.

SOURCE: Excerpts from Studs Terkel, *Hard Times: An Oral History of the Great Depression* (New York: Pantheon Books, 1970), 29–31.

## QUESTIONS

1. Economic historians most frequently cite a decrease in planned investment as one of the major causes for the Great Depression of the 1930s. Explain how a decrease in planned investment, other things being equal, would affect planned expenditure and the aggregate demand curve. How would the resulting shift in the aggregate demand curve affect real output and employment?

2. If wages and prices adjusted immediately and fully to changes in demand, what would happen to unemployment as a result of a decrease in planned investment?

3. What does the story of Ed Paulsen suggest regarding the speed of adjustment of wages and prices to a shift in aggregate demand? What might cause a gradual, rather than a rapid, adjustment?

# CHAPTER *10*

# Strategies and Rules for Monetary Policy

| After reading this chapter, you will understand the following: |
| --- |

1. Why lags, forecasting errors, and time-inconsistency create problems for economic fine-tuning
2. The distinctions among policy instruments, operating targets, intermediate targets, and goals
3. How policy rules, such as inflation targeting, attempt to overcome the limits of fine-tuning
4. How central bank actions affect exchange rates
5. Why some countries choose exchange rates as the principal target for monetary policy

| Before reading this chapter, make sure you know the meaning of the concepts: |
| --- |

1. The aggregate supply and demand model
2. Monetary policy instruments
3. Fiscal policy
4. Money
5. Planned expenditure
6. The multiplier effect
7. Equation of exchange
8. Velocity
9. Transmission mechanism

S TABILITY AND PROSPERITY are the twin goals of macroeconomic policy. Achieving stability means taming the business cycle by moderating short-term swings in real output, inflation, and unemployment. Achieving prosperity means promoting productivity and growth of real output over a longer time horizon; however, if short-term stabilization policy fails, long-run prosperity will prove elusive. To achieve stability and prosperity, monetary and fiscal policy must work together. This chapter focuses primarily on strategies and rules for monetary policy, although some of the ideas it presents apply to both areas of policy. Chapter 11 will undertake a more detailed look at fiscal policy.

## The Limits of Fine-Tuning

The discussion of monetary policy instruments in Chapter 8 and the aggregate supply and demand model developed in Chapter 9 provide a framework for our discussion of stabilization policy. As this chapter will make clear, however, the models are only a starting point. They make stabilization policy look far too easy—as if policymakers were like engineers in a recording studio, who can just twist a few knobs with labels like "monetary base" and "federal funds rate," and presto! Aggregate demand, interest rates, real output, and the price level will slip into harmony with one another. As explained in *Applying Economic Ideas 10.1*, there was a time when some people thought that kind of economic fine-tuning might be possible. Over the years, however, it has become apparent that between the clean, orderly, world of the models and the real world where policymakers operate, there some messy problems that make it frustratingly difficult to fine-tune the economy to a state of harmonious stability.

### The Problem of Lags

The first problem standing in the way of fine-tuning is that of *lags*, a term economists use to refer to unavoidable delays in the execution of monetary or fiscal policy. There are two kinds of these lags. Delays between the time a problem develops and the time a decision is taken to do something about it are known as **inside lags**. Delays between the time a decision is taken and the time the resulting policy action affects the economy are known as **outside lags**. Both kinds of lags are a problem both for monetary and fiscal policy.

**INSIDE LAGS**   Some inside lags arise because of the time required to collect and report economic data. A few kinds of data, like interest rates and exchange rates, are available almost instantly; but other important data take longer to gather. Data on inflation, unemployment, consumer confidence, and several other variables are published monthly. The biggest problem lies with data on GDP and foreign transactions. As explained in Chapter 6, these data are available only quarterly. Furthermore, the first estimates for each quarter, published about three weeks after the close of the quarter, are subject to significant revisions. Final data are not available until nearly three months after the close of the quarter.

Another problem compounds that of delays. All macroeconomic data are influenced by random events and measurement errors that cause unpredictable ups and downs in monthly or quarterly indicators. That means it is usually not enough to base policy decisions on the single most recent observation. It may take several monthly or quarterly observations to establish a clear trend on which a sound policy decision can be based.

The long lags in collection of macroeconomic data, especially data on real GDP and its components, mean that policymakers may not be aware of a turning

**Inside lags**

Delays between the time a problem develops and the time a decision is taken to do something about it

**Outside lags**

Delays between the time a decision is taken and the time the resulting policy action affects the economy

**Applying Economic Ideas 10.1**
## "IT IS NOW WITHIN OUR CAPABILITIES ..."

The 1960s were an exciting decade for the economics profession. Some people had feared that the United States would sink into renewed depression after World War II; instead, the economy returned to prosperity. Although the 1950s were on the whole a good decade for the economy, many people thought the country could do even better. In the 1960s, Harvard-educated President John F. Kennedy brought some of the country's best and brightest economists to Washington, including some of his former professors. His successor, Lyndon Johnson, kept them there. By 1966, the President's Council of Economic Advisers consisted of three of the most distinguished professionals ever to sit on that body: Gardner Ackley, Otto Eckstein, and Arthur Okun.

Armed with refined versions of theories developed in the 1930s by John Maynard Keynes and with newly-available electronic computers, these men were convinced that it was time to attempt more than just to safeguard the economy from deep depression and runaway inflation. "It is now within our capabilities to set more ambitious goals," they wrote in their January 1966 Report to the President. "We strive to avoid recurrent recessions, to keep unemployment far below rates of the past decade, to maintain price stability at full employment, ... and indeed to make full prosperity the normal state of the American economy. It is a tribute to our success ... that we now have not only the economic understanding but also the will and determination to use economic policy as an effective tool for progress."

It was a high-water mark of professional self-confidence. Regrettably, the hope that policymakers would be able to fine-tune the economy to recession-free and inflation-free prosperity proved unfounded. As the figure shows, 1965, with its enviable achievements of 4.5 percent unemployment with just 1.9 percent inflation, was the last really good year before a long period

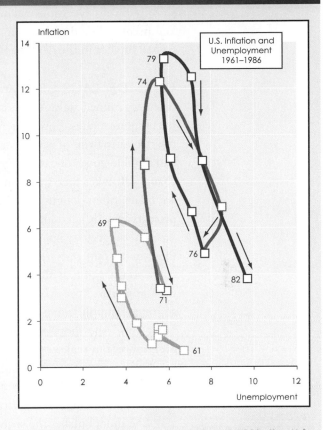

of serious instability. Between 1965 and 1982, the U.S. economy went through three severe cycles of inflation and unemployment. In each cycle, the highest rates of inflation and unemployment exceeded the cycle before. Fine-tuning 1960s-style failed dismally to live up to expectations.

SOURCE OF QUOTATION: *Annual Report of the Council of Economic Advisers, 1966.* Washington, D.C.: Government Printing Office, p. 186.

point in the business cycle until long after it has occurred. Consider the example of the mild recession from January to November 2001, which marked the end of the dot.com boom. In May 2001, when the recession was already half over, the latest government data still showed the economy to be expanding, although at a slowing rate. Only after the recession was over did revised data clearly show that the economy had begun to shrink at the end of 2000.

In addition to delays in data collection, the time needed to take decisions adds to the inside lag. Monetary policy decisions on interest rates and other instruments are usually made at regular meetings of the Federal Open Market Committee, which occur just eight times a year. Before those meetings can take place, the Fed's professional staff must spend weeks of work preparing background materials. The Fed has the power to make emergency changes in policy between regular meetings, but it does so only rarely. Decision-making lags for fiscal policy can be even longer, since many key fiscal policy decisions require action by Congress. Lags in fiscal policy are discussed further in the next chapter.

**OUTSIDE LAGS**   Even after a decision is made, policy actions do not affect the economy immediately. As an example, consider the use of expansionary monetary policy to cut interest rates. Lower interest rates affect aggregate demand by reducing the opportunity cost to firms of new capital investment and the cost to households of buying homes and durable goods on credit. Firms and households do not react instantly to interest rate changes. It takes time for them to make investment decisions; and even when decisions are made, often designs must be drawn up, orders placed, and permits obtained before projects actually get under way.

The aggregate supply and demand model includes allowances for some of the most important outside lags. Suppose a policy change shifts the aggregate demand curve to the right, as shown in Figure 9.6 of the previous chapter. In a period we call the "short run," the economy begins to move up and to the right along the short-run aggregate supply curve, with both prices and output rising. In a period we call the "long run," the short-run aggregate supply curve begins to shift upward. Prices rise even more, but real output begins to fall back toward its natural level. A new long-run equilibrium is not reached until the economy returns to a point where the aggregate demand curve and the short- and long-run aggregate supply curves all intersect at a common point equal to the natural level of real output.

The model makes the sequence of events clear enough, but policymakers need to know more than that. Just how long, according to the calendar, are the abstract intervals of "short run" and "long run" involved in the adjustment process? Econometric studies shed some light on these issues. Studies based on data from both the United States and Europe suggest that the "short run," during which real output increases following a reduction in interest rates (or falls following an increase in rates), lasts for at least one year and sometimes as much as two years. The full effect of an interest rate change on the price level, allowing time for real output to return to its natural level, appears to take three years or longer. By the time the full effects of one policy change are felt, it is likely that new external shocks and policy decisions will be affecting the economy. In reality, the economy is constantly in motion and never reaches a full long-run equilibrium of the kind that is so easily represented with a textbook graph.

## Forecasting Errors

Lags in data collection and policy effectiveness are serious problems, but they would cause less trouble if accurate forecasts were available. In this regard, it may help to compare an economic policymaker to the captain of a giant oil tanker. The tanker captain also faces a problem of lags. If she turns the wheel of her ship or signals for a change in engine speed, it may take up to several miles for the ship to steady on its new course. The difference between the tanker captain and the policymaker is that the captain has accurate charts of the waters she is navigating and radar to show obstacles ahead. Based on the charts and radar, she can give orders well in advance, so that the ship changes

The captain of an oil tanker has accurate charts, but economic policy makers have no accurate way to see what lies ahead.

course long before it goes on the rocks. The economic policymaker has no good way to see into the future. The economic ship may end up on the rocks before anyone knows what has happened.

Instead of charts and radar, policymakers must rely on economic forecasts. In every country, competing teams of economists—some private, some in government agencies like the Fed or the Office of Management and Budget—publish estimates of real GDP, inflation, unemployment, and other variables for the year ahead. Unfortunately, those forecasts are not as reliable as one would like. According to a study by the International Monetary Fund, forecasts of the rate of real GDP growth for a year ahead in industrialized countries are, on average, wrong by more than a full percentage point (disregarding the sign of the error).[1] For two years ahead, the error is nearly two percentage points. For developing countries, accuracy is worse than this by still another full percentage point. What is more, forecasts are least accurate at turning points in the business cycle, just when they are needed most. Looking at an international sample of 72 recessions in the 1990s, the IMF paper found only two cases in which the recession was accurately predicted two years in advance. Even as late as September of the year in which a recession began, only about half of forecasters were predicting that a recession would occur.

Several factors combine to reduce the accuracy of forecasts. First, forecasters themselves face the problem of lags in data collection. They must try to see into the future when they are not yet sure what has happened in the recent past. Second, the real world economy is much more complex than any model—not just more complex than the simplified models of textbooks like this one, but more than even the most sophisticated multivariate models of the best professional forecasters. Also, no matter how complex, models are always based on past observations; but because the structure of the economy is always changing, it may not behave the same way in the future. Third, forecasts may be biased. Government forecasts may be biased toward optimism because politicians do not like to hear or deliver bad news. Private sector forecasters may see a marketing advantage in developing a reputation as being persistently optimistic or persistently gloomy. The private clients of forecasters may reinforce those tendencies when, knowing that forecasts are not accurate, they play it safe by buying forecasts from several sources with differing methodologies and reputations.

## Time Inconsistency

Lags and forecasting errors together make the conduct of economic policy very difficult, but they are not the whole story. One more factor must be added to get a full picture of the difficulties of fine-tuning the economy. Economists call that factor **time-inconsistency**, by which they mean a tendency of policymakers to take actions that have desirable results in the short run, but undesirable long-run results.

Time-inconsistency is not unique to economic policymaking. It occurs in many situations of everyday life. Perhaps some readers may have had the experience of being offered a glass of tequila or vodka at a party. The short-run effects of drinking it are pleasant, so down goes another glass, and then another. The next day the undesirable results are felt in full force. As another example of time-inconsistency, patients with drug-resistant forms of tuberculosis or malaria must take heavy doses of strong medications over a long period in order to be fully cured. Often, such patients feel better after just a few weeks and then stop taking their medicine because of unpleasant side effects. When they stop taking the medications before the cure is complete, they become carriers of drug-resistant forms of the disease. In the long run, they endanger the whole community.

In democracies, time-inconsistency is especially a problem when policymaking interacts with the election cycle. For example, as the aggregate supply and demand model shows, expansionary policies like reductions in taxes or interest rates initially have desirable results. As the aggregate demand curve shifts, the economy moves up and to the right along the short-run aggregate supply curve. Real output increases, incomes increase, unemployment falls, and there is only mild inflation. This process takes place over a short-run time frame of one to two years. Later, as expectations adjust and the short-run aggregate supply curve begins to shift upward, less desirable consequences occur. Real output falls back toward its natural level, and unemployment rises back toward its natural rate. The rate of inflation increases. That process occurs over a time frame of one or two additional years, perhaps longer. Taking all of the lags into account, we can see that if expansionary policy is applied a year or so before an election, the beneficial effects will be at their strongest just as the election approaches; and the harmful effects will not be felt until the election has passed.

For contractionary policy, the sequence of events is reversed. If an increase in interest rates or taxes is used to combat overheating of the economy, the immediate effect will be a leftward shift of the aggregate demand curve and a move down and to the left along the short-run aggregate supply curve. During this painful phase, which lasts a year or two years, unemployment rises, real output and incomes fall, and the rate of inflation slows only a little. Later, after expectations adjust, the short-run aggregate supply curve will begin to shift downward. Real output will again rise toward its natural level, unemployment will fall back toward its natural rate, and additional progress will be made toward slowing, or even reversing previous inflation. In short, from a political point of view, the period just before an election is not a good time to begin an episode of anti-inflationary policy. There will be a temptation to let the economy overheat for a few months longer and begin to apply contractionary medicine only after the election has passed.

---

**Time-inconsistency**

Tendency of policymakers to take actions that have desirable results in the short run, but undesirable long-run results

When lags, forecasting errors, and time-inconsistency are all combined, well-intentioned effects to fine-tune the economy are in danger of producing two types of unintended consequences.

First, because of lags and forecasting errors, there is a danger that expansionary or contractionary policy will be applied too late in the business cycle. Expansionary policies, intended to combat a recession, will not come into full effect until the next upturn of the business cycle has already begun. When they do come into effect, they will push the economy past the point of stability and promote inflationary overheating. Similarly, contractionary policies, intended to prevent overexpansion during a boom, will come into effect only after the economy has already begun to slow. They will make the next recession worse than it would have been if no policy action had been taken. The combined effects of lags and forecasting errors, then, create a danger that policy actions cause the economy to overshoot inflation and unemployment targets at both ends of the business cycle.

Second, when time-inconsistency is added to lags and forecasting errors, there may be a bias toward expansion and inflation. In that case, the economy will tend to overshoot at the top of the business cycle; however, the contraction phase of the business cycle will be cut short while inflation is still relatively high. That happens because policymakers will often want to hurry up the application of expansionary policies like tax cuts, spending increases, or interest rate reductions in order to make things look good in time for the next election. They will also want to delay the application of contractionary policies like tax increases, spending cuts, or interest rate increases.

Is this purely a theoretical danger, or could it actually happen? Look back for a moment to the diagram in *Applying Economic Ideas 10.1* near the beginning of this chapter. A close examination of the figure will show that the inflation rates at the cyclical peaks of 1969, 1974, and 1979 are each time higher than the peak rate of the preceding cycle. Similarly, the unemployment rates at the cyclical troughs of 1971, 1976, and 1982 are also each higher than at the preceding trough. Clearly, the experience of the 1960s and 1970s failed to justify hopes that economists had finally acquired both the tools and the political will to implement successful fine-tuning.

## Policy Rules

**Policy rules**

A set of rules for monetary and fiscal policy that specifies in advance the actions that will be taken in response to economic developments as they occur

Since the 1970s, there has been a widespread shift in the way economists think about the strategy of stabilization policy.[2] Fine-tuning with fiscal or monetary policy is no longer viewed with favor. That does not mean economists think monetary and fiscal policy are ineffective. It does not mean that the government should always take a hands-off approach to the business cycle. It does not mean that emergency measures may not be helpful in extreme situations. What it does mean is a consensus that, in a world of lags and forecasting errors, frequent, active, discretionary tinkering with interest rates, government spending, and tax rates is more likely to be destabilizing than stabilizing and that destabilization is even more likely when politically motivated time-inconsistency is taken into account.

In place of fine-tuning, a majority of economists now favor stabilization strategies based on preset **policy rules**. The idea of rules is that policymakers should announce in advance the way they will respond to unfolding developments in the economy. It is hoped that such rules will minimize the risk that lags and forecasting errors will lead to overshooting at peaks and troughs of the business cycle and will minimize the effects of politically motivated time-inconsistency. If successful, policy rules will provide a stable framework for planning by private firms and households and promote long-run prosperity. This section focuses primarily on rules for monetary policy. We will look at rules for fiscal policy in Chapter 11.

## Instruments and Targets

As background for our discussion of policy rules, it will be useful to distinguish among *instruments*, *targets*, and *goals* of economic policy:

**Policy instrument**

A variable directly under the control of policymakers

**Operating target**

A variable that responds immediately to the use of a policy instrument

**Intermediate target**

A variable that responds to the use of a policy instrument or a change in operating target with a significant lag

**Policy goal**

A long-run objective of economic policy that is important for economic welfare

- A **policy instrument** is a variable that is directly under control of policymakers. For example, open market purchases and the discount rate are policy instruments of the Federal Reserve.

- An **operating target** is a variable that responds immediately, or almost immediately, to the use of a policy instrument. For example, the federal funds rate for interbank lending (an operating target) responds almost immediately to an open market purchase (a policy instrument).

- An **intermediate target** is a variable that responds to the use of a policy instrument or a change in operating target with a significant lag. For example, inflation and real GDP (intermediate targets) respond to a change in interest rates (an operating target), but not immediately.

- A **policy goal** is a long-run objective of economic policy that is important for economic welfare. Stated in their broadest forms, the goals of macroeconomic policy are prosperity and stability.

The hierarchy of instruments, targets, and goals can be illustrated with examples from areas of life other than economics. Returning to our example of the oil tanker, we could say that the wheel and engine speed control are the captain's main policy instruments. The ship's speed and course are operating targets that respond immediately, or almost immediately, to use of those instruments. The captain's intermediate target, on a given voyage, is to get the ship to a certain harbor by a certain date. Long-run goals, over a series of voyages, are to establish a reputation for reliability and earn a profit for the company that owns the ship.

Debates over strategies for stabilization policy do not usually focus on the choice of policy instruments or the long-term policy goals of prosperity and stability. More often, they focus on which operating targets to emphasize and the choosing of intermediate targets that link changes in operating targets to long-term goals. The remainder of this chapter will look at several alternative policy rules, each having its supporters and critics.

## Monetarism: the Grandparent of Policy Rules

Even while enthusiasm for macroeconomic fine-tuning was at its peak in the 1960s, there were dissenters. One of the best known was University of Chicago professor

Milton Friedman. (See *Who Said It? Who Did it? 10.1*.) Friedman was the intellectual leader, although by no means the only prominent member, of a school of economics that came to be known as *monetarism*.

In his most famous work, *A Monetary History of the United States*, co-authored with Anna Schwartz, Friedman argued for a reinterpretation of the causes of the Great Depression. In the book, Friedman and Schwartz took issue with the approach that John Maynard Keynes had taken in the 1930s (See *Who Said It? Who Did It? 4.1*). Keynes' approach emphasized fiscal policy, planned expenditure, and the multiplier as the key variables in macroeconomics. Instead, Friedman saw mistakes in monetary policy as the principal factor that turned an ordinary cyclical recession into a national disaster lasting ten years. He argued that the correct conduct of monetary policy continued to be crucial for stabilization policy in the 1960s. This emphasis on monetary policy gave the monetarist school its name.

A second element of Friedman's thinking was his argument that neither monetary nor fiscal policy should be conducted with an eye to fine-tuning the economy. Instead, the Federal Reserve should conduct its policy according to a simple rule that would avoid the problems of lags, forecasting errors, and time-inconsistency. Specifically, Friedman recommended that the Fed use a steady rate of growth of the money stock, equal to the

---

### Who Said It? Who Did It? 10.1
## MILTON FRIEDMAN AND MONETARISM

In October 1976, Milton Friedman received the Nobel Memorial Prize in economics, becoming the sixth American to win or share that honor. Few people were surprised. Most people wondered why he had to wait so long. Perhaps it was because Friedman had built his career outside the economics establishment, challenging almost every major doctrine of the profession.

Milton Friedman

Friedman was born in New York in 1912, the son of immigrant garment workers. He attended Rutgers University where he came under the influence of Arthur Burns, then a young assistant professor and later chairman of the Federal Reserve Board. From Burns, Friedman learned the importance of empirical work in economics. Statistical testing of all theory and policy prescriptions became a key feature of Friedman's later work. From Rutgers, Friedman went to the University of Chicago for an M.A. and then east again to Columbia University, where he received his Ph.D. in 1946. He returned to Chicago to teach. There, he and his colleagues of the "Chicago school" of economics posed a major challenge to economists of the "Eastern establishment."

It one could single out a recurrent theme in Friedman's work it would be his belief that the market economy works—and that it works best when left alone. "The Great Depression," Friedman once wrote, "far from being a sign of the inherent instability of the private enterprise system, is a testament to how much harm can be done by mistakes on the part of a few men when they wield vast power over the monetary system ot the country."

Friedman strongly favored a hands-off policy by government in almost every area. In his view, the problem was not that government is evil by nature but that so many policies end up having the opposite of their intended effects. "The social reformers who seek through politics to do nothing but serve the public interest invariably end up serving some private interest that was not part of their intention to serve. They are led by an invisible hand to serve a private interest." Not just monetary policy but also transportation regulation, public education, agricultural subsidies, and housing programs were among the many policy areas in which Friedman believed that the government has done more harm than good and for which a free competitive market would do better.

economy's long-run rate of growth of real GDP, as its principal operating target. It would use open market operations as its main instrument for keeping money growth on target.

The link between the operating target of steady money growth and the policy goals of stability and full employment can be expressed by means of the equation of exchange, MV = PQ. As explained in Chapter 8, M stands for the quantity of money, V for the velocity of circulation of money, P for the price level, and Q for real GDP. The concept behind Friedman's money growth rule was that if M grew steadily at the same rate as Q, and V was subject only to minor and predictable variations, the price level P would remain approximately constant in the long run, that is, there would be little or no inflation. Although random events might cause short-term variations in prices, real output, and employment, there could be no risk of run-away inflation or deep, lasting depression.

Friedman's rule was never implemented in its original form. Structural reforms in the banking industry during the 1980s increased the variability of velocity and weakened the link between the growth rate of the money stock and the rate of inflation. However, the idea that policy rules were a better basis for stabilization strategy than fine-tuning prevailed. It was just a matter of finding the right rule.

## Inflation Targeting

**Inflation targeting**

A measure of the average prices of labor, raw materials, and other inputs that firms use to produce goods and services

Today, the most popular policy rule among the world's central banks is **inflation targeting**, a term used to describe any stabilization strategy that is based on a target range for the rate of inflation.

The basic idea behind inflation targeting, like Friedman's money-growth target, can be explained in terms of the equation of exchange, MV = PQ. The money growth target promotes long-term price stability only if both velocity (V) and the growth rate of real output (Q) are fairly stable. If either or both are subject to significant, unpredictable changes, even a steady rate of money growth could lead to undesired inflation or deflation. The idea of inflation targeting is that policymakers can guard against these sources of instability by using the rate of change of the price level, P, as their target rather than the rate of growth of money, M.

**INTEREST RATES AS AN OPERATING TARGET**   Although the concept of inflation targeting is simple, implementing it is not so easy. To begin with, the rate of inflation cannot be used as a short-run operating target because it does not respond fast enough to the use of policy instruments. Instead, as our discussion of the aggregate supply and demand model has shown, inflation responds to policy actions only after a lag of up to several years. Policymakers can use the rate of inflation, averaged over a one- or two-year time horizon, as an intermediate target; but in order to implement an inflation targeting strategy, they must also have a suitable operating target over which they can exercise closer control.

Many central banks have chosen to use short-term interest rates as their principal operating target. This includes not only central banks like those of the U.K. and Australia that have officially adopted an inflation targeting strategy but also many, like the Federal Reserve in the United States and the European Central Bank in the euro area, that pursue a mixed strategy that includes some elements of inflation targeting.

Figure 10.1 shows how an interest rate operating target works.[3] There are three interest rates involved. The first two are administrative rates set directly by the central bank. One is the interest rate that the central bank charges for reserves that it loans to commercial banks. In the United States, this is called the discount rate. The second is the interest rate paid on reserves that commercial banks keep on deposit with the central bank. In the United States, the Fed began paying interest on reserve deposits only recently (October 2008), but the practice has been common for some time in other countries. The third interest rate is the rate on interbank loans of reserves that commercial banks make to one another. In the United States, this is called the federal funds rate. Unlike the first two, the interbank rate is not under the direct administrative control of the central bank. Instead, it is determined by supply and demand in the interbank loan market.

Figure 10.1 also shows commercial banks' demand curve for reserves. As explained in Chapter 8, commercial banks hold reserves of liquid assets to meet their customers' needs and minimize liquidity risk, but the amount of reserves they hold depends on the interest rate. Other things being equal, the lower the interest rate, the lower the opportunity cost of holding reserves, so the greater the quantity of reserves demanded. In the

**FIGURE 10.1  AN INTEREST RATE OPERATING TARGET**

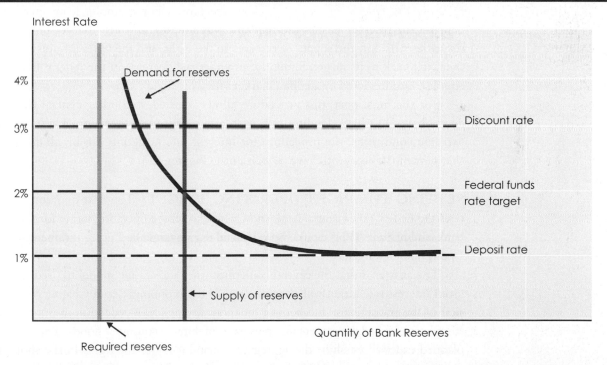

The Fed's discount rate and deposit rate are under its direct administrative control. The Federal funds rate for interbank lending is a market rate set by supply and demand. Commercial bank demand for reserves has a negative slope because lower interest rates mean a lower opportunity cost of holding reserves. To implement an interest rate operating target, the Fed sets a target value for the federal funds rate (2 percent in this case) and sets its administrative rates to form a corridor above and below the target. The Fed then uses open market purchases or sales to adjust the supply of reserves to a quantity such that the supply and demand curves intersect at the target rate of interest.

United States and many (but not all) other countries, the central bank also sets a minimum required level of reserves, shown by a vertical line in the diagram. The demand curve becomes vertical as it approaches the minimum required level of reserves. It becomes horizontal as it approaches the central bank's deposit rate. The horizontal section of the curve is explained by the fact that, if the interbank rate were to fall below the central bank's deposit rate, banks could make an effortless, risk-free profit by borrowing reserves from other banks and depositing them with the central bank.[4]

In this setting, the Fed implements its policy as follows. First, it sets the discount rate and the deposit rate, both of which are under its direct administrative control. Those two rates form a corridor within which supply and demand conditions will determine the federal funds rate. Next, the Fed sets an operating target for the federal funds rate. In our example, the target is 2 percent, in the center of the corridor. Although the Fed cannot directly control the federal funds rate, it can control it indirectly by using open market purchases or sales to adjust the quantity of reserves it supplies to the banking system. As Figure 10.1 shows, adjusting the supply of reserves to the right quantity will ensure that the equilibrium federal funds rate is equal to the target.

Of course, changing market conditions may cause the demand curve to shift, in which case the federal funds rate will temporarily rise above or below the target. The Fed tolerates brief, small moves away from the target; but if the rate moves more than a little, it uses open market operations to adjust the supply of reserves in such a way as to bring the federal funds rate back to the target. For example, if an increase in demand for reserves pushes the federal funds rate up, an open market purchase of securities will shift the supply of reserves to the right; and the federal funds rate will, then, fall back to its target. Similarly, an undesired decrease in the federal funds rate could be counteracted by an open market sale.

For the most part, this procedure allows the Fed, and other central banks, to control the interbank lending rate with a fair degree of precision. Under certain extreme conditions, the procedure for interest rate targeting can break down; but that part of the story will have to wait until Chapter 12.

**SETTING THE RIGHT OPERATING TARGET**   The next question is: How does the Fed or other central bank know where to set the operating target for the interbank lending rate? Why should the federal funds rate target be 2 percent rather than, say, 1 percent or 5 percent?

The answer is that the central bank must use a forecasting model to predict how a given interest rate target will affect the rest of the economy. Recall Chapter 9's discussion of the transmission mechanism for monetary policy. A reduction in interest rates stimulates planned investment and purchases of durable consumer goods. The increased planned expenditure shifts the aggregate demand curve to the right. In the short-run, real output and the price level both increase. In the long run, the price level increases more and real output returns to its natural level. A forecasting model that includes a model of the transmission mechanism is used to estimate the rate of inflation over the next year or two that will result from any given interest rate operating target.

Figure 10.2 shows how forecasting is used as a bridge between the central bank's interest rate operating target and its intermediate inflation target. (For simplicity, we

**FIGURE 10.2    SHIFTS IN THE AGGREGATE DEMAND CURVE**

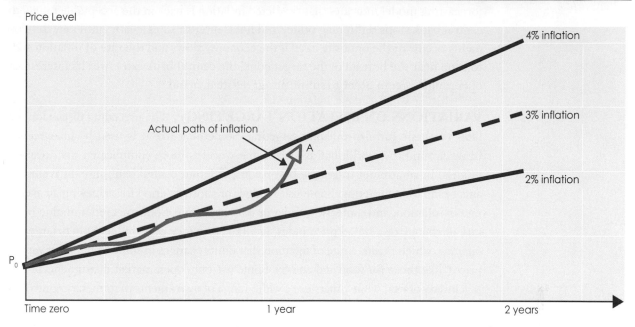

A central bank implements inflation targeting as follows. First, it sets upper and lower limits on the acceptable rate of inflation over a one or two-year time horizon. Here the limits are 2 to 4 percent, which define a cone-shaped area of acceptable values for the price level. Next, it uses a forecasting model to determine an interest rate that will put the expected rate of inflation on a path in the middle of the target cone. As time goes by, unexpected developments may push the actual inflation rate higher or lower than the forecast. If the rate of inflation threatens to move the price level above the acceptable range, as at point A, the central bank raises its interest rate target until the forecast rate of inflation falls back into the target cone.

will consider the case of a central bank that uses a pure form of inflation targeting, not the mixed policy used by the Fed.) First, the central bank sets its intermediate target for the inflation rate. Policymakers know they cannot control inflation precisely; so they name a target range of inflation, for example, between two percent and four percent on average over the next two years. Starting from the current price level $P_0$, the target range for inflation defines a cone-shaped area of acceptable values for the future price level.

Next, the forecasting model is used to find an operating target for the interbank interest rate that appears likely to result in a rate of inflation near the center of the cone. The central bank uses open market operations, as shown in Figure 10.2, to maintain the interbank rate at that level. Looking forward from time zero, it is expected that maintaining that interest rate target will put the economy on an inflation path of 3 percent, right in the center of the cone.

Now comes the tricky part. As we know from our earlier discussion  forecasting models are far from perfect. Even if policymakers maintain their operating target for the interest rate, unforeseen events are likely to cause the actual path of inflation to swing above or below the center of the target cone, as shown in the figure. When the price level threatens to cross the limits of the target cone, as it does at point A in Figure 10.2, the central bank must act. It raises its operating target for the interbank interest rate and uses open market operations to tighten the supply of reserves to commercial banks. Doing so will restrain the growth of aggregate demand. When the forecasting model indicates that predicted inflation is back in the acceptable range, the central bank stops tightening policy and holds interest rates steady until new developments occur. In the opposite case, if the economy slows and the rate of inflation starts to drop near the bottom of the target cone, the central bank can lower its interest rate operating target in order to stimulate aggregate demand.

**VARIATIONS ON INFLATION TARGETING**   The preceding discussion outlines the basic form of inflation targeting. Something like it is used by many central banks around the world; but as always, the world is more complicated than textbook models. In an attempt to get the best results, different central banks use different variants of inflation targeting. Some use a longer or shorter period for achieving an average rate of inflation, and some use a wider or narrower cone. Some measure inflation by the rate of change of a broad price index, like the consumer price index. Others target *core inflation*, which means a rate of inflation that omits changes in some of the most variable prices, like those for food and energy. Some use only open market instruments to control interest rates, while others use a wider range of instruments of monetary control.

**MULTIPLE TARGETS**   The monetary policy of the Federal Reserve, from the mid-1980s through the start of the global financial crisis in 2007, followed a policy that in some ways resembles inflation targeting, but not entirely. The Fed does place a higher priority on price stability than on any other single intermediate policy target. It uses open market instruments to control bank reserves and sets an operating target for the federal funds rate very much as described above. However, there are two important differences between the Fed's policy and pure inflation targeting. First, the Fed has not announced an explicit inflation target although its actual decisions suggest a target of about 2.5 percent, plus or minus one percent or so. Second, the Fed, especially under Alan Greenspan chairmanship from 1987 to 2006, kept an eye on other intermediate targets as well as inflation. Those included the unemployment rate, the growth rate of real output, and in some cases developments in other financial markets.

**Taylor rule**

A rule that adjusts monetary policy according to changes in the rate of inflation and the output gap (or unemployment)

A number of economists have proposed explicit policy rules based on the Fed's practice of watching more than one intermediate target. The best known of these is the **Taylor rule**, proposed by Stanford University economist John Taylor. Under the Taylor rule, the Fed would

The Taylor rule was developed by Stanford University economist John Taylor.

tighten policy by adjusting its interest-rate operating target upward by a specified amount whenever the rate of inflation increased and also raise interest rates whenever real output exceed its natural level, that is, when a positive output gap developed.

Despite its resemblance to what the Fed actually does, implementing an explicit Taylor rule encounters some practical difficulties. One is the question of how much interest rates should be adjusted for a given change in inflation or the output gap. If the adjustment is too small, the policy will not be effective in damping the business cycle. If it is too large, policy might overshoot its goals at cyclical peaks and troughs, making things worse rather than better. Taylor's original formulation also encounters the difficulty that data on the output gap are available to policymakers only with a long lag. A variation of the Taylor rule would instead watch changes in unemployment, which are closely linked to changes in the output gap but are available with a much shorter lag.

In academic writings before becoming Fed chairman in 2006, Ben Bernanke sometimes wrote more favorably of policy rules than his predecessor, Alan Greenspan. Someday the Fed may move more explicitly in the direction of inflation targeting or even a Taylor rule. However, in the climate of crisis that prevails as this is written in 2009, the Fed has other, more pressing short-term objectives. We will return to the Fed's recent policies in Chapter 12.

## Exchange Rates and Monetary Policy

Inflation targeting is the most widely used stabilization policy rule among major economies, but it is not by any means universal. Another type of policy rule that is followed by the central banks of many small economies, and a few large ones, uses the exchange rate, rather than interest rates and inflation, as its principal policy target. This section briefly outlines how countries that choose to maintain a fixed exchange rate for their currency conduct monetary policy, and explains why some countries adopt this strategy.

### *The Structure of the Foreign-Exchange Market*

As a traveler you may have had occasion to exchange U.S. dollars for Canadian dollars, Mexican pesos, or the currency of some other country. This trading in paper currencies is a small corner of the largest set of markets in the world—the **foreign-exchange market**—in which trillions of dollars are traded each day. Such trading reflects the fact that most international transactions in goods, services, or financial assets are accompanied by the exchange of one currency for another.

**Foreign-exchange market**

A market in which the currency of one country is traded for that of another

Large trades in the foreign-exchange market, like large domestic financial transactions, are not conducted in paper currency but rather by transfers of funds among deposits in commercial banks. Large banks in the world's money centers—New York, London, Tokyo, and other cities—which are known as *trading banks*, play a key role. These banks have branches all over the world and accept deposits denominated in many different currencies.

Suppose that a supermarket chain in the United States needs to buy pesos that it will use to purchase a shipment of asparagus from a grower in Mexico. The supermarket will ask the commercial bank at which it maintains its accounts to take funds from its dollar-denominated account and make an increase of equal value in a peso-denominated account in Mexico. The peso account can then be used to pay the Mexican supplier. Similarly, if a Mexican pension fund wants to buy U.S. Treasury bills, it can exchange a deposit denominated in pesos for a deposit denominated in dollars and use those dollars to buy the Treasury bills. The banks charge a fee of a small fraction of one percent for these transactions, proportionately far less than the fee you would pay for currency exchange as a tourist visiting Mexico.

## Supply and Demand in the Foreign-Exchange Market

What determines the number of pesos that a customer gets in exchange for its dollars? Why, on a given day, is the exchange rate 10 pesos per dollar rather than 8 or 12? The rate depends on supply and demand, as shown in Figure 10.3.

**FIGURE 10.3    THE FOREIGN-EXCHANGE MARKET FOR DOLLARS AND MEXICAN PESOS**

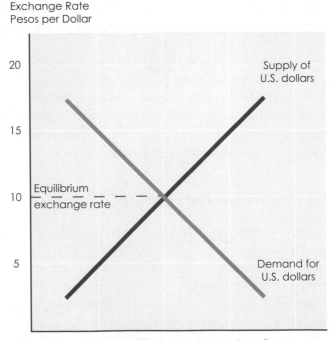

This diagram represents the foreign-exchange market in which U.S. dollars are exchanged for Mexican pesos. The exchange rate is expressed as the number of pesos needed to purchase one dollar. The supply curve of dollars reflects, in part, the activities of U.S. importers of Mexican goods and services, who sell dollars to obtain the pesos they need in order to buy Mexican asparagus, cars assembled in Mexico, and so on. It also reflects the activities of U.S. investors who need pesos in order to buy Mexican stocks, bonds, or other assets. The demand curve for dollars reflects the activities of Mexican buyers of exports from the U.S. They use pesos to buy the dollars they need to buy Boeing aircraft, American corn, and other goods. The demand curve also includes the effects of financial inflows into the United States. For example, a Mexican pension fund that wants to buy U.S. government bonds first needs to exchange pesos for dollars to use in purchasing the bonds.

The supply curve for dollars in Figure 10.3 reflects the activities of everyone who offers dollars in exchange for pesos. They include importers, like the U.S. supermarket chain mentioned earlier and tourists who travel to Mexico. They also include U.S. residents who want to invest in Mexico by buying Mexican securities or making direct investments in Mexican resorts, factories, or other projects. Remittances that Mexicans working in the U.S. send home to their families are a further important supply of dollars in this market.

The demand curve for dollars reflects the activities of everyone who comes to the foreign exchange market with pesos that they want to exchange for dollars. They include Mexican importers of U.S. consumer goods, Mexicans making trips north of the border, Mexican firms buying production equipment or other capital goods from the United States, and Mexican investors buying U.S. assets.

**CHANGES IN EXCHANGE RATES**   Foreign exchange rates—the prices of one currency in terms of another—change from day to day as supply and demand conditions change. Exchange rates are published in many daily newspapers, and up-to-the-minute exchange rates are available on the Internet. Currencies can be quoted in terms of units of foreign currency per dollar, as in our supply and demand diagram, or the other way around, in U.S. dollars per unit of foreign currency.

As supply and demand conditions change, exchange rates also change. If a currency gets stronger, it is said to **appreciate**. For example, in April 2008, one U.S. dollar would buy about 10.5 Mexican pesos. A year later, one dollar would buy 13 pesos. The dollar appreciated relative to the peso over that period. If a currency gets weaker, it is said to **depreciate**. Between April 2008 and April 2009, the Mexican peso would be said to have depreciated relative to the dollar.

A number of factors can cause an appreciation or depreciation. We will give just two of many possible examples, again based on the market where U.S. dollars are exchanged for Mexican pesos.

As one example, consider what happened when there was an outbreak of swine flu in Mexico in the spring of 2009. Vacation travel to Mexico suddenly decreased, which in turn reduced the number of dollars supplied by U.S. tourists in exchange for pesos. The supply curve for dollars shifted sharply to the left, as shown in Part (a) of Figure 10.4. The shift of the supply curve changes the equilibrium exchange rate from 10 pesos per dollar to 15 pesos per dollar—an appreciation of the dollar and a depreciation of the peso.

Our second example shows how changes in financial flows can affect exchange rates. Suppose interest rates increase in the United States while interest rates remain unchanged in Mexico. U.S. bonds and other assets would become relatively more attractive than before to Mexican investors, so net financial outflows from Mexico to the United States would increase. The result would be an increase in demand for dollars and an appreciation of the dollar (depreciation of the peso) as shown in part b of Figure 10.4. Other factors might also affect financial flows. For example, an increase in Mexican taxes on investment income or a threat of political instability in Mexico could also increase financial outflows. The effect would be the same as shown in the figure.

**Appreciate**

Increase in value—such as the value of one country's currency increasing relative to the currency of another country

**Depreciate**

The decrease in value of a currency relative to the value of the currency of another country

**FIGURE 10.4** EFFECTS OF THE SWINE FLUE ON THE PESO-DOLLAR EXCHANGE RATE

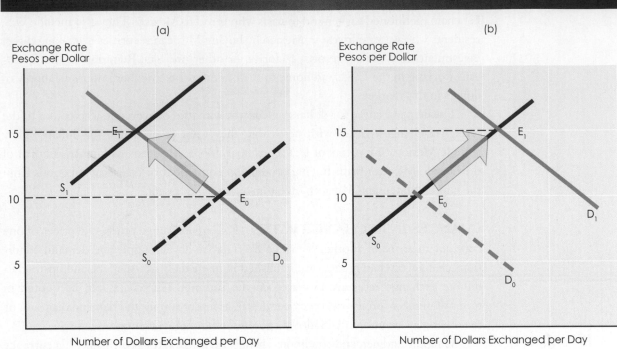

Part (a) shows the effects on the peso-dollar exchange rate of the 2009 outbreak of swine flu in Mexico. A decrease in U.S. tourists to Mexico shifted the supply curve of dollars to the left. As it did so, the exchange rate moved from 10 pesos per dollar to 15 pesos per dollar—an appreciation of the dollar and a depreciation of the peso. Part (b) shows the effects of an increase in U.S. interest rates. The increase in interest rates increases the quantity of dollars supplied by Mexican investors wishing to purchase U.S. bonds. The demand curve shifts to the right. As it does so, there is again an appreciation of the dollar and a depreciation of the peso.

## Central Banks and the Foreign-Exchange Market

In our discussion of central banking in Chapter 8, purchases and sales of assets denominated in foreign currencies were listed as an instrument of monetary policy, together with domestic open market purchases, changes in interest rates, and changes in reserve ratios. Purchases of foreign assets are an instrument of expansionary policy; they increase bank reserves and the monetary base exactly as do domestic open market purchases do. Sales of foreign assets are an instrument of contractionary policy. In addition to their effects on domestic monetary conditions, purchases and sales of foreign assets also affect exchange rates. An example will show how these effects come about.

Figure 10.5 shows how Mexico's central bank, Bank of Mexico, could intervene to maintain an exchange rate of 10 pesos per dollar, if it wanted to do so. (The Bank of Mexico does not currently maintain a fixed exchange rate relative to the dollar, but it has done so at times in the past.) Suppose that originally the supply and demand curves are in the positions $S_0$ and $D_0$. Then, suppose that fast growth of GDP in Mexico increases demand for imports from the United States, and shifts the demand curve for dollars rightward, to $D_1$. If the Bank of Mexico does nothing, the peso will depreciate to a rate of 15 pesos per

**FIGURE 10.5   MAINTAINING A PESO-DOLLAR EXCHANGE RATE**

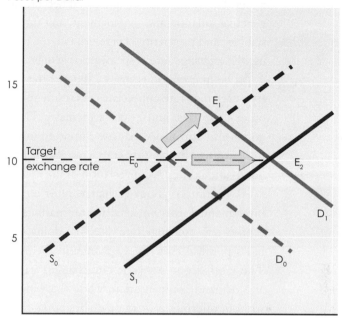

Number of Dollars Exchanged per Day

The Bank of Mexico, Mexico's central bank, could, if it wished, intervene in foreign exchange markets to hold the exchange rate at a target rate of 10 pesos per dollar. Suppose an increase in demand for dollars shifted the demand curve from $D_0$ to $D_1$. Other things being equal, the increase in demand would cause the peso to depreciate (an appreciation of the dollar). To prevent this, the Bank of Mexico could sell dollars from its foreign exchange reserves, shifting the supply curve to S1. The exchange rate would then remain at its target value of 10 pesos per dollar.

dollar, shown by a movement from point $E_0$ to point $E_1$. In order to hold the exchange rate at 10 pesos per dollar, the Bank of Mexico can sell dollars from its foreign exchange reserves. The sales of dollars, added to the dollars already offered for sale by private parties, would shift the supply curve rightward to $S_1$. Instead of moving to $E_1$, the market would move to $E_2$, and the exchange rate would remain at its target level.

On another occasion, the Bank of Mexico might want to offset a different combination of market forces that would tend to cause an unwanted appreciation of the peso. To do so, it would buy dollars to add to its foreign reserves. All the effects described above would then be reversed.

## Why Maintain an Exchange Rate Target?

Up to this point, we have explained how a central bank can intervene in foreign exchange markets to maintain an exchange rate at some level stronger or weaker than what would otherwise be the market equilibrium. What we have not yet explained is why policymakers might want to do so—that is, why they might select a monetary policy strategy that focuses on the exchange rate, rather than some other target.

The exchange rate is the operating target for the central bank, not in itself a goal of policy. Exchange rates are important because of the effects they have on intermediate targets like inflation and employment, and through those, on the ultimate policy goals of stability and prosperity. There are two main reasons why some central banks choose to use the exchange rate as their principal operating target in pursuit of broader goals.

The first reason is that exchange rates influence patterns of trade. When a country's exchange rate appreciates, its residents find it less expensive to buy goods made in other countries; and imports increase. That benefits buyers of imported consumer goods and also firms that use imported inputs. At the same time, an appreciation of the currency harms exporters and also firms that compete with imported consumer goods and inputs. A depreciation of the exchange rate has opposite effects.

Uncertainty about exchange rates increases the risk of international trade and investment. Firms engaged in international trade can take measures to reduce their exposure to exchange rate risks, but doing so is costly. Also, exchange rate uncertainty has a political cost. Every change in the exchange rate produces winners and losers. The losers from exchange rate changes are likely to express anger at the government and demand compensation, while the winners are likely to quietly count their gains without offering to share them. Together, the economic and political costs of exchange rate uncertainty are one factor that makes an exchange rate target attractive.

The second reason to use an exchange rate target as a basis for economic policy is to help control inflation. In the late twentieth century, many countries around the world—Argentina, Brazil, Israel, Russia, and Bulgaria, to name just a few—had periods of extreme inflation. As we will explain in detail in Chapter 12, one policy that has been found effective in bringing inflation under control is to set a fixed exchange-rate link to a stronger, more stable currency—like the dollar or the euro (or, before the euro, the German mark). The expectation of a stable exchange rate acts as an anchor to promote domestic price stability.

For both of these reasons, then, many countries use the exchange rate as their principal operating target. Some of these countries, like Hong Kong, Estonia, and Bulgaria, maintain an exchange rate that is precisely fixed relative to the dollar or euro, allowing not even the smallest variation from day to day. Other countries, like China and Russia, use central bank policy to influence exchange rates and reduce short-term fluctuations without announcing an exact target or eliminating all exchange rate movements.

When all is said and done, there is no simple answer to which monetary policy strategy is best for any given country. The choice of an inflation target, an exchange rate target, or some mixed policy target involves both economic and political considerations. Nonetheless, over the past couple of decades, economists have more and more come around to the view that some kind transparent policy rule, based on preset targets of some kind, does a better job of promoting stability and prosperity than the kind of ad-hoc fine-tuning that many countries attempted in the past.

## SUMMARY

1. **Why do lags, forecasting errors, and time-inconsistency combine to create problems for economic policy?** Simple textbook models make it look as if it would be easy to *fine-tune* the economy. In practice, three problems make fine-tuning difficult. *Lags* create delays between the time problems develop and the time policies take effect. *Forecasting errors* make it difficult for policymakers to overcome the problem of lags by acting before a turning point in the business cycle approaches. *Time-inconsistency* is a tendency for policymakers to take actions that are beneficial in the short run, but make problems worse in the long run.

2. **What are the differences among policy instruments, operating targets, intermediate targets, and policy goals?** *Policy instruments* are variables that are under direct control of policymakers. *Operating targets* are variables that respond immediately, or almost immediately, to changes in policy instruments. *Intermediate targets* are variables that respond to changes in operating targets with a significant lag. *Policy goals* like prosperity and stability are connected to people's long-run economic welfare.

3. **How do policy rules like inflation targeting seek to overcome the limits of fine-tuning?** If policy makers follow transparent, preset policy rules, there is less chance that lags and forecasting errors will lead to overshooting at the top and bottom of the business cycle. Also, preset rules reduce the risk that time-inconsistency will lead to politically motivated destabilizing actions. Under *inflation targeting*, the central bank uses its policy instrument to hold the forecast rate of inflation within a target range over a one to two year time horizon. Under a Taylor rule, the central bank would watch developments both of inflation and of real output or unemployment.

4. **How do central bank actions affect exchange rates?** Exchange rates are determined by the supply and demand in markets where foreign currency is exchanged for domestic currency. Central banks can cause their own domestic currency to *appreciate* relative to foreign currency by selling assets denominated in foreign currency. Central banks can cause their domestic currency to *depreciate* by buying assets denominated in foreign currency. Some central banks use the exchange rate as an operating target, buying and selling foreign assets as needed to hold the exchange rate at its target value.

5. **Why do some countries choose exchange rates as the principal target for monetary policy?** There are two main reasons why some central banks choose to maintain the exchange rate of their currency equal to, or close to, a fixed value relative to some other currency. The first reason is to reduce the risk that exchange rate movements will disrupt patterns of trade. The second reason is that maintaining a fixed exchange rate relative to some stable currency like the dollar or euro can be an effective tool for fighting inflation.

## Key Terms

## Problems and Topics for Discussions

1. **Terms of Federal Reserve governors** The chief policy making body of the Federal Reserve

System is its seven-member Board of Governors. Governors are appointed for terms of 14 years, and usually cannot serve more than one term (except for an additional partial term to fill a vacancy). Terms are staggered, so that one governor's term expires every other year. Governors cannot be removed from office except "for cause," that is, for abuse of their office, not just because of policy disagreements. In what way do the long terms and secure tenure of Federal Reserve governors help to overcome the problem of time-inconsistency in monetary policy? Discuss.

2. **Monetary policy targets in Eudemonia** Suppose that natural real output in the country of Eudemonia grows at a steady rate of 3 percent per year. In the past, velocity has been approximately constant, and the Eudemonian Central Bank (ECB) has maintained a target rate of growth of 4 percent per year for the money stock. What would be the resulting rate of inflation? Now suppose that the introduction of Internet banking allows people to make transactions on line without holding large amounts of currency or bank balances. As Internet banking spreads, velocity begins to increase at a rate of 3 percent per year. What will happen to the rate of inflation? How could the ECB offset the impact on inflation, if any?

3. **Core versus headline inflation** Among central banks that practice inflation targeting, there is a debate over whether to target "headline" inflation or "core" inflation. Headline inflation means the most widely publicized measure of inflation, usually the consumer price index for all items. Some banks favor headline inflation because promising to stabilize a widely publicized inflation measure has maximum psychological impact on public expectations. Core inflation means consumer price inflation adjusted to remove the most variable prices, like those of food and energy. Some central banks favor core inflation on the grounds that food and energy prices are set in world markets and are beyond the control of domestic monetary policy. Compare the rate of inflation for "core" and "head-

line" measures for the country you live in for the most recently reported ten years. How great has the difference between the two measures been? If you live in the United States, a convenient source for this information is the annual Economic Report of the President. You can find the report on line at http://www.gpoaccess.gov/eop/. Click on the link for "statistical tables" and then look for Table B-63, special consumer price indexes.

4. **Exchange rate movements** Exchange rate data is easily available on line for almost every currency in the world. One easy-to-use source for past and present exchange rates is http://www.oanda.com/convert/fxhistory. Select a currency other than the U.S. dollar (for example, the currency of the country where you live or a country you have recently visited). How has the exchange rate of this currency moved relative to the dollar over the past year? Has it appreciated, depreciated, or remained unchanged? Can you find any explanation of recent exchange rate movements for this currency, or for its unchanged exchange rate, if the exchange rate has not moved?

5. **Foreign exchange supply and demand** Draw a diagram for the foreign exchange market for the dollar vs. the euro. Model your diagram on Figure 10.3. Place "euros per dollar" on the vertical axis. Suppose now that rapid growth of the U.S. economy increases U.S. demand for European goods, while there is no change in growth of countries using the euro. Will the increase in U.S. growth affect the demand for euros, the supply of euros, both, or neither? Why? Will the result be an appreciation, depreciation, or no change in the euro? Why?

## Case for Discussion

### Is the Chinese YUAN too weak?

One of the most dramatic events in the global economy in recent decades has been the rise of China as an export powerhouse. China has many advantages that have contributed to its export success. It has low wage rates and an enormous pool of workers willing to acquire industrial skills. It has a high savings rate resulting in high investment, and it has a government that actively encourages export-oriented businesses. By 2008, these advantages had combined to bring the U.S. deficit on trade of goods with China to more than $25 billion per month, the largest bilateral deficit with any country.

One controversial aspect of China's export push concerns the role of the Chinese central bank in regard to the Chinese currency, the yuan. The Chinese central bank intervenes aggressively to influence the value of the value of the yuan. Until mid-2005, it held the yuan closely to a value of about 8.3 yuan per dollar. Without intervention, the yuan would have quickly appreciated. Such an appreciation would increase the cost of Chinese goods to U.S. buyers and would make it easier for U.S. firms to export to China.

Many U.S. politicians, eager to help exporters in their home districts, wanted to see an appreciation of the yuan. President George W. Bush spoke out in favor of such a policy change. A bill was introduced in the U.S. Congress to put pressure on China to allow the yuan to "float" to a stronger value. Finally, on July 21, 2005, China's central bank governor Zhou Xiaochuan gave into pressure and announced a change in policy. At first the appreciation was slight, only about 6 percent over the next year. Gradually, however, appreciation continued. By early 2009, the yuan was trading at around 6.8 to the dollar. Even so, it appeared that the Chinese central bank was still intervening behind the scenes to limit the rate of appreciation.

Some U.S. economists noted that a change in Chinese policy would not be beneficial to the U.S. economy in all ways. A stronger yuan would mean higher prices for consumers of goods imported from China. Furthermore, in order to keep the yuan from appreciating, the Chinese central bank had become a huge buyer of dollars. Its growing official reserves of dollars were invested in U.S. government bonds, helping to keep U.S. interest rates low. They warned that a change in Chinese policy might lead to a rise in U.S. interest rates

that would more than offset the beneficial effect of an a decrease in the trade deficit.

In the end, whether a stronger appreciation of the yuan would help or hurt the U.S. economy will be decided only when it happens. Most observers expect that to happen sooner or later, but just when is anyone's guess.

## QUESTIONS

1. Explain why a weak yuan leads to large net exports from China to the United States.
2. Draw a supply and demand diagram showing yuan per dollar on the vertical axis. Draw supply and demand curves showing an initial equilibrium exchange rate of 8 yuan per dollar. Next suppose rapid growth of the U.S. economy increases demand for imports from China. What will happen to the supply and/or demand curves?
3. In your diagram, show a rightward shift of the supply curve, tending to cause an appreciation of the yuan (fewer yuan per dollar). What could the Chinese central bank do to hold the exchange rate at 8 yuan per dollar? Would this require buying or selling dollars for its international reserves of dollars?
4. Based on your understanding of the elements of planned expenditure, what would be the effect on U.S. GDP of a decrease in net exports (Ex-Im) to China, other things being equal? What would be the effect of an increase in U.S. interest rates? Would these two effects work in the same, or opposite directions? Why?
5. Look on line for recent trends in the exchange rate of the yuan relative to the dollar. (One site where you can find this information is http://www.oanda.com/convert/fxhistory). Has the trend toward appreciated continued since the beginning of 2009?

## End Notes

1. Grace Juhn and Prakesh Lougani, "Further Cross-Country Evidence on the Accuracy of the Private Sector's Output Forecasts," IMF Staff Papers Vol. 49, No. 1 (2002).

2. For an excellent account of the evolution of economists' views on policy rules, see Marvin Goodfriend, "How the World Achieved Consensus on Monetary Policy," *Journal of Economic Perspectives,* (Fall 2007): 47-68.

3. An alternative presentation of interest-rate targeting is given in the appendix to this chapter.

4. For complex technical reasons, the effective federal funds rate in the United States does occasionally fall below not only the Fed's target rate, but also the deposit rate, at least for short periods. However, such episodes do not prevent use of the federal funds rate as a policy target.

# Appendix to Chapter 10:
# SUPPLY AND DEMAND FOR MONEY

As we have seen, central banks control interest rates in two ways. First, the discount rate charged on borrowed reserves and the deposit rate for reserves held on deposit at the central bank are set administratively. Second, interest rates can be controlled indirectly by adjusting the monetary base and the quantity of money using open market operations or other instruments. Some central banks use interest rates as their principal operating target while some use other targets. In the chapter, the operation of an interest rate target is explained in terms of the supply and demand for bank reserves (see Figure 10.1). This appendix takes an alternate approach that explains interest rates in terms of the supply and demand for money itself.

## The Money Demand Curve

What do we mean when we speak of the "demand" for money? If we use the term "money" in the careless way it is often used in daily conversation, as a synonym for "income" or "wealth," the answer would be that people seem to have an unlimited demand for money.

> "I'm studying economics because I want to work on Wall Street and make a lot of money when I graduate," a friend might tell you.
>
> "How much money do you want?" you might ask.
>
> "The more the better!" your friend would say.

When economists discuss the demand for money, they have something different in mind. As we saw in Chapter 9, economists use the term "money" to mean a specific set of liquid assets—the currency, transaction deposits, and other elements that make up M2 or some other specific measure of the money stock. To an economist, the demand for money means how much of those particular assets a person wants to hold at any one time, other things being equal. The "other things" include one's total wealth (that is, the sum of all of one's assets, including less liquid assets like houses, cars, and shares of stock) and also one's income.

The quantity of money demanded, given one's level of income, depends on the opportunity cost of holding money. For an ordinary good, like chicken or movie tickets, the opportunity cost is measured by the market price—the amount of money that must be paid per unit to buy it. People, however, do not "buy" money in the same sense that they buy other goods. Instead, they obtain money by exchanging other assets for it, for example, by selling securities in exchange for bank deposits. In that case, the "price," or more accurately, the opportunity cost, of obtaining money is the rate of interest that could have been earned by holding securities instead of currency or transaction deposits that pay no interest.

In this brief appendix, we will make two simplifications with regard to the opportunity cost of money. First, we will assume that money earns no interest at all. It is true that some forms of money, like saving deposits, do pay a small rate of interest, but we will leave these out of consideration. Second, there are many different kinds of securities that could be exchanged for money, each of which would pay a different interest rate and, therefore, imply a different opportunity cost. To keep things simple, we will consider only one non-monetary asset, namely, a short-term, interest-bearing asset that has zero default risk—for example, T-bills.

Figure 10A.1 shows the demand for money in graphical form. The vertical axis shows the interest rate chosen to measure the opportunity cost of money. The horizontal axis shows the quantity of money. We will represent the quantity of money in real terms, so the horizontal axis is labeled M/P, meaning the quantity of money divided by the price level. It would be possible, instead, to place the nominal money stock, M, on the horizontal axis; but the real-money version of the diagram is the one economists most often use.

Along the money demand curve $MD_1$, the real quantity of money demanded increases as the interest rate decreases. For example, at an interest rate of 4 percent, the quantity of money demanded is \$100 billion (point A). If the interest rate falls to 2 percent, the quantity demanded increases to \$200 billion (point B).

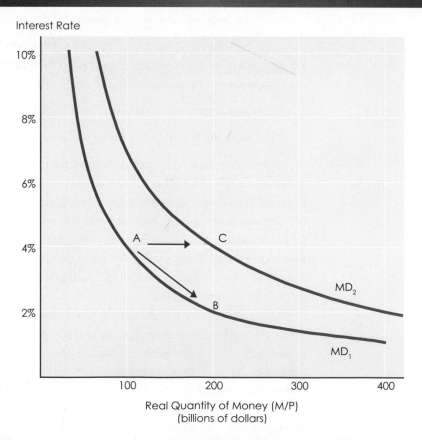

**FIGURE 10A.1  DEMAND FOR MONEY**

The money demand curve shows the real quantity of money balances that people want to hold at any given interest rate. A change in the interest rate causes a movement along a given money demand curve (for example, from A to B). An increase in real income causes a shift in the money demand curve (for example, from $MD_1$ to $MD_2$.)

If real domestic income increases, people will want to buy more goods and services. Other things being equal, more money will be demanded to carry out the greater volume of transactions. An increase in real domestic income thus shifts the money demand curve to the right. For example, suppose that $MD_1$ was drawn for a domestic income of $1 trillion. If domestic income increases to $2 trillion, the money demand curve will shift rightward to $MD_2$. If the interest rate were to remain at 4 percent as domestic income increased, the quantity of money demand would increase to $200 billion (point C).

To summarize, we see that the demand for real money balances is inversely proportional to the interest rate and directly proportional to real domestic income, other things being equal. A change in the interest rate causes a movement along the money demand curve, and a change in real income causes a shift in the curve.

## The Money Supply Curve

The supply of money is controlled by the central bank, which is able to adjust it to any desired value by using open market operations or other instruments. Figure 10A.2 shows how money supply, as controlled by the central bank, interacts with money demand.

Suppose, for example, that the central bank uses open market operations to adjust the real money supply to $200 billion. The result is the money supply curve $MS_1$. If the

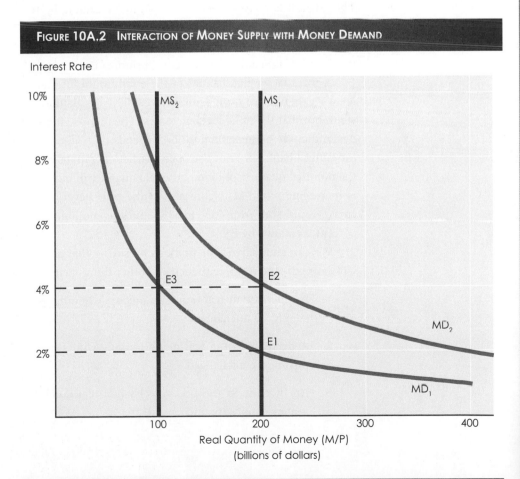

**FIGURE 10A.2  INTERACTION OF MONEY SUPPLY WITH MONEY DEMAND**

money demand curve is in the position $MD_1$, the equilibrium interest rate will be 2 percent, shown by the intersection of $MS_1$ and $MD_1$.

*Starting from point $E_1$, any change in money demand, while money supply was held constant, would change the equilibrium interest rate. For example, suppose that real domestic income increases, shifting the money demand curve to $MD_2$. If the interest rate remained unchanged, people would want more money to carry out the greater volume of transactions associated with their higher income. Firms and households would try to get the money they want by borrowing it from their banks. However, if the central bank held the quantity of money constant, the banking system would not have the reserves needed to supply the desired amount of money. As the demand for loans increased, but with limited reserves available, banks would raise their interest rates. Increasing interest rates, in turn, would cause firms and households to tighten up their cash management practices and find ways to make do with less money per dollar of income. As interest rates rose, the economy would move to a new equilibrium at $E_2$.*

Interest rates would also increase if the central bank used open market sales of securities to reduce the real money supply while real income and the price level remain unchanged. For example, suppose the central bank reduces the real money supply from $200 billion to $100 billion. That would be shown by a leftward shift in the money supply curve from $MS_1$ to $MS_2$. Banks would suddenly find themselves short on reserves. They would have to reduce their volume of lending by refusing to extend new loans when customers paid off existing loans. Competition among borrowers for the limited volume of loans available would drive up interest rates, and the economy would move from equilibrium at $E_1$ to a new equilibrium at $E_3$.

A third factor that can affect the equilibrium interest rate is a change in the price level. Again we start from equilibrium at $E_1$. Now assume that real income remains constant, but that the price level increases. The increase in the price level will not shift the demand curve because its position depends on real, not nominal, income. However, if the central bank does not use open market operations or other instruments to increase the nominal quantity of money, the real quantity of money, $M/P$, will decrease because P is increasing while M is constant. If the price level doubled, the real money supply curve would shift from $MS_1$ to $MS_2$, and the equilibrium interest rate would rise to 4 percent, as shown by $E_3$.

We can summarize our findings by saying that any of the following three events will cause the interest rate to increase, other things being equal:

1. An increase in real domestic income while the price level and the real money supply are unchanged

2. A decrease in the real money supply while the price level and real domestic income are unchanged

3. An increase in the price level while real domestic income and the nominal money supply are unchanged

### Money Supply Target Versus Interest Rate Target

The diagrams in this appendix provide additional perspective on the use of different targets and policy rules by the central bank.

A monetarist policy rule of the kind favored by Milton Friedman would use open market operations to hold the nominal money stock constant. Under such a policy rule, any increase in nominal domestic income, whether in the form of inflation, an increase in real income, or a combination of the two, would cause interest rates to rise. As interest rates rose, credit market conditions would tighten, planned investment would decrease, and the growth of nominal income would down. Similarly, any decrease in nominal income would cause interest rates to fall. Planned investment would be encouraged, counteracting the slowdown of nominal income. In short, under the monetarist rule, countercyclical changes in interest rates would tend to moderate excessive variations in the growth of nominal income.

A central bank that used an interest rate operating target would operate differently. After setting its interest rate target, it would use open market operations to adjust the position of the money supply curve as needed to hit the target. However, the central bank would have to be careful that the interest rate target was set at the right level. If it maintained too low an interest rate target for too long, it would risk an inflationary spiral. When inflation accelerated, it would have to increase the nominal money stock in order to prevent a rising price level from shifting the real money supply curve to the left and, thereby, increasing interest rates. The increase in the nominal money stock, in turn, would feed further inflation. To avoid this trap and prevent unwanted inflation, a central bank must supplement an interest rate operating target with inflation targeting, a Taylor rule, or some other intermediate target that tells it when and by how much to adjust the short-run interest rate operating target.

# CHAPTER *11*

# Fiscal Policy

**After reading this chapter, you will understand the following:**

1. How changes in taxes and expenditures can be used as a tool of stabilization policy
2. Practical problems encountered in implementing fiscal stimulus
3. The meaning of automatic fiscal policy
4. How the federal budget process works
5. Whether the U.S. budget deficit and national debt are sustainable

**Before reading this chapter, make sure you know the meaning of the concepts:**

1. Disposable income
2. Government purchases
3. Transfer payments
4. Net taxes
5. Expenditure multiplier
6. Multiplier effect
7. Output gap
8. Monetary base

**Fiscal policy**

Policy that is concerned with government purchases, taxes, and transfer payments

**F**ISCAL POLICY MEANS policy related to taxes and government expenditures. As we have seen, both taxes and spending affect planned expenditure and aggregate demand. Taxes on households influence the consumption component of planned expenditure by way of changes in after-tax income. Business taxes are important because they affect incentives for investment, another major component of planned expenditure. On the expenditure side of the budget, government purchases of goods and services are themselves a major component of planned expenditure. Finally, the parts of government expenditures that

283

consist of transfer payments affect planned expenditure in the same way as tax cuts, by increasing disposable income and, hence, consumption.

**Budget deficit**

Government expenditures minus tax revenues, or, alternatively, government purchases minus net taxes

Because government expenditures stimulate planned expenditure and taxes reduce it, the government's **budget deficit** is often used as an indicator of the impact of fiscal policy on aggregate demand. As we learned in Chapter 5, the deficit can be expressed in one of two equivalent ways—either as government expenditures minus tax revenues or as government purchases minus net taxes. The deficit or surplus of the government budget is important not only for short-term stabilization policy in the context of the business cycle but also for growth and prosperity in the long term. This chapter will discuss both short-and long-term perspectives.

Fiscal policy is about politics as much as it is about economics. To some extent, of course, this is true of other areas of economic policy, too. If central banks are not adequately shielded from political pressures, they may give way to time-inconsistency. They may pursue overly expansionary policies that produce politically attractive short-run gains at the risk of long-run inflation and instability. Exchange rate policy also may be subject to political pressure, for example, if a country tries to maintain an undervalued exchange rate to serve the interests export industries, or an overvalued rate to curry favor with consumers. However, no area of economic policy is more closely entangled with politics than fiscal policy. Taxes are never paid in the abstract—they are always paid either by one person or another, by businesses or consumers, by the rich or the poor, by farmers or city dwellers. Nor does the government ever spend money in the abstract. It spends on specific things—unemployment benefits, health care, military hardware, or farm subsidies—each of which has its own political constituency. In addition to combining short- and long-term perspectives on fiscal policy, then, this chapter will also have to blend economic and political perspectives.

# Taxes and Spending as Tools of Stabilization Policy

The instruments of fiscal policy are changes in tax rates, changes in transfer payments, and changes in government purchases. The use of these instruments to smooth the short-term ups and downs of the business cycle makes a logical starting point for our discussion of fiscal policy.

## *Using Government Purchases to Combat a Recession*

Figure 11.1 uses the aggregate supply and demand model to show how fiscal policy can be used to combat a recession. Suppose that for some reason, perhaps a drop in demand for the country's exports, a situation has developed in which the aggregate supply curve $AS_1$ meets the aggregate demand curve $AD_1$ at a point like $E_1$, where real GDP is less than its natural level. As the diagram is drawn, there is a negative output gap of $500 billion between the short-run equilibrium value of real GDP,

**FIGURE 11.1    USING FISCAL POLICY TO COMBAT A RECESSION**

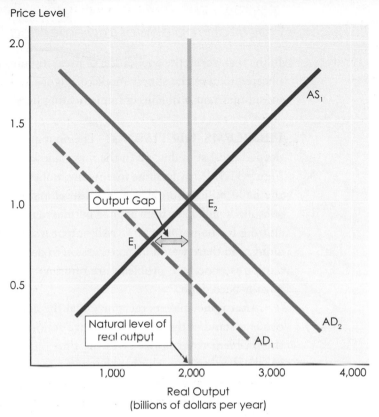

In this figure, a negative output gap has developed at $E_1$. To reach the natural level of real output at $E_2$ without waiting for a downward shift of the aggregate supply curve, the aggregate demand curve could be shifted to the right, from $AD_1$ to $AD_2$. That could be done either by increasing real government purchases or reducing net taxes.

$1,500 billion, and its natural level, $2,000 billion. Unemployment will exceed its natural rate at this point.

As explained in Chapter 9, if aggregate demand were to remain at this low level, the combined effect of high unemployment and low capacity utilization would put downward pressure on prices. As the aggregate supply curve shifted downward and the economy moved down and to the right along $AD_1$, real output would eventually return to its natural level. That kind of adjustment, however, occurs only with a substantial lag. Reluctance of firms to lower their prices and the unwillingness of workers to accept lower nominal wages could make the return to full employment via price and wage decreases slow and painful.

Why wait so long? Suppose that policymakers, impatient with the economy's natural speed of adjustment, want to do something immediately. In the context of the simple model in the figure, the solution seems simple. The aggregate demand curve can be shifted rightward to the desired position $AD_2$, using either an appropriate increase in government purchases or an appropriate reduction in net taxes. Later on, if the initial problem (in this case, a decrease in export demand) corrects itself, the extra fiscal stimulus can be reversed; and the economy will remain in full-employment equilibrium at $E_2$.

## Practical Problems of Implementing Fiscal Stimulus

In the real world, the application of fiscal stimulus to close an output gap is more complicated than in the simple model of Figure 11.1. This section examines some of the most important problems of implementing fiscal policy.

**PROBLEMS OF TIMING**    The first problem is that of correctly timing the needed fiscal stimulus, given the inevitable lags and forecasting errors. Look again at Figure 11.1. With accurate forecasting, policymakers would have been able to prevent the $500 billion output gap from developing in the first place. Fiscal or monetary stimulus would have been applied in time to prevent the aggregate demand curve from shifting to the position $AD_1$, real output would have remained at its natural level all along, and there would be no recession to deal with. In the real world, however, forecasting is imperfect; problems are often not discovered until after much damage has already been done.

After policymakers recognize that the economy has slipped into recession, various lags stand in the way of corrective action. Some are inside lags between the time the problem is recognized and the time a decision is made to do something. Most fiscal policy actions, whether changes in taxes or spending, require legislative action. Occasionally Congress acts with commendable swiftness to fight an economic downturn. On other occasions, legislators take their time.

There is likely to be an additional lag between the times a legislative vote is taken but before policy instruments can actually be deployed. This particular lag is a much bigger problem for fiscal policy than for monetary policy, where instruments like open market operations or discount rate changes can be carried out immediately after a vote by the Fed's Open Market Committee. In the case of fiscal policy, if the chosen instrument is a tax cut, new schedules for withholding must be published or rebate checks mailed, either of which can take weeks or months. If the instrument is a change in government purchases, the lag may be even longer. Sometimes federal, state, or local governments have "shovel ready" projects, for example, highway repairs, on which work can begin immediately. Often, however, government spending projects require extended periods of planning, design, permitting, bidding, and hiring before they are begun, and up to several years before they can be completed.

Fiscal policy actions in 2008 and 2009 illustrate these lags. According to the Business Cycle Dating Committee of the National Bureau of Economic Research, the U.S. economy entered recession in December 2007; however, this finding was not officially announced until December 2008, a full year later. Meanwhile, there were growing signs that the economy was slowing. Policymakers did not want to wait until all the data were in, so Congress passed the Economic Stimulus Act of 2008 in February. That act authorized some $100 billion in tax rebates to U.S. households, but the rebate checks ($1,200 each for most families) were not actually mailed until April and May. By that time, the rebates were too little to achieve more than a brief pause in the downturn.

The Economic Stimulus Act of 2008 authorized $100 billion in tax rebates to U.S. households ($1,200 each for most families).

The contraction became much more severe in the fall of 2008. In response, the following February, Congress passed a much larger fiscal stimulus package called the American Recovery and Reinvestment Act of 2009. That legislation had a nominal value nearly eight times larger than the 2008 stimulus package, but it, too, did not go into effect immediately. The first spending from the new package did not begin to flow until the spring of 2009, more than 15 months after the official start of the recession.

Even after tax rebates are paid out or government purchases are made, there are more lags before intermediate targets like output, employment, and the price level respond. As explained in the previous chapter, these lags add up to at least a year or two. Putting it all together, in contrast to the ease of shifting curves in our textbook models, several years are likely to elapse, in the real world, between the onset of a recession and a return of the economy to its natural level of real output.

**HOW LARGE A STIMULUS?**   The second problem in implementing fiscal policy is how large a stimulus to apply. In part, the problem is one of measuring the output gap. The output gap of $500 billion is easy to measure in Figure 11.1; but in reality, policymakers do not have such a tidy diagram. They must make do with data on prices and real GDP that are incomplete and forecasts that, although helpful, are far from fully accurate. These problems are shared by fiscal and monetary policy.

For fiscal policy, there is the additional problem of knowing how much new aggregate demand will be produced by any given fiscal stimulus. In Figure 11.1, the aggregate demand curve would have to shift horizontally by $1 trillion to close the $500 billion output gap, but it does not necessarily require a $1 trillion increase in government purchases to shift the curve by that amount. As explained in Chapter 5, any increase in government purchases has a *multiplier effect*, which means the new government spending causes additional planned expenditure outside the public sector. Suppose, say, that the government spends $100 billion on highway repairs. Those government purchases are themselves a direct addition to planned expenditure, and they also trigger further, secondary expenditures. For example, newly hired construction workers might increase their spending on restaurant meals, restaurant staff might use some of their tips to buy gasoline, and so on.[1]

The amount of new government purchases needed to close a given output gap depends on the size of the multiplier. For example, if the multiplier were 2, a $500 billion increase in government purchases would be enough to shift the aggregate demand curve by $1 trillion when secondary increases in consumption expenditure are included.

Tax cuts also have a multiplier effect, although it tends to be somewhat weaker than the multiplier for government purchases. The reason is that tax cuts are not themselves additions to planned expenditure but rather additions to the disposable income of households. Tax cuts stimulate planned expenditure only to the extent that households spend part of any new disposable income, as do others who benefit from the increased business they do with the immediate beneficiaries of the tax cuts. In the simplest case, the amount of new consumption expenditure would be equal to the amount of the tax cut multiplied by the marginal propensity to consume. However, the amount of new spending may sometimes be less because people tend to use part of temporary tax rebates to pay off debt, especially credit card debt. Some estimates suggest that households may have spent as little as 15 to 20 percent of their 2008 tax rebates.

Just how large, effectively, is the multiplier for fiscal policy in the U.S. economy? The truth is—economists do not really know. In January 2009, presidential advisers Christina Romer and Jared Bernstein released a paper that estimated that each $100 million in new government purchases would add about $160 million to real GDP, an effective multiplier of 1.6.[2] This estimate formed the basis for the policy proposals of the incoming Obama administration. The multipliers used by Romer and Bernstein are near the high end of recent estimates, however. Other studies suggested that the effective fiscal multiplier might be much less than they thought—perhaps as little as 0.5. That would mean that a $1 trillion of government purchases would add only about $500 billion to real GDP.

The wide range of estimates for the fiscal policy multiplier stem from differences in models and assumptions. One of the differences lies in assumptions about monetary policy. A given increase in government spending will have maximum effect if the Fed **accommodates** the fiscal policy by holding interest rates constant, even if doing so requires an increase in bank reserves and the money stock. If the Fed does not fully accommodate the fiscal stimulus, interest rates will rise as aggregate demand increases. The increase in interest rates, in turn, will tend to reduce private investment spending, partially offsetting the initial increase in government purchases. The strength of this tendency, which is called the **crowding-out effect**, depends critically on what kind of policy rules the Fed follows. For example, if the Fed pursues an explicit or implicit inflation target, it may need to raise interest rates to counteract the impact of fiscal policy on the price level. In that case, the crowding out effect will be strong, and the effective fiscal policy multiplier will be small.

**Accommodating monetary policy**

A policy in which the central bank holds interest rates constant in response to a fiscal stimulus

**Crowding-out effect**

The tendency of expansionary fiscal policy to raise the interest rate and thereby cause a decrease in real planned investment

In evaluating the multiplier that would apply to the fiscal stimulus applied in the winter of 2009, economists largely agreed that in the short run the Fed would keep interest rates low in order to minimize any crowding out effect. Accordingly, even relative pessimists found that the multiplier would be greater than one in the short run. Over a longer time horizon, those who expected the Fed to raise interest rates more sharply as the economy recovered expected a smaller impact from fiscal stimulus.

Another source of difference in multiplier estimates has to do with assumptions about how fiscal policy affects expectations. Some economists argue that because fiscal stimulus increases the budget deficit in the short run, people will anticipate that taxes will be raised in the future to return the budget to balance. If so, they will be more cautious in their current consumption and investment spending. Such caution will reduce the effective fiscal multiplier.

In short, economists simply do not know exactly how much fiscal stimulus is needed to close a given output gap. Once again, the real world is much more complicated than the textbook model.

**REVERSIBILITY AND TIME-INCONSISTENCY**   A third problem concerns the reversibility of fiscal stimulus. If fiscal policy is to succeed in moderating the business cycle, it should add to deficient aggregate demand during contractions and then be reversed to restrain excessive demand during the expansion. Policies that were inappropriately timed or not symmetric over contractions and expansions could instead cause the economy to overshoot peaks and troughs, making the business cycle more, not less, severe.

The problem of reversibility affects both monetary and fiscal policy, but not equally. The Fed, which is able to implement its policy instruments quickly by administrative decision and is at least partially insulated from day-to-day politics, can reverse its policy fairly easily. Fiscal policy can be harder to reverse. The two-year Congressional election cycle in the United States, together with the lags that are inherent in fiscal policy, create a serious problem of time-inconsistency. With an election never more than two years away, it is always a good time, politically, to cut taxes or increase government spending. It is never a good time, politically, to raise taxes or cut spending.

The extensive tax cuts enacted in 2003, early in the administration of George W. Bush, illustrate the problem of reversibility. Originally, the tax cuts were justified as necessary to speed recovery from the mild recession of 2001. Accordingly, they were subject to "sunset" provisions that would have phased them out in 2009 and 2010. Whether because of the tax cuts or for other reasons, the economy did expand strongly over the next several years; but as the date for phase out approached, Republicans in Congress and the White House argued strongly for making the tax cuts permanent. By 2009, when a new Democratic administration took over, the economy was in recession again; so phase-out of the 2003 tax cuts was once again postponed.

**THE PROBLEM OF PRIORITIES**   A final problem is that of reconciling short-term fiscal stimulus with longer-term spending priorities. At one time, it was thought that the multiplier was larger than it now appears to be, perhaps as large as 8 or 10. In that case, only a small fiscal stimulus would be needed to get the economy moving, and it would not matter much what the money was spent on. Economists used to joke about stimulating the economy by hiring one team of workers to bury jars of money and another team to dig them up again. Today, when few economists think the effective multiplier is even as large as 2, a much larger dose of spending is thought to be needed to close a given output gap. The larger the amount spent, the more important that it is used for something the country really needs. However, that is easier said than done.

For one thing, there may be conflicts between long-term priorities and the short-term goal of getting stimulus money flowing as fast as possible. The fiscal stimulus package passed by Congress in February 2009 is a case in point. Some of the money in the package was devoted to construction projects and other short-term spending, but only a limited number of projects could be found that were both worthwhile and shovel-ready. Other parts of the stimulus were devoted to some of the Obama administration's long-term priorities, for example, computerization of medical records and other health care reforms. However, spending that part of the stimulus required more preparation and was expected to extend over a much longer period. Accordingly, it had less short-term impact.

Politics can also make it hard to reconcile short-term stimulus spending with long-term priorities, especially when spending decisions are made in a hurry. Consider the case of the Emergency Economic Stabilization Act of 2008. In its original form, the act was conceived purely as a financial-sector rescue plan and contained little by way of conventional fiscal stimulus. When it was first put to a vote in Congress on September 28, 2008, it was narrowly rejected. Over the next week, it was hastily "sweetened" with $132 billion in fiscal stimulus measures, including both new spending and tax breaks. It passed Congress in its new form on October 3. Unfortunately, many of the added sweeteners seemed more like political pork than long-term national priorities. For example, the package included tax breaks for makers of children's wooden arrows, rum distillers in the Virgin Islands, makers of adult films, and automobile racetracks.

**FISCAL STIMULUS AS A WEAPON OF LAST RESORT**   When we compare them in terms of lags, reversibility, and freedom from short-term political pressures, monetary policy looks more flexible and reliable than fiscal policy. Most economists would agree that in normal times, a responsible central bank, guided by transparent, preset rules, can do a better job of stabilization than the more politicized and unpredictable apparatus of fiscal policy. However, times are not always normal. In times of very low inflation and rapid collapse of aggregate demand, combined with crisis conditions in financial markets, monetary policy may lose much of its effectiveness. Chapter 12 will discuss the reasons for possible failure of monetary policy in more detail.

In the atmosphere of economic crisis that prevailed in 2008 and 2009, many economists and policymakers saw fiscal policy as the weapon of last resort. The result was application of fiscal stimulus on an unprecedented scale not just in the United States, but in many other countries, as well. As this is being written, it is too early to know how effective those policies will be; but it is certain that careful dissection of the results will dominate discussion of the economics of fiscal policy for years to come.

## Automatic Fiscal Policy

The type of fiscal policy discussed so far—changes in the laws regarding government purchases, taxes, and transfer payments that are designed to increase or decrease

## Discretionary fiscal policy

Changes in the laws regarding government purchases and net taxes

## Automatic fiscal policy

Changes in government purchases or net taxes that are caused by changes in economic conditions given unchanged tax and spending laws

## Automatic stabilizers

Those elements of automatic fiscal policy that move the federal budget toward deficit during an economic contraction and toward surplus during an expansion

## Structural budget deficit or surplus

The deficit or surplus that would prevail in any year given that year's tax and spending laws, assuming real GDP to be at its natural level

aggregate demand—is known as **discretionary fiscal policy**. There is also a second aspect of fiscal policy—**automatic fiscal policy**—that concerns the way taxes and government spending respond to changes in income, unemployment, and the price level even when laws remain unchanged.

As the economy moves through the business cycle, changes in real output and employment affect both tax revenues and outlays. An increase in real output increases real revenues from all major tax sources, including income taxes, social security payroll taxes, taxes on corporate profits, and sales taxes. At the same time, an increase in real output cuts real government outlays for transfer payments, largely because increases in real output are associated with decreases in the unemployment rate. Taking both effects together, an increase in real GDP tends to reduce the federal budget deficit in both real and nominal terms.

Changes in price level can also affect taxes and government expenditures. With real output held constant, an increase in the price level tends to increase federal tax receipts. Because marginal tax rates are higher at higher income levels, nominal taxes rise more than in proportion to nominal income. At the same time, an increase in the price level tends to increase nominal expenditures on transfer payments. That happens because most transfer programs are now indexed to the cost of living. On balance, an increase in the price level, other things being equal, tends to increase revenues by more than expenditures.

Taking all these effects together, as real output and the price level rise and unemployment falls during an expansion, the government budget moves toward surplus in real terms. Automatic fiscal policy thus operates to moderate aggregate demand during an expansion. By the same token, when the economy slows down, inflation and the growth rate of real output decrease and unemployment rises. As a result, the budget swings toward deficit during a contraction.

Because automatic fiscal policy operates to offset changes in other elements of planned expenditure, budget components like income taxes and unemployment benefits are known as **automatic stabilizers**. These mechanisms serve to moderate the economy's response to exogenous changes in consumption, private planned investment, and net exports. As reported in *Economics in the News 11.1*, the strength of automatic stabilizers varies substantially from one country to another. The United States lies somewhere near the middle of the spectrum.

## Cyclical and Structural Deficits

One way to measure the size of automatic stabilizers is to ask how large the budget deficit would be with and without their influence. As a baseline for the measurement, we can choose a year when real GDP is equal to its natural level. Depending on policies that are in force, the budget may be either in surplus, deficit, or balance in such a year. The position of the budget when real GDP is at its natural level is called the **structural deficit** or **structural surplus**. Suppose the next year that the economy enters a recession and a negative output gap develops, but there are no changes in any tax or spending laws. As incomes shrink, tax collections will fall; and as unemployment rises, more people will receive unemployment compensation, food aid, and other government benefits. As a

Economics in the News 11.1
### AUTOMATIC VERSUS DISCRETIONARY FISCAL STIMULUS:
### AN INTERNATIONAL COMPARISON

Fiscal stimulus was a major point of discussion.

In April 2009, the presidents and prime ministers of 20 of the world's major economic powers gathered for the G-20 summit meeting in London. When the leaders of United States, the European Union, Japan, China, Russia, Brazil and others sat down around the conference table, one of the major points of discussion was fiscal stimulus. Six weeks earlier the U.S. Congress had passed an enormous fiscal stimulus bill.

The U.K., Japan, and China were taking similar actions. However, some countries of continental Europe were less eager to commit to large increases in discretionary spending. They pointed out a major difference between their fiscal systems and those of the United States or China. France, Germany, and several other EU members have much higher tax rates and much broader social safety nets. As a result, automatic stabilizers are stronger in proportion to their economies, as shown in the chart. It is true that during expansions, high taxes and broad social safety nets can act as a drag on growth, and for that reason, they are subject to much criticism; but during a downturn, they have a protective function. In the end, it was decided that there was no such thing as a one-size-fits-all fiscal policy. The G-20 meeting ended with no across-the-board commitment to increased discretionary fiscal stimulus.

SOURCE OF FIGURE: David Leonhardt, "Stimulus Thinking, and Nuance," *New York Times*, April 1, 2009, http://www.nytimes.com/ 2009/04/01/business/economy/01leonhardt.html?_r=1.

### Spending as Share of Gross Domestic Product, 2008–2010

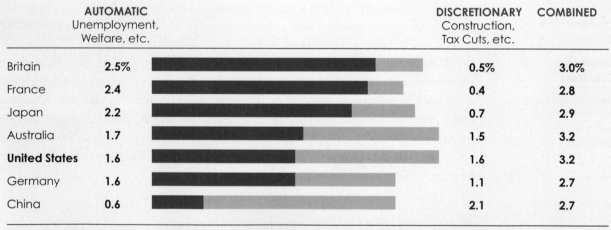

| | AUTOMATIC<br>Unemployment,<br>Welfare, etc. | | DISCRETIONARY<br>Construction,<br>Tax Cuts, etc. | COMBINED |
|---|---|---|---|---|
| Britain | 2.5% | | 0.5% | 3.0% |
| France | 2.4 | | 0.4 | 2.8 |
| Japan | 2.2 | | 0.7 | 2.9 |
| Australia | 1.7 | | 1.5 | 3.2 |
| **United States** | 1.6 | | 1.6 | 3.2 |
| Germany | 1.6 | | 1.1 | 2.7 |
| China | 0.6 | | 2.1 | 2.7 |

SOURCE: International Monetary Fund                                        *The New York Times*

## Cyclical deficit or surplus

The difference between the deficit or surplus shown in the structural budget and that shown in the actual federal budget

result, the budget will move toward deficit. The difference between the actual deficit in that year and the deficit that would have been reported if real GDP had remained at its natural level, with unchanged tax and spending laws, is called the **cyclical deficit**. As the economy approaches a cyclical peak and a positive output gap develops, the operation of automatic stabilizers makes the deficit smaller than its structural value; and there is said to be a **cyclical surplus**. A cyclical surplus might reflect an actual surplus, or simply a smaller deficit than there would be if the output gap were zero.

Figure 11.2 shows movements of the actual and structural deficits of the U.S. federal budget since 1970. Most of the time, the budget has been in deficit, with the exception of a few years in the late 1990s and early 2000s. The actual deficit is more variable than the structural deficit. Major shifts in the direction of fiscal policy, like the large tax cuts and defense expenditures of the 1980s and early 2000s, show up as sharp changes in the structural deficit.

## The Role of State and Local Government Budgets

Up to this point, we have focused entirely on the federal government budget. Doing so significantly understates the total size of the government sector. The federal government accounts for only about 60 percent of all government receipts and expenditures in the United States, with state and local governments making up the rest. In terms of the

**FIGURE 11.2   ACTUAL AND STRUCTURAL SURPLUS OR DEFICIT OF THE U.S. FEDERAL BUDGET**

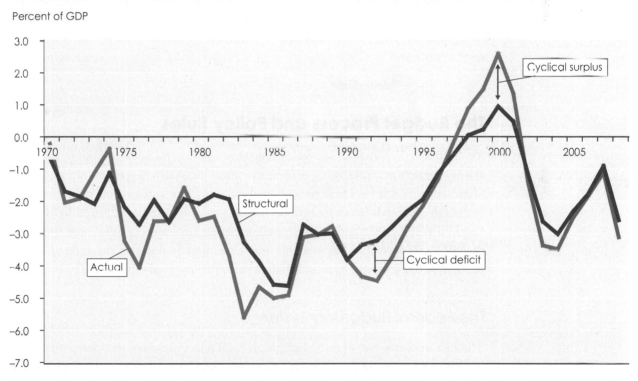

This figure shows two views of the U.S. federal surplus or deficit from 1962 to 2008. The actual surplus or deficit measures the difference between each year's revenues and outlays. The structural deficit is corrected to remove the influence of the business cycle. It can be interpreted as showing what the deficit would have been, given each year's tax and spending laws, if the economy had been at its natural level of GDP in that year. In years like 1992 when the economy is near the trough of a business cycle, the actual deficit is below the structural deficit, showing that automatic stabilizers are adding to the deficit. In years like 2000, near the peak of a business cycle, the actual surplus is larger than the structural surplus, showing that automatic stabilizers are adding to the surplus.

SOURCE: Congressional Budget Office, Historical Budget Data, Table E-13 (http://www.cbo.gov/budget/historical.xls).

impact on planned expenditure and aggregate demand, a dollar of state or local government revenue or expenditure is exactly equivalent to a dollar at the federal level.

When it comes to stabilization policy, however, state and local government budgets are less important than their size would indicate. Most state and local governments are required by law to balance their budgets. They undertake little discretionary fiscal policy. When the budgets of all units of government below the federal government are added together, they typically show a slight surplus, usually less than 1 percent of GDP. Occasionally the consolidated state and local government show a very small deficit.

Because their budgets are kept close to balance year in and year out, state and local governments contribute little to automatic fiscal policy. To the extent that they contribute at all, their effect is slightly destabilizing, or *procyclical*, as economists like to say. The reason is that when the economy slips into recession, state and local government revenues fall; thus, spending must be cut in order to keep deficits from exceeding permissible limits. An equal reduction in revenue and expenditure has a slightly contractionary effect on aggregate demand.

The procyclical effect of state and local balanced budget requirements is somewhat offset by grants from the federal budget to state and local governments. These grants average about 15 percent of federal expenditures or about 2 percent of GDP. During recessions, federal grants to support state spending on education, unemployment benefits, and the like increase. Although the increase does not fully offset the need of state and local governments to tighten their belts during a recession, it helps.

## The Budget Process and Policy Rules

As discussed in Chapter 10, following preset policy rules can mitigate problems arising from lags, forecasting errors, and time-inconsistency for monetary policy. Some countries have implemented explicit rules like inflation targeting or fixed exchange rates, while others rely on implicit rules like those followed by the Fed. Could a rule-based approach also help with the problems of implementing fiscal policy? This section addresses that question, first looking at the federal budget process of the United States and then at possible improvements to the process.

### The Federal Budgetary System

The first important set of rules that govern fiscal policy are those that define the federal budget process. Aside from limited emergency funds, executive branch of government cannot simply spend money whenever the mood strikes. Congress must authorize expenditures, following rules set by the Constitution and its own past budget legislation.

**Fiscal year**

The federal government's budgetary year, which starts on October 1 of the preceding calendar year

**THE BUDGET CYCLE**   The U.S. government operates on a **fiscal year** that runs from October through September. For example, the fiscal year 2010 means the period from October 1, 2009, through September 30, 2010. About eighteen months before the beginning of a fiscal year, the executive branch begins preparing the budget. The Office of Management and Budget (OMB) takes the lead in this process. It receives advice from the Council of Economic Advisers (CEA), the Department of the Treasury, and other sources. After an outline of the budget has been drawn up, it is sent to the various departments and agencies. Within the executive branch, a period of bargaining ensues in which the Pentagon argues for more defense spending, the Department of Transportation for more highway funds, and so on. During this process the OMB is supposed to act as a restraining force, keeping macroeconomic goals in mind.

By January—nine months before the fiscal year starts—the president must submit the budget to Congress. After the budget has been submitted, Congress assumes the lead. Its committees and subcommittees look at the president's proposals for the programs and agencies under their jurisdiction. The Congressional Budget Office (CBO) employs a staff of professionals who advise the committees on economic matters, in somewhat the same way that the OMB advises the president. In the spring, the House and Senate are expected to pass a first budget resolution that sets forth overall spending targets and revenue goals.

Bargaining among committees—between the House and the Senate and between Congress and the executive branch—continues throughout the summer. During this period committees prepare specific spending and tax laws called *appropriations bills*, without which no money can actually be spent. The appropriation bills are supposed to be guided by the budget resolution and completed before the start of the fiscal year on October 1.

**LIMITATIONS OF THE BUDGETARY PROCESS**   In practice, many things can—and do—go wrong with the budget process.

The first and most basic problem is that macroeconomic goals—full employment, price stability, and economic growth—carry little weight. Tax and spending decisions are made in dozens of subcommittees, where interest group pressures, vote trading, and the desire of each member if Congress dominate them. Many years ago Herbert Stein, then chairman of the Council of Economic Advisers, wrote, "We have no long-run budget policy—no policy for the size of deficits and for the rate of growth of the public debt over a period of years." Each year, according to Stein, the president and Congress make short-term budgetary decisions that are wholly inconsistent with their declared long-run goals, hoping "that something will happen or be done before the long-run arises, but not yet."[3] What Stein wrote remains very much true today.

A second problem is that Congress has not been willing to follow its own rules. The required budget resolutions often are not passed on time; and if they are passed, they are not treated as binding. More often than not, the fiscal year starts before all twelve of the required appropriations bills have been passed. Then the agencies of government must operate on the basis of "continuing resolutions," meaning that they can go on doing whatever they were doing the year before.

Sometimes not even a continuing resolution can be passed, in which case the government is limited to performing a narrow range of essential functions. In one of the worst episodes, in November 1995, the government shut down for six days when Congress failed to pass either appropriations bills or a continuing resolution. It was estimated that the government shutdown cost more than $700 million, including $400 million to furloughed federal employees who were paid, but did not report to work.

Often, to avoid a government shutdown at the expiration of a continuing resolution, Congress short-circuits the appropriations process by rolling several of the twelve separate appropriations bills into a single "omnibus-spending" bill. The omnibus bills are not always assembled as carefully as appropriations bills should be. In particular, they are often packed with spending provisions called *earmarks* that are requested by individual members of Congress and bypass merit-based evaluation. For example, a $410 billion omnibus-spending bill passed by Congress in February 2009 contained more than 9,000 earmarks worth an estimated $13 billion. These included very prosaic items, like school sidewalks, along with some more exotic ones like a tattoo removal program.

**ENTITLEMENTS**   Not all government spending is subject to the annual appropriations process. More than half of the federal budget consists of so-called mandatory items governed by long-term laws that are not subject to annual review. The biggest mandatory items are entitlements like social security, military retirement pay, and Medicare. Congress could control entitlement costs by passing new laws to replace the current ones, but doing so is not part of the normal budgetary process. Another major mandatory item is interest on the national debt. Interest expense depends on market interest rates, which are beyond the control of fiscal policy.

Finally, there are emergency items that cannot be predicted. Modest amounts are included in regular budgets to cover costs of natural disasters like hurricanes, but some expenses exceed the budgeted emergency allowances. Sometimes even very large budget items are placed in the emergency or unpredictable category. For example, the administration of George W. Bush excluded hundreds of billions of dollars in spending on the Iraq war from its regular budget. Instead, the war was financed by annual supplemental appropriations that bypassed the normal budget process. (As of fiscal year 2010, the costs of the wars in Iraq and Afghanistan will be included in the regular budget.)

**ATTEMPTS AT BUDGET REFORM**   Over the years, there have been several attempts to introduce stronger rules to govern the federal budget process. None of these has been fully successful. One of the more ambitious efforts at reform was the PAYGO (pay-as-you-go) system, which existed from 1990 to 2002. Under that system, no new spending or tax cuts were permitted unless they were accompanied by offsetting spending cuts or revenue increases elsewhere in the budget. If the Office of Management and Budget certified that the rules had been violated, the President was authorized to enforce "sequestration," that is, to make proportional, across-the-board cuts in discretionary spending to bring the budget back in line with the rules.

Some observers believe that the PAYGO rules made a significant contribution to the emergence of federal budget surpluses in 1998 through 2001, the first in many years. However, the surpluses themselves created a temptation to weaken budget rules, much as a person might celebrate a 5-pound weight loss by eating a pint of ice cream. At first, technical changes were made in the "scorecard" for PAYGO, so that some kinds of spending no longer came under its limits. The rules were abandoned altogether early in the Bush administration when it became clear that tax cuts, Medicare drug benefits, and Iraq war costs could not be accommodated. The House of Representatives made an attempt to reestablish pay-as-you-go rules in 2007, but the effort did not last long. The onset of the economic crisis later that year and the fiscal stimulus programs of the next two years changed the game altogether, leaving both Congress and the White House to make up new rules as they went along.

# Fiscal Policy in Long-Run Perspective

So far, we have looked at the fiscal policy mainly in a short-run context. In this section, we turn to the role of fiscal policy in promoting a balanced and prosperous economy in the long run.

## Achieving a Balanced Economy

Any doctor knows that a patient with a normal temperature can still have serious health problems. In much the same way, an economy that keeps the short-term business cycle within reasonable bounds can still have long-term structural problems. Examining the balance, or imbalance, among the four main components of GDP—consumption, investment, government purchases, and net exports—can often identify structural problems.

**BALANCE OF SAVING AND INVESTMENT**    One kind of balance to look for is that between saving and investment. At a bare minimum, just in order to keep the standard of living from decreasing, a country needs enough investment to replace structures and business equipment as they wear out. In the United States, that requires about 12 percent of GDP. Additional investment beyond that contributes to long-term economic growth.

As the circular flow analysis of Chapter 5 explained, investment could be financed from several sources. Saving from household income is one possible source. Household savings rates vary widely around the world. Koreans and Italians save more than 20 percent of their disposable income. Canadians and Swedes save 10 percent or more. U.S. households saved 8 to 12 percent of disposable income until the early1990s, but after that, saving dropped sharply. By 2006, household saving was actually negative; on average, for the whole country, ordinary families spent more each year than they earned. When household saving is low, some other way must be found to finance investment.

Business saving helps. Reinvestment of undistributed corporate profits amounts to about 3 percent of U.S. GDP, and constitutes the largest single component of private saving. By itself, however, business saving is not enough even to replace capital as it wears out.

A third possible source of saving would be a surplus in the government budget, but in the United States, the combined federal, state, and local budget has been in surplus in only five of the past 40 years. In many years, the deficit is large enough to offset all business saving. When household, business, and government saving are all added together, then, the United States has a large, chronic imbalance between domestic saving and domestic investment.

**EXTERNAL BALANCE**    Even without an adequate source of domestic saving, a country can continue to invest by borrowing from abroad, that is, by drawing on the saving of other countries. In its international accounts, the borrowing will be reflected in a current account deficit (imports greater than exports), balanced by a financial inflow. An external imbalance between imports and exports is thus, in a sense, the twin of an imbalance between domestic saving and investment. The government budget deficit is not the sole cause of the external deficit, but it is a significant contributing factor. (Details of the twin deficit syndrome for the United States were given in *Applying Economic Ideas 5.1* in chapter 5.)

Economists differ as to how seriously low domestic savings and the large U.S. current account deficit threaten the long-term prosperity of the U.S. economy. Some take an optimistic view and see the ability of the U.S. economy to attract foreign investment as a sign of strength. Others point out that imbalances in the U.S. international accounts are not entirely that country's fault. To some extent, they can be seen as reflecting opposite imbalances in the economies of trading partners. *Applying Economic Ideas 11.1* describes imbalances in the Chinese economy, which in some ways are the mirror image of those of the United States. Still, many observers warn that the United States as a whole has been living beyond its means. A day of reckoning could come if the oil-rich Gulf States, the Chinese, the Russians, and others were to stop funding the deficit by buying U.S. government securities at low interest rates. Without the cheap financial inflows on which the United States has become dependent, growth could slow and living standards for future generations of Americans could be undermined.

**BALANCE VERSUS CYCLICAL RECOVERY**    When a country with an imbalanced economy enters a recession, policymakers face a dilemma. Long-term imbalances like deficient household savings, large government deficits, and persistent current account shortfalls may well have been part of the cause of the recession to begin with. However, the quickest way to eliminate the output gap and return to full employment may be to restore the economy to its state before the recession started, imbalances and all.

Suppose, for example, that household saving during the boom preceding a crisis had fallen to zero, whereas the economy would be better balanced in the long term if saving rose to 5 percent of GDP. After rebalancing, the extra 5 percent formerly devoted to consumption could be divided among additional government spending on national priorities like education or infrastructure, additional business investment, and reduction of the current account deficit.

If the circular flow of income and product were filled with some uniform substance like water, rebalancing the economy would be easy. A few valves could be adjusted and less would flow through the consumption channel while more flowed through the investment channel. In reality, though, the circular flow is filled with a heterogeneous mix of donuts, building supplies, high school teaching, and Caterpillar tractors. It is not possible to change the ratio of the consumption flow to the investment or net export flow without moving specific workers and produc-

## Applying Economic Ideas 11.1
## REBALANCING THE CHINESE ECONOMY

Americans are so used to dire warnings about trade deficits, budget deficits, spendthrift consumers, and underinvestment that a country without these problems might easily be seen as an economic paradise. Consider China. There is a country that has enjoyed 10 percent growth or better year after year. Its current account surplus has exceeded 12 percent of GDP. Investment, at 45 percent of GDP, is the highest in the world. On top of that, the government budget, in most years, has shown a healthy surplus. What more could one want?

It can come as a surprise, then, to learn that the Chinese, and economists elsewhere who specialize in China, see serious structural imbalances that threaten future growth and stability.

Take the question of saving vs. consumption. Where American families are among the world's most profligate, Chinese households are the world's thriftiest. Household savings run around 30 percent of disposable income. Consumption is extremely low—barely over 40 percent of GDP—the lowest percentage anywhere. What lies behind the high saving rate? Surveys suggest that high savings are, to a large extent, motivated by economic insecurity. China's social safety net is weak. Public financing of healthcare, education, pensions, and unemployment benefits is minimal. Household access to credit is underdeveloped. As a result, Chinese families, even those with very low incomes, must scrimp and save to educate their children and be ready for their own illness or retirement.

What about all that investment? Yes, up to a point high investment is one of the sources of China's rapid growth, but there is also a lot of wasted investment. Bloated state-owned steel mills and cement factories, with no shareholders to answer to, spend billions on expansion of low-tech, dirty, and relatively unproductive facilities. A study by the McKinsey Global Institute found that the amount of investment needed to produce one unit of additional output—the so called *incremental capital-output ratio*—is lower in China than in neighboring Japan or South Korea, and is getting worse, not better.*

Surely, though, the huge trade surpluses are a blessing, are they not? Well, not entirely. For one thing, not all of China's trade surpluses have been invested wisely. As the U.S. budget deficit approaches record levels, Chinese leaders have even begun worrying publicly about the safety of the billions they have invested in U.S. Treasury bills. Moreover, economies, like China's, that depend too much on exports can find themselves in a very vulnerable position when the growth of their trading partners slows. When the U.S. economy sank into recession after 2007, tens of millions of Chinese workers were laid off in export industries. As they headed back to their villages, the government became nervous about possible political unrest.

In short, Goldilocks may have been right. An economy may be healthiest when it is neither too hot nor too cold, when it has neither excessive surpluses nor excessive deficits, and when it gives its consumers a standard of living that is neither too far above nor too far below its real productive capabilities.

*McKinsey Global Institute, "Putting China's Capital to Work: The Value of Financial System Reform," May 2006. http://www.mckinsey.com/mgi/publications/china_capital/index.asp

Year after year, China has had an economic growth rate of 10 percent or better.

tion equipment from one industry to another, but retraining auto workers as nurses or reconfiguring an assembly line to produce excavators rather than Pontiacs takes time. During a recession, when the highest priority is putting unemployed people back to work, such structural changes may actually slow recovery. There is a great temptation to restore the economy just as it used to be and put off worrying about restructuring until later. When "later" comes and the economy is back at full employment, restructuring no longer seems like such a high priority.

## *Sustainability of the Deficit and the Debt Pyramid*

Although government deficits are sometimes a sign of an imbalance that threatens long-term prosperity and stability, that is not always the case. Government borrowing to finance development projects like improved public health, education, and infrastructure can boost long-term economic growth and, in doing so, help to generate the resources needed to repay debt. The same can be said of financial inflows, especially when they take the form of foreign direct investment accompanied by transfers of technology and management skills. In this section, we develop some criteria to distinguish between sustainable and unsustainable imbalances and look at the consequences of non-sustainability. Our discussion will focus on sustainability of the government budget deficit, but many of the same principles also apply to current account deficits and foreign borrowing.

**Government budget constraint**

The relationship between what the government buys and the sources of funds needed to make the purchases

**THE GOVERNMENT BUDGET CONSTRAINT**   Governments, like private households and firms, face a budget constraint. They do not, with only a few exceptions, just take goods and services without paying for them. Normally they buy goods and services in market transactions with firms and households. The **government budget constraint** states the relationship between what a government buys and the sources of the funds it needs to make the purchases.

The first step in understanding the government budget constraint is to divide government expenditures into two parts by separating interest payments on the government debt from all other expenditures, including both purchases of goods and services like computers and salaries of employees, and transfer payments like unemployment benefits and farm subsidies. The government's expenditures are covered, at least in part, by tax revenues. The difference between the government's ordinary expenditures (excluding interest) and tax revenues is called the **primary deficit** (or *primary surplus*, if taxes exceed ordinary expenditures.) As long as interest expenses are greater than zero, the total deficit will be greater than the primary deficit.

**Primary deficit**

Government expenditures, excluding interest cost, minus tax revenues

For example, in 2008, the total deficit of the U.S. federal budget was $455 billion, of which $249 billion reflected interest on the debt; so there was a primary deficit of $206 billion. In contrast, in 2007, the total deficit was only $162 billion. Interest costs in 2007 were $237 billion, so in that year, there was a primary surplus of $75 billion.

Interest costs are among the least controllable items of the budget. Market forces determine interest rates; and once securities have been sold, the government has a legal obligation to pay interest as it comes due. The primary deficit is more controllable. Changing tax and spending laws can change the primary deficit. Changing the laws that govern social security, Medicare, and similar items can change even the entitlement part of the primary deficit, which is not set by annual appropriations.

If the budget runs a deficit, the next question is—How can the government find the funds to cover it? Normally, selling newly issued government securities finances most of the government's deficit. In the United States, these are classified as Treasury bills (T-bills) if short-term, notes if medium term, and bonds if long-term. They are sold through an auction process and earn a rate of interest determined by supply and demand conditions at the time.

A deficit can, instead, be financed by means of newly created money rather than newly issued securities; but normally only a small part of the budget can be financed in this way. When the government finances a significant portion of its budget in this way, it is often said to be "printing money." In a modern economy, this expression must be understood more figuratively than literally. Historically, in times of war and revolution, it is true that governments have sometimes literally printed new currency to pay their bills. It was done in the United States during the revolutionary war and in the Confederate states during the Civil War. In modern, well-managed economies, however, governments do not finance their deficits with paper currency.

Rather than printing paper currency, they use an indirect, four-step process. First, the country's treasury sells bonds or other securities to the central bank, which credits the equivalent amount to a special account held by the treasury. Second, the treasury draws on this account, using checks or electronic transfers, to make its purchases. Third, businesses and households deposit the government payments in their own accounts in commercial banks. Fourth, when they do so, reserves of the commercial banks increase, thereby increasing the monetary base. The phrase "printing money" is journalistic shorthand for this four-step process that results in an increase in the monetary base. The process is more accurately described as **monetizing the deficit.**

**Monetizing the deficit**

Financing a government budget deficit through an increase in the monetary base

Putting together what we have learned, we can now formalize the government budget constraint. In words, it can be written as follows:

Primary budget deficit + interest costs = new borrowing + newly created money

Alternatively, we can express the budget constraint in the form of the following equation:

$$(G - T)^* + rD = \Delta D + \Delta B$$

In this equation, the term $(G - T)^*$ stands for the primary budget deficit; r is the interest rate and D is the size of the outstanding government debt, so that rD is the annual interest cost. $\Delta D$ is the increase in the outstanding debt, that is, the amount borrowed through the issue of new securities; and $\Delta B$ is the change in the monetary base, that is, the part of the deficit financed by monetization. All variables in this equation, including the interest rate, are adjusted for inflation and expressed in real terms or as a percent of GDP.

Figure 11.3 uses a diagram called the *debt pyramid* to illustrate what we have learned about government finance. Suppose a country begins in Year 0 with no debt. In that year, it needs to raise sufficient funds to only cover its primary deficit, $(G - T)^*$. To keep things simple, we will ignore the possibility of monetization and assume that the entire deficit is financed by borrowing. We use the term $\Delta D0$ to represent the amount of borrowing in Year 0—that year's increase in the government debt. In Year 1, the government must again borrow enough to finance its primary deficit, plus an added amount to pay interest on the amount it borrowed in Year 0. Using r to stand for the rate of interest, debt service costs in Year 1 are represented by $r\Delta D0$ (that is, the interest rate times the amount of debt issued in Year 0). In Year 2, it must borrow enough to finance the primary deficit—plus another year's interest on debt issued in Year 0, plus interest on new debt that was issued

## FIGURE 11.3   THE DEBT PYRAMID

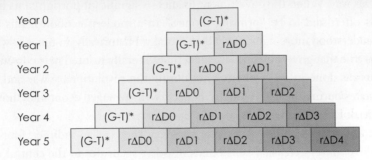

Suppose a country begins with no debt. In Year 0, it needs to borrow enough only to finance its primary deficit, (G-T)*. In Year 1, it must again borrow enough to finance the primary deficit, plus enough to pay interest on the amount it borrowed in Year 0. Using r to stand for the rate of interest and ΔD0 to stand for the amount of borrowing in Year 0, interest costs in Year 1 are represented by rΔD0. In Year 2, the government must borrow enough to finance the primary deficit, plus another year's interest on debt issued in Year 0, plus interest on new debt that was issued in Year 1. As time goes by and the government debt accumulates, more and more "bricks" are added to the debt pyramid.

in Year 1. As time goes by and the government debt accumulates, more and more "bricks" are added to the debt pyramid; and the cost of debt service grows.

**SUSTAINABILITY OF THE DEBT PYRAMID**   How fast can a debt pyramid grow before debt service costs become unsustainable? To be sustainable in the long run, the base of the pyramid (including interest on the government debt) must not grow faster than real GDP. If it did so, and the government struggled to borrow more and more each year to keep up with interest payments, financial markets would become saturated with government debt. At some point, either the government would find itself unable to sell securities at all or could do so only with punitively high interest rates. Something would have to be done—but what?

A government that persistently runs an unsustainable budget deficit has just three alternatives. At one time and place or another, each has been used.

The first alternative is to default on the debt. The government simply tells bondholders, "Sorry, we can't pay the interest and principal we owe. You are out of luck!" The bondholders either get nothing or are forced to settle for a fraction of the face value of their debt. Recent examples of countries that have taken this alternative are Russia, in 1998, and Argentina, in 2001. Holders of defaulted Russian debt received virtually nothing. Argentine bondholders eventually obtained a partial payment.

The second alternative is to monetize the deficit. When it becomes impossible to borrow enough to pay for government purchases, the treasury begins selling its bonds directly to the central bank instead of to the public. The central bank, in turn, creates enough new money to pay the government's bills using the four-step process described earlier. Technically there is no limit to how much money the government can issue, but excessive monetization has a cost of its own—inflation. As shown by the equation of exchange, $MV = PQ$, an increase in M (money) beyond the rate of increase of Q (real GDP) will cause the price level to rise. In the next chapter, we will look in more detail at the extreme inflation that can occur in countries like Zimbabwe that rely on money creation to finance their deficits.

The third alternative for dealing with a runaway debt pyramid is to raise taxes or cut spending by enough to bring the government's borrowing needs back within the limits of sustainability. This alternative is called **fiscal consolidation**. Politically speaking, fiscal consolidation can be the hardest of all the alternatives, but it is the only one that avoids lasting damage to the economy. It can be done. Ireland and Denmark in the 1980s are examples of countries that once had unsustainable deficits but successfully achieved fiscal consolidation.

**Fiscal consolidation**

The process of reducing government spending and increasing revenues by enough to make the deficit sustainable

### Is the U.S. Budget Deficit Sustainable?

Having looked at the question of sustainability, in general, we will conclude by looking at the question of whether the federal budget deficit of the United States is sustainable in the long run. As this is written, in mid-2009, the situation with the budget and the entire economy is highly fluid. No final answer to the question of sustainability can yet be given. Still, we can look at past and current trends, making some educated guesses about what might be done or what might need to be done, in order to achieve sustainability.

**IMPACT OF RECESSION AND FISCAL STIMULUS** Figure 11.4 presents data on the past and projected federal budget deficit and federal debt held by the public.[4] U.S. federal government debt reached an all-time high of 120 percent of GDP at the end of World War II. After reaching a low of 24 percent of GDP in 1974, it grew again until the mid-1990s and resumed its upward trend after 2001.

The recession and fiscal stimulus sharply increased the deficit beginning 2009, leading to an abrupt jump in the size of the federal debt. What happens beyond 2010 will depend on future developments both in the world economy and in U.S. budget policy.[5] The Office of Management and Budget, which is part of the executive branch, and the Congressional Budget Office, a nonpartisan agency that provides technical advice to the Congress both provide projections of future debt and deficit trends. The OMB's projections tend to be somewhat more optimistic since they assume that Congress will pass all of the President's budget requests. OMB projections suggest that the debt will stabilize after 2011 at about 60 percent of GDP. The CBO uses somewhat more pessimistic assumptions that assume some programs will remain unchanged until Congress actually passes new budget measures. Its projections show the debt continuing to rise through 2019 and beyond.

**REASONS TO THINK THE DEFICIT IS SUSTAINABLE** Despite the large size and recent growth of the U.S. federal budget deficit, not all observers consider the federal government's financial position to be hopeless. Clearly, deficits like that of 2009, which exceeded 12 percent of GDP, could not be sustained. However, much of the record 2009 deficit consisted of a cyclical component reflecting the operation of automatic stabilizers and one-off fiscal stimulus measures. It is not intended that deficits of that magnitude would continue for long.

**FIGURE 11.4** **REVENUE AND SPENDING TRENDS FOR THE U.S. FEDERAL GOVERNMENT**

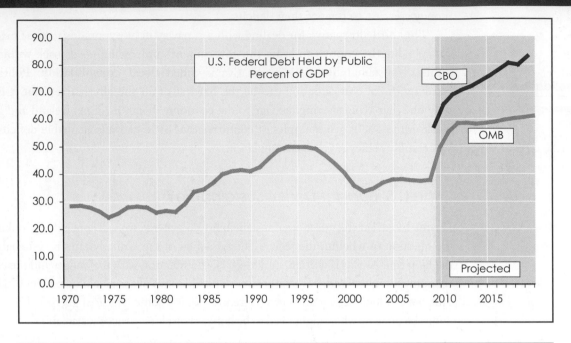

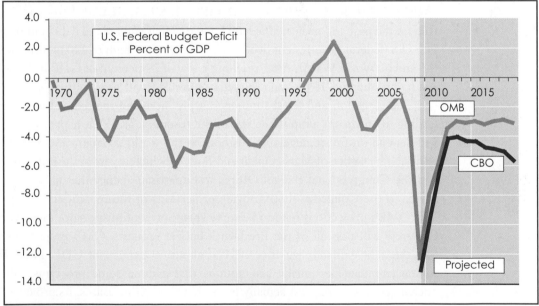

The U.S. federal government debt reached an all-time high of 120 percent of GDP at the end of World War II. After reaching a low of 24 percent of GDP in 1974, it grew again until the mid-1990s and resumed its upward trend after 2001. The very large deficits resulting from recession and fiscal stimulus beginning in 2009 guarantee that the federal debt will reach its highest level in half a century, but the debt will probably remain below the World War II peak. What will happen beyond 2010 depends on further developments both in the world economy and in U.S. budget policy. As of 2009, the Office of Management and Budget was projecting that the debt would stabilize as a percentage of GDP after 2011, while more pessimistic estimates by the Congressional Budget Office suggested that it would continue to grow for at least a decade.

SOURCES: Congressional Budget Office and Office of Management and Budget

As we have seen, the basic requirement for sustainability is that the size of the total debt (the base of the debt pyramid) should grow no faster than GDP. If the deficit is sustainable, the debt will eventually stabilize at some constant fraction of GDP. The equilibrium debt ratio can be calculated by dividing the deficit by the rate of growth of nominal GDP.[6] Suppose the average rate of growth of nominal GDP to be 5 percent per year, consisting of about 2.5 percent inflation and about 2.5 percent real growth. These estimates are broadly consistent with real growth trends over recent decades and the Fed's implicit inflation target. Given these estimates, the debt would stabilize at about 60 percent of GDP if the deficit could be brought back to 3 percent of GDP and held there, once the current crisis has been resolved.

These numbers do not seem beyond the realm of the possible. Figure 11.5 provides some international comparisons. The data come from the Organization for Economic Cooperation and Development (OECD), a group of thirty countries

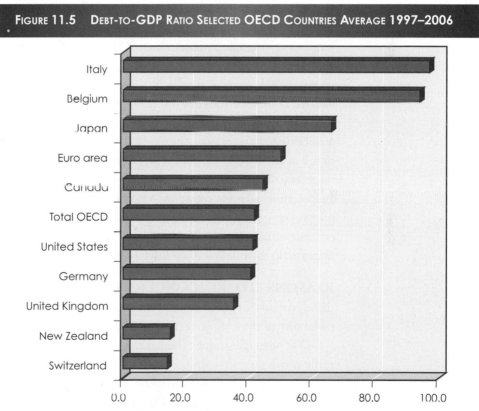

**FIGURE 11.5    DEBT-TO-GDP RATIO SELECTED OECD COUNTRIES AVERAGE 1997–2006**

The Organization for Economic Cooperation and Development (OECD), a group of 30 countries with market economies and democratic political systems, includes countries with both high and low ratios of debt to GDP. This figure shows average debt to GDP ratios for selected countries for the pre-crisis period 1997–2006. At that time the United States was close to the OECD average. A few OECD countries, like Norway, not shown here, have accumulated foreign assets that exceed domestic government debt and have negative debt ratios. Debt ratios are expected to rise in all OECD countries as a result of the global financial crisis.

SOURCE: OECD, Economic Outlook 84, Statistical Annex Table 33.

with market economies and democratic political systems. The figure shows average debt-to-GDP ratios over a ten-year period before the start of the recent global financial crisis. The U.S. debt ratio during this period was about equal to the OECD average and was lower than the average for the euro area. Although the OECD does not set any standard regarding the acceptable level of government debt, the European Union, to which two-thirds of the members of the OECD belong, requires that countries maintain a debt ratio below 60 percent of GDP. Still, even EU members like Italy and Belgium that have not met this guideline, and also Japan, outside the EU, have been able to maintain high debt ratios for many years without collapse of their government finances. All in all, then, if the U.S. federal debt rises to 60 percent of GDP, or even a little more, it will still not be impossibly high by international standards.

We also need to consider the exceptional, world-wide breadth of the market for U.S. securities. It is true, as discussed above, that excessive foreign borrowing, linked to a large current account deficit, can seriously unbalance an economy. However, if a country does decide to borrow abroad, being able to do so in its own currency is a big advantage. The United States can borrow abroad in its own currency more easily than any other country. Most small countries cannot sell any securities abroad that are denominated in their own currencies. Japan, the U.K., and euro area countries can borrow abroad in their own currencies to some extent, but the markets for their securities are not nearly as large as for those of the U.S. Treasury.

The ability to borrow abroad in one's own currency is important for financial sustainability for two reasons. First, if a country can easily borrow abroad, it does not have to sell as many securities at home. That reduces the possibility that domestic financial markets will become saturated with government securities, driving interest rates higher and creating a larger crowding-out effect. Second, if a country borrows abroad in its own currency, the cost of debt service is not affected by changes in exchange rates. In contrast, smaller countries that borrow abroad in dollars or euros can experience sharp increases in their debt service costs when their exchange rates depreciate.

**REASONS TO BE CONCERNED ABOUT SUSTAINABILITY**    Despite these grounds for optimism, there remain reasons for concern about the long-run sustainability of the U.S. government deficit and debt.

One open question is whether the large fiscal stimulus programs begun in 2009 will really prove reversible. Initial reactions of Congress were more favorable to immediate spending proposals than to longer-term measures for increasing revenues or reducing spending once recovery began. Deficit-cutting proposals like cuts in agricultural subsidies or introduction of pollution charges for carbon emissions are by no means sure to win Congressional approval. If the executive and legislative branches of government cannot work together to close the deficit, once recovery begins, the debt ratio will continue to grow rather than flattening out at a sustainable level. As the time this is being written, it is too early to say what will happen. The reader should watch for the latest developments in news sources and the web sites of government agencies like OMB and CBO.

Another cause for concern is the way deficits are being financed. From the time of the first fiscal stimulus measures in 2008, the Fed's monetary policy became strongly accommodating. As explained earlier, this meant keeping interest rates low as federal borrowing increased, even though doing so meant allowing bank reserves and the money stock to increase rapidly. The accommodating monetary policy did not cause any immediate upward pressure on inflation and was not expected to do so as long as the recession continues. Instead of being reflected in higher prices, increases in bank reserves were initially absorbed in a lower money multiplier and lower velocity. Economists at the Fed and elsewhere were aware all along, however, that the situation could change rapidly once a recovery begins. As the money multiplier and velocity return to normal, the Fed will have to work quickly to pull back the extra bank reserves injected during the crisis. In principle, that should be possible; but if unforeseen difficulties arise, monetary accommodation of fiscal stimulus during 2008 and 2009 could cause inflationary pressure in the future.

**ENTITLEMENTS AND THE IMPLICIT FEDERAL DEBT** Future entitlement obligations are a final reason to be concerned about the long-run sustainability of the federal deficit and debt. The debt shown in Figure 11.5 includes only the value of government securities owned by the public. However, the government has additional future obligations in the form of promised social security and Medicare benefits, for which no adequate funding provisions now exist. These constitute an additional, implicit government debt.

Of the two main entitlement programs, Medicare is in worse shape. As of 2009, Medicare is funded by a 2.9 percent payroll tax. Revenue from the tax is paid into a trust fund; and money for benefits, in turn, is drawn from the trust fund. If there is not enough in the trust fund to pay benefits—and this was already starting to be true in 2009—the difference must be made up from the government's general revenues. Under the projections of the fund's trustees, by 2014 the trust fund will be able to cover less than half of benefits; and by 2019 it will be exhausted altogether. In order to keep the fund solvent over the long term, the Medicare payroll tax would have to be raised from 2.9 percent to 6.44 percent. Alternatively, benefits could be cut by 51 percent, something that would be hard to do at a time when opinion polls show that people want more, not less, government support of health care.

The Social Security program is in better shape, but only relatively so. Social Security trust fund revenues are projected to begin falling short of outlays in 2017, and the fund will be exhausted in 2041. Restoring solvency would require an immediate increase in the Social Security

The Social Security program is an example of a future entitlement obligation from the government.

payroll tax rate from 12.4 percent to 14.1 percent or an immediate 12 percent cut in benefits or some combination of the two.

In short, when the government's future obligations under entitlement programs are included, the federal deficit and debt are not even close to sustainable. That is not just the alarmist conclusion of think-tank economists—it is the considered opinion of the entitlement programs' own trustees, headed by the Secretary of the Treasury. To quote the trustees' 2008 report, "The financial condition of the Social Security and Medicare programs remains problematic. Projected long run program costs are not sustainable under current financing arrangements. . . . We are increasingly concerned about inaction on the financial challenges facing the Social Security and Medicare programs. The longer action is delayed, the greater will be the required adjustments, the larger the burden on future generations, and the more severe the detrimental economic impact on our nation."[7]

**THE CONSEQUENCES OF NON-SUSTAINABILITY**   The consequences of non-sustainability are familiar from the experience of many countries. The first sign that a debt pyramid is growing beyond the limits of sustainability is increased difficulty in selling new government securities. Buyers become unwilling to take on additional debt without higher interest rates that include a heavy risk premium. As total debt increases and maturing securities are rolled over at ever-higher interest rates, the cost of debt service rises geometrically. Eventually it becomes impossible to borrow enough, at any interest rate, to cover the deficit. If the United States were to find itself in that position, it would face the same three choices as any other country: default, monetization, or fiscal consolidation.

For two reasons, default is the least likely option for the United States. First, too much debt—more than half the total—is held by foreign governments, many of which the United States would be reluctant to offend. China, Japan, Middle Eastern oil exporters, and Russia together hold nearly 40 percent of total U.S. debt. Second, as mentioned earlier, U.S. debt, unlike that of many countries, is denominated almost entirely in its own currency, the dollar. That reduces the risk of exchange rate changes as a trigger for default, as has happened in other countries.

If forced to choose between default and monetization, the U.S. government would more likely opt for the latter. To implement monetization of the deficit, the Fed would increasingly accommodate the borrowing needs of the Treasury. It would act as a buyer of last resort for securities that could not be sold at acceptable interest rates through financial markets. The monetary base would grow dollar-for-dollar with the Fed's purchases of securities. News media would begin to write that the Fed was "printing money" to finance the deficit, an assertion that would be metaphorically, if not literally, true. As bank reserves and currency in circulation grew, the rate of inflation would rise. Although faster inflation would push up nominal market interest rates, thereby increasing interest costs in nominal terms, it would also reduce the real value of past debt, especially long-term debt that had been sold at low, fixed interest rates while inflation was still low. In principle, when the ratio of real debt to real GDP fell back to a sustainable level, the government could stop the process of monetization and begin borrowing again.

Critics would be sure to point out that reducing the real value of the debt through inflation is just default by another name. However, many countries, when pushed to the wall by their inability to control their budgets, have found indirect default via inflation to be politically and legally more palatable than outright repudiation of their debt.

If neither default nor monetization were considered acceptable, the option of fiscal consolidation would remain. What would fiscal consolidation look like for the United States?

In popular discussions, the most widely mentioned way of cutting the deficit is to eliminate waste in government. The quickest search can uncover dozens, even hundreds of purportedly wasteful programs—a manned mission to mars, farm subsidies, unneeded weapons programs, the U.S. Geological Survey, the Corporation for Public Broadcasting, the Rock and Roll Hall of Fame Museum—these all have made the lists of one or more self-appointed budget watchdogs. Some of them claim that wasteful projects may total as much as $200 billion per year.

Still, although eliminating waste in government provides many good talking points, it is likely to play only a limited role in fiscal consolidation. One reason is that there is not enough agreement on exactly which programs are wasteful. What one person attacks as waste, others defend passionately as a national priority. Another reason is that the relatively few programs that make almost everyone's list—for example, farm subsidies for large agribusinesses—have been targets of waste-busters for generations without effect. Most of all, when entitlements, defense, and homeland security are set to one side, all remaining discretionary programs amount to only about 13 percent of federal spending. However worthy the goal of eliminating waste, trimming fat from the discretionary non-defense budget with even the sharpest knife can make only a limited contribution to long-term fiscal consolidation.

Real fiscal consolidation for the United States means making hard choices. Choices like either raising payroll taxes by a third or cutting social security and Medicare benefits by similar amounts. Choices like abandoning the goal of universal healthcare for all Americans or admitting that meeting the goal will require tax increases. The United States, after fiscal consolidation, might look like Sweden or France with high taxes and extensive social benefits. It might look like a pre-Depression United States where taxes were low and government was small, while social services were left to families and churches. It might look like Japan or New Zealand, which spend less than 1 percent of GDP on national defense, trusting to diplomacy to provide national security. Only one thing is sure. The United States, after fiscal consolidation, cannot possibly continue to be a low-tax country with an ever-expanding social safety net and a superpower-class defense establishment.

# Summary

1. **How can changes in taxes and expenditures be used as a tool of stabilization policy?** Fiscal policy means policy that is related to government purchases and net taxes. If a decrease in private planned expenditure threatens to send the economy into a recession, an increase in government purchases or a cut in net taxes can help to fill the output gap. Properly executed, such a policy can help the economy return more rapidly to full-employment equilibrium.

2. **What practical problems are encountered in implementing fiscal stimulus?** Lags and forecasting errors are one source of problems in implementing fiscal policy. In contrast with the ease of shifting curves in textbook models, several years may elapse in the real world between the onset of a recession and a return to full employment. A second problem is determining how large a stimulus is needed, given uncertainties about the size of the multiplier and the crowding-out effect. Reversing fiscal stimulus once and expansion is underway is a third problem; failure to reverse a stimulus in time can lead to over-shooting during the next expansion. Finally, it is difficult to align short-term fiscal stimulus with long-term budget priorities.

3. **What is meant by automatic fiscal policy?** The term automatic fiscal policy refers to the tendency for the government budget to move toward surplus as the economy expands and toward deficit as it contracts. This occurs as the result of the operation of automatic stabilizers like income taxes and unemployment benefits that increase or decrease over the business cycle even if tax and spending laws remain unchanged.

4. **How does the federal budget process work?** The federal budget operates on a fiscal year that runs from October through the following September. The budget process begins when the executive branch submits a budget proposal in January. In the spring, Congress passes a non-binding budget resolution that sets out priorities. During the summer, these are supposed to be converted into specific appropriations bills. If appropriations bills are not passed on time, the government must operate on the basis of continuing resolutions. A little over half of the budget consists of entitlements and the costs of debt service, which are not subject to the annual appropriations process.

5. **What is meant by long-term balance of the economy?** An excessive budget deficit can contribute to long-term imbalance of the economy. One area of concern is the balance between saving and investment. In the United States, saving by domestic households and businesses are insufficient to fund investment, and a chronic government budget deficit further increases the imbalance between investment and domestic saving. This is reflected in an external imbalance characterized by a large current account deficit matched by large financial inflows. Many observers see these imbalances as signs that the country is living beyond its means and threats to the future growth of living standards.

6. **Are the U.S. government budget deficit and debt sustainable?** A country must finance any budget deficit either by borrowing or by increasing bank reserves and the monetary base. Borrowing leads to a growth of the national debt and constantly increasing debt service costs. If the debt grows faster than GDP, it becomes unsustainable beyond some point. A country with an unsustainable deficit must choose among the options of default, monetization of the deficit with the likely result of inflation, or fiscal consolidation. When future entitlement costs are taken into account, the U.S. budget deficit and debt are not sustainable. At some point, the government will have to make a choice among these three alternatives.

## Key Terms

## Problems and Topics for Discussion

1. **Military spending**  Suppose that in response to a foreign crisis, the government increases defense spending by $50 billion. How would the increase in defense spending affect the economy? How would the effects differ depending on the size and sign of the output gap when the crisis began? Illustrate your answer with an aggregate supply and demand diagram.

2. **Kennedy tax cuts**  Use your favorite Internet search engine to do a little historical research using the search term "Kennedy tax cut." How large were the tax cuts proposed by President John F. Kennedy in comparison with later tax cuts during the administrations of Ronald Reagan and George W. Bush? How long were the lags involved in enacting them?

4. **A balanced budget amendment**  From time to time it has been proposed that a law or constitutional amendment be passed that will force the federal government to balance its budget every

year, as many state and local governments are required to do. How would such a requirement affect the conduct of discretionary fiscal policy? Automatic fiscal policy? If you were designing such an amendment, do you think it would be better to require that the actual budget deficit be kept at zero each year, or should the aim be only to keep the structural deficit at zero? Discuss.

5. **Entitlement programs**  The Social Security Administration annually publishes a Trustees Report. (Look for it on line at www.ssa.gov/OACT/TR/.) This chapter quoted from the 2008 report. Look up the most recent available report. Has the financial position of the Social Security and Medicare programs improved or deteriorated since 2008? Are you aware of any currently active efforts to change the programs in major ways? If so, describe them and relate them to the issues discussed in this chapter.

## Case for Discussion

### Hungary: the Politics of Fiscal Lies

In September 2006, a wave of political demonstrations exploded in Hungary's capital of Budapest. Riot police, using water cannon, battled in the street with crowds that overturned cars and made barriers of burning tires. It was not the image that Hungary, a new and usually well-behaved member of the European Union, was happy to display to the world.

The source of the rioting was a speech on fiscal policy that Hungarian Prime Minister Ferenc Gyurcsany delivered to a closed meeting of members of his Socialist government. In his speech, Gyurcsany used unusually candid language about the past performance of his government and the tactics his party had used to win a narrow victory in national elections the preceding April. He was quoted as saying, in part, "We screwed up. Not just a bit. A lot ...

It was perfectly clear that what we were saying wasn't true … You cannot mention a single major government measure we can be proud of … I almost died when I had to pretend that we were actually governing. We lied morning, noon and night."

Unfortunately for Gyurcsany, the speech, intended as a private scolding of party insiders with the intent to improve performance in the future, was leaked to the press. When members of the opposition learned that the prime minister had openly admitted lying to win the election, they took to the streets in protests that soon turned violent.

The specific subject of the lies in question concerned Hungary's government budget. In the run-up to the election, everyone knew that the country had a deficit problem, but government officials tried to assure the nation that the deficit for 2006 would be no more than 4.7 percent of GDP. That would be well above the European Union norm of 3 percent of GDP, but not a disaster. Instead, after the election, it became plain that the deficit for the year would be closer to 10 percent of GDP and that the government had known this all along.

Unfortunately, the steps needed to reduce Hungary's budget deficit are politically painful. They include cutting the number of public employees; cutting costs of an inefficient health system, possibly through partial privatization; reforming a system of social welfare in order to focus payments on the truly poor; and reducing generous transportation subsidies. No one in Hungary even talks about tax increases since taxes are already considered too high.

If all parties could agree to cooperate on a package of reforms, the goal of fiscal consolidation could be achieved. In Hungary, however, each party seems intent on daring the other to bear the political cost of painful expenditure cuts; but any party that actually undertook the needed reforms, without cooperation of the opposition, would surely lose the next election. As Jean-Claude Junker, Prime Minister of Luxembourg, once said, "We all know what to do, we just don't know how to win the election afterwards."

## QUESTIONS

1. In the years leading up to 2006, Hungary's economy has been growing at 4 percent or so per year, resulting in GDP that is probably close to its natural level. From such a starting point, what would be the short-term impact on the economy of cutting government spending while taxes remained unchanged? What would be the longer-term impact of the budget cuts? Could these impacts be mitigated by monetary policy? If so, how? Answer in terms of the economic models of this and preceding chapters.

2. Hungary has national elections every five years. From a political point of view, taking into account both the short-term and long-term effects of budget cuts, what would be the safest time for a government to attempt policy reforms? What would be the riskiest time?

3. Do a little Internet research on the current state of Hungary's government budget. (A good starting point would be to look at the web site of the OECD, www.oecd.org, and follow the "by country" link for information on Hungary.) Has Hungary made any progress with fiscal consolidation since 2006?

## End Notes

1. See the appendix to Chapter 5 for details on the multiplier effect. In the simplest case, the multiplier is equal to 1/mpc, where mpc is the marginal propensity to consume.

2. Christina Romer and Jared Bernstein, "The Job Impact of the American Recovery and Reinvestment Plan," released January 9, 2009 by the office of the President Elect.                    (http://otrans. 3cdn.net/45593e8ecbd339d074_l3m6bt1te.pdf)  Strictly speaking, the ratio of GDP change to change in government purchases estimated by Romer and Bernstein is not the same as the simple expenditure multiplier discussed in the appendix to Chapter 5. The simple expenditure multiplier assumes that prices and interest rates remain constant as GDP increases, while most practical discussions allow for changes in prices, interest rates, bank

reserves, and other variables. Loosely speaking, however, these estimates are often referred to as multipliers. We will refer to them with the informal term "effective fiscal multiplier." For a thorough critique of the Romer and Bernstein estimates, see John F. Cogan et al., "New Keynesian vs. Old Keynesian Government Spending Multipliers," Center for Economic Policy Research, Discussion Paper DP7236, March 2009.

3. Herbert Stein, "After the Ball," *AEI Economist* (December 1984): 2.

4. Debt held by the public includes all securities held by individuals, financial and nonfinancial firms, and foreign governments. In addition, large quantities of government securities are held by government agencies, principally the Federal Reserve System and the Social Security Trust Fund. Only debt held by the public matters for the issue of sustainability. Interest paid on debt held by government agencies is recycled into the budget as revenue, so it adds nothing to net interest costs.

5. Our emphasis in this chapter has been on debt that is issued in order to cover the difference between government purchases of goods and services and net taxes. The size of the debt can also be affected by off-budget financial operations of the Treasury. For example,

Chapter 7 described the TARP program, under which the Treasury exchanges newly issued government debt for private assets like mortgage-backed securities and stock in financial institutions. If the assets the government acquires in this way are worth as much as the government securities sold to obtain them, there is no impact on the government's net worth, and the debt pyramid is neither more nor less sustainable than before. However, if the private assets acquired turn out to be worth less than the government debt they were exchanged for, the government's financial position does become less sustainable than before.

6. Let $(G - T)$ be the deficit, expressed as a ratio to GDP, q be the rate of growth of real GDP, p be the rate of inflation, and D be the debt expressed as a ratio to GDP. The debt will be constant as a percent of GDP if $(G - T) = (q + p)D$. The right-hand part of this equation is the deficit and the left-hand part is the amount of new borrowing that will leave the debt ratio unchanged. Solving for D gives the equation $D = (G - T) / (q + p)$ for the equilibrium debt-to-GDP ratio associated with any given deficit.

7. U.S. Social Security Administration, Status of the Social Security and Medicare Programs, Summary of the 2008 Annual Reports Social Security On Line, http://www.ssa.gov/OACT/ TRSUM/trsummary.html.

# CHAPTER *12*

# Fighting Inflation and Deflation

---

**After reading this chapter, you will understand the following:**

1. The distinction between demand-side and supply-side inflation
2. The Phillips curve and how it can be interpreted
3. Hyperinflation and how it can be combated
4. Why demand-side deflation is harmful and what policies can prevent or reverse it
5. Supply-side deflation driven by productivity
6. The dangers of asset price bubbles

---

**Before reading this chapter, make sure you know the meaning of the concepts:**

1. Aggregate supply and demand
2. Exchange rates
3. Accommodating policy
4. Equation of exchange
5. Deflation
6. Real and nominal interest rates
7. Operating targets and intermediate targets
8. Taylor rule

---

CHAPTER 10 LOOKED at strategies for safeguarding economic stability. We saw that it is unrealistic to aim for complete elimination of the business cycle. The economy is subject to many shocks from within and without, and the reality of lags and forecasting errors make precise fine-tuning impossible. However, by following preset rules and avoiding short-sighted, politically motivated policies that make matters worse rather than better, it should be possible to avoid extremes of instability.

Unfortunately, mistakes are made, and we do sometimes experience booms and busts. This chapter will look at how episodes of instability come about and at policies that can set things right when they do occur. First we will look at inflation and its variants, which were the most common form of instability in the second half of the twentieth century. Then we will turn to deflation, a problem that last afflicted the United States in the 1930s and which again began to pose a danger during the global economic crisis that began in 2008.

# Inflation

Since Chapter 9, our main tool for understanding stabilization policy has been the aggregate supply and demand model. We have shown how changes in the planned expenditures of households and firms, and in fiscal and monetary policy, can shift the aggregate demand curve to the right or left. We have seen how the short-run aggregate supply curve shifts up or down with changes in expectations about the level of wages and other input prices. We have seen how the economy tends to move, with a lag, toward a long-run equilibrium at the natural level of real output, although new shocks may disturb it again before the adjustment is complete. In this section, we start our discussion of inflation by using the aggregate supply and demand model to distinguish between different types of inflation and looking at the dynamic processes that set inflation in motion.

## *Demand-Side Inflation*

**Demand-side inflation**

Inflation caused by an upward shift of the aggregate demand curve while the aggregate supply curve remains fixed or shifts upward at no more than an equal rate

We begin with the case of **demand-side inflation**. Demand-side inflation occurs when the aggregate demand curve shifts up and to the right while the short-run aggregate supply curve remains fixed or shifts upward at no more than an equal rate.

In the simplest form of demand-side inflation, there is a one-time shift in the aggregate demand curve, beginning from an initial state of equilibrium. In response, the economy first moves up and to the right along the short-run aggregate supply curve to a new short-run equilibrium. Real output and the price level increase during this initial phase of inflation while the unemployment rate decreases. After a lag, expectations regarding wages and other input prices begin to adjust and the short-run aggregate supply curve starts to shift upward. If the aggregate demand curve remains in its new position, the economy moves up and to the left along it to a new long-run equilibrium where real output returns to its natural level and unemployment returns to its natural rate.

Such an isolated, one-time shift in the aggregate demand curve is not the only form demand-side inflation can take, or even the most common one. Instead, as shown in Figure 12.1, sustained expansionary policy often allows aggregate demand to grow continuously. In that case, as the short-run aggregate supply curve is shifted upward by firms' expectations of ever-higher input prices ($AS_2$, $AS_3$), the aggregate demand curve keeps pace with it ($AD_2$, $AD_3$). Real output does not fall back toward its natural level; rather, the economy moves straight upward along the path from E1 to $E_2$ to $E_3$ and beyond.

FIGURE 12.1     DEMAND-SIDE INFLATION

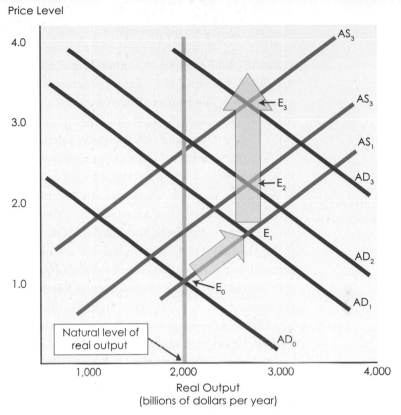

Demand-side inflation begins when a rightward shift in the aggregate demand curve moves the economy up and to the right along the short-run aggregate supply curve, from $E_0$ to $E_1$. Soon, the short-run aggregate supply curve begins to shift upward as increases in final-goods prices filter through to cause expected increases in wages and other input prices. If expansionary policy continues to shift the aggregate demand curve as shown, real output can be kept above its natural level for a sustained period. However, the cost of doing so will be ongoing inflation.

The scenario shown in Figure 12.1 has major implications for economic policy. In the short run, starting from a state of long-run equilibrium, expansionary fiscal or monetary policy is effective in stimulating real economic growth and lowering unemployment as the economy moves from $E_0$ to $E_1$. The initial cost is only a little inflation. However, those initial gains in real output can be sustained only at the cost of ongoing demand-side inflation. Although it is not directly apparent from Figure 12.1, a rate of inflation that is constant from year to year may not be enough to hold unemployment below its natural rate. Under plausible assumptions regarding the way expectations of inflation are formed, inflation must accelerate to a higher rate each year to sustain a positive output gap.

Once the initial benefits of the expansion have been realized, policymakers will face a dilemma. One choice is to stop the stimulus. If they do that, inflation will slow and eventually stop; however, output will fall back to its natural level, and unemployment will increase. The other choice is to continue the expansionary policy. In that case, the positive output gap can be maintained for an extended period. Choosing that path, however, will mean year after year of ever-faster inflation.

## Supply-Side Inflation and Supply Shocks

Demand-side inflation can instead be caused by an upward shift in the aggregate supply curve while the aggregate demand curve stays in place or shifts upward more slowly. The upward movement of the aggregate supply curve is caused by increases in expected wages and other input prices, which push up costs of production. The result can be called **supply-side inflation**.

**Supply shocks** are one source of supply-side inflation. A supply shock is an event that changes the average level of expected input prices but does not arise from changes in aggregate demand. The world-wide increase in commodity prices (oil, food, and metals, and others) that occurred in the first half of 2008 is an example of a supply shock. A rise in the price of commodities increases expected input prices through two main channels. First, commodities like oil and metals are inputs for many firms; their prices directly affect the expected costs of production. In addition, firms will expect that increases in prices of commodities like food and fuel will affect the cost of living for their workers, so that nominal wages will sooner or later have to be adjusted.

Changes in global commodity prices are one of the most common sources of supply shocks, but not the only one. Unusually bad weather affects expected costs in farming, construction, and transportation. Natural disasters, like earthquakes or hurricanes, raise costs of doing business in the affected areas; they may also drive up input prices more widely via changes in demand for construction materials or other goods needed for recovery. Finally, changes in exchange rates affect the prices of inputs that a country imports. In the United States, a depreciation of the dollar relative to foreign currencies makes imported inputs (say, imported steel used by an appliance maker) more expensive. At the same time, it may also increase demand for U.S. exports of intermediate goods such as chemicals that are traded on the world market, thereby driving up their prices.

Supply shocks can work both ways. Just as increases in world commodity prices in early 2008 raised expected input prices, the subsequent sharp fall in commodity prices reduced them. Similarly, unusually good weather leading to bumper crops or an appreciation of a country's currency would tend to cause a decrease in expected input prices.

Figure 12.2 illustrates the short-run effects of a supply shock. In the figure, the economy begins

**Supply-side inflation**

Inflation that is caused by an upward shift in the aggregate supply curve while the aggregate demand curve remains fixed or shifts upward more slowly

**Supply shock**

An event not arising from changes in aggregate demand that changes the average level of expected input prices

A natural disaster like hurricane Katrina can cause a supply shock.

**FIGURE 12.2   SHORT-RUN EFFECTS OF A SUPPLY SHOCK**

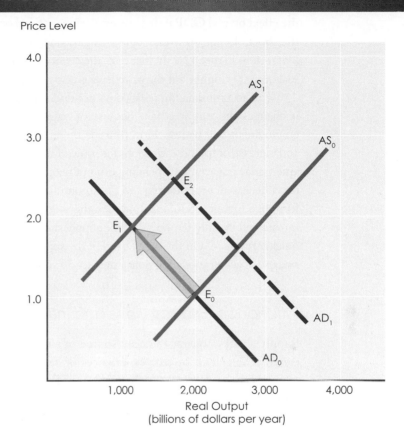

Beginning from $E_0$, suppose a supply shock shifts the aggregate supply curve from $AS_0$ to $AS_1$. If there is no change in aggregate demand, the economy will move from $E_0$ to $E_1$ along $AD_0$. The economy will experience supply-side inflation accompanied by falling real output. If the Fed uses expansionary monetary policy to partially accommodate the supply shock, shifting the aggregate demand curve to $AD_1$, the economy will instead end up at $E_2$. The supply shock will then have less impact on real output, but there will be more inflation.

in equilibrium at $E_0$. At this point, something—say a devastating hurricane—causes an increase in the expected level of input prices. As firms adjust their expectations, the short-run aggregate supply curve shifts upward from $AS_0$ to $AS_1$. With the higher expected level of input prices, but no matching increase in aggregate demand, firms must revise their production and pricing plans. As they raise prices to cover increased production costs, they find that it is no longer profitable to produce as much as before. The whole economy moves upward and to the left along aggregate demand curve $AD_0$ to $E_1$.

What happens next depends on how policymakers adjust aggregate demand. The hurricane has caused real damage to the economy. Even if people work just as many hours as before, the total quantity of goods and services available for consumption, investment, government purchases, and net exports will be less. If, as is likely, some people are put out of work because their places of employment are destroyed, there will be even more economic damage. No possible policies can fully offset it. However, policymakers can soften the effect on real GDP if they use expansionary fiscal or monetary policy to accommodate the shock. Doing so would shift the aggregate demand curve to the right, to a position like $AD_1$ in Figure 12.2. In that case, the economy will move toward a point like $E_2$, where real output is higher but the price level is also higher than at $E_1$.

The accommodating policy does not undo all of the harm from the supply shock, but it changes the way it is felt. Because of increased demand, the impact on output and employment will be less. Firms outside the area affected by the hurricane can add shifts and increase output, creating jobs for some of the people thrown out of work by the storm; emergency government spending can put people to work repairing storm damage; and so on. There is an economic cost to the accommodating policy, however. That cost takes the form of a higher rate of inflation than there otherwise would have been. The inflationary impact will be only temporary if the supply shock is a moderate one and its effects can be quickly reversed. On the other hand, if the supply shock is severe and long lasting, excessive use of accommodating policy may set off sustained demand-side inflation.

## Inflationary Expectations and Inflationary Recession

Supply shocks are not the only source of supply-side inflation. Supply-side inflation can also be caused by past experiences of demand-side inflation. To understand why, we need to look more closely at the way firms and workers form their expectations about input prices.

Up to this point, we have assumed that firms expect input prices in the current year to be equal to the level of final goods' prices in the previous year. In practice, though, they may expect prices to continue rising in the future and not to come to a halt at the level to which they were carried by last year's inflation. If so, that will affect their pricing and production plans for the coming year. A simple assumption that captures this behavior is that firms expect wages and other input prices in the coming year to increase by the same percentage as they did the year before. Such a tendency of firms and workers to expect prices to continue rising in the future at the same rate as in the immediate past is called **inflation inertia or inflation momentum**.

Figure 12.3 shows what happens when inflation inertia becomes established. The story begins from a situation of ongoing demand-side inflation similar to the one shown in Figure 12.1. Expansionary fiscal or monetary policy has held output above its natural level for some time. The economy is moving upward along the arrow through $E_1$ and $E_2$. As a result of past inflation, firms and workers expect more inflation in the future and have adjusted their plans to cope with it as best they can. The inflation momentum built into their plans is reflected in a series of upward shifting short-run aggregate supply curves.

What happens if, after the economy has reached $E_2$, policymakers attempt to stop inflation by halting the growth of aggregate demand? (We are talking not about reducing the level of aggregate demand but only about stopping its growth.) The result, in Figure 12.3, is to stop the upward shift of the aggregate demand curve, leaving it in the position $AD_2$.

**Inflation inertia (inflation momentum)**

A tendency of firms and workers to expect prices to continue rising in the future at the same rate as in the immediate past

**FIGURE 12.3    INFLATIONARY RECESSION**

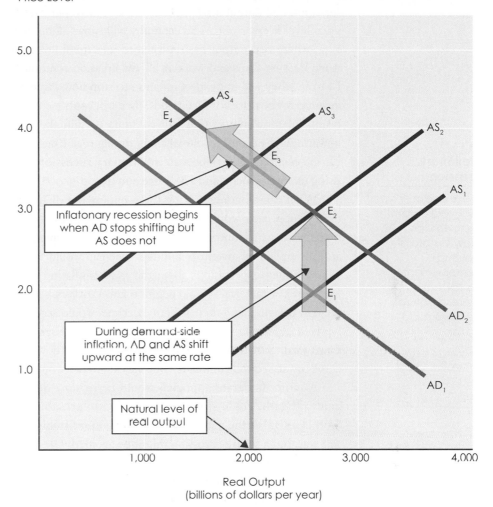

An inflationary recession occurs when aggregate demand slows or stops growing following a period of sustained inflation. In this figure, the aggregate demand curve stops shifting after the economy reaches $E_2$. Firms expect the level of input prices to continue to rise; thus, the short-run aggregate supply curve moves on up to $AS_3$ in the next year and to $AS_4$ in the year after that. As it does, the economy enters a recession during which the price level continues to rise. For a time the inflation rate may actually increase as real output falls.

Halting the growth of aggregate demand will not stop inflation in its tracks. Firms and workers have grown used to inflation and expect it to continue. Workers, expecting their costs of living to rise further, will have done their best to make contracts with their employers that give them compensating wage increases as the cost of living rises. Firms expect their input prices to rise further and will have become used to passing the increases along to their customers. As long as firms expect their input prices to continue rising and set their prices and output plans on that basis, the short-run aggregate supply curve will continue to shift upward.

With the aggregate supply curve moving upward while the aggregate demand curve stays put, real output starts to decrease and unemployment to increase. Meanwhile, the price level keeps rising. The economy will move along $AD_2$ toward point $E_3$ in Figure 12.3, where real output has returned to its natural level; but that is not the end of the story. Because firms and workers all saw inflation continue as the economy moved from $E_2$ to $E_3$, they will not expect inflation to stop now. As long as firms anticipate a further increase in the prices of final goods, they will continue to expect rising input prices. As a result, inflation momentum will continue to shift the aggregate supply curve further upward. As the economy moves along the aggregate demand curve toward a position like $E_4$, the economy experiences an **inflationary recession**—an episode in which inflation, rising unemployment, and a negative output gap all occur at the same time.[1]

What can be done to bring the economy out of an inflationary recession? A "cold turkey" approach would be to sit tight and keep the lid on aggregate demand. At $E_4$, there is a negative output gap, accompanied by a rising unemployment, declining sales, and an unplanned inventory buildup. The gap would, in time, cause firms and workers to revise their expectations about the rate of inflation for both inputs and final goods. Prices of raw materials would begin to fall. Workers, seeing first a slowing of the rise in the cost of living, and then an actual decline, would accept lower nominal wages. Lower levels of expected input prices would cause the aggregate supply curve to begin shifting downward. Slowly the economy would slip back down along the aggregate demand curve toward equilibrium at $E_3$, but the experience would be a painful one.

A more moderate approach would be to slow the growth of aggregate demand gradually rather than stopping it cold. With luck, this could bring the economy to a "soft landing" at the natural level of real output. It might take longer to slow inflation this way, but a severe recession might be avoided.

In practice, though, there is a danger that politically driven time-inconsistency will prevent smooth adjustment. Instead, policymakers may first respond to pressures to "do something" about inflation by stopping the growth of aggregate demand altogether and then react to pressures to "do something" about unemployment by renewing demand growth before inflation inertia been broken. Such a "stop-go" policy would result in a highly unstable path for the economy over time.[2]

The truth is that no one knows a quick, painless way to stop inflation once it has become embedded in public expectations. That is why, as discussed in Chapter 10, it is better to keep inflation under control in the first place by using inflation targeting or some other preset rule.

## The Phillips Curve

At several points, our examples have suggested an inverse relationship between inflation and unemployment. The initial effect of expansionary policy is to move the economy up and to the right along the short-run aggregate supply curve. As it does so, unemployment falls and inflation rises. Over a longer period, unemployment can be kept below its natural rate by a policy of continuous expansionary policy, but doing so has a side effect

**Inflationary recession**

An episode in which real output falls toward or below its natural level and unemployment rises toward or above its natural rate while rapid inflation continues

of accelerating inflation. On the down side, contractionary policy aimed at slowing inflation has the initial effect of reducing real output and raising unemployment.

This inverse relationship between inflation and unemployment can be represented in the form of a graph called a **Phillips curve**, named for A. W. H. Phillips, who first described it in a 1958 paper (see *Who Said It? Who Did It? 12.1*)[3].

**THE PHILLIPS CURVE AS A POLICY MENU**  A representative Phillips curve is drawn in Figure 12.4a. During the 1960s, when the curve first attracted economists' attention, some viewed it as a menu of policy choices. Political liberals argued that policymakers should choose a point such as L on the Phillips curve; this point would "buy" full employment and prosperity at the price of a modest inflation rate. Conservatives objected to any but the slightest degree of inflation

**Phillips curve**

A graph showing the relationship between the inflation rate and the unemployment rate, other things being equal

## Who Said It? Who Did It?  12.1
## A. W. H. PHILLIPS AND THE PHILLIPS CURVE

The reputation of Alban W. H. Phillips, known to his friends as Bill, is based on a single paper, written on the right topic and published at the right time. In the late 1950s, the connection between inflation and unemployment was a major focus of macroeconomic theory. In an article published in the journal *Economica* in 1958, Phillips presented a set of graphs that suggested a stable, inverse relationship between inflation and unemployment. The paper did not contain much by way of a theory to explain the relationship, but the author's curves became a peg on which all future discussions of the problem would be hung. Every subsequent article on inflation and unemployment discussed the shape of the Phillips curve that best served as a policy target, how the Phillips curve could be shifted, and so on. Today the term is so familiar that Phillips' name enjoys a sort of immortality, even though Phillips left further development of the inflation-unemployment relationship to others.

Phillips was born in New Zealand in 1914. He moved to Australia at the age of 16, worked there as an apprentice electrician in a mine, and learned electrical engineering skills. In 1937, he immigrated to Britain. He served in World War II and was taken prisoner by the Japanese. After the war, he studied at the London School of Economics and later joined the faculty there. He stayed at LSE until 1967, when he moved to Australian National University.

Phillips's early hands-on engineering training seems to have influenced his approach to economic problems. One of his early projects at LSE was to construct a hydraulic analog computer called the Monetary National Income Automatic Computer (MONIAC). The device was designed to simulate the circular flow of income and product in the economy. By adjusting valves on the computer, flows of water representing saving, taxes, government spending, and other variables could be sent through a series of pipes and tanks. The MONIAC foreshadowed the widespread use of computers in modern economic research. Several copies of Phillips' machine were made, some of which are preserved in working order to this day.

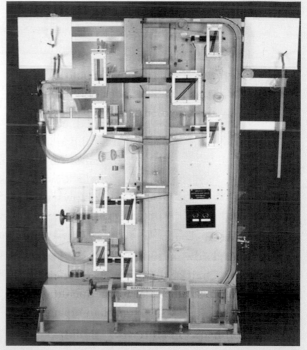

The Phillips economic computer

**FIGURE 12.4   A REPRESENTATIVE PHILLIPS CURVE**

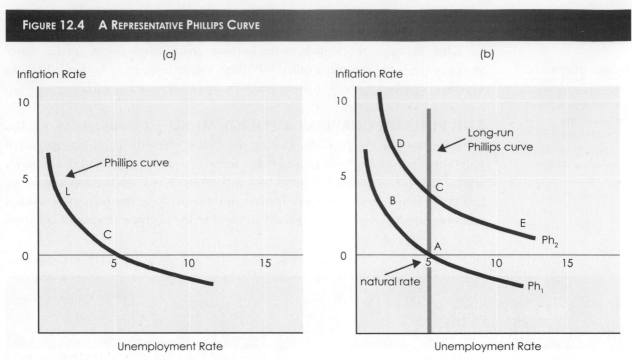

When the Phillips curve was first introduced, it was seen by many as a policy menu, as shown in Part (a) of this figure. Political liberals could choose a point of permanent low unemployment with some inflation (L), while conservatives could choose permanent low inflation with higher unemployment (C). Later it became apparent that the Phillips curve shifts over time as inflation expectations adjust to past inflation. In Part (b), if inflation increased from 0 to 4 percent, the economy would at first move from A to B along $Ph_1$. Once people came to expect 4 percent inflation, the curve would shift up to $Ph_2$. Further changes in inflation would move the economy along $Ph_2$ in the short run, until expectations changed again.

and argued for a point such as C, which would achieve price stability at the expense of some jobs.

Economists soon discovered a problem with viewing the Phillips curve as a policy menu: the choices it offered kept changing while the meal was in progress. As the 1960s unfolded, economists began to notice that inflation-unemployment points for recent years did not fit the curves they had plotted using data from the 1950s. It became common to speak of an upward drift of the Phillips curve. A given level of inflation would "buy" increasingly smaller reductions in unemployment.

Had the upward drift of the Phillips curve been caused by factors outside their control, policymakers could have chosen their preferred point on a new, higher Phillips curve. In the 1970s, however, perceptions of the Phillips curve started to change. It began to appear that shifts in the Phillips curve were caused by the very policies that had sought to move the economy along the curve.

**THE PHILLIPS CURVE IN THE LONG-RUN**   The key to this new view of the Phillips curve is provided by the distinction between long-run and short-run effects of changes in aggregate demand. A once-and-for-all rise in the level of aggregate demand leads only to a temporary reduction in unemployment. The reason is that expectations soon adjust to past inflation, causing an upward shift in the aggregate supply curve. Real output can rise above its natural level only as long as the short-run aggregate supply curve does not completely catch up with the shifting aggregate demand curve.

In the aggregate supply and demand model, unemployment is at its natural rate only when expected inflation rate equals the actual inflation rate and when the inflation rate is neither accelerating nor decelerating. Those conditions can be met when the expected and actual inflation rates of inflation are both zero, but that is not the only possibility. Unemployment can also be at its natural rate when the economy is in a moving equilibrium with a constant, positive inflation rate to which everyone has become accustomed.

The modern view of the Phillips curve is illustrated in Figure 12.4b. Two short-run Phillips curves are shown, each corresponding to a different expected inflation rate. If no inflation is expected, the Phillips curve takes the position $Ph_1$. The intersection of that Phillips curve with the horizontal axis occurs at the natural rate of unemployment, assumed to be 5 percent in our example. If the actual inflation rate unexpectedly goes up to 4 percent per year, the economy will initially move upward and to the left along Phillips curve $Ph_1$ from point A to point B. The same movement would be shown with an the aggregate supply and demand diagram as a movement upward and to the right along the economy's short-run aggregate supply curve, with real output and the price level both increasing.

If the inflation rate remains at 4 percent per year, people will sooner or later adjust their expectations accordingly. In the aggregate supply and demand model, that would be shown as an upward shift in the aggregate supply curve. In Figure 12.4b, the same adjustment of expectations causes an upward shift of the short-run Phillips curve to $Ph_2$. As a result, the economy moves to point C.

Once the Phillips curve has shifted, the economy can make short-run movements upward or downward along it depending on what happens to inflation. If inflation increases to 8 percent while people expect it to remain at 4 percent, the economy will, in the short run, move from C to D along the $Ph_2$. If inflation slows to 2 percent while people expect it to remain at 4 percent, the economy at first will move from point C to point E. However, those movements along the short-run Phillips curve will not represent new points of long-run equilibrium. If some inflation rate other than 4 percent persists long enough for people to adjust to it, the short-run Phillips curve will shift again.

All of this can be summarized by saying that, in addition to a whole set of short-run Phillips curves, there must also be a vertical long-run Phillips curve, as shown in Figure 12.4b. That conclusion follows from the ideas that unemployment is at its natural rate whenever the actual and expected inflation rates are equal and that any given steady rate of inflation will be expected to continue. The vertical long-run Phillips curve intersects the horizontal axis at the natural rate of unemployment. Each short-run Phillips curve intersects the long-run Phillips curve at the expected inflation rate for which the short-run curve is drawn. Unemployment will be at its natural rate only when the actual and expected inflation rates are equal.

## Hyperinflation

The Phillips curve and the aggregate supply-demand model are based on the experience of economies with low to moderate inflation. The United States, where inflation

**Hyperinflation**

Very rapid inflation

in the past 100 years has rarely exceeded 10 percent, is such a country. Other countries have sometimes experienced more extreme inflation, known as **hyperinflation**. There is no precise cutoff between moderate inflation and hyperinflation. One classic study drew the line at an inflation rate of 50 percent per month which, when compounded, is equivalent to about 14,000 percent per year. Others consider rates of 1,000 percent per year or more to be hyperinflation. Some of the symptoms of hyperinflation begin to appear at rates as low as 100 percent per year. The upper limits of hyperinflation are extremely high, as discussed in *Economics in the News 12.1*.

**THE ORIGINS OF HYPERINFLATION** Hyperinflation always begins in the same way. A government, because of war, revolution, or an unsustainable debt pyramid, can neither raise enough taxes nor borrow enough money to pay its bills. As a last resort, it starts printing money, or more exactly, monetizing the deficit. As the quantity of money starts increasing rapidly, a chain reaction sets in that involves all of the variables of the equation of exchange, $MV = PQ$.

## Economics in the News 12.1
## HYPERINFLATION, THEN AND NOW

One hundred trillion dollars for a loaf of bread? Impossible? Not if the price is in Zimbabwe dollars. In fact, when Zimbabwe's inflation rate hit a high of 518 quintillion percent per year in 2008, the largest bill printed by the central bank, 100 trillion dollars, was not quite enough to buy a loaf of bread. At the peak of its hyperinflation, Zimbabwe's economy was in a state of total collapse. Almost nothing was being produced, and more than half the labor force was out of work. That experience has been shared, to a degree, by all countries that have experienced hyperinflation. Their economies, and often their governments, too, simply fall apart. With prices changing so fast, money loses its ability to function as a store of value and unit of account. Without money, any but the most primitive economic activity is impossible.

Even at 518 quintillion percent, Zimbabwe's inflation was not an all-time record. The record is still held by Hungary, which, in 1946-47, saw prices increase at a rate of ... well, it is hard to put it in words. Most people don't even know what a "quintillion" is. (It is a 1 followed by 18 zeros.) Even fewer people would be able to properly express Hungary's inflation rate as "three octillion percent" (a 3 followed by 27 zeros).

Cases like Hungary and Zimbabwe make the 1993 hyperinflation in Yugoslavia, at 3 trillion percent, seem tame. The most famous hyperinflation in history, 1923 in Germany, was a mere 300 million percent; but even that caused enough damage to help set the stage for the rise of Hitler's Nazi party a few years later.

Astronomical numbers are not needed for inflation to be harmful, however. Inflation of 2,000 percent per year

in Argentina in 1991 brought down the government. Inflation at about the same rate in Russia in 1992, the year after the collapse of the Soviet Union, did not cause the fall of the government, but it undermined the credibility of the country's young democracy and market economy in ways that have not yet been forgotten. Fortunately, hyperinflation is not common, but it is so frightening that central bankers around the world make avoiding even the possibility of hyperinflation one of their highest priorities.

In 2008, Zimbabwe saw an inflation rate of 518 quintillion percent. The largest bill printed, one trillion Zimbabwe dollars, was not enough to buy a loaf of bread.

First, as the money stock, M, grows faster than real output, Q, there is upward pressure on P, the price level. Inflation tends to interfere with orderly tax collection; as inflation speeds up, the real deficit increases, and the money stock grows even faster. Excessive monetary growth is just the beginning of the hyperinflation story, however.

As inflation accelerates, the next thing that happens is that velocity, the V in the equation of exchange, begins to increase. Velocity means the number of times per year, on average, each unit of the money stock is used to make purchases. When inflation becomes so rapid that prices are rising daily, people learn that as soon as possible after they receive any money, they should spend it on something. The faster people run to the store to buy things, the less time they hold on to their money, and the more rapidly the money circulates through the economy. It is easy to see that with both M and V increasing rapidly, the right hand side of the equation, PQ, must rise rapidly as well.

The final element of the chain reaction occurs when inflation gets so rapid that it undermines production of real goods and services. As the economy collapses, real output, Q, not only stops increasing—it decreases. With M and V both growing rapidly and Q falling, the price level, P, is squeezed from all sides. The resulting pressure of M, V, and Q acting together is what forces inflation to millions of percent per year, or more.

**ENDING HYPERINFLATION**   The good news about hyperinflation is that it does not go on forever. Sooner or later, suddenly or gradually, it comes to an end. Most hyperinflations end in one of two ways.

Hyperinflation in the lower range of extreme—for example, Russia's 2,000 percent inflation—can sometimes be ended with conventional tightening of monetary policy. After 1993, the Russian government gradually stopped monetizing its deficit. It began to borrow more, both on domestic and foreign credit markets, and printed less money. As inflation slowed, it became possible to reduce the deficit itself. By 1996, inflation was down to about 10 percent per year. Not everything went smoothly. A failure to complete the process of fiscal consolidation led to a debt pyramid collapse in 1998, followed by a default and a brief return of inflation. Full economic stabilization was not achieved until rising prices of energy exports helped bring the budget into balance in 2000 and after.

Conventional policy like Russia's is not the only way to end hyperinflation, nor is it always the best. Many countries have instead used an approach called **exchange-rate based stabilization (ERB stabilization)**. Exchange-rate based stabilization is an approach to control hyperinflation that emphasizes a fixed exchange rate relative to some stable currency, like the dollar, the euro, or before the euro, the German mark. The exchange rate acts as a "nominal anchor" that provides a fixed point of reference for everyone in the economy. People no longer have to deal with nominal values—nominal wages, nominal interest rates, nominal taxes—that increase by thousands or millions of percent each month and make it difficult to focus on the underlying real values when making production and investment decisions. Instead, ERB stabilization introduces a stable unit of account, based on the chosen stable currency, that allows everyone to get back to the real business of working, running a firm, or providing for a family.

An important part of the nominal-anchor principal is its impact on velocity. As long as the local currency is subject to rapid inflation, no one wants to hold on to paper

**Exchange-rate based stabilization (ERB stabilization)**

A policy that uses a fixed exchange rate as the principal tool for ending hyperinflation

currency or bank balances. Everyone tries to spend money as fast as possible, driving up velocity and making inflation worse. As soon as money is redefined as having a fixed value relative to a reliable currency, people's attitudes change. There is now no "inflation tax" to pay if a person decides to hold on to some of Friday's pay to spend for groceries on Monday. As can be seen from the equation of exchange, a decrease in velocity immediately slows—or even reverses—the rate of increase of the price level. During the period of a few weeks or months that it takes for velocity to return to normal, the government has a chance to bring the budget under control and slow the growth of money; and private firms have a chance to get their businesses in order and restore the growth of real output. If all goes well, the economy returns to stability.

There is more than one way to implement ERB stabilization. Some countries directly adopt another country's stable currency as their legal tender. Ecuador adopted the U.S. dollar as its currency in 2000 to end a hyperinflation, a process called *dollarization*. Other countries keep their own currency in name only and peg it at a fixed ratio to a stable currency following an arrangement called a *currency board*. Argentina successfully ended a hyperinflation in 1991 using a currency board linked to the dollar; Estonia and Bulgaria used currency board links to the German mark to end hyperinflation and later transferred the link to the euro when it replaced the mark. Still other countries use less rigid forms of fixed exchange rates to accomplish the same purpose. For example, Latvia used a link to a weighted average of stable currencies. Poland and Hungary used exchange rates that were not rigidly fixed but instead followed a sliding scale that adjusted at a pre-announced rate. Zimbabwe's recent hyperinflation seems finally to have come under control, not because of any decisive action by its government, but simply because people spontaneously gave up using the nearly worthless Zimbabwe dollar and began using the U.S. dollar or South African rand instead.

**THE LIMITS OF ERB STABILIZATION**   Policies using a fixed exchange rate to stop hyperinflation are not always fully successful in restoring long-run stability. Two problems are especially likely to cause trouble.

First, ERB stabilization will not work if the government's commitment to economic reform is not credible. As explained above, much of the effect of a fixed exchange rate comes from its impact on velocity. Velocity is determined largely by psychology. If people believe a government's promise that a currency will have a stable value, they will use it as a store of value, unit of account, and means of exchange. The monetary system will then return to normal. If the government says the currency will be stable but does not back up its words with credible reforms, like fiscal consolidation and respect for independence of the central bank, people will see through the sham. They will go right on spending their money as fast as they can, and the impact on inflation will be momentary, at best. Argentina, which successfully used ERB stabilization in 1991, had spectacularly failed in a previous attempt in the 1980s, when a fixed exchange rate was not backed up with real reforms.

Second, even if an ERB strategy is successful in ending hyperinflation, it may leave the country with a fixed exchange rate policy that is not suitable in the long run. The issue of whether a country's economy will perform better over time with a fixed or flexible exchange rate is a complex one. The choice depends on such factors as how closely the country's trade is tied to its currency partner, how flexible its labor markets are, and how exposed it is to external economic shocks. Suffice it to say that in the long run, a fixed exchange rate suits some countries, but not all.

If a country is not suited to live with a fixed exchange rate in the long run, it should attempt ERB stabilization only as a short-run tool for ending hyperinflation and have an exit strategy at the ready. Israel did this to end an episode of hyperinflation in the mid-1980s. It introduced a new version of its currency, the shekel, with a fixed exchange rate to the U.S. dollar and implemented budget reforms to increase the credibility of the policy. After hyperinflation ended, the government phased out the fixed exchange rate and returned to a more flexible policy regime. Argentina in the 1990s provides an unfortunate contrast. The introduction of a currency board fixed to the U.S. dollar successfully ended hyperinflation in 1991, but the country could not live with a fixed exchange rate in the long run. Ten years later the currency board suffered a spectacular collapse that brought down the government and caused a severe recession. Since that time, Argentina has recovered under more flexible exchange rate rules; but its failure to find an orderly exit strategy from its earlier currency board caused a lot of harm.

## Deflation

After the preceding discussion of the evils of inflation, it might seem that deflation—a prolonged period of falling prices—would present a lesser set of problems. If inflation is bad, shouldn't we expect its opposite to be good? Instead, we find that deflation can be just as much of a curse as inflation. Only under special circumstances can an economy remain healthy for long while prices of goods and services fall.

**Demand-side deflation**

A period of falling prices caused by a decrease in aggregate demand

Like inflation, deflation can exist in both demand-side and supply-side variants, as illustrated in Figure 12.5. Part a shows **demand-side deflation**. Suppose that beginning from equilibrium at $E_0$, something happens to reduce aggregate demand—a slowdown in investment, a decrease in net exports, or a reduction in any other element of planned expenditure. As the aggregate demand curve shifts leftward, the economy moves down and to the left along its aggregate supply curve from $E_1$ to $E_2$. The price level and real output both decrease in the short run. If there were no further change in aggregate demand, expectations would eventually begin to adjust. As a result, the short-run aggregate supply curve would shift downward; and the economy would, with a lag, return to an equilibrium (not shown) at its natural level of real output.

**Supply-side deflation**

A period of falling prices caused by a decrease in the expected costs of production

Part b of Figure 12.5 shows **supply-side deflation**. Beginning from equilibrium at $E_0$, suppose a favorable supply shock occurs, for example, a decrease in world commodity prices or an appreciation of the country's exchange rate. Because inputs suddenly become cheaper, firms will expect a decrease in costs of production. This is reflected in a downward shift of the short-run aggregate supply curve. If there is no change in aggregate demand, the economy moves from $E_0$ to a new short-run equilibrium at $E_1$. In the process, firms react to the expectation of lower production costs partly by increasing output and partly by passing along lower costs to their customers through price reductions. If the favorable supply shock is only temporary, the economy will later return to its starting point at $E_0$. The long-run effects of a lasting supply shock are more complex. We will return to them shortly.

FIGURE 12.5   SUPPLY-SIDE AND DEMAND-SIDE DEFLATION

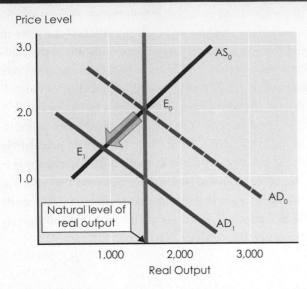 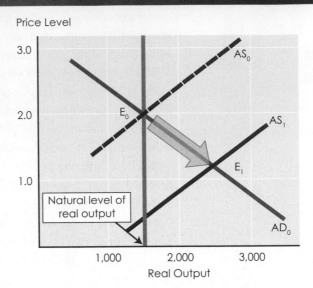

Deflation, like inflation, can exist in demand-side or supply-side variants. Part a shows demand-side deflation. Beginning from equilibrium at $E_0$, something happens to reduce aggregate demand (for example, a slowdown in investment or a decrease in net exports). The economy moves down and to the left along its aggregate supply curve from $E_0$ to $E_1$. The price level and real output both decrease. Part b shows supply-side deflation. A favorable supply shock (for example, a decrease in world commodity prices or an appreciation of the country's exchange rate) causes firms to expect a decrease in costs of production and shifts the short-run aggregate supply curve downward. The economy moves from $E_0$ to a new short-run equilibrium at $E_1$. Firms react to the expectation of lower production costs partly by increasing output and partly by passing along lower costs to their customers through price reductions. As this happens, real output increases and the price level falls.

Demand-side and supply side deflation pose different problems for economic policy. We will begin with the more common, demand-side variant.

## Asymmetries of Demand-Side Deflation

In the aggregate supply and demand model, demand-side deflation looks like the mirror image of demand-side inflation. If that were the case, no separate treatment would be needed. Policymakers could react to demand-side deflation in one two ways. One would be simply to wait for the economy to return to equilibrium on its own as expectations, catching up with past changes in the price level, shifted the aggregate supply curve downward. The alternative would be to try to speed the adjustment with countercyclical monetary or fiscal policy, which would shift the aggregate demand curve back to the right.

In reality, though, the economy is not perfectly symmetrical in its upward and downward movements. There are similarities between demand-side inflation and deflation, but there are important differences as well.

**ASYMMETRIES IN LABOR MARKETS**   One of the important asymmetries between inflation and deflation concerns the ease with which labor markets adjust to increases and decreases in labor demand. Suppose first that demand for labor increases, say, because of an increase in demand for a country's exports. Export industries would immediately start to expand production, partly by increasing workers' hours and partly by recruiting new workers. Wages in the export sector would start to rise, both because of overtime pay and because employers would need to offer premium wages to draw in workers from other parts of the economy. As workers started to switch jobs to the export sector, labor shortages would develop for firms that produce for domestic sale. Wages in those sectors would also rise. It would not matter much whether workers were unionized or not. If workers were organized, union leaders would take advantage of rising labor demand to negotiate better contracts. If workers were not organized, employers would still have to offer better wages to retain the workers they have and hire the new ones they need. Not all of this would happen immediately. It would take some time for employers to interview job candidates, workers to move to new job sites, and unions to negotiate new contracts. Still, the lags would not be long because everyone—workers and employers—would want to be among the first to take advantage of the changed situation.

If labor demand were instead to fall, because of decreasing exports or for any other reason, the adjustment would not go so smoothly. Export industries would cut back output, shorten hours, and begin to lay off workers; but they would find it harder to lower wages. Some workers would be protected by union contracts. If so, it might be hard even to begin negotiations before the contract expired. Even where workers were not unionized, it would be hard to get them to accept lower wages. People tend to have a psychological resistance to losing something they already have that is greater than their appreciation of getting something new. The psychological resistance to accepting nominal wage cuts can persist even in periods when deflation is lowering the cost of living, so that the lower nominal wage can buy the same real goods and services as before. Furthermore, any employer that attempted to cut wages would find its best workers quitting first—they would be the ones who would most easily find new jobs.

In a rising job market, workers that are just entering the labor market or who are temporarily unemployed can be drawn to expanding sectors by higher wages. In a falling labor market, it is harder for newly entering or unemployed workers to find jobs. In a world of pure economic rationality, unemployed workers might approach employers and offer to work for less than people who already have jobs; but in practice, social and cultural stigmas are attached both to workers who propose undercutting their neighbors' wages and firms that agree to hire them on those terms. In countries that experience strong deflationary pressures, nominal wages do eventually begin to fall; however, the process can be slow and painful. For example, in the United States during the first years of the Great Depression, nominal wages did decrease. They did not fall as fast as the price level, however, which meant that

During the early stages of the Great Depression, rising real wages helped push the unemployment rate to nearly 25 percent of the labor force.

real wages increased. With real wages increasing at the same time labor demand was decreasing, unemployment rose to nearly a quarter of the labor force.

**ASYMMETRIES IN FINANCIAL MARKETS**    Financial markets, too, react differently to deflation than to inflation. During the recent downturn, some of the most striking differences have been found in markets for home mortgages.

During a boom, when jobs are plentiful and wages are rising, people are eager to move up to better housing. Banks willingly lend them the money to do so, based on their income and employment prospects. Soon housing prices begin to rise, and people begin to see a house not just as a place to live but also as a sure-fire investment. Lenders accommodate the eagerness of home buyers by offering loans with low down payments. If a banker extends a loan of 90 or even 100 percent of the value of a house, the collateral may be barely adequate at first. Both the borrow and lender know, though, that as house prices rise, a comfortable cushion of equity will be created between the amount owed on the loan and the sale price. The equity will protect the bank in case the borrower becomes unable to pay. Expansion of the housing sector feeds on itself.

When the economy turns down, the dynamic of the mortgage market becomes much more difficult. As incomes level off, and the increase in housing prices slows and is then reversed, people who bought at the top find themselves in homes they cannot really afford. Their financial situation is fragile. If they lose their jobs or even see their hours cut, they may find it hard to keep up with mortgage payments. Moving down the market to a cheaper house can be difficult because the one they are in now cannot be sold for enough to pay off the mortgage. Foreclosures begin to rise, and a glut of unsold houses begins to build. As that happens, the construction industry grinds to a halt, and more people are thrown out of work. Lenders find they are no longer able to count on the collateral value of homes in case of foreclosures. Forced sales below loan values cause losses for banks, which then become unwilling or unable to make new loans even for people who have kept their jobs. Soon tightening of credit markets spreads beyond the housing sector. Firms find it difficult to borrow to expand production and perhaps may not even be able to borrow the working capital they need to stay in business. Now it is the contraction that feeds on itself.

**THE ZERO INTEREST RATE BOUND**    As financial markets begin to spiral downward, the economy runs into still another major asymmetry of deflation. This one concerns the way that interest rates behave during inflation and deflation. To understand this asymmetry, we need to draw on the distinction between real and nominal interest rates, first discussed in Chapter 4. Nominal interest rates are those that are stated in financial contracts—3 percent interest on a savings account, 6 percent interest on a home mortgage, 18 percent on a credit-card bill, or whatever. Real interest rates are corrected for the effects of inflation by subtracting the rate of inflation from the nominal interest rate. In equation form,

$$\text{Real interest rate} = \text{Nominal interest rate} - \text{rate of inflation}$$

If the rate of inflation is, say, 5 percent, the 18 percent nominal rate on the credit card bill becomes a real rate of 13 percent, the nominal 6 percent on the mortgage becomes a real rate of just 1 percent, and the 3 percent nominal rate on the savings account becomes a real rate of *minus* 2 percent. A negative real rate means that the holder of the savings account does not even get enough interest to compensate for the 5 percent per year loss in purchasing power of the money left on deposit.

When inflation varies within a moderate but positive range, nominal interest rates tend to adjust to inflation automatically under the influence of supply and demand. For example, suppose the rate of inflation is at first 3 percent, at which time a bank is making auto loans at a nominal rate of 7 percent. The next year, the rate of inflation goes up to 5 percent. If both borrowers and lenders expect the new rate of inflation to last at least for the life of the loan, the nominal interest rate on auto loans will adjust upward to 9 percent by mutual consent. Borrowers will be willing to pay the extra amount because they expect their wages to rise 2 percent faster during the life of the loan. Bankers are willing to accept the extra 2 percent interest as compensation for the greater annual loss in the purchasing power of money. The real interest rate remains unchanged. At first it was a nominal 7 percent minus 3 percent inflation for a real interest rate of 4 percent. Later it became a nominal 9 percent minus 5 percent inflation, still a real interest rate of 4 percent.

When deflation sets in, though, it can become impossible to adjust the nominal interest rates downward by enough to keep the real interest rate constant. Consider what would happen, in our example, if there were deflation of 5 percent per year (that is, inflation of minus 5 percent). To keep the real interest rate at 4 percent, the nominal rate would have to fall to minus 1 percent. As you learned in grade school, "minus a minus makes a plus," so the math would look like this: (Nominal rate of − 1 percent) − (inflation rate of −5 percent) = (real rate of + 4 percent).

There is a problem here, however. Although we can write out the equation, it is not possible, in reality, for a lender to offer loans at a negative nominal interest rate. Think what would happen if you walked by your local bank and saw a sign advertising loans at minus 1 percent. That would mean you could borrow $1,000 today, and a year from now, you would owe the bank just $990. Good deal, right? You could borrow the $1,000, put $990 safely away in a drawer to repay the loan when it comes due, and buy lunch with the $10 that is left over.

The minus 1 percent interest rate is such a good deal; why not borrow ten thousand dollars, or 10 billion? As the example shows, nominal interest rates can never fall below zero because as they approach that level, the demand for loans becomes infinite. Economists call this principle the **zero interest rate bound (ZIRB)**. Because the ZIRB raises real interest rates during deflation, credit becomes more expensive. People become less willing to take out loans to build houses, buy cars, and upgrade production equipment. Falling investment reduces aggregate demand—still another reason why deflation, once started, feeds on itself.

**Zero interest rate bound (ZIRB)**

The principle that nominal interest rates cannot fall below zero

## Policies to Fight Demand-Side Deflation

The zero interest rate bound is a troublesome constraint for central banks trying to reverse a demand-side deflation. As we saw in Chapter 10, many central banks use interest rates as their principal operating target. The Federal Reserve, whose main operating target is the federal funds rate (the interbank lending rate), is one of these.

When the Fed wants to tighten monetary policy, it raises its target interest rate. Doing so raises the opportunity cost to commercial banks of holding reserves. They, in turn, raise their loan rates and tighten lending standards. Borrowing slows down; aggregate demand decreases. With a lag, real output growth and then inflation begin to fall. When the Fed wants to loosen monetary policy to stimulate the economy, it does the opposite. It lowers its federal funds target, making it cheaper for banks to hold reserves. Lending increases, aggregate demand strengthens, and with a lag, inflation and real output speed up.

**THE LIQUIDITY TRAP** The interest rate operating target works well until deflation causes nominal interest rates to approach zero. The federal funds rate, which is a very short-term, very low-risk interest rate, is among the first to approach the ZIRB. As it does so, the opportunity cost to banks of holding reserves also falls to zero. Banks lose their normal incentive to put reserves to work quickly by lending them out to firms and consumers. As excess reserves accumulate in the banking system, lending slows down, investment falls, aggregate demand decreases, and the problem of deflation becomes worse.

The accumulation of excess reserves in the banking system is not the only problem for monetary policy. As nominal interest rates approach zero, the opportunity cost to firms and households of holding money decreases. Normally, neither consumers nor firms want to accumulate large money balances. The reason is that they earn little or no interest on money held in the form of currency or transaction deposits. Once their immediate liquidity needs are met, they invest any excess cash in some form of interest-bearing asset. For consumers, certificates of deposit at their bank are a convenient resting place for money that is not needed immediately; for business firms, short-term securities may be a good use for idle money balances. The reluctance of people to hold money balances beyond their immediate liquidity needs means that money keeps circulating around the economy, and velocity stays at a normal level.

When interest rates approach zero, there is no longer much incentive to manage cash carefully. Interest rates on alternative, safe, short-term investments are so low that firms and households simply allow funds to accumulate in transaction deposits, or even as paper currency. Velocity slows. As we know from the equation of exchange, MV = PQ, a reduction in velocity, other things being equal, will cause either P (the price level) or Q (real output) or both to decrease. The accumulation of excess money by firms and households, thus, makes deflation worse once it is underway.

Together, the accumulation of liquid reserves by banks and money balances by households and firms reduces the effectiveness of monetary policy as nominal interest rates approach zero. This combination of circumstances is called a **liquidity trap**. The name comes from the fact that the economy is "trapped" in a state of low aggregate demand from which monetary policy cannot easily free it.

Figure 12.6 shows symptoms of a liquidity trap in the U.S. economy beginning in the fall of 2008. Normally, the monetary base (bank reserves plus currency) and the money stock (M2) move closely together because the money multiplier (the ratio of the money stock to the monetary base) is approximately constant. M2 and nominal GDP also nor-

**Liquidity trap**

A situation in which monetary policy loses its effectiveness as nominal interest rates approach zero

## FIGURE 12.6    SYMPTOMS OF A LIQUIDITY TRAP IN THE U.S. ECONOMY, 2008–2009

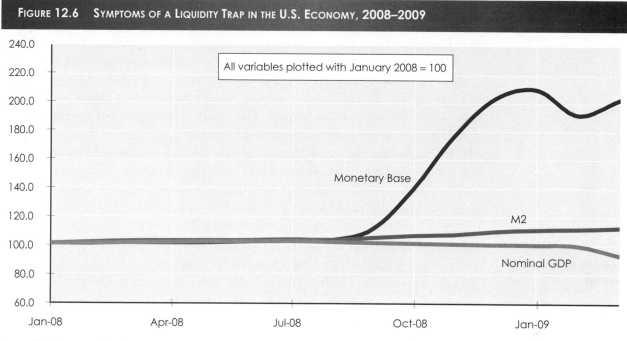

Normally, the monetary base and the money stock (M2) move closely together, as they did until mid-2008, because the money multiplier is approximately constant. M2 and nominal GDP also normally move together because of approximately constant velocity. In the fall of 2008, expansionary monetary policy sharply increased the growth rate of the monetary base, especially bank reserves; but the money multiplier fell, so M2 increased only a little. At the same time, firms and households accumulated money balances. As they did so, velocity decreased, with the result that nominal GDP decreased even while M2 continued to rise. On balance, expansionary monetary policy succeeded in increasing the monetary base but failed to restore growth of nominal GDP. These are the classic symptoms of a liquidity trap.

DATA SOURCE: Federal Reserve Board of Governors; Federal Reserve Bank of St. Louis.

mally move together. The reason is apparent from the equation of exchange, $MV = PQ$, applied to normal times when velocity is approximately constant. The figure shows that in the first half of 2008, the monetary base, the money stock, and nominal GDP all moved closely together, as they had for several years previously. Then, in the fall of 2008, these normal relationships broke apart. Expansionary monetary policy sharply increased the growth rate of the monetary base, especially bank reserves. However, because interest rates were very low, banks accumulated reserves rather than lending them out. As banks stopped converting excess reserves to money by extending new loans, the money multiplier fell. On balance, the huge increase in bank reserves had only a slight positive impact on the growth rate of M2. At the same time, low interest rates reduced the opportunity cost to firms and households of accumulating money in the form of currency and transaction deposits. As they did so, velocity decreased. The result, as the chart shows, was that nominal GDP decreased even while M2 continued to rise. The combined result of these effects was that expansionary monetary policy succeeded in expanding the monetary base but failed to restore growth of nominal GDP. These are the classic symptoms of a liquidity trap.

**BREAKING OUT OF THE LIQUIDITY TRAP**    Policymakers in the United States and other countries did not sit on their hands as the threat of deflation developed during 2008 and 2009. They took vigorous measures to try to break out of the liquidity trap before full-scale deflation became established. Both monetary and fiscal policies were brought to bear.

On the monetary policy side, the Fed began by pushing interest rates as low as it could. For technical reasons, a target of exactly zero for the federal funds rate was not feasible; but on December 16, 2008, the Fed announced a target range for its key interest rate of 0 to 0.25 percent. The rate paid on deposits of reserves was cut to 0.25 percent and the discount rate to 0.5 percent.

To increase the rate at which reserves were injected into the banking system, the Fed also began purchasing a wider range of assets than in the past. Rather than limiting itself to purchases of short-term Treasury bills, it began buying long-term government bonds, commercial paper (short-term corporate debt), assets related to securitized mortgages, student loans, and other securities. Policies of this nature, which aim to increase the quantity of reserves even after interest rates have reached the zero bound, are known as **quantitative easing**. Quantitative easing was used by the Japanese central bank during a period of deflation in the 1990s, with mixed success. Opinions differ as to how effective the policy will prove to be in the United States.

Worried that monetary policy alone would not be enough to reverse deflationary pressures, fiscal stimulus was added to the mix. As explained in Chapter 11, discretionary fiscal policy, considered by many to be a clumsy tool of stabilization policy in normal times, comes into its own when there is a threat of deflation. The record $787 billion stimulus package adopted in February 2009 was a case in point. The Fed made every effort to ensure that the fiscal stimulus would be effective. It kept interest rates near zero to accommodate the fiscal stimulus and minimize any crowding-out effect that might undermine it.

**Quantitative easing**

The use of central bank policies that increase the quantity of bank reserves and money in order to stimulate the economy after interest rates have hit the zero bound

**WHY PREVENTION IS THE BEST CURE**    At the time this is written, it is too early to tell whether the combination of vigorous monetary and fiscal policies will be sufficient to avoid prolonged deflation in the United States. It is also too early to know whether, when the time comes, the Fed will be able to reabsorb all of the excess liquidity created by quantitative easing quickly enough to avoid a post-recession burst of inflation. What is already clear is that when demand-side deflation threatens, policymakers need to use every tool at their disposal to ward off disaster; even their maximum efforts may barely be enough.

Because full-scale demand-side deflation is so hard to stop, it is widely accepted that prevention is the best cure. Policymakers are normally willing to risk a small amount of inflation to avoid a risk of deflation. That is why countries that practice inflation targeting do not set their target exactly at zero. They aim for an inflation rate of two or three percent that gives a margin of error in case the economy is hit with unexpected deflationary shocks. Because of asymmetries in labor and financial markets, the harm done by inflation of a few percent per year is thought to be less than the same rate of demand-side deflation.

## Supply-Side Deflation

Just one topic—supply-side deflation—remains to be covered before we complete our survey of macroeconomics and stabilization policy. Although both involve a falling price level, supply-side deflation raises a very different set of issues than demand-side deflation. Both kinds of deflation turn out to be relevant, but in different ways, to the global economic crisis that began in 2008.

**DEFLATION AND SHORT-TERM SUPPLY SHOCKS**   Supply-side deflation, as shown earlier in Figure 12.5, occurs when a favorable supply shock lowers expected production costs and shifts the short-run aggregate supply curve downward. Often such shocks are temporary, caused by a decrease in prices of imported commodities, unusually good weather, or an appreciation of the exchange rate. Temporary shocks of that kind are not likely to have major policy implications.

For one thing, the favorable short-run supply shock may occur during a period when the price level has already been rising, rather than from a stationary equilibrium, as was the case in Figure 12.5. That is especially likely to be the case if policymakers set a moderately positive inflation target for normal times. An example would be the fall in world oil prices in the second half of 2008, which followed an earlier oil price increase that had temporarily raised the inflation rate. Under such conditions, a deflationary supply shock only slows a previously established upward drift of the aggregate supply curve caused by inflationary momentum. Neither the aggregate supply curve itself nor the price level need actually fall.

Even if a temporary favorable supply shock hits when inflation is already low or zero, so that prices do begin to fall, the effect may not continue long enough to bring nominal interest rates to zero. Financial markets tend to mark up nominal interest rates above real interest rates by an amount that reflects the rate of inflation expected over the life of loans currently being made. Even if the price level decreases briefly, lenders and borrowers are likely to expect price stability or moderate inflation to return. Until prices fall for long enough that people come to see falling prices as the norm, financial markets will be able to function without the danger of a liquidity trap.

**DEFLATION AND LONG-TERM PRODUCTIVITY GROWTH**   Long-term productivity growth can cause a more problematic form of supply-side deflation. This case is illustrated in Figure 12.7. The events shown begin from a point of long-term equilibrium at $E_0$. Next some improvement in technology or the organization of production begins to increase productivity. The productivity growth has two effects. First, the economy's long-term natural level of real output increases because the existing stock of labor and capital can now produce more output than before. That effect is shown as a rightward shift of the vertical long-run aggregate supply curve from $N_0$ to $N_1$. Second, improved productivity lowers the expected cost of production because fewer units of input will be needed to produce any given quantity of output. That effect is shown as a downward and rightward shift of the short-run aggregate supply curve from $AS_0$ to $AS_1$. If aggregate demand remains unchanged, the economy will move along the aggregate demand curve, from $E_0$ to $E_1$. The price level will fall while real output increases. The unemployment rate does not need to change because real output stays at its natural level. Because of productivity improvements, the same number of labor hours as before now produce more output, more cheaply.

Supply-side deflation caused by productivity growth is less likely to have harmful consequences than demand-side deflation.[4] For one thing, it does not

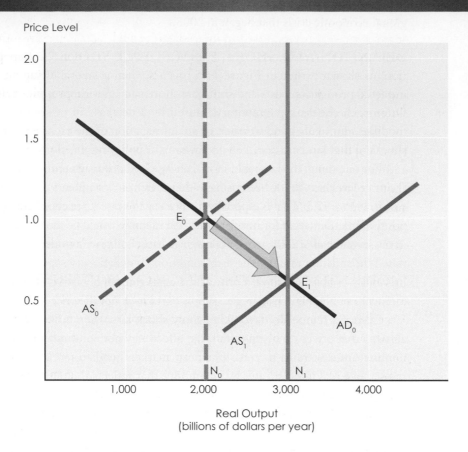

**FIGURE 12.7  EFFECTS OF PRODUCTIVITY GROWTH**

Beginning from equilibrium at point $E_0$, productivity growth has two effects. First, the economy's long-term natural level of real output increases from $N_0$ to $N_1$, shifting the long-term aggregate supply curve rightward. Second, improved productivity lowers the expected cost of production, shifting the short-run aggregate supply curve both downward and to the right, from $AS_0$ to $AS_1$. If aggregate demand remains unchanged, the price level will fall while real output increases; and the economy will move to a new equilibrium at $E_1$.

disrupt the operation of labor markets in the way demand-side deflation does. In demand-side deflation, nominal wage rates must fall in order to bring the economy to a new long-run equilibrium. Workers, whether unionized or nonunionized, are likely to resist nominal wage cuts, even if the price level is also falling. In contrast, productivity-driven supply-side deflation does not require a decrease in nominal wages. Productivity growth causes real wages to increase. The increase in real wages most often takes the form of nominal wage that rises faster than the rate of inflation for goods and services. However, in the case shown in Figure 12.7, it can instead take the form of a nominal wage that remains constant while falling prices reduce the cost of living. Either way, productivity growth makes workers better off. Deflation does not trigger either institutional or psychological disruption of labor markets.

Furthermore, productivity-driven deflation is less likely to disrupt financial markets. For one thing, productivity growth does not usually occur in sudden jumps but rather at a rate of a few percent per year. If the price level were to fall by a steady one or two percent per year, nominal interest rates could remain positive—they would be lower than the real interest rate, but above zero. In addition, because productivity-driven deflation would not be accompanied by falling output, rising unemployment, and falling real incomes, there would be less danger of widespread loan defaults, foreclosures, and collapsing collateral values.

The most recent occurrence of prolonged productivity-driven deflation in the United States was in the 1920s, which was a decade of period of prosperity and growth until the stock market crash of 1929. During all of the nineteenth century, in both the United States and the U.K., the price level fell on average one decade after another, interrupted only during periods of war. Both countries experienced steady growth and rising living standards. Economists who characterize supply-side deflation as benign in contrast to harmful demand-side deflation often cite these episodes.

**PRODUCTIVITY GROWTH AND INFLATION TARGETING**   No country in recent years has experienced the kind of deflation shown in Figure 12.7, but that is not because there has been no productivity growth. On the contrary, productivity growth in the United States and many other countries was unusually strong in the 1990s and early 2000s. (See Figure 4.2 in Chapter 4, for a chart of recent productivity growth in the United States.) The reason there was no productivity-driven deflation during this period was that monetary policy did not allow it.

Figure 12.8 shows how monetary policy can prevent deflation even when productivity is growing. In the example, the central bank is assumed to follow a strict form of inflation targeting that aims at complete price stability. As the long-run and short-run aggregate supply curves shift to the right, expansionary monetary policy is applied to shift the aggregate demand curve from $AD_0$ to $AD_1$. The rapid growth of aggregate demand is enough to hold the price level constant at its original level of 1.0 despite shifts in the aggregate supply curves. In the process, real output grows even faster than in the case that was shown earlier in Figure 12.7. By the time the economy reaches $E_2$, real output is $3,600 billion. There is a positive output gap of $800 billion compared with the new natural real GDP of $2,800 billion ($N_1$).

**UNINTENDED CONSEQUENCES**   At first glance, the circumstances produced by the combination of inflation targeting and productivity growth look like the best of all possible worlds. There is no inflation or deflation. Real output grows even more rapidly than it otherwise would. What is more, the unemployment rate falls as real output grows beyond its natural level, and firms add shifts in a struggle to keep up with booming demand. However, economists, we all know, are a gloomy lot. They see unintended consequences and hidden trouble even in the sunny scenario shown in Figure 12.8.

The unintended consequences stem from the interest-rate policy that is needed to keep demand growing fast enough to hold the price level constant. In order to prevent deflation, the central bank must push real output well above its natural level. Interest rates must be kept very low to produce such a big shift in aggregate demand. The

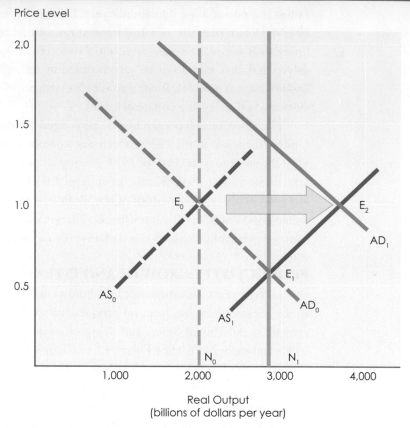

**FIGURE 12.8  PREVENTING DEFLATION WITH MONETARY POLICY**

Expansionary monetary policy can keep the price level constant even while productivity growth is shifting the long- and short-run aggregate supply curves. In this example, the central bank follows a zero-inflation target. Strongly expansionary policy shifts the aggregate demand curve from $AD_0$ to $AD_1$ as the aggregate supply curve moves from $AS_0$ to $AS_1$, so the economy moves from $E_0$ to $E_2$ instead of to $E_1$. The actual level of real output increases faster than the natural level of real output, a positive output gap develops, and there is no deflation.

banking system must be flooded with liquidity. Credit must be become very cheap, and lending standards must be lenient. Households and businesses must be able to borrow as much as they want for almost any purpose.

The result of such a policy, say the critics, is the emergence of **asset price bubbles**. Remember, the price level shown on the vertical axis of the aggregate supply and demand diagram is an index of prices of final goods and services. Prices of assets—like real estate, stocks, and commodities—are not included. Some of the easy credit available during the boom spills over into asset markets; and asset prices can rise to unsustainable levels even if prices of final goods and services do not.

It is hard to predict just where asset price bubbles will first develop in any particular case. In the United States in the 1990s, high-tech stocks were the most affected. In the course of the decade, the NASDAQ composite stock index, heavily weighted with

**Asset price bubbles**

A situation in which the prices of assets (stocks, real estate, commodities, etc.) rise to unsustainable levels compared to prices of goods and services

stylish "dot.com" companies, soared from under 500 to nearly 5,000 before it crashed again. In Japan in the 1980s and Thailand in the 1990s, the bubble was in commercial real estate; and in the United States in the early 2000s, home prices were the focus of the bubble, as we saw in Chapter 7.

Whatever particular asset is at the center of the bubble, people will invest in producing more of it. During the dot.com bubble, billions of dollars-worth of capital was poured into investment in technology startups, a few of which were successful, but most of which failed. During the housing bubble, the investment poured into construction of new homes. People bought larger homes and second homes that they could not afford, in the hope of quickly "flipping" them at higher prices to other buyers who would later arrive at the party.

When a bubble collapses, there is no smooth way to get the economy back to equilibrium. Much of the investment made during the boom turns out to have been wasted. Unwanted software code or subdivisions, produced at the cost of millions of labor-hours and billions of dollars, cannot now be converted to something more useful, like shoes or schools. Borrowers default, and banks find that the collateral that backed their loans is worthless. Credit dries up, and the economy plunges from boom to bust.

## What to Do about Asset Price Bubbles

What should be done to counter the risk that a combination of inflation targeting, productivity growth, and asset price bubbles will lead to an unsustainable boom-bust cycle? The aggregate supply and demand model suggests an apparently simple answer: Rather than holding the price level constant as productivity grows, the central bank could follow a policy of planned, gradual deflation that is just sufficient to keep real output close to its natural level. The economy would follow a path closer to Figure 12.7 than to Figure 12.8, and the goals of prosperity and stability would be achieved. However, as is often the case, our textbook models oversimplify matters. In practice, such a policy is not easy to achieve.

One problem is that a willingness to accept productivity-driven supply-side deflation might increase the risk of harmful demand-side deflation. The reason is that policymakers cannot always be sure at the time with what kind of deflation they are dealing. They cannot watch aggregate supply and demand curves in real time; instead, they have to work with lagged data and imperfect forecasts. As we saw earlier, one of the ways to guard against harmful demand-side deflation in an world of lags and forecasting errors is to set an inflation target that is a little above zero, say two or three percent. That way, small downturns in demand can be absorbed in a slowdown of inflation without immediately causing a downward deflationary spiral. However, during a productivity boom, an inflation target of two percent or so, rather than the zero-inflation target shown in Figure 12.8,would make matters worse, not better.

What kind of practical rule might allow policymakers to balance the risks of deflationary contractions against the risks of unsustainable bubbles and booms? One suggestion is that policymakers should use preset rate of growth for nominal GDP as their principal intermediate target. The logic of a nominal GDP target can easily be understood in terms of the equation of exchange, $MV = PQ$, where the right-hand term, $PQ$, is equal to nominal GDP (price level times real output). The target growth rate for nominal GDP would be set equal to, or a little above, the long-term average growth rate of natural real output. Suppose, for example, the average growth rate of natural real GDP is 3 percent and the nominal GDP target is set at 5 percent. If natural real GDP, in fact, grows at 3 percent, there will be 2 percent inflation. If productivity growth slows down, a positive output gap will develop and inflation will speed up a little, but not too much. If productivity growth speeds up, inflation will automatically slow down, or even turn slightly negative. That will reduce the likelihood of asset price bubbles and a boom-bust cycle.

On paper, a nominal GDP target makes sense, but it is subject to significant practical problems. As we have seen, GDP, both real and nominal, is hard to forecast and is subject to long lags in data collection. When there are changes in the linkages between operating targets and the growth of nominal GDP—for example, changes in the money multiplier, velocity, or the multiplier for fiscal policy—policymakers may miss their intended target for nominal GDP growth. If they are unlucky enough to miss the target in the wrong direction at the wrong time, the risk of demand-side deflation or productivity-driven asset bubbles could reappear.

These risks cause some economists to be skeptical not only about nominal GDP targeting but also about any policy rule based entirely on a single economic indicator. Instead, they think policymakers should watch several variables at once. A Taylor rule, discussed in Chapter 11, is one example. The original Taylor rule called for changes in interest rates in response both to changes in inflation and to changes in the output gap.

In order to overcome lags in data for the output gap, a modified Taylor rule could instead watch employment trends. Employment indicators, unlike GDP, are available with relatively short lags. If rising unemployment signaled the development of a negative output gap, they could apply expansionary policy to avoid development of demand-side deflation. If falling unemployment signaled development of a positive output gap, they could tighten policy to avoid overheating. John Taylor himself, for whom the rule is named, has argued that if the Fed had followed his rule, it would have raised interest rates earlier in the mid-2000s—and the worst of the housing boom and following bust would have been avoided.

A more controversial idea is that, in addition to watching inflation and employment indicators, policymakers should also watch asset prices. If they saw something abnormal going on in the stock market, or real estate, or commodity prices, they could take that as a warning sign of overheating. To prevent the problem from getting out of hand, they could then try to deflate the bubble by raising interest rates.

In the past, the Fed has resisted suggestions that it target asset price bubbles. In a 2002 speech, Ben Bernanke, then a board member and now chairman of the Federal Reserve, commented that "Understandably, as a society, we would like to find ways to mitigate the potential instabilities associated with asset-price booms and busts. Monetary policy is not a useful tool for achieving this objective, however. Even putting aside the great difficulty of identifying bubbles in asset prices, monetary policy cannot be directed finely enough to guide asset prices without risking severe collateral damage to the economy."[5] Bernanke's first concern was that the Fed could not accurately second-guess asset markets in order to determine what was a bubble and what was a justified increase in prices. In addition, he was worried that aggressive action to "pop" a bubble could trigger a crisis. At most, he guardedly endorsed a policy of gently "leaning against the bubble."

Still, in the aftermath of the recent crisis, the idea that central banks should pay more attention to asset price bubbles is not likely to go away. In retrospect, it is clear that housing price bubbles, not just in the United States but also in the U.K., Spain, and other countries, were a key contributing factor to the crisis. There is a strong argument that those bubbles grew out of control, in part, because central banks, including the Fed, kept interest rates too low for too long during the preceding expansion. Some observers argue that rather than "popping" the bubble with tight monetary policy, better financial regulation at the microeconomic level would have been enough to limit the damage. Our own discussion in Chapter 7 looked at several areas in which better regulation could have helped. Others argue that both better regulation and some form of asset-price targeting are needed. All we can really hope for is that policymakers, at both the microeconomic and macroeconomic level, will be more vigilant next time and that the current crisis does not repeat itself any time soon.

## Summary

1. **How does demand-side deflation differ from supply-side deflation?** Inflation caused by an increase in aggregate demand is known as *demand-side inflation*. In the short run, an increase in aggregate demand will move the economy up and to the right along its short-run aggregate supply curve. As increases in final goods prices come to be reflected in expected input prices, the aggregate supply curve shifts upward. If continued expansionary policy shifts the aggregate demand curve upward at the same rate, the economy can be held above its natural level of real output for an extended period, but at a substantial cost in terms of inflation. If the short-run aggregate supply curve shifts upward while the aggregate demand curve stays in place or shifts upward more slowly, the economy will experience *supply-side inflation*. Real output will fall, and the economy will enter an *inflationary recession*. One source of supply-side inflation is a *supply shock*, such as an increase in the price of a key input such as petroleum. Another is the momentum of inflationary expectations generated by previous demand-side inflation.

2. **What is the Phillips curve and how can it be interpreted?** The short-run *Phillips curve* shows that for a given expected inflation rate, lower actual inflation rates tend to be associated with higher unemployment rates. When first introduced, the Phillips curve was sometimes interpreted as a policy menu. In the modern view, an increase in the expected inflation rate tends to shift the short-run Phillips curve upward. The long-run Phillips curve is a vertical line at the natural rate of unemployment. Unemployment will be at its natural rate only when the actual inflation rate equals the expected inflation rate.

3. **What is hyperinflation and how can it be combated?** Hyperinflation is very rapid inflation, in the thousands or millions of percent per year, or even higher. Hyperinflation begins when a government uses money creation to finance a deficit. Soon, rising velocity and falling real-output make inflation worse. Hyperinflation can sometimes be brought under control by conventional contractionary monetary policy and fiscal reforms. More often, exchange rate based stabilization is used, based on a fixed exchange rate

with a stable currency. If a country is not suited to use of a fixed exchange rate in the long run (and not every country is), it should use ERB stabilization only as a short-term measure and have an exit strategy at the ready.

4. **Why is demand-side deflation harmful, and what policies can prevent or reverse it?** Demand-side deflation is harmful because of three key asymmetries between inflation and deflation. First, labor markets do not function well because of resistance to cutting nominal wages. Second, financial markets run into trouble because of falling collateral values and increased loan defaults. Third, once the nominal interest rates hits the zero interest rate bound, real interest rates rise, further damping aggregate demand. Once demand-side deflation becomes established, it is hard to reverse. The economy enters a liquidity trap, which weakens the effectiveness of monetary policy. It may take a combination of super-expansionary monetary policy (*quantitative easing*) and fiscal stimulus to get the economy moving again.

5. **How can productivity growth cause demand-side deflation?** When productivity increases, two things happen to aggregate supply. First, the economy's capacity to produce goods and services increases, so the long-run aggregate supply curve shifts to the right. Second, per-unit costs of production decrease, so the short-run aggregate supply curve shifts downward. If aggregate demand remains unchanged, the result will be a combination of deflation and growing real output, as was the case in the United States for much of the nineteenth century. Productivity-driven supply-side deflation is less likely to be harmful than demand-side deflation because it is less likely to disrupt the workings of labor and financial markets.

6. **What are asset price bubbles and what can be done about them?** Asset price bubbles develop when the prices of assets like real estate, stocks, or commodities rise to unsustainable levels even while prices of goods and services remain under control. The sectors subject to asset price bubbles attract disproportionately large amounts of investment, some of which becomes worthless when the bubble collapses. The collapse of an asset price bubble can trigger an economy-wide contraction. One of the current controversies of monetary policy is whether central banks should try to "pop" asset price bubbles, try to lean gently against them, or do nothing about them.

## Key Terms

## Problems and Topics for Discussion

1. **Inflation or deflation?** Go to the web site of the Bureau of Labor Statistics and find the most recent information on the Consumer Price Index. This data can be found by following the link to CPI tables, beginning from http://www.bls.gov/cpi. Has the United States experienced inflation, deflation, or a mix of the two over the most recent year? Two years? Do you think the inflation or deflation shown is of the demand-side or supply-side variety?

What other information, from other data sources or news sources, might help you answer the supply-side/demand-side question?

2. **Phillips curve** Turn to the chart given in *Applying Economic Ideas 10.1* in Chapter 10. Look closely at the segment of the diagram that plots inflation/unemployment points for the years 1961 to 1969. Do you think that segment of the chart is best interpreted as a set of points from a single Phillips curve, or a set of points from a set of short-run Phillips curve that shifts over time? Explain the reason for your answer, based both on your understanding of the Phillips curve and on information contained in the text of the box.

3. **Phillips curve versus AS/AD** Now, look at another part of the chart given in *Applying Economic Ideas 10.1*—this time the segment that goes from 1976 to 1982. That diagram is drawn using a Phillips curve framework, that is, unemployment on the horizontal axis and inflation on the vertical axis. In contrast, the aggregate supply and demand diagram uses real output on the horizontal axis and the price level on the vertical axis. What do you think the pattern of year-to-year movements from 1976 to 1982 would look like if you plotted them on an AS/AD type of diagram? Try doing this. You will not be able to put exact numbers on your diagram or draw the exact positions of the curves—there is not enough information. However, you should be able to put points for each year in their correct relationship to each other (movement to the left or right, movement up or down) based on whether the price level and real output increased or decreased from year to year. Of the various types of events described in this chapter (deflation, supply shock, inflationary recession, etc.), which one do you think best describes the pattern you have plotted?

4. **Supply shocks from oil prices** The U.S. Energy Information Agency supplies current and historical data for world crude oil prices. The data can be found on their web site, http://tonto.eia.doe. gov/dnav/pet/pet_pri_wco_k_w.htm. Look both at current and historical data on world crude oil prices. Over the last six months, do you think the price of crude oil has produced an upward or a downward supply shock, or neither? How can you tell? Looking at historical data, when did the most recent oil-related supply shocks occur?

5. **Zimbabwe update** Use your favorite search engine to find recent news items on inflation in Zimbabwe. At the time this chapter was written (early 2009), there were preliminary indications that the long period of hyperinflation in Zimbabwe was coming to an end. Did hyperinflation really end at that time, or has it come back again? Can you find any information in your news story about what currency is being used for day-to-day purchases? Is the Zimbabwe dollar in use, or are foreign currencies like the U.S. dollar or South African rand being more commonly used?

6. **The U.S. housing bubble** The U.S. Federal Housing Finance Authority publishes an index of home prices. You can find it at http://www.fhfa. gov, and follow the link for FHFA House Price Index. When did the U.S. housing price bubble peak? Has the decline in housing prices ended? If so, when did it end?

## Case for Discussion

### Japan's Lost Decade

From the 1960s through the 1980s, the Japanese economy was the envy of the world. As Japanese cars, consumer electronics, and industrial goods flooded the world and set new standards of quality, its economy boomed. Japan became the world's second-largest economy, and it became the first Asian country whose living standards were on a par with those of North America and Western Europe. Books with titles like *The Japanese Century* became best sellers.

Then, in the 1990s, all this began to fall apart. One of the first signs of change came from the Consumer Price Index. Japan had never been a high inflation country, but in the early 1990s, inflation slowed sharply from its already moderate rate. After dipping below zero in 1995, and rising slightly in 1996 through early 1998, the rate of inflation became persistently negative after 1999. Deflation continued for six more years.

This long period of deflation, which has become known as Japan's "lost decade," was accompanied by very poor performance of the real economy. One measure of this is the output gap—positive when real GDP is above its natural level, negative when the economy is performing below potential. The chart shows that the Japanese output gap was negative throughout the period of deflation. Although the unemployment rate remained at moderate levels by the standards of other countries, the weak labor market brought big changes to Japan. Among other effects, it undermined the "jobs for life" tradition that had been a hallmark of the Japanese economy.

In 2006 and 2007, the Japanese economy finally showed signs of recovery. Few countries have ever been so happy to see consumer prices on the rise. Unfortunately, the recovery fell apart before it got far. In the second half of 2008 and over the next year or more, the spreading global recession undermined demand for Japan's exports. Sales of cars and consumer electronics fell by more than half, and the economy plunged back into renewed deflation.

## QUESTIONS

1. Was Japan's deflation of the demand-side or supply-side variety? How can you tell from the information given?
2. From 1999 to the end of 2005, Japan's central bank held nominal short-term interest rates between one tenth and one one-thousandth of a percent per year. What happened to the real rate of interest over this period? In what year did the real interest rate reach its highest value, and approximately what was the value?
3. Go to the web site of the Organization for Economic Cooperation and Development (www.oecd.org). Follow the link for "Browse—by country" to find the latest report on the Japanese economy. Is the Japanese economy beginning to recover, or is there a danger that it will fall into another "lost decade?"

## End Notes

1. This situation is sometimes called *stagflation*, but the term is not apt. The term *stagflation*—a combination of "stagnation" and "inflation"—was coined in the 1970s to describe a situation of slow or zero growth in real output, high inflation, and unemployment in excess of its natural rate. The term *inflationary recession* is more suitable for periods that combine high inflation rates with decreasing real output.
2. The instability of the U.S. economy in the 1960s and 1970s, which was discussed in *Applying Economic Ideas 10.1* (Chapter 10), appears to fit this pattern of repeated inflationary recessions and time-inconsistent overreactions to them.
3. A. W. H. Phillips, "The Relationship between Unemployment and the Rate of Change of Money Wage Rages in the United Kingdom, 1861–1957," *Economica*, new series, 25 (November 1958): 283–299.
4. For an excellent review of the literature on supply-side deflation, see David Beckworth, "Aggregate Supply-Driven Deflation and Its Implications for Macroeconomic Stability," *Cato Journal* (Fall 2008): 363-384. http://www.cato.org/pubs/ journal/cj28n3/cj28n3-1.pdf
5. Ben Bernanke, "Asset Price 'Bubbles' and Monetary Policy," Speech before the New York chapter of the National Association of Business Economists, October 15, 2002. http://www. federalreserve.gov/BoardDocs/Speeches/2002/20021015/ default.htm.

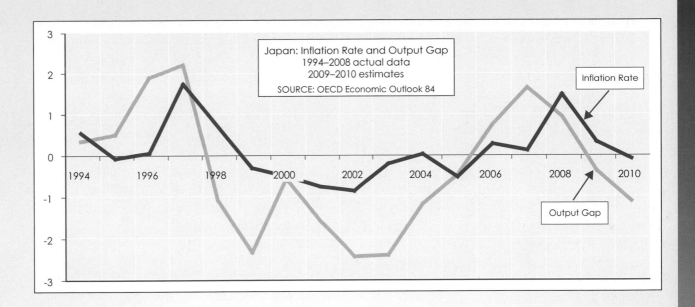

Japan: Inflation Rate and Output Gap
1994–2008 actual data
2009–2010 estimates
SOURCE: OECD Economic Outlook 84

# Glossary

**Accommodating monetary policy** A policy in which the central bank holds interest rates constant in response to a fiscal stimulus

**Aggregate demand** Total real planned expenditure

**Aggregate demand curve** A graph showing the relationship between aggregate demand and the aggregate price level

**Aggregate supply** Total real output of final goods and services (real GDP)

**Aggregate supply curve** A graph showing the relationship between real output (real domestic product) and the average price level of final goods

**Appreciate** Increase in value—such as the value of one country's currency increasing relative to the currency of another country

**Asset price bubbles** A situation in which the prices of assets (stocks, real estate, commodities, etc.) rise to unsustainable levels compared to prices of goods and services

**Assets** All the things that the firm or household owns or to which it holds a legal claim

**Automatic fiscal policy** Changes in government purchases or net taxes that are caused by changes in economic conditions given unchanged tax and spending laws

**Automatic stabilizers** Those elements of automatic fiscal policy that move the federal budget toward deficit during an economic contraction and toward surplus during an expansion

**Balance sheet** A financial statement showing what a firm or household owns and what it owes

**Bank** A financial institution whose principal business consists of accepting deposits and making loans

**Base year** The year that is chosen as a basis for comparison in calculating a price index or price level

**Budget deficit** Government expenditures minus tax revenues, or, alternatively, government purchases minus net taxes

**Business cycle** A pattern of irregular but repeated expansion and contraction of aggregate economic activity

**Capital** All means of production that are created by people—including tools, industrial equipment, and structures

**Central bank** A government agency responsible for carrying out monetary policy and often, also, for regulating the country's banking system

**Change in demand**   A change in the quantity of a good that buyers are willing and able to purchase that results from a change in some condition other than the price of that good, shown by a shift in the demand curve

**Change in quantity demanded**   A change in the quantity of a good that buyers are willing and able to purchase that results from a change in the good's price, other things being equal, shown by a movement from one point to another along a demand curve

**Change in quantity supplied**   A change in the quantity of a good that suppliers are willing and able to sell that results from a change in the good's price, other things being equal; shown by a movement along a supply curve

**Change in supply**   A change in the quantity of a good that suppliers are willing and able to sell that results from a change in some condition other than the good's price; shown by a shift in the supply curve

**Circular flow of income and product**   The flow of goods and services between households and firms, balanced by the flow of payments made in exchange for goods and services

**Closed economy**   An economy that has no links to the rest of the world

**Comparative advantage**   The ability to produce a good or service at a relatively lower opportunity cost than someone else

**Complementary goods**   A pair of goods for which an increase in the price of one results in a decrease in demand for the other

**Conditional forecast**   A prediction of future economic events in the form "If A, then B, other things being equal"

**Consumer price index (CPI)**   A price index based on the market basket of goods and services purchased by a typical urban household

**Consumption**   All purchases of goods and services by households for the purpose of immediate use

**Credit default swap**   An arrangement in which one party buys protection against the risk of default on a bond by paying an agreed premium to another party, the seller of protection, in return for which the protection seller agrees to compensate the protection buyer if the bond

**Cross-elasticity of demand**   The ratio of the percentage change in the quantity of a good demanded to a given percentage change in the price of some other good, other things being equal

**Crowding-out effect**   The tendency of expansionary fiscal policy to raise the interest rate and thereby cause a decrease in real planned investment

**Currency**   Coins and paper money

**Current account balance**   The value of a country's exports of goods and services minus the value of its imports of goods and services plus its net transfer receipts from foreign sources

**Cyclical deficit or surplus**   The difference between the deficit or surplus shown in the structural budget and that shown in the actual federal budget

**Cyclical unemployment**   The difference between the observed rate of unemployment at a given point in the business cycle and the natural rate of unemployment

**Deflation**   An episode during which the price level falls for a sustained period

**Demand**   The willingness and ability of buyers to purchase goods

**Demand curve**   A graphical representation of the relationship between the price of a good and the quantity of that good that buyers demand

**Demand-side deflation**   A period of falling prices caused by a decrease in aggregate demand

**Demand-side inflation**   Inflation caused by an upward shift of the aggregate demand curve while the aggregate supply curve remains fixed or shifts upward at no more than an equal rate

**Deposit multiplier**  The quantity of total deposits that can be created for each dollar of total reserves in a simple banking system where deposits are the only form of money, equal to 1/Reserve ratio

**Depreciate**  The decrease in value of a currency relative to the value of the currency of another country

**Direct relationship**  A relationship between two variables in which an increase in the value of one variable is associated with an increase in the value of the other

**Discount rate**  The interest rate charged by the Fed on loans of reserves to banks

**Discount window**  The department through which the Federal Reserve lends reserves to banks

**Discouraged worker**  A person who would work if a suitable job were available but has given up looking for such a job

**Discretionary fiscal policy**  Changes in the laws regarding government purchases and net taxes

**Disposable income**  Income minus taxes

**Domestic income**  The total income of all types, including wages, rents, interest payments, and profits, paid in return for factors of production used in producing domestic product

**Econometrics**  The statistical analysis of empirical economic data

**Economic efficiency**  A state of affairs in which it is impossible to make any change that satisfies one person's wants more fully without causing some other person's wants to be satisfied less fully

**Economics**  The social science that seeks to understand the choices people make in using scarce resources to meet their wants

**Efficiency in distribution**  A situation in which it is not possible, by redistributing existing supplies of goods, to satisfy one person's wants more fully without causing some other person's wants to be satisfied less fully

**Efficiency in production**  A situation in which it is not possible, given available knowledge and productive resources, to produce more of one good without forgoing the opportunity to produce some of another good

**Elastic demand**  A situation in which quantity demanded changes by a larger percentage than price, so that total revenue increases as price decreases

**Elasticity**  A measure of the response of one variable to a change in another, stated as a ratio of the percentage change in one variable to the associated percentage change in another variable

**Empirical**  Based on experience or observation

**Employed**  A term used to refer to a person who is working at least one hour a week for pay or at least fifteen hours per week as an unpaid worker in a family business

**Employment-population ratio**  The percentage of the noninstitutional adult population that is employed

**Endogenous**  Term applied to any variable that is determined by other variables included in an economic model

**Entrepreneurship**  The process of looking for new possibilities—making use of new ways of doing things, being alert to new opportunities, and overcoming old limits

**Equation of exchange**  An equation that shows the relationship among the money stock (M), the income velocity of money (V), the price level (P), and real domestic product (Q); written as MV = PQ

**Equilibrium**  A condition in which buyers' and sellers' plans exactly mesh in the marketplace, so that the quantity supplied exactly equals the quantity demanded at a given price

**Excess quantity demanded (shortage)**  A condition in which the quantity of a good demanded at a given price exceeds the quantity supplied

**Excess quantity supplied (surplus)**  A condition in which the quantity of a good supplied at a given price exceeds the quantity demanded

**Excess reserves**  The difference between the amounts of reserve a bank actually holds and the minimum required by regulations

**Exchange-rate based stabilization (ERB stabilization)**  A policy that uses a fixed exchange rate as the principal tool for ending hyperinflation

**Exogenous**  Term applied to any variable that is determined by noneconomic considerations, or by economic considerations that lie outside the scope of a given model

**Exports**  An injection into the circular flow that consists of payments received for goods and services sold to the rest of the world

**Factors of production**  The basic inputs of labor, capital, and natural resources used in producing all goods and services

**Federal funds market**  A market in which banks lend reserves to one another for periods as short as 24 hours

**Federal funds rate**  The interest rate on overnight loans of reserves from one bank to another

**Federal Reserve System (the Fed)**  The central bank of the United States, consisting of twelve regional Federal Reserve Banks and a Board of Governors in Washington, D.C.

**Final goods and services**  Goods and services that are sold to or ready for sale to parties that will use them for consumption, investment, government purchases, or export

**Financial inflow**  Purchases of domestic assets by foreign buyers and borrowing from foreign lenders; also often called capital inflows

**Financial inflow**  Purchases of domestic assets by foreign buyers and borrowing from foreign lenders, also often called capital inflows

**Financial outflow**  Purchases of foreign assets by domestic residents or loans by domestic lenders to foreign borrowers—also often called capital outflows

**Financial outflow**  Purchases of foreign assets by domestic residents or loans by domestic lenders to foreign borrowers, also often called capital outflows

**Fiscal consolidation**  The process of reducing government spending and increasing revenues by enough to make the deficit sustainable

**Fiscal policy**  Policy that is concerned with government purchases, taxes, and transfer payments

**Fiscal policy**  Policy that is concerned with government purchases, taxes, and transfer payments

**Fiscal year**  The federal government's budgetary year, which starts on October 1 of the preceding calendar year

**Fixed investment**  Purchases of newly produced capital goods

**Foreign-exchange market**  A market in which the currency of one country is traded for that of another

**Frictional unemployment**  The portion of unemployment that is accounted for by the short periods of unemployment needed for matching jobs with job seekers

**GDP deflator**  A weighted average of the prices of all final goods and services produced in the economy

**Government budget constraint**  The relationship between what the government buys and the sources of funds needed to make the purchases

**Government expenditures (government outlays)**  Government purchases of goods and services plus transfer payments

**Government purchases of goods and services (government purchases)**  Purchases of goods by all levels of government plus purchases of services from contractors and wages of government employees

**Government Sponsored Enterprises (GSEs)** Privately owned but government-sponsored specialized intermediaries that engage in the business of securitizing home mortgage loans and, sometimes, other loans

**Gross domestic income (domestic income)** The total income of all types, including wages, rents, interest payments, and profits, paid in return for factors of production used in producing domestic product

**Gross domestic product (GDP)** The value at current market prices of all final goods and services produced annually in a given country

**Gross domestic product (GDP)** The value, at current market prices, of all final goods and services produced annually in a given country

**Hierarchy** A way of achieving coordination in which individual actions are guided by instructions from a central authority

**Hyperinflation** Very rapid inflation

**Imports** A leakage from the circular flow consisting of payments made for goods and services purchased from the rest of the world

**Income elasticity of demand** The ratio of the percentage change in the quantity of a good demanded to a given percentage change in consumer incomes, other things being equal

**Indexation** A policy of automatically adjusting a value or payment in proportion to changes in the average price level

**Inelastic demand** A situation in which quantity demanded changes by a smaller percentage than price, so that total revenue decreases as price decreases

**Inferior good** A good for which an increase in consumer incomes results in a decrease in demand

**Inflation** A sustained increase in the average level of prices of all goods and services

**Inflation inertia (inflation momentum)** A tendency of firms and workers to expect prices to continue rising in the future at the same rate as in the immediate past

**Inflation targeting** A measure of the average prices of labor, raw materials, and other inputs that firms use to produce goods and services

**Inflationary recession** An episode in which real output falls toward or below its natural level and unemployment rises toward or above its natural rate while rapid inflation continues

**Injections** The government purchase, investment, and net export components of the circular flow

**Input prices** A measure of the average prices of labor, raw materials, and other inputs that firms use to produce goods and services

**Inside lags** Delays between the time a problem develops and the time a decision is taken to do something about it

**Insolvency** A state of affairs in which the net worth (capital) of a bank or other business falls to zero

**Intermediate target** A variable that responds to the use of a policy instrument or a change in operating target with a significant lag

**Inventory** A stock of a finished good awaiting sale or use

**Inventory investment** Changes in stocks of finished goods ready for sale, raw materials, and partially completed goods in process of production

**Inverse relationship** A relationship between two variables in which an increase in the value of one variable is associated with a decrease in the value of the other

**Investment** The act of increasing the economy's stock of capital—that is, its supply of means of production made by people

**Investment** The sum of fixed investment and inventory investment

**Labor** The contributions to production made by people working with their minds and muscles

**Labor force**   The sum of all individuals who are employed and all individuals who are unemployed

**Law of demand**   The principle that an inverse relationship exists between the price of a good and the quantity of that good that buyers demand, other things being equal

**Leakages**   The saving, net tax, and import components of the circular flow.

**Liabilities**   All the legal claims against a firm by nonowners or against a household by nonmembers

**Liquidity**   An asset's ability to be used directly as a means of payment, or to be readily converted into one, while retaining a fixed nominal value

**Liquidity trap**   A situation in which monetary policy loses its effectiveness as nominal interest rates approach zero

**M1**   A measure of the money supply that includes currency and transaction deposits

**M2**   A measure of the money supply that includes M1 plus retail money market mutual fund shares, money market deposit accounts, and saving deposits

**Macroeconomics**   The branch of economics that studies large-scale economic phenomena, particularly inflation, unemployment, and economic growth

**Marginal propensity to consume**   The proportion of each added dollar of real disposable income that households devote to consumption

**Market**   Any arrangement people have for trading with one another

**Merchandise balance**   The value of a country's merchandise exports minus the value of its merchandise imports

**Microeconomics**   The branch of economics that studies the choices of individual units—including households, business firms, and government agencies

**Model**   A synonym for theory; in economics, often applied to theories that are stated in graphical or mathematical form

**Monetary base**   The sum of currency and reserve deposits, the monetary liabilities of the central bank

**Monetizing the deficit**   Financing a government budget deficit through an increase in the monetary base

**Money**   An asset that serves as a means of payment, a store of purchasing power, and a unit of account

**Money multiplier**   The total quantity of money that can be created for each dollar of the monetary base

**Multiplier effect**   The tendency of a given exogenous change in planned expenditure to increase equilibrium GDP by a greater amount

**National income**   The total income earned by a country's residents, including wages, rents, interest payments, and profits

**National income accounts**   A set of official government statistics on aggregate economic activity

**Natural level of real output**   The trend of real GDP growth over time, also known as potential real output

**Natural rate of unemployment**   The rate of unemployment that prevails when real output is at its natural level

**Natural resources**   Anything that can be used as a productive input in its natural state, such as farmland, building sites, forests, and mineral deposits

**Negative slope**   A slope having a value less than zero

**Net exports**   Payments received for exports minus payments made for imports

**Net taxes**   Tax revenue minus transfer payments

**Net worth**   A firm's or household's assets minus its liabilities, also called equity or capital

**Nominal** In economics, a term that refers to data that have not been adjusted for the effects of inflation

**Nominal interest rate** The interest rate expressed in the usual way: in terms of current dollars without adjustment for inflation

**Normal good** A good for which an increase in consumer income results in an increase in demand

**Normative economics** The area of economics that is devoted to judgments about whether economic policies or conditions are good or bad

**Open economy** An economy that is linked to the outside world by imports, exports, and financial transactions

**Operating target** A variable that responds immediately to the use of a policy instrument

**Opportunity cost** The cost of a good or service measured in terms of the forgone opportunity to pursue the best possible alternative activity with the same time or resources

**Originate-to-distribute model** A model of banking that emphasizes the sale of loans soon after they are made, and use of the proceeds from the sale to make new loans

**Originate-to-hold model** A model of banking that emphasized making loans, and then holding the loans until maturity

**Output gap** The economy's current level of real output minus its natural level of real output

**Outside lags** Delays between the time a decision is taken and the time the resulting policy action affects the economy

**Perfectly elastic demand** A situation in which the demand curve is a horizontal line

**Perfectly inelastic demand** A situation in which the demand curve is a vertical line

**Phillips curve** A graph showing the relationship between the inflation rate and the unemployment rate, other things being equal

**Planned expenditure** The sum of consumption, government purchases, net exports, and planned investment

**Planned investment** The sum of fixed investment and planned inventory investment

**Planned inventory investment** Changes in the level of inventory, made on purpose, as part of a firm's business plan

**Policy goal** A long-run objective of economic policy that is important for economic welfare

**Policy instrument** A variable directly under the control of policymakers

**Policy rules** A set of rules for monetary and fiscal policy that specifies in advance the actions that will be taken in response to economic developments as they occur

**Positive economics** The area of economics that is concerned with facts and the relationships among them

**Positive slope** A slope having a value greater than zero

**Price elasticity of demand** The ratio of the percentage change in the quantity of a good demanded to a given percentage change in its price, other things being equal

**Price elasticity of supply** The ratio of the percentage change in the quantity of a good supplied to a given percentage change in its price, other things being equal

**Price index** A weighted average of the prices of goods and services expressed in relation to a base year value of 100

**Price level** A weighted average of the prices of goods and services expressed in relation to a base year value of 1.0

**Price stability** A situation in which the rate of inflation is low enough so that it is not a significant factor in business and individual decision making

**Primary deficit** Government expenditures, excluding interest cost, minus tax revenues

**Producer price index (PPI)**   A price index based on a sample of goods and services bought by business firms

**Production possibility frontier**   A graph that shows possible combinations of goods that can be produced by an economy given available knowledge and factors of production

**Quantitative easing**   The use of central bank policies that increase the quantity of bank reserves and money in order to stimulate the economy after interest rates have hit the zero bound

**Real**   In economics, a term that refers to data that have been adjusted for the effects of inflation

**Real interest rate**   The nominal interest rate minus the rate of inflation

**Real output**   A synonym for real gross domestic product

**Recession**   A cyclical economic contraction that lasts six months or more

**Reserve ratio**   The ratio of a bank's reserves (reserve deposits at the central bank plus vault cash) to its own deposit liabilities

**Reserves**   Cash in bank vaults and banks' deposits with the Federal Reserve System

**Revenue**   Price multiplied by quantity sold

**Saving**   The part of household income that is not used to buy goods and services or to pay taxes

**Savings deposit**   A deposit at a bank that can be fully redeemed at any time, but from which checks cannot be written

**Scarcity**   A situation in which there is not enough of a resource to meet all of everyone's wants

**Securitization**   A process in which a specialized financial intermediary assembles a large pool of loans (or other assets) and uses those loans as a basis for issuing its own securities for sale to investors

**Slope**   For a straight line, the ratio of the change in the y value to the change in the x value between any two points on the line

**Spontaneous order**   A way of achieving coordination in which individuals adjust their actions in response to cues from their immediate environment

**Structural budget deficit or surplus**   The deficit or surplus that would prevail in any year given that year's tax and spending laws, assuming real GDP to be at its natural level

**Structural unemployment**   The portion of unemployment that is accounted for by people who are out of work for long periods because their skills do not match those required for available jobs

**Subprime mortgage**   Mortgages with features like low down payments, variable interest rates, and prepayment penalties that make them attractive to low-income borrowers

**Substitute goods**   A pair of goods for which an increase in the price of one causes an increase in demand for the other

**Supply**   The willingness and ability of sellers to provide goods for sale in a market

**Supply curve**   A graphical representation of the relationship between the price of a good and the quantity of that good that sellers are willing to supply

**Supply shock**   An event not arising from changes in aggregate demand that changes the average level of expected input prices

**Supply-side deflation**   A period of falling prices caused by a decrease in the expected costs of production

**Supply-side inflation**   Inflation that is caused by an upward shift in the aggregate supply curve while the aggregate demand curve remains fixed or shifts upward more slowly

**T-account**   A simplified version of a balance sheet that shows only items that change as a result of a given set of transactions

**Tangent**   A straight line that touches a curve at a given point without intersecting it

**Target reserve ratio** The minimum amount of reserves a bank needs to hold that is consistent with regulations and safe banking practices

**Tax incidence** The distribution of the economic burden of a tax

**Tax revenue** The total value of all taxes collected by government

**Taylor rule** A rule that adjusts monetary policy according to changes in the rate of inflation and the output gap (or unemployment)

**Theory** A representation of the way in which facts are related to one another

**Time deposit** A deposit at a bank or thrift institution from which funds can be withdrawn without payment of a penalty only at the end of an agreed-upon period

**Time-inconsistency** Tendency of policymakers to take actions that have desirable results in the short run, but undesirable long-run results

**Total factor productivity** A measurement of improvements in technology and organization that allow increases in the output produced by given quantities of labor and capital

**Transaction deposit** A deposit from which funds can be freely withdrawn by check or electronic transfer to make payments to third parties

**Transfer payments** Payments by government to individuals not made in return for services currently performed, for example, unemployment compensation and pensions

**Transfer payments** Payments to individuals that are not made in return for work they currently perform

**Transmission mechanism** The set of channels through which monetary policy affects aggregate demand

**Unemployed** A term used to refer to a person who is not employed but is actively looking for work

**Unemployment rate** The percentage of the labor force that is unemployed

**Unit elastic demand** A situation in which price and quantity demanded change by the same percentage, so that total revenue remains unchanged as price changes

**Unplanned inventory investment** Changes in the level of inventory arising from a difference between planned and actual sales

**Value added** The dollar value of an industry's sales less the value of intermediate goods purchased for use in production

**Vault cash** Paper currency and coins that are held by banks as part of their reserves of liquid assets

**Velocity (income velocity of money)** The ratio of nominal GDP to the money stock; a measure of the average number of times each dollar of the money stock is used each year to purchase final goods and services

**Zero interest rate bound (ZIRB)** The principle that nominal interest rates cannot fall below zero

# Photo Credits

# Index